DATE DUE

FEB 02 1985		
FEB 18 1985		
OCT 04 1989		
JAN 05		
FEB 23 1992		
MAR 3 1 1994		

GAYLORD   PRINTED IN U.S.A.

❧❧❧

Portrait of André Gide

❧❧❧

PENCIL SKETCH OF ANDRÉ GIDE (1915)
BY THÉO VAN RYSSELBERGHE

PORTRAIT OF

ANDRÉ GIDE

A CRITICAL BIOGRAPHY

by JUSTIN O'BRIEN

OCTAGON BOOKS

A DIVISION OF FARRAR, STRAUS AND GIROUX

New York   1977

Copyright 1953 by Justin O'Brien

Reprinted 1977
by special arrangement with Alfred A. Knopf, Inc.

OCTAGON BOOKS
A DIVISION OF FARRAR, STRAUS & GIROUX, INC.
19 Union Square West
New York, N.Y. 10003

Library of Congress Cataloging in Publication Data

O'Brien, Justin, 1906-1968.
    Portrait of André Gide.

    Reprint of the ed. published by Knopf, New York.
    Bibliography: p.
    Includes index.
    1. Gide, André Paul Guillaume, 1869-1951—Biography. 2.
    Authors, French—20th century—Biography. I. Title.
[PQ2613.I2Z6568   1977]   848'.9'1209   76-56751
ISBN 0-374-96139-5

Manufactured by Braun-Brumfield, Inc.
Ann Arbor, Michigan
Printed in the United States of America

for Isabel

Mon plus secret conseil et mon doux entretien . . .

PREFACE

A NDRÉ GIDE knew I was writing this book, but we almost
never talked of it. We first met in June 1939 to discuss
plans for a French edition of my doctoral dissertation, for which
he had been so kind as to find a publisher and a translator.
From then on, except for the years of enemy occupation of
France, we corresponded irregularly. Having learned from his
publisher in 1945 that I had been commissioned to translate his
monumental journals, he wrote cordially from Egypt to express
his confidence. The following year I was able to spend a month
in almost daily converse with him—an opportunity that was renewed each year until his death in 1951. My notes on our many
conversations reveal that, although I frequently drew our talk
to such subjects as his readings at one or another period of his
life and his intentions in this or that work, I consistently shied
away from any description of this book, probably for fear that
he might unintentionally influence its form or content. I was
eager not to lose the advantage of perspective deriving from the
fact that I was a foreigner writing far from Paris.

Without fully knowing it, then, André Gide sat to me for his
portrait. During our long conversations in the various rooms of
his rue Vaneau apartment, in the bright house of Richard Heyd
overlooking the Lake of Neuchâtel, in a hotel dining-room, in a
speeding jeep, and once as I hurried to keep pace with him on
the crowded sidewalks of Paris, I constantly observed him with
a now critical, now indulgent eye. Everything about him interested me—from his thoughts on religion to his embarrassed
habit of noisily sniffing, from his comments on his art to his

manner of dressing and of heating his apartment. If I ever annoyed him with a series of direct questions (while hiding behind the necessity of fully annotating his *Journals*), he forgave me at once.

When I would return home on each of those trips to France, Gide continued to sit for his portrait in his works. For each time, besides continuing to translate the *Journals*, I would plunge again into the rereading of his novels and plays and essays and early treatises to discover hidden elements in them, echoes of earlier preoccupations or anticipations of later themes.

Since 1940, in fact, with the exception of three years of absence on military assignment, I have conducted nearly every year a one-semester seminar on André Gide at Columbia University. Designed for doctoral candidates in French, it adopted a different approach each year following a limitation based on chronology, on *genres*, or on aspects of Gide's mind. The ideal seminars varied between eight and fifteen carefully chosen students convinced that Gide had them in mind when he wrote in his *Journals* under date of 21 July 1921: "I should long ago have ceased to write if I were not inhabited by the conviction that those to come will discover in my writings what those of today refuse to see there, and which I nevertheless know that I put there." Each year, from rereading the writings of André Gide and guiding the ever-stimulating discussions of the students, I certainly learned more than I taught. Obviously it is impossible now to distinguish in every case my precise debt to individual students except when they crystallized their findings in published articles or M.A. essays or went on to write Ph.D. dissertations devoted to Gide. Such specific indebtedness, like that to the many authors of books and articles on Gide, is acknowledged in the notes. In principle, I have tried to read everything of value on the subject.

In addition, certain friends of André Gide, either in conversation or by correspondence, have generously provided information not otherwise available. Such information, like that derived from frequenting Gide himself, may not always have found its way directly into this study and hence deserve recording in the notes, but it certainly forms much of the indispensable background. That is why it is essential, as well as pleasurable, to thank specifically M. Jean Amrouche, Gide's regular opponent at chess; Mme Yvonne Davet, who has devoted her life to the reputation of Gide; MM. Dominique Drouin, the writer's nephew; Julien Green, the novelist; Richard Heyd, the publisher; Jean Lambert, Gide's son-in-law; Roger Martin du Gard, the novelist; Arnold Naville, the writer's almost lifelong friend and bibliographer; and Maurice Saillet, the literary critic. To the John Simon Guggenheim Memorial Foundation, whose grant of a Fellowship made work in France possible, my gratitude is very great.

All quotations are given in English and in my translation in order to preserve a single tone rather than suggesting that *Paludes, Les Nourritures terrestres*, and *Saül*, for instance, were written by three different persons. Furthermore, this system permits giving references in the notes to the French editions, so that a reader who checks those references will find confirmation in the original text for any passage quoted here. Notes are limited to such references and are consequently relegated to the back of the book. The titles of Gide's writings are consistently given in the original and translated parenthetically on their first appearance. A list of "Works by André Gide" in the Appendix, with French and English titles in parallel columns, will serve as a check and reminder. The epigraphs to each chapter are from the work of Gide and are identified in the notes.

JUSTIN O'BRIEN

CONTENTS

ILLUSTRATIONS

All the photographs were graciously furnished by M. Dominique Drouin from a family album at Cuverville.

Portrait of André Gide

⤟⧸ 3 ⧹⤞

I. INTRODUCTION

THE MERE title of this book suggests something between a critical study and a biography, or perhaps a combination of the two; indeed, it was chosen to do just that. It is still too early for the world to be interested in a laboriously detailed life of André Gide, and it would be a mistake ever to present him in the dehydrated form of a schematic monograph of the traditional *vie-et-oeuvre* type. To be sure, Gide's work cannot be wholly divorced from the facts of his life, nor his biography from the primordial fact of his literary achievement. The one projects light upon the other, making it possible for us to understand both.

"I took out my sheaf of notes," Gide wrote at the beginning of his capital book on Dostoevsky; "it seemed to me as I reread them after an interval that the ideas I had noted down deserved our prolonged attention, but that the chronological order of exposition, which a biography would require, was perhaps not the best. It is often awkward to unravel the tangle of those ideas, which Dostoevsky braids tightly together in each of his major works; but from book to book we find the same ones; they are what matter to me [. . .] Pursuing those ideas from book to book, I shall try to isolate them, to get hold of them and to set them forth for you at once as clearly as their apparent confusion will allow." So I shall attempt to do for Gide himself, in the hope that such an exposition may shape into an intellectual and spiritual portrait of a most complex man as seen in his work. The task should be easier with him than with the Russian novelist inasmuch as—besides frequently presenting those ideas in relation to the characters who express them as Dostoevsky always does—Gide has more often and more eloquently spoken in his own name than Dostoevsky ever did.

In that same series of lectures on Dostoevsky, which by no means aims to provide either a complete or an impartial portrait, Gide points out that, however good the resemblance may be, a portrait always reflects the painter almost as much as it does the model. And he adds: "Probably the most admirable model is the one who authorizes the most diverse resemblances and lends himself to the greatest number of portraits." This Gide decidedly does, as is evident to anyone who compares the many images of him in black and white or colors, in clay or stone left by so many artists to whom he sat. My portrait, coming after so many others, pretends to no greater objectivity than does the pencil sketch by Sir William Rothenstein or the bust by Jo Davidson. Simply, instead of catching André Gide at a single moment and in a particular mood, it offers the advantage of trying to fix many moments and numerous moods. Furthermore, as a portrait in the medium of words, it can have recourse to Gide's own words and thus try to understand the subject, in part at least, from the inside. If for this reason it may occasionally seem to partake overmuch of the self-portrait and even to be partial to his own view of himself, that danger should be offset by the added vividness that can only come from a sympathetic collaboration between subject and portraitist.

It is noteworthy that Gide speaks specifically of Dostoevsky's *ideas* as his primary interest in the Russian novelist. Such a statement implies no disregard for the form in which those ideas are expressed, for to Gide form is the external, symbolic presentation of an idea and the two are indivisible. "The work of art is the exaggeration of an idea," he wrote in an early page of his *Journals*. As in his *Dostoïevsky,* it may often seem that the writer is being portrayed here in terms of his fundamental, recurrent ideas—his attitudes toward various major problems. But it must never be forgotten that all life long Gide was primarily a consummate literary artist rather than a philosopher, a sociologist, or a critic. It is, to be sure, the combination he offers of a complex body of coherent thought with a subtle and individual style that justifies his unique position in modern letters.

As a young aesthete in the nineties, André Gide lived exclusively for art, and as he grew older he more than once stated that he wanted his work to be judged from the aesthetic point of view. Yet he did not revert to that attitude until after he had been frequently attacked by men who, opposed to his ideas on moral, religious, or political grounds, systematically refused to consider his works as art. Of all the critics and commentators who have written on Gide, only one resolutely followed his recommendation and excluded all considerations other than the aesthetic. In so doing Jean Hytier, then professor at the University of Algiers, brought out in 1938 the most profound and most valuable study of the writer that has yet appeared.

Toward the end of his life, however, Gide admitted that it was no longer desirable or even possible to omit any pertinent considerations in the study of his work. After all, he was even then portraying himself without indulgence in an essay, intended for posthumous publication, that took but little account of his published writings. At present, when Gide is no longer living, some of the dust raised by the bitter polemical battles raging about his name has settled. And now for the first time he can be judged dispassionately. This means that, while fully appreciating the artistic qualities for which we read and reread his books, we can for the first time also give proper weight to their moral, social, and religious implications. As this study progresses to such considerations, the aesthetic point of view may of necessity seem somewhat neglected, as it occasionally seemed to be by Gide himself. This is in part why I have devoted the last chapter to a brief scrutiny of the craftsman in André Gide: to re-establish the balance and to leave the reader with the final conviction that above all he belongs among the great literary artists.

Now, to portray André Gide through a series of familiar myths is simply to isolate the most remarkable features of his spiritual physiognomy. Although he might not have approved of the method, there is ample justification for it in his writings. His readers must be struck by the constant use he made of classical mythology throughout his career, from the *Traité du Narcisse* (*Treatise of the Narcissus*) of 1891 to the *Thésée* (*Theseus*) of 1946. For many of his best years, he planned to write a "Treatise of the Dioscuri" or *Castor et Pollux*, of which, unfortunately, but a few highly suggestive pages ever appeared under the more descriptive title of *"Considérations sur la mythologie grecque"* ("Reflections on Greek Mythology"). In them he vaunts the ever-new, the constantly fecundating quality of ancient legend:

"Greek fable is like Philemon's pitcher that no thirst empties when one drinks with Jupiter. (Oh, I invite God to my table!) And the milk that my thirst finds in it is certainly not the same that Montaigne drank here, I am well aware—as I am that Keats's or Goethe's thirst was not identical with that of Racine or Chénier. Others will come, like Nietzsche, whose fevered lip will have other impatient demands. But whoever, devoid of respect for the God, breaks the jug in order to see the bottom and expose the miracle, will soon have nothing but potsherds in his hands. And it is such broken fragments of the myth that mythologists most often give us; strange fragments in which can still be admired, as in the remains of an Etruscan vase, an accidental appearance, a gesture, a foot raised in dance, a hand held out toward the unknown, an ardent pursuit of some once-fleeing prey, an isolated link in the perfect chorus of the Muses whose unbroken garland presumably circled the vase . . ."

André Gide has written extensively—to mention only those legendary characters who figure directly in the titles of his works—of Narcissus, Prometheus, Philoctetes, Ajax, Candaules, Persephone, Corydon, Oedipus, and Theseus. And there are many more who do not play title-rôles. In view of such a consistent exploitation of mythology, it seems justifiable to treat Gide himself in terms of a series of myths. At best, his portrait can only be a composite image, so great is his diversity. In his *Journals* he noted: "The Greeks, who not only in the multitude of their statues, but also in themselves, left us such a beautiful image of humanity, recognized as many gods as there are instincts, and the problem for them was to keep the inner Olympus in equilibrium, not to subjugate and subdue any of the gods." With this statement as a cue, if we look upon a series of myths as forming Gide's "inner Olympus," they may point a way through his complex labyrinth.

It may be objected that it is unjust to identify an author with his heroes, as it is unfair to treat their utterances as if he had written them in his own name. Yet these are two quite different things. The writer of Gide's type often creates a character in order to have someone say things of which he would be incapable: but he would be utterly incapable of creating the character at all if he did not contain at least a germ of that character within himself. Gide has often discussed the terms "objective" and "subjective," pointing out that if Werther is in Goethe, Goethe is not altogether in Werther; that though Browning does not exactly confess himself in *Sludge* or *Andrea del Sarto*, yet he does momentarily identify himself with each of them in turn. Elsewhere he says that "if it happens that I use myself as a model (and sometimes it seems to me that there can be no other exact way of painting), this is because I first began by becoming the very one I wanted to portray." Again and again he attempted to clarify this relationship between creator and creature.

If he has chosen to recreate such as Narcissus, Prometheus, Oedipus, and Theseus, this is because he found them within himself. No single one of them sums up André Gide; yet each of them corresponds to a dominant aspect of his character and work and can thus serve as a symbol. What is more likely, in fact, to reveal his ideals, his affinities, and his antipathies?

As might be expected, André Gide's interpretation of the

myths is a personal one, for he claimed "to interrogate the Greek fable in a new way," bringing out its psychological significance. Otherwise, there would be no reason to retell the story, for instance, of Oedipus. One must not be surprised, then, to see Narcissus contemplating Adam in Paradise, to find Prometheus lecturing to men on the necessity of an eagle, to see an obese and rich Zeus strolling on the Paris boulevards, or to hear Theseus telling how he half-intentionally neglected to change his black sail on returning from Crete. In his *"Considérations sur la mythologie grecque,"* though insisting upon the rational basis for each legend, Gide warns against seeing a myth as the mere poetic expression of physical laws in which Fate plays a major rôle. The less Fate is emphasized in the fable, the more apparent becomes the psychological truth. Accordingly Gide played down the "amor fati" that Nietzsche admired, except in so far as it reflected an inner fatality. In this he was merely following the lead established in the mid-nineteenth century by the brilliant Louis Ménard, as Gilbert Highet points out in his remarkably comprehensive and stimulating study of *The Classical Tradition,* where he adds: "It was through him and his pupil Leconte de Lisle that Greek legends, instead of being merely pretty rococo decorations, became, for the French Parnassians, grand and beautiful expressions of profound truths." It so happens that Gide encountered Greek mythology in Leconte de Lisle's translations.

Now, the myth which best suggests elusive complexity—and which Gide enjoyed applying to himself—is that of Proteus. Wily old Proteus, bound to Neptune and demi-god himself, served as herdsman of the unsightly seals and other monsters of the deep. He had the power, according to the legend, of assuming all manner of shapes in order to elude whoever would pursue him. But when held down in fetters, he would, after many frightening transformations, eventually resume his original shape. Then, from his vast knowledge of past, present and future, the aged seer was obliged to answer questions.

Applying to this myth, which charmed both Homer and Virgil, the method of logical exegesis that Gide commonly used in similar cases, we may say that the answer was framed by the very metamorphoses themselves on which the daemon relied. Whoever held him until he had writhed through the whole gamut of his possibilities finally knew his authentic and intimate outlines. By forcing André Gide as Aristaeus forced Proteus, may we likewise wrest from him his secrets. Through his complex evolution and the multiple shapes he assumes, we shall gradually trace his lineaments in an appropriately fluid portrait to which our restless "sitter" will have himself contributed the most telling details. In the process, we shall also inevitably dredge up many a deeply submerged monster and swimming enigma to confuse and confound us.

II. INTERROGATING PROTEUS

"To tell the truth, I don't know what I think of him. He is never the same for long. He never clings to anything, yet nothing is more gripping than his flight. You haven't known him long enough to judge him. His personality is constantly dissolving and taking on new forms. You think you have caught him . . . but he is Proteus. He assumes the shape of whatever he loves. And in order to understand him, one must love him."

THE COMPLEXITY of André Gide's character and writings has long been legendary. He himself frequently wondered at it, and almost all his commentators, according to their views, have admired or deplored his abundant or devious, but ever surprising, resources. To some the epitome of French classicism, to others an outstanding example of current Alexandrianism, he has variously appeared as a profound religious thinker and a devil's henchman, an apostle of sincerity and a crafty purveyor of guile, a broad humanist and an egocentric introvert, a moral teacher and a calculating perverter of youth. His old friend, Charles Du Bos, who felt after years of subtle converse with Gide that he had penetrated the secret, characterized him as a "lattice-work labyrinth."

Indeed, Gide's dynamic equilibrium—this is a word he uses with particular and frequent affection—rests upon a number of familiar antinomies, such as the soul and the flesh, life and art, ethics and aesthetics, ardor and austerity, expression and restraint, the individual and society, classicism and romanticism, Christ and Christianity, God and the devil.

Within the Gidian complexity, and forming an integral part of it to the greater annoyance of his critics, contradictions abound. It would be quite possible, and even amusing, to construct of such contradictions, drawn literally from his writing and brutally lifted from their context, a prolonged dialogue between two André Gides, each genuine. "It is through his contradictions," he once noted apropos of the poet Francis Jammes, "that an individual interests us and reveals his sincerity."

It is particularly tempting to hear such a dialogue as spoken, for the first voice, by the young Gide in his late twenties, during that period of ardent ferment which produced poetry, satires, *Les Nourritures terrestres* (*The Fruits of the Earth*), his first plays, and prophetic criticism; and, for the second voice, by the Gide of sixty-five, at the height of his flirtation with Communism, the great number of his major works behind him and enjoying an assured position in world letters.

The meeting would have taken place in the large study hidden deep in the top-floor apartment on the rue Vaneau to which André Gide had moved in August 1928. The walls lined with books in neat array, many behind glass, and the narrow gallery giving access to the second storey of books darken this room, to which none but intimates are admitted. Above the grand piano the death-mask of Leopardi catches the light and over a large table Severn's drawing of Keats on his deathbed makes another luminous spot. The young man would be seated nonchalantly on the bench before the piano, his long body, half-draped in a flowing black cape, turned toward his interlocutor as his large right hand caresses a bronze statuette by Maillol. He has only just abandoned the Lavallière necktie and shaved off the rough beard that had masked his youthful emotion, but a silky mustache *"à la Gauloise"* still projects beyond the sharp line of his cheeks. He still wears his hair long in back, but already it is receding from his high forehead. Opposite him at the narrow table built into a nook under the stairs leading to the gallery, would sit the older Gide in shirt sleeves rolled up to his elbows. The vigor of his still athletic body strikes the visitor at once. He is lean, hard, smooth-shaven, and his baldness adds to the austerity of his appearance. One can imagine him as ready to start on another arduous voyage through the Congo, like the one of eight years earlier. Indeed, hardly a month has passed in recent years without his traveling somewhere, to Germany, Italy, the south coast, or to the desert and oases that already mean so much to the younger man. As he lights cigarette after cigarette, his attentive, piercing eyes never leave his visitor's face, not even to glance out the small window at his elbow into the old closed gardens below. . .

It is tempting, yes, to envisage the speakers thus, but it would be false to do so. The dates at which the following statements were actually made will not justify such a neat confrontation. If they did, the divergences being uniformly attributable to an intellectual evolution, the interest of this juxtaposition would be considerably diminished. In a sense, it would be ideally appropriate, rather, if the dates of any two conflicting statements were identical. Gide has so often noted in himself the "cohabitation of extremes" resulting from his inability to renounce any authentic part of himself that we must accept him, at any moment in his life, as the creature of dialogue he calls himself.

Without attempting, then, to visualize two André Gides at different stages of development, let us simply listen to the conversation, noting the contradictions. "The bad novelist constructs his characters," Gide tells us in the notes he kept while writing *Les Faux-Monnayeurs* (*The Counterfeiters* or *The Coiners*); "he directs them and makes them speak. The true novelist listens to them and watches them act; he hears them talk, even before knowing them, and only according to what he hears them say does he gradually understand *who* they are." He then tells us that he began his novel by writing some of the dialogues, without yet knowing how he was going to use the characters. Similarly, let us attentively listen, giving the floor, as will be necessary throughout this book, to André Gide, who will thus portray himself. The artificial dialogue of contradictions, made up of actual statements, would run like this:

A: "I find just as much profit in cultivating my hates as my loves."

B: "I am and shall remain incapable of hating."

A: "Absence of sympathy = lack of imagination."

B: "I find great danger in a too ready sympathy."

A: "There is almost nothing left in me that does not sympathize."

B: "Heretic among heretics, I have always been drawn by most widely separated opinions, by extreme intellectual detours, by divergences. Each mind interested me solely by what made it differ from others. I thus came to banish sympathy, ceasing to see in it anything but the recognition of a common emotion."

A: "Equilibrium is perfect 'health'; what M. Taine calls a happy accident, but it is physically unrealizable because of what we were saying: realizable only in the work of art. The work of art is an equilibrium outside of time, an artificial health."

B: "That state of equilibrium is attractive only when one is on a tight-rope; seated on the ground, there is nothing wonderful about it."

A: "Loathing for my sin rises to my lips."

B: "I have ceased to believe in sin!"

A: "Grant me not to count among the fortunate, the satisfied, the satiated, among those who are applauded, who are congratulated, and who are envied."

B: "Just the same it takes a certain dose of mysticism—or of something—to go on speaking, writing, when you know that you are absolutely not being listened to."

A: "At times I get to the point of thinking that the absence of
echo of my writings, for a long time, allowed them everything that constituted their value. [. . .] Ah, the happy
time when I was not listened to! And how well one speaks so
long as one speaks in the desert!"

It would be both easy and futile to continue such a dialogue
at much greater length. But from this sample it is sufficiently
clear with what problems and what sport Gide has provided his
critics. Not satisfied with the weapons he puts in their hands,
those most bitterly opposed to him on doctrinal grounds habitually resort to two unfair devices: misquotation and the attribu-
tion to Gide of the ideas expressed by his characters. By bitter
experience he knew how unwise, if not dishonest, it is to hold a
writer responsible for every thought voiced by his creatures.
Fortunately, however, for the scrupulous commentator, the writings in which he speaks in his own name are numerous at all
periods of his long career; despite the advice of Oscar Wilde
and, twenty-five years later, of Marcel Proust, Gide never feared
the first person singular.

Nothing is easier, in fact, than to convict André Gide of
contradicting himself. He was the first to accept the charge, readily seeing in this the index of an active, open mind. He who is
ever consistent, erecting a system that holds in all circumstances,
never gets outside of himself. A victim of intellectual sclerosis,
he might as well be dead, for there is no possibility of growth in
him. "They talk of constructing a system. Artificial construction
from which all life immediately withdraws. I let *my* system
grow up slowly and naturally. What eludes logic is the most
precious element in us, and one can draw from a syllogism
nothing that the mind has not put there in advance. I let the most
antagonistic proposals of my nature gradually come to agreement without violence. Suppressing the dialogue in oneself
really amounts to stopping the development of life. Everything
leads to harmony. The fiercer and more persistent the discord
had been, the broader the reconciliation blossoms." Harmony,

equilibrium, always appeared to Gide as the *natural* outcome of his discord and his attraction to extremes.

The problem in dealing with Gide, then, is not to resolve the contradictions but, rather, to preserve the conflicts and present his ambivalence as an indigenous and constant element of his nature. Few things are more revealing in this connection than his predilection for Baudelaire's remark: "There are in every man, at every moment, two simultaneous postulations: one toward God and the other toward Satan." Gide claims that the whole interest of Baudelaire's luminous discovery lies in the single word *simultaneous*. He would prove the truth of the statement from his own experience, as from that of Dostoevsky, in whom he likewise recognized himself. But the difficulty lies in reproducing that very simultaneity of the contrary impulses. All who have written on Gide have suffered from the unfortunate necessity of presenting in sequence a number of traits that are really coexistent in him. He himself acknowledged this defect in his memoirs: "Doubtless a need of my mind urges me, in order to draw each line more faithfully, to simplify everything excessively; draftmanship involves choice; but the most awkward thing is having to present, as successive, states of confused simultaneity. I am a creature of dialogue; everything in me is at war and in contradiction."

Where others tend to see but vacillation and inconsistency, it is characteristic that Gide should note, on the contrary, fidelity. Most men, "learning from life," compromise with their innate, original truth and cling instead to borrowed truths. "It takes much more precaution to deliver one's own message, much more boldness and prudence, than to sign up with and add one's voice to an already existing party. Whence that accusation of indecision and uncertainty that some hurl at me, precisely because I believed that it is above all to oneself that it is important to remain faithful." The discordant dualism of his nature, with its attendant quest of harmony, was but one of the evidences that he had been truly "chasing after his youth." And to it, doubtless, he owed in part the extraordinarily youthful spirit that marked him even in his eightieth year.

Aware of his complexity even to the point of vaunting it, André Gide had his own theory as to its source: "Nothing is consistent, nothing is fixed or certain, in my life. By turns I resemble and differ; there is no living creature so foreign to me that I cannot confidently approach. I do not yet know, at the age of thirty-six, whether I am miserly or prodigal, temperate or greedy . . . or rather, being suddenly carried from one to the other extreme, in this very balancing I feel that my fate is being carried out. Why should I attempt to form, by artificially imitating myself, the artificial unity of my life? Only in movement can I find my equilibrium. Through my heredity, which interbreeds in me two very different systems of life, can be explained this complexity and these contradictions from which I suffer."

The earliest mention Gide makes of his conflicting heredity occurs in the flippant, though appropriate, opening to his review in early 1898 of Maurice Barrès's *Les Déracinés* (*The Uprooted*). In that important novel the young *député*, who had already charmed the youth of the nineties with a proud and fervent trilogy preaching "the cult of the ego," first extolled tradition and provincial roots in what he was later to call "the cult of the earth and the dead." Now Gide, seven years younger than Barrès, began his review thus: "Born in Paris of a father from Uzès and a mother from Normandy, where, M. Barrès, do you expect me to take root?" Over thirty years later, he was to note in his *Journals*: "I have discovered quite by chance and without much believing in astrology that it just happens that on the 21st of November, my birthday, our earth leaves the influence of Scorpio to enter that of Sagittarius. Is it my fault if your God took such great care to have me born between two stars, the fruit of two races, of two provinces, and of two faiths?"

By now André Gide has reinforced the hereditary opposition by adding to the geographical contrast another of race or blood (but are we not all the *"fruit de deux sangs"*?) and a third of religion. Geographically he did not have to stretch a point, for his father came from Uzès in the Gard Département (a part of ancient Languedoc) and his mother from Rouen, the old capital of Normandy. In a sensitive essay, *"La Normandie et le Bas-Languedoc,"* written in 1902 for the monthly *L'Occident* and curiously omitted from the *Œuvres complètes (Complete Works)*, though it was included in *Prétextes*, André Gide, understanding both the Langue d'Oc and the Langue d'Oïl, loving both the deep woods and the moors, "the apple blossom in its whiteness and the white almond-blossom," contrasts the two provinces. The south means to him hills of scorched rock dotted with silver olive trees and the sharp foliage of the ilex, an air charged with dazzling sunlight, perfumed with thyme and lavender, and strident with the buzz of cicadas. It is an almost Latin land, known for grave laughter and lucid, severe poetry. The Calvados region of Normandy, on the other hand, suggests the heavy grass of pasture-lands, ever moist with rain, the bending branches of fruit trees, and shady sunken roads disappearing into dense woods. There all is softness and luxury.

When it comes to the "two faiths," however, we should be less inclined, today and outside of France, to give much weight to the distinction. To be sure, the Gide family of Uzès had been Calvinist since the Reformation. André's grandfather, Tancrède Gide, was an "austere Huguenot, very tall, strong and angular, excessively scrupulous, inflexible, and carrying his confidence in God to a sublime degree." After having been Président du Tribunal, or chief judge, in Uzès, he devoted the end of his life to charity and to his Sunday school classes. The Rondeaux family of Rouen, on the other hand, had been traditionally Catholic, like most Norman families, until 1839, when André's grandfather, Édouard Rondeaux, himself baptized a Catholic in 1789, married a Protestant before a Protestant minister and consented to have his children brought up in the Reformed Church.

It was he who definitively established the family's fortune, abandoning his drysaltery in Rouen to join his father-in-law in the manufacture of printed calico. A substantial citizen who served as judge, town councillor, and deputy mayor, he acquired a large house in the rue de Crosne, a country house on the Seine called La Mivoie, and the two châteaux of Cuverville-en-Caux and La Roque-Baignard, at which his grandson was to spend such happy days. By a typical abjuration he became a Catholic again on his deathbed in 1860.

His third son Henri, who had shocked the family by receiving Catholic baptism in 1849, may have been responsible for this re-conversion. In 1874 Henri inherited the impressive house in the rue de Crosne, where André Gide was to stay during his childhood visits to Rouen. This fact justifies Gide's statement in his memoirs that "at the time of my earliest recollections, the house of my parents had become Catholic again, more Catholic and orthodox than it had ever been."

But the grandmother, Julie Pouchet Rondeaux, and four of her five children remained staunchly Protestant, perhaps intensifying their faith as a protest against Henri's attitude. The important facts are that the family's conversion took place thirty years before André Gide's birth and that his mother, Juliette Rondeaux, was just as fervent and strict a Protestant as Paul Gide, the young law professor whom M. Roberty, the local minister, introduced to her mother in the early sixties. The youngest of the five children, Juliette nevertheless was to receive a considerable share of a very solid fortune. She was regarded as a "good match." In reply to an interested inquiry made in 1859, the distinguished statesman and historian, François Guizot, who spent his summers in a neighboring château, wrote of her: "The daughter is not pretty, nor yet ugly; somewhat awkward in manner. She has been very well brought up by a person of great merit who has inculcated in her in all regards good sentiments and good habits. My daughters say she has a solid education and a taste for good literature."

Mme PAUL GIDE

PAUL GIDE

Paul Gide, who was born three years before her in 1832, had received his doctorate at the University of Aix and had recently taken first place in the rigorous competitive examinations for the *agrégation* in law. Having substituted at the University of Grenoble for a few months, he was awaiting a permanent assignment, which he eventually received to the chair of Roman law at the University of Paris. The marriage was celebrated in Rouen in February 1863, one of the witnesses who signed the declarations being Dr. Achille Flaubert, the brother of the novelist; and the young couple went immediately to Paris, where they settled within the shadow of the University.

It was there, in an apartment at 19 rue de Médicis, that their only child, André-Paul-Guillaume, was born on Monday, 22 November 1869. As Paul Gide died in October 1880 when André had not quite turned eleven, it is not surprising that his son recalls very little of him. "It is according to a photograph," the memoirs tell us, "that I see my father, with a square beard and rather long and curly black hair; without that image I should have remembered only his extreme kindness." But the mature writer had not forgotten his father's impressive sanctuary, the dark, book-filled study in which he spent the day preparing his courses and which the boy could enter only when invited. He also remembered the long walks, on summer evenings, up the Boulevard Saint-Michel and through the Luxembourg Gardens, where father and son often wandered until the guard rolled his drum for closing time. Much of Gide's childhood, indeed, centered in those beautiful gardens. There he played in summer and skated in winter. Later he used to cut across the Luxembourg to reach his school on the rue d'Assas, and still later that verdant paradise in the heart of the Latin Quarter was the scene of interminable adolescent discussions such as those which figure in the first chapter of *Les Faux-Monnayeurs*. During the same years another, slightly younger, child who was also to contribute signally to modern letters was growing up in the Champs-Elysées on the other side of the Seine, for though Marcel Proust's father was also a professor at the University, the family lived on the more fashionable Right Bank. Gide left a less detailed and less charming record of his childhood than did Proust, perhaps for the same reason that his work dwells less upon himself than does Proust's. All the information we have as to his early years is to be found in the fat volume of memoirs entitled *Si le grain ne meurt . . . (If It Die . . .)*, written after the age of forty and with a specific purpose in mind, which Proust may have unconsciously strengthened by the example of his writings. From the very first page those tendentious memoirs reveal a desire to tell the truth at the expense of the author's vanity and even of the reader's susceptibilities. Although Gide's intention is diametrically opposed to that of Rousseau, which was to prove that he was different from all other men, we find here, as in the famous *Confessions*, an evident pleasure in shocking and a predilection for whatever reveals the author in an unlovely light. Early in the memoirs the tone is set: "At that age of innocence when the soul is said to be altogether transparence, affection, and purity, I see in me nothing but darkness, ugliness, guile." That this, however sincere, is a gross exaggeration becomes apparent to every reader. André Gide's childhood was not, to be sure, all sweetness and light; neither was it all nastiness and masturbation.

André Gide's most vivid memory of his father remains attached to the jurist's reading aloud to him in the sombre study. Scorning the books specially designed for children, which were then of poor quality, the father would read scenes from Molière, passages from the *Odyssey*, the medieval farce of Pathelin, the adventures of Sinbad or Ali-Baba, or comic scenes from the Italian *commedia dell'arte*.

Of his mother, in the shadow of whose absorbing love and strict principles he lived until her death in 1895, when he was twenty-five years old, André Gide has more to say in his memoirs: "She was forever striving toward something good, toward something better, and never relapsed into self-satisfaction. It was not enough for her to be modest; she constantly strove toward diminishing her imperfections, or those she surprised in others, toward correcting herself or others, toward educating herself. While my father was alive, all this was dominated and absorbed by a great love. Her love for me was doubtless scarcely less, but all the submission she had showed toward my father she now demanded of me. From this there resulted conflicts that helped to convince me that I resembled only my father; the deepest ancestral resemblances come out only late in life." In general he depicts his mother as a creature of convention, a victim of her typical *bourgeois* upbringing, but on at least two occasions he expresses admiration for the unconventional way in which she braved the whole family and went to care for the farmers on her estate at La Roque when they were suffering from an epidemic of typhus. It was she who caused him to begin the study of the piano at seven. Through modesty she never played alone, but with his first teacher his mother used to launch vigorously into duets. Usually they were taken from a Haydn symphony, preferably the finale, "which, she thought, involved less expression because of the rapid tempo—which she would precipitate even more as she approached the end. She would count aloud from one end to the other of the piece."

It is impossible for her son, as for anyone else who knew her, to visualize Mme Paul Gide without seeing beside her the dignified and beautiful figure of Miss Anna Shackleton. Calmness, purity, severity characterized her noble features. In speaking of her long after her death André Gide would have liked "to invent more vibrant, more respectful, and more affectionate words." Miss Anna, as she was then known, had entered the Rondeaux family in 1850 or 1851 as governess to Juliette, then in her late teens. The presence of this Scottish girl in France is explained by her father's having been brought over to Rouen as foreman of a foundry connected with the laying of the Paris-Havre railway. Very soon the pretty, gay girl, but little older than her charge, was considered as Juliette's *dame de com-*

pagnie. Then she lost altogether her semi-domestic status, until people came to speak without distinction of *"ces demoiselles."* Upon Juliette's marriage, Anna Shackleton followed the couple to Paris and took an apartment not far away: having remained a spinster, she was not to have any other family than the one lent her by the Rondeaux and the Gides. "However harmoniously calm the expression of her face, her gait, and her whole life," Gide says of her, "Anna was never idle." When alone she translated, for she read English and German as well, and Italian almost as well, as she did French. When with others, she worked on interminable, subtle embroideries, often consulting a blue and white pattern on the table beside her. Moreover she drew well and painted water-colors, many of which have remained in the family.

But Anna Shackleton's chief occupation and study was botany. Besides attending lectures at the Museum of Natural History, she went on regular Sunday field trips made up almost exclusively of old maids and amiable cranks, each with a green metal box slung over his shoulder. Little André sometimes went along, carrying his butterfly net and stuffing his pockets with glass tubes in which to asphyxiate his victims with benzine fumes or cyanide of potassium. With Anna's help he made an herbarium and also helped to fill out her very large collection of fine examples delicately held down by gummed paper and labeled in her neat hand.

It was chiefly at La Roque, where Anna Shackleton accompanied the family every summer, that the collection of plants reigned supreme. As far back as André Gide could recall, he spent his Christmas and New Year at Uncle Émile's in Rouen, his Easter holidays at grandmother Gide's in Uzès, and the long summer vacations at La Roque. This château in Calvados, some seven or eight miles west of Lisieux, had been bought in 1851 by his grandfather, Édouard Rondeaux. On the death of his grandmother in 1874, it had come to his mother, who in turn left it to him when she died in 1895. Five years later, because of the heavy responsibilities it entailed, he was reluctantly to sell the domain with its 593 acres divided into eight farms and its 370 acres of woodland. Of the manor-house built in 1577 and destroyed by revolutionaries in 1792 there remained but an elegant postern gate with drawbridge, a dovecote, and the kitchen wing, all in a characteristic Renaissance combination of brick and white stone. The central part of the château had been rebuilt in the same style in 1803 and had, according to Gide, "no other charm than the mantle of wistaria covering it." But, most important of all, the château was surrounded by a deep moat, which was fed by a flower-lined stream that broke into a murmuring waterfall beneath Anna's window.

From the little gravel courtyard in front of the house, over the parapet of the moat and beyond the garden, the view plunged deeply down a valley. Behind the house a steep meadow rose to a little gate leading into the woods that covered the hill and extended, with all their impenetrable mystery, the little boy knew not how far.

In Rouen the family used to stay in the large house in the rue de Crosne where Mme Paul Gide had been brought up. The ground floor included a kitchen, a stable, a carriage-room, a storeroom for the stock of Rouen prints manufactured by Uncle Henri, and a small office heavy with cigar smoke. Opposite the courtyard entrance the inner stairway rose four flights with green velvet benches on each landing where the child would stretch out prone to read.

The center of young André's life when in Rouen, or in Normandy at all for that matter, was his cousins—not so much the children of Uncle Henri, who were a bit too old, as those of Uncle Émile Rondeaux, who lived somewhat more modestly in the dull rue de Lecat. They were five: Madeleine, two and one half years older than André, Jeanne, a year and one half older than he, Valentine, born in June 1870, Édouard and Georges, born respectively in November 1871 and December 1872. For reasons of discretion, Gide in his memoirs has changed the

names of the girls, calling Jeanne "Suzanne" and rebaptizing
Valentine as "Louise." For Madeleine, whom he was later to
marry, he kept the pseudonym he had already used in *Les
Cahiers d'André Walter* and in his *Journals*: "Emmanuèle."
Édouard and Georges appear under their own names.

In the early years "the boys"—as the others scornfully
called them—were negligible quantities because too young.
In the beginning Madeleine was too quiet for André's taste, always quitting the play when it became noisy or questionable,
forever isolating herself with a book. "She never disputed; it
was so natural for her to yield to the others her turn, her place,
her share, and always with such smiling grace, that one wondered if she were not doing so rather from inclination than
from virtue and if she would not have had to force herself to act
otherwise." Bold, lively, and spontaneous, Jeanne was the one
with whom André most enjoyed playing, as he did with Valentine when she was in a good mood. With the three girls he not
only played but studied, for they had classes together under the
same tutor; they shared the same desires and plans, forming
their taste along the same lines. When their parents would separate them at nightfall, he used to think: "This has to be since
we are still young; but a time will come when even the night
will not separate us."

The happy childhood memories associated with the Rondeaux cousins have as background the large house in the rue de
Crosne, Uncle Henri's important textile-printing plant at Le
Houlme just outside of Rouen, and, during the summers, the
château of La Roque and that of Cuverville-en-Caux, which belonged to the girls' father, Uncle Émile. Upon Émile Rondeaux's
death in 1890, the large house surrounded by a seventeen-acre
park and 185 acres of farmlands, to which were added the 142
acres of adjoining Gonneville with its six farms, fell to Madeleine. Hence André Gide's marriage five years later made him
proprietor of both La Roque and Cuverville and, inasmuch as

he was to sell the former estate in 1900, Cuverville was to play an important part in his mature life.

The long, three-storey house dates from the eighteenth century, of which it has the typical mansard roof and small-paned windows. In front of the house a wide, shaded lawn is surrounded by walls, over which can be seen the farmyard with its avenue of beeches. To the west, behind the house, lies the garden, its paths outlined by espaliered fruit trees and protected by a thick curtain of tall trees. Beyond and down a few steps, the vegetable garden extends to a high brick wall sheltering a small door that opens onto a thicket of woods. From the southern façade one can look over these gardens, the wall, and the grove to a plateau covered with rich grain.

This is the domain that directly inspired the beautiful description of Fongueusemare in *La Porte étroite*, from which the above details are taken. When André Gide was writing his memoirs years later at Cuverville, he could look out on the garden circle surrounded by clipped yews where he and his cousins used to play in the sand and on the silvery linden in the shade of which Madeleine so timidly and Jeanne so daringly used to indulge in gymnastics. In front of the house the big cedar in which each of the children had arranged a "room" had become enormous; he and Jeanne used to climb to the very top and shout down to those below: "We can see the sea!"

If the winter holidays and summer vacations were regularly spent in Normandy among the Rondeaux, Easter always brought the family back to the paternal relatives in the south. One can imagine young Mme Paul Gide's shock, after a childhood spent in industrial Rouen and the lush pasturelands of Calvados, upon getting off the train in Nîmes and riding for miles in a carriage over dusty roads to the little town of Uzès, which nineteenth-century progress had apparently neglected. In the grandmother's apartment all the rooms communicated, so that in order to reach their room André's parents had to go through the dining-room, the drawing-room and another smaller parlor in which his bed had been set up. Grandfather Tancrède Gide having died before André's birth, and most of the children having succumbed in their early years, the family consisted merely of the grandmother and Uncle Charles. At that time the future economist of the Collège de France, whose international fame was for long to eclipse that of his literary nephew, was "a tall young man with long black hair plastered down behind his ears, somewhat short-sighted, somewhat odd, silent, and as intimidating as possible."

It would be impossible, thought the grandson, to imagine anyone older than his grandmother. Nothing about her gave a hint as to what she might once have been. Still she outlived her son Paul Gide by many years, during which André and his mother returned to Uzès each spring to find her but slightly more deaf than before.

Little André would spend his time roaming the heaths accompanied by his mother's Swiss maid, Marie, or on rainy days he would take the clocks apart and, to his grandmother's amazement, set them working again. One day in a diagonal knothole that descended deep into the cupboard door in the dining-room his finger encountered something round and smooth. The aged servant Rose told him that it was a marble his father had dropped in there when he was about André's age. This information only excited him the more, and he constantly slipped his little finger into the hole in an effort to pull up the marble, which merely rolled over with a little scraping sound. On his return to Uzès the following spring, he ran at once to that door, for, despite the ridicule his mother and Marie had heaped upon him, he had let the nail of his little finger grow to an extraordinary length. As soon as he got his nail under the marble and pulled, it popped out into his other hand. "My first impulse," he relates in his memoirs, "was to run to the kitchen and cry victory; but, immediately anticipating the pleasure I should get from Rose's congratulations, I foresaw it as so slight that this stopped me.

I remained for a few moments before the door staring at that gray marble in the hollow of my hand, henceforth just like any other marble, now quite without interest as soon as it had left its hiding-place. I felt utterly foolish and sheepish for having tried to be smart. . . Blushing, I dropped the marble back into the hole (it is probably still there) and went to cut my nails without telling anyone of my exploit."

It is not surprising that André Gide's earliest happy memories should derive from the vacation periods, for his formal schooling did not begin auspiciously. After attending, at the age of five, the private classes conducted by Mlle Fleur and Mme Lackerbauer, he entered the ninth form, taught by M. Vedel, of the École Alsacienne in the rue d'Assas. The very first day he received his first zero for obstinately refusing to grasp the principle of synonyms. Although but eight years old, he rapidly became accustomed to a regular weekly "zero in deportment" and to the last rank in studies. As he tells us, it was as if he had not yet been born. Only a few weeks later he was temporarily suspended: "M. Brunig, who was in charge of the lower forms, gave me three months to cure myself of those 'vicious habits' which M. Vedel had easily discovered because I did not take great care to hide them, not having really understood that they were so reprehensible; for I was still living (if this can be called living) in the half-awake state of imbecility that I have depicted."

Three months later he was back in class, apparently cured, but soon thereafter a case of the measles persuaded his parents to take him to La Roque without waiting for the holidays. Repeating the ninth form the following year, he began to have good marks, and this gave him a new interest in his studies. Although the École Alsacienne had nothing but day pupils, some of the teachers took a small number of boarders into their homes; thus as André Gide entered the eighth form in the autumn of 1880 he took board and lodging in the house of M. Vedel, though his own home was just across the Luxembourg

Gardens. This experience did not last long, for it was in late October of that year that his father died. Having decided to withdraw to Rouen for the winter, Mme Gide took her son along, and again his education was interrupted. To be sure, he studied with tutors both then and the following summer, spent at La Roque, but years later he wondered that so interrupted a schooling could have given him anything.

The ways of parents are often inscrutable even when resulting, as in the case of Mme Gide, from serious deliberation and consultation; and the mature Gide disclaims knowing why his mother took him the next winter to Montpellier, within a few miles of the Mediterranean, where his Uncle Charles was then living. However dull and ugly the apartment that mother and son and the faithful Marie found near the Esplanade, the Lycée which André attended made home seem a paradise. The pupils were divided into two camps according to whether they were Catholics or Protestants, and even the best of them were interested chiefly in cannons and home-made firecrackers. Furthermore, André's first recitation of poetry, in which he expressed the feeling and rhythm as he had been taught in Paris, by drawing a compliment from the teacher aroused the hostility of all his classmates. Chased and ambushed every day as he left school, he often got home with his clothes torn and mud-covered and his nose bleeding. Providentially he fell ill, and the doctor's diagnosis of smallpox saved him from his pursuers.

His dizziness on first getting up several weeks later suggested exaggerating his weakness, for the doctor had just given the unwelcome news that he could return to school in a few days. "And while I was imagining," he says in the memoirs, "already I could feel what a relaxation of strain, what a relief I should enjoy by yielding to the urging of my nerves. A backward glance to choose the spot and make sure of not hurting myself too much when I fell. . ." The success of this initial fall encouraged him to invent other movements, convulsive or rhythmical, until he had a veritable repertory.

In general the mature Gide judges this phase of his childhood with a mingling of severe reprobation and sincere perplexity, unable to say where the real malady left off and the simulation began. At any rate, a consultation of three doctors, two of whom even wore white beards, treated him most seriously and he accordingly spent the spring and autumn taking the iron-and-acid baths at Lamalou-les-Bains and the intervening summer under treatment at Gerardmer. When he finally returned to the École Alsacienne after ten months of intellectual inactivity, dreadful headaches made him give up again at the end of a month. Again he is unable to say just how real his sufferings were, but thirty-five years later he was unable to forgive the doctor who prescribed a regime of bromide and chloral for a growing child.

By this time, two years after his father's death, anyone would have augured very ill of the thirteen-year-old André Gide. Until then his education had been of the most spotty nature possible, and this is particularly serious in France, where so much is crammed into the first ten years of school. For the next five years he was to study under private tutors, living as a boarding pupil or half-boarder in the homes of different teachers, before returning to the École Alsacienne in the autumn of 1887. He had reached then, at the end of 1882, the lowest point in his spiritual development. In the words of his memoirs, "Decidedly the devil had his eye on me; I was enveloped in darkness and nothing gave a hint as to where and whence a ray of hope might fall upon me. Then it was that the angelic intervention I am about to relate came to tear me from the Evil One. An infinitely modest event in appearance, but as important in my life as revolutions are for empires, the first scene of a drama that is not yet finished."

The incident, in fictional form, is known to readers of *La Porte étroite* (*Strait is the Gate*), but the true version given in the memoirs is even more stirring. He was in Rouen in December, where he found his three cousins again. Though he played most often and naturally with the two younger girls, it was Madeleine whom he preferred for her very reserve and gravity. However serious he became to please her, he felt that he was still a child whereas she had ceased to be one. He strove to share her tastes and thoughts even to the childish point of going without dessert when, to test him, she did so. "I did not discover gradually, as one most often does, the secrets of a soul, the secret sadness that was so precociously maturing my cousin. It was the total and sudden revelation of an unsuspected world, on which my eyes opened all at once, like the eyes of the man born blind when the Lord had touched them."

Having left his cousins toward evening and not finding his mother at home at the rue de Crosne, he returned unexpectedly to the rue de Lecat, full of the joy of taking his cousins by surprise. A maid, obviously awaiting a visitor at the outer door, expressed annoyance at his return. Noiselessly he climbed the stairs and as he passed his aunt's brilliantly lighted bedroom he saw her languidly lying on a sofa while Jeanne and Valentine fanned her. An instinct told him that Madeleine was not there. In her room on the top floor, he found her kneeling by her bed. As she gently reproached him for coming back, and he felt her tears in the dark, a light dawned upon him, for he sensed her anguish if not the "abominable secret" that caused it.

In *Si le grain ne meurt . . .* this account directly precedes the following capital commentary: "I think today that nothing could be more cruel, for a child who was all purity, love, and affection, than having to judge her mother and disapprove her conduct. And the torment was intensified by having to keep to herself and hide from the father she venerated a secret she had discovered in some way and which had crushed her—that secret about which the town was gossiping and the maids snickering and which took advantage of her sisters' carefree innocence. No, I was not to understand any of this until later; but I felt that this little creature whom I already cherished was filled with a great and unbearable grief, a sorrow such that it would

require all my love and my whole life to cure. What more shall
I say? . . . Until that day I had wandered aimlessly; I suddenly discovered a new Orient to my life. [. . .] I hid in the
depths of my heart the secret of my destiny. Had it been less
contradicted and crossed, I should not be writing these memoirs."

From this point onward his cousin Madeleine was to be in
his thoughts constantly. She was, indeed, the dominant influence
of his adolescent years. Each step in his intellectual and spiritual development had to be taken, not only in full view of her,
but even in unison with her. While reading he would write her
initials opposite every sentence that he wanted to share with her.
Away from her, he wrote innumerable letters, which later struck
him as odiously artificial. But how could he be natural when
seeking his path amidst such a complex tangle of possibilities?

Already at eleven, shaken by some indefinable anguish, he
had fallen into his mother's arms sobbing: "I am not like the
others! I am not like the others!" Much has been made of that
incident, some seeing in it an improbable foreshadowing of his
emotional and sensual unconventionality, whereas others interpret it as a barely conscious awareness of the artist's eternal
isolation and uniqueness. When faced for the first time with the
brutalities of life, most men have obscurely felt their own individuality and expressed some symbolic revolt against one or
more aspects of the human condition. And it is but reasonable
that the artist should do so earlier than others. However that
may be, three years later, when a canary lighted on his head
as he was crossing a Paris street, the young André Gide took this
as confirmation of his own feeling that he was predestined. But
what his vocation might be, it would have been impossible to say.

At that stage of his adolescence no one would have predicted
for him a literary career. It would have been easier to foresee
him as a scientist or a concert pianist. Having begun his musical education at seven, he had already endured the lessons of
several indifferent teachers before being entrusted to the sympathetic and inspired care of Marc de La Nux. Born in 1830 on

Reunion Island in the Indian Ocean, Marc de La Nux had come to France at eleven and had studied at the Nîmes Conservatory and under Franz Liszt, through whom he met Chopin. A tall, dark-skinned man with a languid air, in his long Prince Albert and high collar twice encircled by a silk cravat he greatly resembled Delacroix's self-portrait. For sixty years he taught in Paris, forming many accomplished pianists who recall that up to his death in 1914 he knew by heart all the Beethoven sonatas. His infectious enthusiasm inspired his pupil to develop his memory so that after the first few weeks the young Gide knew several Bach fugues by heart without having opened the music. Suddenly he felt as if he had become able to speak a divine language whose sounds he had previously repeated without understanding. Years later he learned that Marc de La Nux had begged his mother to sacrifice the rest of his education to music by entrusting him, without charge, to this single teacher. Fortunately Mme Gide decided that her son could do better in life than to interpret the work of others. The veneration André Gide felt for such a master during his four years of study never diminished after Marc de La Nux told him that he had learned to do without lessons. Nor did it become any the less when, under the transparent pseudonym of M. de La Pérouse, Gide recorded conversations with him in the *Journals* and used him as the starting-point for a character in *Les Faux-Monnayeurs* (*The Counterfeiters*).

Every Sunday Mme Gide and her son would dine with her older sister Mme Claire Desmarest and nephew Albert, twenty years older than André. After dinner, while the ladies enjoyed a game of cards, the two cousins would sit down at the piano and play everything that was then available in transcription for four hands, but principally the trios, quartets, and symphonies of Mozart, Beethoven, and Schumann.

At the age of ten the boy had begun attending concerts with his mother, first those of Pasdeloup and then those of the Conservatory. His most vivid musical recollection of those years is associated with the series of concerts that Anton Rubinstein gave in the winter of 1883, tracing the evolution of piano music from its origins. André Gide attended three of his concerts devoted respectively to ancient music, to Beethoven, and to Schumann. He wanted to hear the Chopin concert also, but his mother considered Chopin "unhealthy" and refused to take him.

Such a taboo is particularly piquant in view of André Gide's later implied choice of Chopin as his favorite composer. There is none other whom he has played more consistently nor studied more fervently for sixty years; there is none on whom he has written so pertinently and at such length. Indeed, G. Jean-Aubry doubted if Chopin had ever known a more faithful and less sentimental devotion, and the French critic, M. Fred Goldbeck recommended in 1949 that the Chopin centenary be celebrated by each individual before his own piano with Gide's *Notes sur Chopin*, "the best interpretation one can listen to just now."

Very few amateurs give music such an important place in their lives as André Gide consistently gave it. His journals abound in notations of the joy he always took in playing and of the hours spent at his piano. Except for rare periods, he regularly devoted several hours daily to his practice; occasionally, as in 1913 and again in January 1931, he noted that he was spending as much as five hours at the piano each day; in October 1926, soon after returning from a year in the Congo, this figure rose even higher. Even when away from home, he did not forego his practice: at Biskra in his twenties he had a piano sent at great expense from Algiers as, during a winter spent in the Jura mountains, he had one sent out from Geneva. Although he frequently refers to his playing of Beethoven and Schumann, Albéniz and Granados, he returned most insistently to Bach and Chopin.

Upon the death of his wife in 1938, André Gide closed his piano with the intention of never opening it again, perhaps because Mme Gide was the only one with whom he could share his music (his *Journals* are full of comments revealing his inability to play properly before an audience even of intimate friends). Thus his lifelong communion with music remained, because of such self-consciousness, a purely personal matter without the usual satisfaction of vanity. In January 1939 he noted: "When I think of the farewell I said to music,

My heart almost bursts

and it does not seem to me that death can take anything from me, now, that has meant more to me."

Throughout his life André Gide was to teach many others to play, often continuing his lessons—as in the case of his niece Françoise Gilbert—for years. He is quite justified when he states in his memoirs that if he had to earn his living he would become a piano teacher, adding: "I have a passion for teaching and, if the pupil is worth it, a never-failing patience."

The other career that Gide specifically recognized he might have followed instead of the one in which he distinguished himself is that of the natural sciences. Thinking back, in his forties, to his early years, he reflects that if he had then met a naturalist, he would most eagerly have followed him, deserting literature, so great was his taste for the natural sciences. This taste manifested itself very early, for in a letter written by his mother to his father in 1873 she said that the four-year-old "André would be very nice if he didn't have a mania for standing a long time absolutely still at the foot of a tree, watching snails." As a boy, on his walks near Uzès with his mother's maid, he used to collect caterpillars, those of the hawk-moth with a horn on their rear and those of the swallow-tailed butterfly which, when stroked, "put forth above their neck a sort of forked trunk, very odorous and of unexpected color." In Normandy he communicated his enthusiasm to his cousin Jeanne, until she became accustomed to turning over cow-pies and carcasses in search of carrion-beetles. One of the great joys of his childhood was finding, in an old pile of sawdust, a colony of *oryctes nasicornes* or rhinoceros-beetles and their eggs, which he tried to keep in sawdust until their pupation. His family must have taken this interest quite seriously, for in his early teens they gave him the collection of coleoptera made by his grandmother's first cousin, Félix-Archimède Pouchet, the naturalist who obstinately upheld the theory of spontaneous generation against Pasteur.

"It is not given to everyone to have a cousin named Archimède," Gide says flippantly after inheriting the twenty-four cork-lined boxes which made his own collection seem paltry. Nor, he might have added, is it given to everyone to have a several-times-great uncle named Father Incarville, who, as a Jesuit missionary to Pekin in the eighteenth century, had built up a valuable collection of exotic plants now preserved at the Natural History Museum and a great-great-grandfather named Charles Rondeaux de Montbray who won a first prize in botany before he was fourteen, later composed a "Tableau of Living Nature, drawn from the best Authors," and in 1778 catalogued the Rouen Botanical Garden.

Although entomology was André Gide's first love among the natural sciences, he early became passionately interested, doubtless through the influence of Anna Shackleton, in botany as well. At the age of thirteen the important events of his stay at Hyères on the south coast were his first encounter with eucalyptus trees and the discovery of a little hooded arum. A few years later he kept beside his desk in boarding-school a gladiolus he had planted. Struck by the rapid growth of the green spear emerging from the soil, he stood a white stick in the pot and noted on it each day's upward progress. Thus he calculated that the leaf grew at a rate of three-fifths of a millimeter every hour and he was disappointed not to be able to discern the actual growing.

His *Journals* reveal that his vivid interest in botany and entomology never flagged. During his travels in Andorra, Turkey, Italy, and Germany he constantly notes the new flora he observes. In the Congo and the Chad he regrets having no one to whom to show the rare botanical specimens, and from there he returns with a precious insect collection. He decidedly and consistently has more taste for natural history than for history —the fortuitous, as he says, interesting him less than the necessary.

Many traces of these interests are found in the creative work, whether Gide chooses a banal but misunderstood flower as a subtle symbol in *Paludes*, writes his vivid observations of the lemur called Dindiki, which he tamed in Africa, or uses the accumulated records of natural history as arguments in his *Corydon*. In a pious and turgid article on the relations between art and science in Gide's work, the Swiss biologist Jean Strohl does homage to this writer who might have been a naturalist because he joins a "profound passion for everything living [. . .] with the divine gift of relating discoveries in exquisite and delicate words."

Yet the young André Gide's intense enthusiasm for natural phenomena by no means dampened his religious ardor. At home a puritanical mother brought him up according to the strictest principles. In this she was seconded by Anna Shackleton, whose death in May 1884 was a great loss to the family, and to a lesser degree by her sister Claire Desmarest. Outside the home he was subject to the same influences. Of the three teachers in whose houses he boarded before returning to the École Alsacienne in October 1887, one had prepared for the ministry and the second played the organ Sundays at the Protestant Church in the rue Madame. The homes of these two gentlemen were to fuse years later and, with the name of the third teacher, M. Vedel, to form the Pension Vedel of *Les Faux-Monnayeurs*. In the summers Mme Gide invited the son of a poor minister, Armand Bavretel, to La Roque as a companion for André; he was to enter the same novel almost unchanged and his father was to contribute many a trait to the fictional M. Vedel.

M. Couve, the minister who prepared the boy for his first Communion, was a pious, dull man whose very voice had an orthodox ring as he analyzed the Bible to the little class in his dining-room. Aware of a certain doctrinal dryness in the exposition of the dogma, the young Gide came to wonder whether the Protestant religion responded to his need, whether his heart in quest of God was approaching the altar most suited to him. He spoke of his doubts to M. Couve, who gave him a treatise on Catholic doctrine which chilled his enthusiasm and counterbalanced the emotion he felt upon reading Bossuet, Fénelon, and Pascal. Thrown back upon himself, he began to read the Bible from beginning to end, greedily but methodically; each evening he would read a few chapters of the historical books, a few of the poetical books, and a few from the prophets. Though studying by himself rather than attending school, he adhered to a rigorous program:

"Up before dawn, I would plunge into the icy water with which I had carefully filled a tub the night before; then, before setting to work, I would read a few chapters of the Scriptures, or rather re-read those I had marked the night before as most appropriate to start my meditation on this day; then I would pray. My prayer was a sort of visible impulse of the soul to penetrate God more deeply; and I would renew that impulse from hour to hour; thus I would interrupt my study, never changing its object without again offering it to God. Out of a sense of mortification I used to sleep on a board; in the middle of the night I would get up and kneel again, not so much through mortification as through the impatience of my joy. At such times it used to seem to me that I was attaining the very summit of happiness."

It was during his methodical and personal reading of the Bible that he discovered the Gospel and felt as if he had found the source and purpose of love. He developed the habit of carrying a New Testament in his pocket to read at all times, even in odd places such as street-cars or during recess at school, offering up to God his embarrassment caused by the jibes of his schoolmates. The feeling that the Gospel aroused in him seemed identical with that he experienced for his cousin, Madeleine, the one emotion deepening and justifying the other.

At about the same time, his mind beginning to open to all manifestations of beauty alike, he discovered the Greeks in the translations of Leconte de Lisle. "Through them," he says in his memoirs, "I contemplated Olympus, and man's suffering and the Gods' smiling severity; I learned mythology; I embraced Beauty, hugging it to my eager heart." As Gide, in his maturity, records this double and simultaneous enthusiasm for Christ and the ancients, he expresses wonder that he could harbor such contraries. Yet his unawareness of the contradiction at the time is most significant, for throughout his life his Christianity will be tempered by an equally inherent classicism.

In looking back over André Gide's antecedents and childhood, knowing what he was later to become, we are struck, as he says of the Greek myths, less by the obscure play of fate than by the underlying psychological truth. Heredity and environment combined to make of him at this stage of his adolescence a physically delicate, highly sensitive boy of artistic taste and attentive, curious mind, affectionate but inordinately shy, proud without being vain. Often solitary, he had developed to a high degree the gift of introspection. Over-scrupulous as a result of a puritanical upbringing and a tendency to self-examination, he might have been considered prudish. Little about him as he entered his last year of formal schooling in October 1887 could have revealed the man he was to be but ten years later.

At this point he is leaving behind his childhood and crossing the threshold of manhood. He is in that transitional period of self-discovery—for him, possibly because there was more to discover, it will last longer than it usually does—which can best be symbolized by the myth of Narcissus.

Now, the second of André Gide's works to be published, which appeared before he was twenty-two, was entitled precisely *Le Traité du Narcisse* (*Treatise of the Narcissus*). And with these words the little poem in prose opened:

"Books are perhaps not a very necessary thing; in the beginning a few myths sufficed; a complete religion was embodied in them. The masses were impressed by the exterior of the fables and without understanding, adored; attentive priests, bending over the depths of the images, gradually penetrated the intimate meaning of the hieroglyph. Then it seemed desirable to explain; books amplified the myths;—but a few myths sufficed.

"So it was with the myth of Narcissus: *Narcissus was utterly beautiful and this is why he was chaste; he scorned the Nymphs because he was in love with himself. No breath of wind troubled the spring in which, motionless and leaning over, all day long he contemplated his image. . .* You know the story. Yet we shall relate it again. All things have been said already; but, since no one listens, it is essential to repeat again."

III. THE NARCISSUS POSE

"His hands on the frame, now, he leans
over, in his traditional posture."

LOOKING back to his early years, André Gide twice sees
himself in the pose of Narcissus; between the two occasions there is a world of difference, however, far greater than
the few intervening years would imply. The first relates to a
childhood sojourn on the Mediterranean when, visiting the
island of Saint-Marghérite off the coast of Cannes, he used to
revel in the deep bays divided into numerous pools by the ero-
sion of the rocks: "I had only to remain motionless, leaning
like Narcissus over the surface of the waters, to wonder as I
saw gradually emerge from a thousand holes, a thousand an-
fractuosities of the rock, everything that my approach had put
to flight. [. . .] Translucid, bizarre, strange-acting creatures
loomed up out of the tangle of sea-weeds; the water became
peopled; the light sand covering the bottom began to stir in
spots, and, at the end of colorless tubes that had seemed nothing but old reeds, one saw a frail corolla, at first still somewhat
timid, blossom forth with little convulsive movements." This
was in the spring of 1883 when the boy was thirteen.

The second occasion records an oft-repeated experience of
his nineteenth and twentieth years: "Since I had posed for
Albert (he had just finished my portrait) I had been greatly
concerned with my personage; anxiety to appear as the artist
I felt I was, I wanted to be, went so far as to keep me from
being anything and made of me what is called a *poseur*. In the

mirror of a little secretary-desk inherited from Anna that my mother had put in my room and at which I used to work, I would contemplate my features, tirelessly, study them, train them like an actor, and seek on my lips and in my eyes the expression of all the passions I longed to experience. . . At that time I could not write (and I might almost say think), it seemed to me, unless facing that little mirror. In order to be aware of my emotion, of my thought, it seemed to me that I had first to read it in my eyes. Like Narcissus, I used to bend over my image; every sentence I wrote then is somewhat distorted in consequence."

From the rock pool (could it be that the title of Cyril Connolly's first novel was suggested by the passage from *Si le grain ne meurt . . .?*) to the mirror over the writing desk is a considerable jump; yet the two passages enlighten one another. In the first instance, where solely the pose is narcissistic, we are reminded of the precocious naturalist; and it was precisely that congenital interest in nature and the world beyond himself that kept the later and typically adolescent self-scrutiny from becoming a permanent attitude in Gide.

In the interval between the two instances, the schoolboy torn by a multiplicity of interests had acquired focus, and during his last two years of formal schooling a strong literary vocation had become discernible. The memoirs provide disappointingly little information as to his earliest extra-curricular reading. We know that during his teens his sympathetic Aunt Lucile, who always tried to give him gifts he wanted, made one birthday memorable with a set of Sainte-Beuve's solid critical essays and another with the entire *Comédie humaine*. At thirteen—that is three years before Victor Hugo's death in 1885—he used to recite Hugo's bombastic plays with his tutor; and at sixteen, with the young François de Witt, great-nephew of the historian Guizot and a Protestant like himself, he read such Catholic classics as Bossuet, Fénelon, and Pascal; soon thereafter he discovered that model of Protestant introspection, Amiel's *Journal*.

At about the same time, his mother finally consented to give him access to his father's library, though maintaining close control over his choice and requiring him to read aloud to her. Thus it is that they waded together through the five volumes of Saint-Marc Girardin's mid-nineteenth-century lectures on dramatic literature at the rate of a chapter a day. But, after an embarrassing experience with a poem of Théophile Gautier which was not intended for reading *en famille*, Mme Gide prudently withdrew and let him browse at will. Charmed by the Greek and Roman classics, lovingly chosen by his father and handsomely bound, he was drawn even more by the attractive editions of the French poets. Already he had formed the habit of taking a volume of Hugo with him on his walks and learning the poems by heart.

As is natural at that age, he adds in *Si le grain ne meurt . . .*, he considered art synonymous with poetry and took pleasure in the subtleties of verse technique. Yet perhaps his greatest discovery in the well-stocked library was the poems of Heine in translation, for the forsaking of rhyme and metre offered a model that he felt he himself could follow. Less than two years later, in the autumn of 1887, when the most brilliant student in the class approached during the afternoon recess and asked him what he was reading, he was proud to display a copy of Heine's *Buch der Lieder*, which he was then reading in the original.

This was a decisive encounter, for that fellow-student, graced with charm of person and vivacity of mind, was Pierre Louis, who was destined to play an important part, with his voluptuous *Chansons de Bilitis* (1894) and his famous novel *Aphrodite* (1896), in the neo-classical literature of the *fin de siècle*. A few months younger than Gide but intellectually and socially more mature than any in the class, Louis—who had not yet imagined the preciously archaic orthography of Louÿs— was already known to his classmates as a versifier. And on that day for the first time, in the rigorously competitive system of

French education, he had lost the first place in French composition—and to this shy youth who had been out of school for
years, and who now, ignoring the rough games going on about
him in the yard, was solemnly reading Heine in German.

After the first charming hesitations and a brief period of
somewhat frightened reserve on both parts similar to that of a
pair of lovers, their common passion for literature made these
two boys of eighteen inseparable companions. Dazzled by the
facility that Pierre Louis already showed in writing and following the pernicious example of the Parnassian poet, Sully-
Prudhomme, then at the height of his fame, Gide strove painfully to "translate into verse" his adolescent thoughts and
emotions. To excuse his evident ineptitude in these exercises, he
confessed to his companion that he was completely absorbed by
a projected work in prose into which he was pouring all his
interrogations and anxieties, his perplexities and intimate conflicts. But principally—and this he doubtless did not tell his
friend—it was to reflect his ardent love for his cousin Madeleine Rondeaux. In his mind it was to be not only his first
work but the very essence of its author. Beyond it he saw nothing but death and dissolution, for it was to absorb him utterly.

More than a year was to pass before he could devote himself
completely to this book. But, as he tells us, "I had got into the
habit of keeping a journal, through a need to mould a confused
inner agitation; and many a page of that journal was transcribed
without change into those *Cahiers.* The preoccupation in which
I lived had this serious disadvantage of absorbing introspec-
tively all my faculties of attention; I wrote and longed to write
nothing that was not intimate; I scorned history, and events
seemed to me impertinent interlopers. Today when I admire
perhaps nothing so much as a well-constructed narrative, I am
seized with irritation upon re-reading those pages; but, at that
time, far from realizing that art lives only in the particular, I
aimed to remove it from contingencies, considered as contingent
any sharp outline, and dreamed only of quintessence." During

this period of preparation for his first book, *Les Cahiers d'André Walter* (*The Notebooks of André Walter*), the young Gide finished his year of *rhétorique* at the École Alsacienne, at the end of which both he and Pierre Louis moved to the state *lycée* for their final year of schooling. Whereas Louis entered the Lycée Janson de Sailly on the Right Bank for his *philosophie* (as that final year is called), Gide registered at the older Lycée Henri IV, nearer to his home. But, less than three months later, he abandoned the courses in order to finish his preparation by himself.

His initiation to philosophy, he tells us, took place at this time with Schopenhauer's *World as Will and Idea*, which he read with an "indescribable rapture"; he must also have read many other philosophers, to judge from the references in his early works and from his own statement that at this period he read a book a day. This did not prevent him, however, from failing the second part of his baccalaureate in July and having to repeat the examination in October 1889. During the summer of 1889, between the two examinations, he traveled through Brittany making notes on the spectacular landscape and on the feast of Saint-Anne d'Auray. His mother, who would have preferred him to join a mountain-climbing club and visit Switzerland, managed to catch up with him every two or three days with a fresh supply of linen. The journey was not lost on the young artist, for two years later he was to publish some of his sensitive and rather self-conscious verbal sketches under the title of "Little Studies in Rhythm." In middle life, when writing his memoirs, he was to recall most vividly an encounter with three young painters at Le Pouldu who were brashly working in pure colors with what seemed like a childish technique. When he met Paul Gauguin at Mallarmé's shortly thereafter, he recognized the group of Le Pouldu to have been composed of Gauguin, Séruzier, and Filiger.

With his examinations behind him, André Gide resolved to launch out into his career, feeling curiously free yet obligated

by his love and by the plan of his book. Indeed, the two interests fused, for the book appeared to him as a long declaration
of love so moving and so peremptory that after its publication
neither Madeleine nor their parents could refuse to sanction
their marriage. This was, as we shall see upon examining *The
Notebooks of André Walter*, a very sanguine prognostication.
In the meantime, Madeleine's father had died, nursed by the
two young people in his last illness; it even seemed to André that
their formal engagement had been somehow consecrated by their
common grief.

In order to please his mother, however, he undertook some
special work with one of his former professors in the autumn and
spent the winter of 1889–90 reading voraciously, practicing the
piano, and conversing endlessly with Pierre Louis. Following the
lead of his more worldly-wise companion, he began to widen his
circle of acquaintance, first meeting such classmates of Louis
as the future poet Franc-Nohain and the brilliant Marcel Drouin,
who entered the rigorous École Normale Supérieure with the
highest rank that year and emerged an accomplished Germanist to marry Madeleine Rondeaux's younger sister, Jeanne. Soon
the charming, self-confident Louis and the deplorably shy
Gide, "paralyzed with reticences and scruples," were braving
the literary circles, beginning with the regular Saturday afternoon gatherings at the home of the Parnassian poet, José-Maria
de Heredia, where Louis was eventually to choose a wife among
the poet's daughters. From there they moved on to the Symbolist conversations every Tuesday evening at the rue de Rome
apartment of the master whom they called "Saint Mallarmé."
Many have described the calm, almost religious atmosphere of
that little dining-living-room where young poets and painters
gathered to hear their spiritual director. But perhaps no one
has seized its essence better than André Gide in his memorial
article written shortly after the poet's death in 1898: ". . . at
first one was struck by a great silence; at the door all the noises
of the street died; Mallarmé began to speak in a soft, musi-

cal, unforgettable voice—forever stifled now, alas! Oddly, HE THOUGHT BEFORE SPEAKING!" And Gide continues: "For Mallarmé literature was the aim, yes, the very end of life; here one felt it to be authentic and real. In order to sacrifice everything to it as he did, one had to believe in it to the exclusion of all else. I do not think that, in all our literary history, there is an example of a more intransigent conviction."

The appreciation of Stéphane Mallarmé's own highly condensed, hermetic poetry and prose required a long initiation, which only his little group of fervent admirers possessed at that time. As Gide says in the same essay, he had "preserved his work from life; life flowed around him as a river flows by a ship at anchor; he was never carried along." Eminently untimely, his delicate, intellectual poems seemed already to have stood the test of the ages and to occupy a unique position remote from the ravages of time.

Around Mallarmé's table the young disciples seemed subject to some mysterious injunction to combat realism and turn their backs on reality. Lovers of the absolute, they disdained what one of them was later to call "the prismatic diversity of life." André Gide, fresh from his reading of Schopenhauer, fell an easy victim to this half-formulated credo that was to become the basis of the Symbolist movement. It was there and at Heredia's that he met many of his contemporaries who were destined to develop into leaders of that movement. The tall, thin, haughty Henri de Régnier, five years older than he, with his prominent chin, long drooping mustache, and ribboned monocle, was already known for subtly chiseled poems in the Parnassian mood; years later he was to become the official representative of Symbolism in the French Academy. Beside him the stocky figure of the American-born Francis Vielé-Griffin, with his taste for paradox and literary quarrels, formed almost a ridiculous contrast. But he already enjoyed a reputation as a vers-librist and poet of the joys of country life. Ferdinand Hérold, known for his enormous beard and vast knowledge of philology, was at all the gatherings and ever eager to accompany his interlocutor home at midnight (for which Mme Gide felt particularly grateful to him) in order to prolong the conversation; he was to enrich Symbolism more by his translations of Greek and Hindu dramas than by his subtle imagistic poems. Bernard Lazare, a Jew from Nîmes who had been born Lazare Bernard, rather frightened Gide with his ugly aspect and scornful manner; the hidden possibilities Gide felt in him suddenly emerged during the Dreyfus case when, abandoning literature, he became the articulate champion of revisionism. But in 1890 he was fellow-editor with Vielé-Griffin of a little monthly review, *Les Entretiens politiques et littéraires*, which already published Régnier and Mallarmé and to which Gide was soon to contribute. Another, slightly older little magazine, *La Wallonie*, was published in Liége by the Belgian poet, Albert Mockel, who belonged to the same group. His amazing clarity and subtlety of mind, which made Gide feel heavy and vulgar, readily won him a position as one of the first and keenest theoreticians of Symbolism.

In such surroundings and with such companions, all five or six years older than Gide and Louis, it is not surprising that the literary ambitions of the two youths of twenty should have been maintained at white heat. In a journal-entry transposed into his *Cahiers d'André Walter*, Gide notes receiving a letter from Louis speaking of the literary struggle and first triumphs in Paris; he is upset and intoxicated by the feverish air of competition, feeling in it "so many latent reputations" and fearing to arrive too late. Yet at about the same time, with remarkable clairvoyance, Pierre Louis wrote to a friend that Gide had "by far the most future" of them all.

It was to realize that future that André Gide retired to an isolated spot in the country, in the Spring of 1890, to compose the book he had been developing in his mind for some time. Apparently he did not even consider his mother's estate of La Roque as a possible refuge. Indeed, he even abandoned a pleasant spot he had found at Pierrefonds, north of Paris, because Pierre Louis had discovered his secret and pursued him there. After long searching in the region of Grenoble, he settled into two rooms at Menthon on the beautiful Lake of Annecy. Surrounded by his books and with a rented piano sent out from the nearest town, he could devote himself uninterruptedly to self-analysis.

That analysis was to be so intense that the author might be said to have seen himself seeing himself, for into his book of passionate confession he introduced himself in the act of writing that book. Surely this is the height of self-conscious narcissism. Then, through shyness and native reserve, he had *Les Cahiers d'André Walter* published anonymously in February 1891. In order to maintain the fiction of its being the posthumous work of a real André Walter, a brief preface signed with the initials P.C. (for Pierre Chrysis, the first pseudonym of Pierre Louis) informed the reader that the author, born in Brittany in 1870, had withdrawn to Brittany in March 1889, after the death of his mother, to write the notebooks, and that ten months later he had died there of a cerebral fever.

The work is divided into two almost equal parts, the "White Notebook" and the "Black Notebook." The first part, beginning in the present with the death of André's mother and her exacting a promise that he give up her orphaned niece Emmanuèle whom she has taken into the family and is now engaging to a certain T***, is chiefly made up of fragments written in the past. After the marriage of Emmanuèle and T***, André calls on God to bless him for having followed the narrow path. He then takes out and puts in order the pages he had written, which recall his happy days with his cousin, and thus the idea of his projected book, *Allain*, is revived. His journal-entries record life with Emmanuèle, intoxicated by a common spiritual ardor, their readings together of the Greek classics, Shakespeare, Pascal, Bossuet, the French poets, and Flaubert, his playing of Chopin and Schumann to her, their reading the Bible and praying together, and their souls' mingling in "an immaterial kiss."

André Walter would reject the confusion of the physical with the spiritual: "Oh, the poet's blindness!—believing in the inspiration of the Muse when it is merely puberty stirring within him; then strolling out on moonlight nights with the illusion that he has sung the ideal . . . and, when the verse refuses to take shape, expressing the flood of poetry surging within him through dalliance in the arms of a courtesan . . . Dogs likewise bark at moonlight." Accordingly he refuses a friend's advice to liberate his soul by giving his body what it wants, for he resolutely prefers his dream. He would like, indeed, at twenty-one (this entry was written at sixteen), when passion is unleashed, to tame it through intense work. He sees himself enjoying the *voluptés farouches* of monastic life, sleeping on a board in a bare cell.

Yet he is tormented by a need for caresses, suffering in front of the cold immobility of statues. The first notebook, composed of entries dating from 1886 through 1888 set in a commentary of 1889, ends with a recall of Emmanuèle's marriage and André's going away to write his book.

The second part, entitled "Black Notebook," begins on the first of July 1889 with André Walter ready to write his *Allain*. From his elliptical notes we learn that with a single character, divorced from external events and setting, the entire drama— a purely psychological one—is to take place between the soul and the flesh. The novel is to be a theorem, a transposition of Spinoza's *Ethics*. The form is to be lyrical, even musical, though in prose. André recalls his past with Emmanuèle and suffers from the beauty of nature. He plans to write a poem about the "nausea of being caught like others in this blind rising of new sap" and the desire to take refuge in pure thought and abstract speculation. He studies Schopenhauer, Kant, John Stuart Mill, and Spinoza. Tormented by the echoes of others' embraces, he travels on foot in Auvergne "to dominate the unrest of a vagabond puberty." On approaching the Grande Chartreuse, he turns away without visiting the monastery for fear of spoiling a long-cherished dream: "Oh, how sweet is the bitterness of one's regret for the things one has not known!" (Forty years later in his *Journals,* on visiting the monument at last, Gide notes that in 1889 he went only as far as Saint-Pierre-de-Chartreuse, "out of *André-Waltérisme;* that was the period when I kept from touching what I most wanted. This amounted to plowing up the field for the demon and already sowing fine regrets for later on! Some days the memory of all I did not do and might have done obsesses me.") He dreams of his soul's eternally embracing the soul of Emmanuèle, like Paolo and Francesca, and even regrets that her soul is captive in her body.

Just at this point, André learns of Emmanuèle's death on 31 July. He communes with her in spirit, but is still tormented by desires and thinks even of visiting a prostitute. He has reached the depths of shame and despair. Meanwhile his hero, Allain, comes to live entirely in the ideal, convincing himself that since Emmanuèle's death he possesses her soul more fully than ever. Yet, inasmuch as Allain is still alive and his flesh has its own demands, his vital conflict can lead only to madness. André concludes that we live to manifest, that "life is but a means, not an end; I shall not seek it for itself." (This suggests the famous outcry of Villiers's *Axël,* steeped in metaphysics, who scorns living, which we can delegate to our servants.) He resolves to treat his flesh harshly in order to conquer the demon. But he traverses a period of spiritual dryness, finding his prayers inadequate and beginning to doubt. He has hallucinations. Working furiously at his novel, he is yet tortured by musical obsessions, which no amount of playing or striking of discords will drive away. He recognizes that he is going mad and wonders whether he or his hero will be mad first. "Ah! Ah! the epitaph:

> Here lies Allain who went mad
> Because he thought he had a soul."

He concludes that at last, because she is dead, he truly possesses Emmanuèle, telling her: "You live because I dream you,

when I dream you and only then; that is your immortality."
Visual obsessions follow the musical obsessions. Allain goes
mad, but only a few days thereafter André succumbs to cerebral
fever.

Such is André Gide's first book. It was compounded of far
more literary reminiscences than this synopsis suggests. No
fewer than thirty-two quotations from the Bible punctuate its
feverish pages, though its author confesses that, on the advice
of an older cousin, he removed two-thirds of the Scriptural passages before publication. Quotations in Greek, Latin, Italian,
and German abound, doubtless to impress the reader, though
on examination all the Italian proves to be from Dante and all
the German from Goethe. The references to French literature
range from the *Roman de la Rose* to Verlaine, the Goncourts,
and Taine, and many of the world's chief philosophers receive
mention by the way. All this seems characteristically youthful;
yet, in a penetrating premonition of his later brilliant lecture
on influence, the author candidly notes: "Influences model us,
to be sure; we must therefore discern them. . . Let us choose
our influences."

Already at the age of eighteen, Gide chose his influences
well. He could have found no better models than the Bible,
Dante, Shakespeare, Goethe, and the best of French literature.
In fact, despite the stamp of the epoch, this first book even dares
comparison with the early work of such giants as Goethe and
Dante. For it is inevitable that *Les Cahiers d'André Walter*
should remind us of *Die Leiden des jungen Werthers* and the
Vita Nuova, two other accounts of unrealizable youthful love.
Werther's love for Charlotte, who (like Emmanuèle) had been
betrothed to another at her mother's deathbed, leads to a suicide that had repercussions throughout Europe. His sad, romantic story is told in the first person through his letters to a
friend, who, like Pierre Chrysis, provides a frame for the narrative by writing a brief introduction and then giving an account of the hero's death at the end. As in Gide's work, a book

figures within the book, for Werther's translation of Ossian seems to Charlotte and him to echo the tragedy of their own fate. But not satisfied with this microcosm of his novel, Goethe has rather abruptly introduced an account of a young servant who becomes a murderer because he is discharged and replaced by the young widow he serves and loves hopelessly. After defending him in vain before the court, Werther notes: "Unhappy being! You cannot be saved! I see clearly that *we* cannot be saved!" Furthermore the character of Werther, an ineffectual artist submerged in his own introspection, foreshadows that of André Walter; and is it fanciful to see in the Germanic name of the latter a discreet allusion, conscious or not, to Goethe's famous hero?

Renée Lang, who was the first to suggest a parallelism between the two youthful works, quite pertinently finds in their respective author's severity toward those works in later life indication of a personal catharsis. Both Goethe and Gide liberated themselves from a sterile romanticism by writing their quasi-autobiographical novels. It is significant that when André Gide re-read *The Sorrows of Young Werther* in 1940 he did so "not without irritation"—just as he could no longer open his own *Cahiers d'André Walter* in 1930 "without suffering and even mortification." Although he does not mention this particular work of Goethe either in the *Cahiers* or in his *Journals* of the same period, it seems reasonably certain that he already knew *Werther*. In the Spring of 1890, while Gide was writing his own book, Pierre Louis sent him a letter of advice containing the following remark: "Forget that there exists a *Werther* or an *À Rebours*, and without straining toward oddness, be extremely original *especially in your outline*." Inasmuch as Louis and Gide shared enthusiasms and, omnivorous readers, lent each other their books, it is most unlikely that the one was wrong in assuming that the other knew Goethe's novel.

There is less evidence that he knew the *Vita Nuova*, despite André Walter's reference to a melody "like a cloudy Beatrice,

ANDRÉ GIDE (1890)

fior gittando sopra e d'intorno" (for this is the Beatrice of the *Purgatorio*) and Gide's statement in his *Journals* for September 1893 that he thought of translating the *Vita Nuova*. Years later, in *La Porte étroite* he was to make two capital references to Dante's early work, and Charles Du Bos states that "several times Gide told me that the *Vita Nuova* was the only book that had remained always present in his mind while he was writing *La Porte étroite*." This is more significant than it seems at first, for, as we shall see, *La Porte étroite* is a rehandling in another key of the basic situation already used in the *Cahiers d'André Walter*. Thus if the Alissa of the later book can be compared to the young Beatrice, so can Emmanuèle.

From 1889 until late 1893, André Gide was deeply imbued with German romanticism (Heine, Novalis, the early Goethe) and with German philosophy (Schopenhauer, Fichte, Leibnitz), which, as Renée Lang has demonstrated, conformed to the aesthetics of the new Symbolist movement. His initial work might also be said to be imbued with the mysticism of the *Vita Nuova* and to present even more striking parallels with that work than with *Werther*. Both Dante and Gide have depicted the ideal love of an adolescent (the first sonnet on Beatrice was written during the poet's eighteenth year), impossible of realization. Through the death of the beloved, the youth in both cases is forced to idealize his love even further; in Dante this leads to Heaven, whereas in Gide, thanks to the modern emphasis on conflicts, it leads to madness and death. Furthermore, both writers solve a technical problem in much the same way. The pivot on which the *Vita Nuova* turns is the death of Beatrice; in the *Cahiers* the same rôle is played by the marriage of Emmanuèle. For the book to have any beauty or meaning at all, it was essential to present the beautiful relationship between Emmanuèle and André before her marriage to another. In a first-person narration, this could be done only by giving us the hero (that is, the narrator) at two moments in his life—both *before* and *after*. This Gide achieves by devoting the first notebook almost completely to extracts written by André during his earlier period of happiness, from 1886 through 1888. Although that notebook begins and ends in the present with the fatal marriage, most of it is given over to André's reviewing of the happy past, with a running commentary written in the present, as he puts order into his journal-entries. In the *Vita Nuova*, as Charles Singleton has made so clear in his recent *Essay on the Vita Nuova*, there is likewise such a double vision; for Dante, the writer of a gloss, is writing after the death of Beatrice; whereas Dante, the poet, had written most of his sonnets and canzoni before her death. Hence, though Beatrice is dead when the first line of prose was written and her death is prefigured by visions granted to the poet, yet when she actually dies, the event is meant to strike the reader with surprise.

Although one can readily imagine the young André Gide to have been impressed by the similarity between the Florentine lover's situation and that of his own hero and particularly struck by Dante's solution to an awkward technical problem, the parallel between the two works may well be fortuitous. So may that between *Werther* and the *Cahiers*. But even if one were to deny Gide originality in so far as his initial work recalls those of earlier writers, one would have to grant him great originality in another, more important regard. For in that work, while still an adolescent himself, he clearly saw and depicted the crisis of adolescence, which presumably men had been experiencing, with different degrees of intensity, ever since there were men.

Neither Dante nor Goethe—nor for that matter any of their contemporaries—was concerned with that problem. Rousseau came as close as anyone to giving a faithful picture of that transitory and often painful period in his *Confessions*. Yet most nineteenth-century writers furnish but a half-portrait, such as Flaubert's *Novembre*, limited to the sexual awakening, or Balzac's *Louis Lambert* and Taine's *Etienne Mayran*, both exclusively concerned with the intellectual awakening. A study entitled *The Novel of Adolescence in France* found that the literary interest in that tormented passage from childhood to maturity (which was to become one of the most popular themes in the years 1920–35) began in France around 1890. With the exception of Gide's, the first novels belong to the Naturalist tradition and tend to confuse adolescence with puberty. But Gide recognizes here—and he was one of the first to do so—that the intellectual and spiritual puberty is often as tormenting as the physical; and, furthermore, that the crisis is the more acute when the two impulses come into conflict. As François Mauriac was to write in 1926: "It is the period of debauch and holiness, the period of melancholy and joy, of mockery and admiration, of ambition and of sacrifice, of avidity, of renunciation. . ." Gide had discovered this almost forty years earlier, at a time when physiologists and psychologists were barely beginning to give special attention to the adolescent, simply by observing himself. If this be the result of narcissism, let there be more narcissists!

One sees again, and condones, the painfully self-conscious André Walter studying his expressions in the mirror, as he notes: ". . . eyes peering into eyes, and, at night, almost hypnotized by the ever-changing play of deep pupils, seeking how much of emotion is revealed on the exterior in eyes that shine or weep, what level of the lids, what narrowing of the eyebrows, what furrowing of the brow must accompany words of passion, enthusiasm, or melancholy. . . Comedian? Perhaps . . . but I am playing no other part than myself. The cleverest are the most readily understood."

Probing himself, André Walter finds the familiar Pascalian antithesis of the angel and the beast. On the one hand, his pure love for Emmanuèle in harmony with, and even intensifying, his new enthusiasm for poetry and metaphysics; and on the other his obscure longing for caresses, his erotic dreams, his obsession with prostitutes and the sound of kissing in the dark. At one moment he glorifies desire and ridicules chastity; at the next he praises constraint and the exercise of the will, crying: "I am

pure! I am pure! I am pure!" This is the classic adolescent conflict which must be resolved before maturity can be achieved.

Doubtless in Gide's case the crisis was intensified and prolonged by his peculiar nature, the secret of which he was not
to discover until he was twenty-four years old. If there is one
assertion on which all specialists in the subject agree, it is that
adolescence cannot be defined in terms of years. Obviously
Gide's adolescence was prolonged; indeed, it might even be
pointed out that throughout life he has shown a tendency, characteristic not only of his André Walter, but of all adolescence, to
divorce love and sex, whereas most men eventually identify the
two. Nonetheless a normal, sensitive youth conditioned as André
Walter was and dominated by such a lofty love might well experience the same crisis as Gide's hero. In judging the *Cahiers*
it would seem that the author had forgotten his own oft-repeated
insistence that art achieves the general only through the particular.

Yet André Walter is not devoid of self-criticism—as is
proven by his writing a novel about himself, attributing all his
conflicts and excesses to his hero, Allain. Through the use of a
novel within his novel (a device which was to become an immediately recognizable signature in the years ahead), Gide was
able to transmit to *his* hero his own desire to objectify his
painful dialogue. It is noteworthy that the *Cahiers*, though to
all intents and purposes a novel, is in the form of an intimate
journal with all the interruptions, incoherences, and fragmen-
tary aspect inherent in that form. In his own *Journals* as early
as October 1891 (when the *Cahiers* had already been published), Gide notes: "A diary is useful during conscious, intentional, and painful spiritual evolutions. Then you want to
know where you stand. . . An intimate diary is interesting especially when it records the awakening of ideas; or the awakening of the senses at puberty; or else when you feel yourself to
be dying." We know that many pages of André Walter's notebooks, particularly the first or "white notebook," were taken

bodily from Gide's *Journals*; this is why that intimate and monumental record of a lifetime, as we know it today, begins in 1889 rather than two years earlier. As the author admits, the private diary is an essentially youthful form—one might say: almost a necessity at a certain period of development. More sophisticated than Gide, Maurice Barrès had recognized this fact and taken advantage of it—as he confessed in the dedication to his novel *Un Homme libre* (*A Free Man*) of 1889: "Eager solely to be of help to the schoolboys who mean so much to me, I am limiting myself to the most childish form that can be imagined: a diary." In July 1950 the University of Paris included on the baccalaureate examination, intended for those from eighteen to twenty years of age, the question: "Do you think there is any advantage in keeping an intimate journal?" to which young Claude Forget, who received the highest grade, answered: "It often occurs to us in life, especially at the time when the first emotions of adolescence make their appearance, to feel a more or less violent need of romantic ideal. Then it is that are revealed our intimate reflections, our idealized ideas about a life that we did not imagine as it now faces us, our hopes, our fears, and our anxieties. We live in a world of our own made up of strange dreams which seem mad and which, most often, our elders have ceased to understand. Consequently we hesitate to confide in anyone. [. . .] Then it is that we have recourse to a notebook in order to confide to it our acts and thoughts." It is interesting that this schoolboy of 1950—who almost certainly has never read the *Cahiers d'André Walter*— takes such a book for granted, thus justifying André Walter and the André Gide who created him.

By substituting an imaginary André Walter for himself, Gide manages to objectify—that is, to rid himself momentarily—of his narcissism and of his shattering crisis. It is significant that Walter dies of his sufferings, whereas Gide goes on living, with a measure of health and equilibrium. The fictional hero thus acts as a scapegoat, preserving the author's sanity by assuming the author's spiritual conflict and carrying it to its logical extreme. Now, André Walter in turn tries to do this by passing his contagion to *his* creature, Allain; but, unlike Gide, he is unsuccessful, for he identifies himself too closely with Allain, eventually engaging his hero in a race toward madness.

This, like the epitaph of Allain, is not the least of the ironies contained in the work. In later years André Gide was to be much appreciated for his irony, which most critics first find either in *Paludes* (*Marshlands*) of 1895 or *Le Voyage d'Urien* (*Urien's Travels*) of 1893. It is particularly surprising, however, to find the same trait already emerging in a work composed between the ages of eighteen and twenty and one that at first seems least likely, by its subject and intimate relationship to the author, to permit of the detachment necessary to irony. Yet, how else can one characterize André Walter's passage on the confusion between inspiration and puberty or his remark that by blocking them his parents revealed his desires to him? At another point he says: "Then we went back to our childhood readings, originally performed classically with deflowering admirations," where the very choice of the adverb "classically" with the implication of "in class" already has a peculiarly Gidian flavor. So, indeed, does André's attitude when Emmanuèle tells him that she would rather suffer from not believing than to believe in a lie, for he simply notes: "Ah! Protestant!"

Apparently none of the contemporary critics saw the irony or appreciated the technical innovations of the *Cahiers* in 1891. That bulwark of the young monthly *Mercure de France* and future articulate spokesman for the Symbolist movement, Remy de Gourmont, eleven years older than Gide, went so far as to predict that some day the anonymous author of this "condensation of a whole retiring and timid youth" would awake armed with irony, "the coefficient of his spiritual value." Henri de Régnier, then a mere acquaintance, told the readers of the Belgian review *La Wallonie* that the book summed up a fashion of understanding love peculiar to a certain type of thoughtful and serious youth. "There is more here than the exposition of an individual case and the book has a chance of corresponding to many a secret experience," he stated, as if to disprove in advance the author's later refusal of generality to André Walter. The young Belgian poet, Maurice Maeterlinck, barely seven years older than Gide, replied to Jules Huret's "Enquiry as to the Literary Evolution" then appearing serially in the *Écho de Paris* by grouping the *Cahiers*, among his artistic preferences, with Puvis de Chavannes, Baudelaire, and Laforgue. But he himself, on the basis of a single play, had recently been called by Octave Mirbeau "the French Shakespeare." That was enough to upset anyone's scale of values! Two months later, having learned the author's name from his friend Mockel, he wrote to Gide characterizing the *Cahiers* as "the melancholy and marvelous breviary of virgins." In *L'Observateur français* for 26 May 1891, Charles Maurras, a year older than Gide, who had not yet dreamed of becoming the vigorous polemicist and powerful political leader he was to make of himself through *L'Action française*, said: "This Faust fallen into childhood will remain the type of the generation which immediately preceded ours; paleographers will count it as a variety, perhaps the most curious, of the decadent type," and then added this loyal postscript: "I learn that Walter is not dead or, at least, that the deceased Walter is a myth. I have been deceived by M. André Gide, a very young man of wholly sound mind. And thereupon I suspect a very large part of his book, the very part that shocked me, of being a *tour de force* and a literary curiosity."

In addition to the reviews, André Gide received a number of letters from writers, both the few he had met and those who remained names to him, from Mallarmé, who called the book "a phase of youth now dead," through Marcel Schwob and J.-K. Huysmans, the author of the epoch-making *À Rebours*, to the popular psychological novelist Paul Bourget, who found that the author "seemed to give promise of becoming a real writer." Those letters are reproduced in the re-edition of 1930 of *André Walter*. But the earliest and surely the most gratifying of the letters is not there; it came from Gide's new and already close friend, Paul-Ambroise Valéry, and arrived early in March.

In June 1890, while Gide was still on the Lake of Annecy finishing his book, Pierre Louis had attended the sixth centenary of the University of Montpellier in the south of France. There he had met Valéry, who lived in the town and attended the university, and had written Gide enthusiastically about this youth two years younger than he who was already writing alexandrines. In December of that year Gide had gone to Montpellier, where he had once spent an unhappy season in the *lycée*, in order to visit his Uncle Charles, now a professor at the Law School. As soon as he had met Valéry, he had found in him a kindred spirit burning with the same enthusiasms; Valéry in turn had discovered in the young Parisian the most discreet confidant and most perspicacious critic. Over fifty years later, after Paul Valéry had achieved his rightful position as the great French poet of our time and had died glorious, Gide was to write of him: "His work, indeed, is immortal in so far as any human work can claim to be, whose reknown will continue to spread through space and time. . . I lose in him my oldest friend. A friendship of more than fifty years, without lapses, without clashes, without flaws and such, in short, as we doubtless deserved, however different we were from each other."

Of the three friends—Gide, Louis, Valéry—Gide was the first to publish a book. The event was therefore of great importance for all three. Louis, with whom Gide had discussed his plan in advance, had already shown enthusiasm when the writing had hardly begun. Yet in the Spring of 1890 he had written the author warning him not to publish in haste, for "Autobiographic novels are *possible* only in middle life." After all, Chateaubriand had been thirty-seven when he wrote *René*; Fromentin, forty-three when he wrote *Dominique*; and Benjamin Constant, forty-eight when he wrote *Adolphe*. And, most significant example of all, Flaubert had never finished his youthful *Novembre*. But in Montpellier in December, standing in his hotel room, Gide had read some of the proofs to an approving Valéry. And now in March 1891 came Paul-Ambroise's letter declaring: "Never have I felt my own intimate existence and the painful youth of an intellectual as in your *André Walter*." Thanking Gide for his "opening in a minor key" and then rising to the heights of religion, philosophy, and poetry, Valéry read the message of the book as: "One must create, one must love, one must believe."

Such encouraging words from a deeply sympathetic fellow-poet were the first tangible response to the publication of *Les Cahiers d'André Walter*. Impatient for success and counting on the interest of the public, the twenty-one-year-old author had arranged in advance for two editions, one ordinary and the other more carefully printed on fine paper. Through hesitations and delays on the part of the printer, the ordinary edition (the only one to contain the preface signed "P.C.") was ready first and went on sale in late February 1891. When the finer printing issued from the press in April, it was already clear that the book's sale was negligible. Dissatisfied, besides, by the number of misprints in the first printing, Gide himself picked up at the bindery the entire ordinary edition, less some seventy complimentary copies that had already gone out, and sold it for pulp.

Disappointed by such an utter lack of success, he thereupon resolved not only not to court the public, but even to flee it. This attitude, which he maintained throughout most of his career, has been so severely criticized that he devotes four pages of his memoirs to explaining it: "I do not want to depict myself as more virtuous than I am: I have passionately desired fame; but it soon appeared to me that success, such as is ordinarily granted, is but a pale imitation of it. I like to be liked for the right reason and suffer from praise if I feel that it is bestowed on me through a misunderstanding." Having had a "mortifying

number" of copies of his first book printed, he would henceforth
have just enough, even a bit fewer than enough, printed of his
following books. Thus he could select his readers.

As for the other, more personal, objective he had hoped to
achieve by the *Cahiers*, the result was much the same. For,
though his cousin did not tell him what she thought of his book,
she rejected the proposal that followed its publication—doubtless accompanied by one of the two or three fine-paper copies of
the first printing in which, as that consummate bibliophile
Henri Mondor tells us, the name of the "heroine" appeared as
"Madeleine." The young author protested that he would not consider her refusal as definitive and that, as in the conquest of the
public, he would wait.

This disappointment and Madeleine Rondeaux's subsequent
silence contributed more than anything to the atmosphere of
that *selva oscura* (Gide shows a predilection in this connection
for Dante's appropriately sombre image) in which, at this time,
he led himself astray. He calls this the most troubled period of
his life, one of unrest and frivolous waste of time, which continued until his departure for Africa in late 1893. Then it was
that he circulated among the young writers, that he assiduously
frequented such high-priests of the cult of poetry as Mallarmé
and Heredia, an austere, forbidding youth in black, paralyzed
by modesty and appearing supercilious in his very reserve.
Everything about his appearance—his hair falling to his shoul-
ders, his flowing cape, his broad-brimmed felt, and his Lavallière necktie—proclaimed him a poet.

One can visualize him at this time backed into a corner by
the opinionated and peremptory Robert de Bonnières, poet,
journalist, and count, who maintained vigorously that the work
of any writer must lend itself to ready summary in a slogan that
would assure its survival. Now, as he asked for the slogan that
would summarize Gide's future work, the young writer, loathing
his elder for such indiscreet insistence, though already in possession of a lapidary formula, fairly hissed at Bonnières: "We

must all represent." In his memoirs Gide explains his slogan, which must, even without this, suggest some meaning to those familiar with his subsequent work: "I no longer admitted of anything but individual rules of conduct, which often presented opposing imperatives. I convinced myself that each person, or at very least each of the elect, had a part to play on earth, his very own which resembled no other; so that any attempt to submit to a common rule became treason in my eyes; yes, treason, which I likened to that great unforgivable sin against the Holy Ghost, through which the individual creature lost his specific, irreplaceable meaning, his 'savor' that could not be restored to him."

Yet, despite his theory of "manifesting," despite his associations and external appearance, despite the obviously rhythmical prose, often breaking into lines of free verse, of the *Cahiers*, André Gide had not proved himself as a poet. From another point of view it might be said that, in an age when everyone wrote in verse, he had had the courage to begin his career with a work in prose. To be sure, he had, among the numerous quotations in verse, inserted into André Walter's notebooks a few of his own attempts at versification. Like most of the true journal-entries, they were composed before the actual writing of the book; the manuscript of one of them bears the notation in the young author's hand: "Conceived during the preparation of the baccalaureate" and a Shakespearian epigraph followed by the indication "Hamleth"—a particularly touching mistake in view of Gide's much later translation of Shakespeare's master-piece. As befits a schoolboy fed on the French classics, those few lines are regular alexandrines regularly rhymed except where the poet has attempted, with indifferent success, an internal rhyme.

Soon after the publication of the *Cahiers*, André Gide paid fuller homage to the *mores* of the epoch by composing in less than a week at his mother's estate of La Roque a collection of twenty poems. When they appeared in early 1892 in an edition

limited to one hundred and ninety copies, they did so anonymously under the title of *Les Poésies d'André Walter*. By that
time the anonymity had become but a literary subterfuge, for
informed circles (and they were all that mattered to the young
writer) had easily penetrated the secret, which Charles Maurras
had even revealed publicly in his review of May 1891. In his
preface of 1930, where he reserves for the poems an indulgence
he does not show to the *Cahiers*, Gide admits that there was
something artificial in attributing the verses to an imaginary
André Walter, adding: "It does not even seem to me that the
André Walter of the *Cahiers* would have been quite capable of
writing them; I had already gone beyond him."

The poems, composed in a minor key and inspired by disabused irony, reflect the poet's gentle frustration. In the first of
them he and his unnamed feminine companion, an even more
shadowy Emmanuèle, would half-heartedly like to get away
from their winter books and their false syllogisms, but can at
most press their fevered foreheads against the panes, watching
the night outside. As if they had slept several seasons while absorbed by their "great concepts," they miss Spring altogether
and find that it is again Autumn (which in French rhymes quite
satisfactorily with "monotone," as Verlaine was well aware).

"There has been no Spring this year, my dear;
    No songs beneath the flowers and no flowers this year,
    No April, no laughter, and no metamorphoses;
    We have not woven garlands of posies."

Thus begins the first poem, setting the negative tone for the
whole slim volume; it ends:

"We turned up our lamps during the rain
    (They were dimmed by this red Autumn sun)
    And began waiting all over again
    For the bright new Spring to come."

By the fourth poem the poet and his companion manage to leave
their low room at night, each with a frail torch which the warm
wind soon blows out, leaving them to wander in darkness. In

the eighth poem they are referred to as "two poor little souls" and her soul is seen as the double or shadow of his. As the author confesses in the second poem,

"But all this rather lacks lyricism
And our lamps do not cast much light."

In the original edition the booklet bore the sub-title: "Symbolic Itinerary." But the voyage is an inner one, a voyage of self-discovery, inasmuch as the peregrinations of the two souls neither take them far afield nor lead to any satisfaction. They are unable to enter the park, the high wall of which they skirt listening in tears to the sounds of a fête within. Nor can they walk in the sun-drenched fields that they perceive at a distance from the mountains they climb. Nor can they enter the church, toward which they see others hastening at night, because their lamps go out and, lost in the swamplands covered with brambles and unmarked by roads, they arrive too late. Sitting on the steps and weeping, they listen to the music of the organ as it filters under the door.

They do, however, catch glimpses of unusual landscapes— such as that described in the poem entitled "Polders" (an odd word Gide is to use again which signifies a piece of reclaimed land protected from the sea or river by dikes)—consisting of "verdigris-coated grass" with a sheep grazing between banks of green mud. Elsewhere, more cheerfully, there is a heath of pink briar, which, at sunset, seems reflected in the pink sky.

Such landscapes, like indeed the whole of the *Poésies d'André Walter*, illustrate a theory dear to the young Gide of the identity between landscape and emotion. Already in the *Cahiers* he had noted: "not the landscape itself; the emotion caused by it" and in the "little studies in rhythm" published by *La Wallonie* in the Summer of 1891 under the title of *"Notes d'un voyage en Bretagne"* he had clearly stated his discovery of what we call the pathetic fallacy. In the same spirit his first letter to Paul Valéry, dated 16 January 1891, proposed that each of their letters "should be some subtle landscape of the

soul, full of shimmering half-tints and delicate analogies."
More maturely and explicitly, he was to crystallize his theory in
1894 in the "Preface for a second edition of the *Voyage
d'Urien*" where he holds that an emotion produced by a landscape should be able to communicate itself through the evoca-
tion of the same landscape. For "this involves a sort of aesthetic
algebra; emotion and manifestation form an equation; one is
the equivalent of the other. Whoever says *emotion* will consequently say *landscape,* and whoever reads *landscape* must consequently know *emotion.* (Or it's too bad.)" Gide would not
have insisted so much, in the years 1891–94, on this personal
theory of the reversibility of emotion and landscape if it had
not seemed to him central to his work. It will be essential, then,
to bear this relationship in mind while examining his writings,
at least of this period. Obviously the barren, forbidding landscapes of the *Poésies*—often craggy or swampy or otherwise
impassable and generally dull in color—correspond to the
thwarted, astringent emotions of the poet.

Appropriately the last poem ends thus:
"Perhaps all this is a dream
And we shall wake up.
                    You said to me:
'I think we are living in another's dream
And that is why we are so docile.'
It cannot always go on like this.
'I think the best thing we might do
Would be to try going back to sleep.' "

There *is* a turgid, dream-like quality in the "symbolic itinerary"
that takes André Walter nowhere. That quality, moreover, is reflected in the loose form of the poems, with their free or "liberated" verse enjoying the suppleness of prose, their often poor
rhymes frequently satisfied with mere assonance, and their
languid rhythms. Without obvious debts to the past, these poems
nonetheless suggest relationships in mood, and sometimes in
manner, with Heine, with Jules Laforgue, the disabused Pierrot

who died while Gide was still in school, and with Maeterlinck, whom Gide had probably just met. Indeed, the young Belgian poet had brought out in 1889 his first poems entitled *Serres chaudes* (*Hothouses*), in which such lines as the following seem to foreshadow André Walter:

> "In my eyes I see dreams;
> And my glass-enclosed soul,
> Lighting its hothouse bowl,
> Under blue glazing gleams."

Maeterlinck, like Gide, probing into his own eyes in the pose of Narcissus, sees his soul below the blue surface and likens it to a plant reaching upward under the glass of a hothouse.

As in the *Cahiers*, perhaps the most remarkable element of the *Poésies* is the muted irony with which the poet views his soul's ennui. And the two months separating the two books mark a progression in this regard, for by now the attitude of amused detachment prevails throughout the whole work. The *Poésies* could not have been written if the author had not gone beyond and transcended the states it reflects; in this sense the original André Walter would have been quite incapable, as his creator said, of writing the poems. Some of the contemporary reviewers chided Gide for pointing out that his poetry lacked lyricism or for patently enjoying such a verbal combination as

> "The hemostatic rumpled water."

Yet others delighted in a Laforguian couplet like

> "While with his mechanical trills
> A nightingale in darkness drills"

or the pseudo-naïve confession of "Polders":

> "And our melancholy weeps away
> In lines it has not learned."

Though the young André Gide, as it now seems, should have recognized that prose was his medium, he continued—doubtless in homage to the prevailing custom, and influenced by the example of Louÿs and Valéry—to write occasionally in verse. The thirteen poems published between 1892 and 1897 in reviews such as *Ibis, La Wallonie, Le Mercure de France, L'Ermitage* and collected for the first time in the initial volume of his *Œuvres complètes* show greater ease than those he attributed to André Walter. Nine of the poems form a calendar of months in which each poem fixes a mood in harmony with the season. "August" recaptures, but with greater maturity, the negative emotion of the first verses by Walter, whereas "September"— in which the poet follows his frolicking desires onto the beach and watches them play with the flotsam and seaweed—prefigures his play *Saül.*

Of all the poems, "December" is the most evocative with its contrast between the bleak winter landscape and the poet's fireside comfort surrounded by the rich product of the summer's sun: fruits dreaming of the espalier, dried flowers and herbs, preserves, honey, and wine. . .

> "The whole Autumn is in my bins,
> The whole Spring is in my loft,
> All the wines are in my cellar:
> I harvested well and oft."

To one familiar with Gide's later work these and the closing lines must foreshadow the beautiful song of the farm in the *Nourritures terrestres (The Fruits of the Earth)*, together with the entire aesthetic of that work. Perhaps it is even more significant, however, that the final lines of "December" prefigure Gide's much later use of the Gospel image of the corn that falls into the ground and dies to beget new grain:

> "All that yesterday in today breeds
> Tomorrow will repeat; and Spring again
> Awaits and sleeps in the ripened grain;
> Springs awaits the reviving sperm
> And Summer lives within the germ."

The remaining four poems, after "Calendar," bear the general title of "The Dance of Death." Prosaic and flatly ironic, they ridicule a certain kind of poet, a certain kind of humble folk, a certain kind of untrue love. The poem entitled "The Abstainers" begins thus:

> "When they die, not content with their platitudes,
> They will claim they have much to thank
> And will think they have special aptitudes
> For a heaven they saw as a blank."

Finally, after Gide has likened them to frail, willful skiffs refusing to approach any harbor, he makes them say:

> " 'And we shall have navigated seas
> Where no sirens dwell
> Without the slightest tease
> Of songs that rise and swell,
>
> Or of perfumes which alone nearly delight.
> We did not die of illness. Amen! Good night.' "

Not much can be said for such versifying, even though it is slightly better in the original French. Throughout his long career André Gide was occasionally to write in verse but never with very happy results. Like the original *Nourritures terrestres* of 1897, the *Nouvelles Nourritures* (*New Fruits*) of 1935 is a combination of verse and prose; some of the dramas, even the late *Perséphone* of 1934, are in verse; and the *Journals* contain a very few poems, with one dated as late as the Spring of 1944. But by far the most beautiful of Gide's poems, and perhaps the only true poem to survive him, is beyond question the prose *Retour de l'enfant prodigue* (*The Prodigal's Return*).

Looking back upon his adolescence, the mature Gide notes in his memoirs: ". . . the friend I ought perhaps to have had was someone who would have taught me to be interested in others and taken me outside of myself: a novelist. But at that time my only interest was the soul, my only taste was for poetry." To have known a novelist, however, he would have had to go outside the groups he then frequented, for the young men who sat at the feet of Mallarmé were in open revolt against the excesses of the Naturalists; to them the novel appeared vulgar and formless. Those Symbolists could not have been expected to discourage the youth's narcissism. Indeed, listening to and observing them, he saw that Narcissus was a symbol of Symbolism as they understood it, and accordingly Gide's second published work, coming between the *Cahiers* and the *Poésies*, was his brief *Traité du Narcisse* in prose with the subtitle: "Theory of the Symbol."

IV. NARCISSUS AND THE MULTIPLE MIRRORS

> "This terrifies me: to think that the present, which we are living this very day, will become the mirror in which we shall later recognize ourselves; and that by what we have been we shall know what we are."

TWO encounters may have contributed to Gide's choice of the myth of Narcissus. In 1891 he met and dined with Oscar Wilde, then at the height of his fame. Although there were four at table, Wilde was the only one to talk. "At the end of the meal, we went out," Gide tells in his essay on Wilde. "My two friends walking together, Wilde took me aside: 'You listen with your eyes,' he said rather abruptly. 'That is why I shall tell you this story.'" And he then proceeded to relate his original tale of Narcissus, which he was to preserve as "The Disciple" in his *Poems in Prose*. But already in December 1890 in Montpellier, Paul Valéry and André Gide had gone to the famous botanical garden and meditated over the supposed tomb of Eliza Young, the daughter of the English poet who had called her Narcissa in his *Night Thoughts*. She had died of tuberculosis and probably been buried elsewhere, but legend had made a pilgrimage spot of this tomb with its inscription in marble: *Placandis Narcissae manibus*. These words were to become the epigraph of Valéry's *Narcisse parle* (*Narcissus Speaks*), which he was then writing. In March 1891 his fifty-line poem, later to be greatly enlarged, was the chief feature of the first issue of *La Conque*, the Parisian review that Louÿs had founded, after Gide had carefully read and commented on the manuscript.

Gide's "Treatise of the Narcissus" first appeared in late 1891 in a private edition of thirteen copies—the first trade edition, of fewer than a hundred copies, not coming out until the following year; between the two printings it was also published in the January 1892 issue of the monthly *Entretiens Politiques et Littéraires*, a little review edited by Bernard Lazare and Vielé-Griffin. Though the young poet insisted on choosing his public, he wanted to be doubly sure of reaching that select audience.

For Gide, Narcissus is a symbol and a pretext. The "Treatise" is divided into three parts—concerned respectively with Adam, Narcissus, and the Poet—and a prologue to set the stage. In the prologue, Narcissus, seeking a mirror, leans over the river of Time, a lethargic canal of gray water almost indistinguishable from the colorless landscape. In it the years flow by and the image Narcissus sees is always the present, which constantly and boringly repeats the past. Because the images are forever reappearing in the same form, he concludes that they must be imperfect and striving toward an original lost form, "paradisaical and crystalline." And Narcissus dreams of Paradise.

Part I takes place in that Platonic Paradise, small because containing but one perfect example of each form. "Whether it was or was not, what do we care? . . . But this is the way it was, if it was." Everything in that garden of Ideas was perfect and motionless because nothing longed for change. In the center of Eden stood the logarithmic tree Ygdrasil, with its roots of life plunged deeply into the earth and its heavy shade round about. Propped against its trunk was the book of Mystery containing all essential truth, and all day long the wind deciphered the necessary hieroglyphs.

Adam, still unsexed, listens in religious silence as he sits in the shade of the tree. The center of the spectacle, he watches it unfold and is profoundly bored because his rôle is passive and his power remains hypothetical so long as he has not asserted it. "As a result of contemplating them, he is unable to distinguish himself from these things: not to know one's limits— not to know how far one extends! For, after all, this is bondage if one dares not risk a gesture without spoiling the entire harmony.—And yet, come what may, this harmony gets on my nerves with its uninterrupted common chord. A gesture! A little gesture, just to find out—a dissonance, what the devil!—Come now, a touch of the unexpected!" In order to emphasize Adam's daring deed, Gide brusquely shifts to the first person and from the grand style to the familiar.

The moment Adam breaks a twig of Ygdrasil with his "infatuated fingers," the tree totters and a sudden storm carries away its leaves as well as those of the sacred book. Time is born. In an instant, shuddering in anguish, Man finds himself a divided Androgyne stirring with desire for "this almost identical half of him, this woman suddenly materialized here." And Gide continues: "Sorry race scattered over this world of twilight and prayers! The memory of Paradise lost will sadden your raptures, of the Paradise you will seek everywhere—of which you will hear from prophets, and from poets, such as I, who will piously gather the leaves torn from the immemorial Book that contained all essential truth."

Part II returns without transition to Narcissus in his traditional posture. If he were to turn round, he would see something stable, a tree or flower, which he now sees in broken reflection in the flowing water. When will the river cease moving, when will time stop its flight to let the divine forms be seen? Paradise constantly has to be reconstituted; it is not remote, but close at hand, lying beneath appearances. Yet whenever one thinks time is slowing down and about to end, at each tragic crisis in the life of mankind, a single gesture renews the motion and forces the eternal repetition to begin again—"because a caster of dice did not stop his vain gesture, because a soldier wanted to win a garment, because someone was not paying attention. For the mistake is always the same, through which we are constantly losing Paradise anew: the individual who thinks of himself while the Passion is being enacted, and, arrogant supernumerary, refuses to subordinate himself."

Part III concerns the Poet, he who keeps his eyes open and sees Paradise. Paradise is everywhere. Like the scholar, the Poet sees beyond appearances to seize the archetype of things and to recreate a simple world in which everything is ideally and normally ordained.

Meanwhile Narcissus contemplates the vision from the bank, falls in love with his own image, tries to embrace it, and destroys the image. He recognizes that he must be satisfied with contemplation and, a growing symbol, he remains poring over the external appearance of the World.

In its original form the *Treatise* closed with the following paragraph, a recall of the initial paragraph already quoted:

"This treatise is perhaps nothing very necessary. In the beginning a few myths sufficed. Then people wanted to explain: pride of the priest who wants to reveal the mysteries in order to get himself adored—or else a lively fellow-feeling and that apostolic love that makes one unveil and profane by showing them off the most secret treasures of the temple, because one is unhappy to admire alone and would like others to adore."

Thus to André Gide Narcissus came to stand for humanity absorbed in the contemplation of externals; the last view of him leaning over the river pictures him as "vaguely feeling, integrated within him, the passing human generations." At least Narcissus senses the existence of Paradise with its perfect forms, and his dream again furnishes Gide a story within a story to satisfy the need for composition in depth. For in that dream of an Eden so Platonic that even the creation of Eve harks back to *The Symposium*, Adam's sin is that of Narcissus: preferring himself.

It so happens that the young poet-philosopher, apparently

fearing he had not made his meaning sufficiently explicit, added a long footnote to the body of his treatise; and because this did not figure in the original editions, he saw fit to add that "the note was written in 1890, at the same time as the treatise." The substance of that most important note, which reflects the philosopher more than the poet, is contained in its central paragraphs:

"We live in order to manifest. The rules of ethics and aesthetics are the same: any work that does not manifest is useless and bad. [. . .]

"Every representative of the Idea tends to prefer himself to the Idea he manifests. Preferring oneself is the error. The artist, the scholar must not prefer himself to the Truth he intends to set forth: this is his entire ethic; nor the word nor the sentence to the Idea they intend to reveal: I am inclined to say that this is the whole of aesthetics."

Now, this afterthought provides the key to Gide's second, so important and so misunderstood, work. The *Traité du Narcisse* expressly tells us that the Paradise Adam lost by his rash act can be recovered only by the Poet's penetrating beyond appearances and recapturing at once the true form and original harmony. Narcissus, possessing but a dim vision of the truth, is not the true poet, for as the capital footnote says: "Truths remain behind the Forms-Symbols. Every phenomenon is the Symbol of a Truth. Its sole duty is manifesting this; its sole sin, preferring itself." The *fin de siècle* poets may have recognized in Gide a spiritual brother; externally he gave every indication of being so. But Gide's long footnote should have given pause to such poets and perhaps even suggested the schism that was soon to separate him from the Symbolists.

At least Pierre Louÿs sensed this, for in 1893 he brought out a little poetic tale entitled *Leda, or In Praise of Blessed Obscurity* which leads up to this conclusion: "Symbols must never be explained. They must never be penetrated. Have confidence. Oh, do not doubt. He who fashioned the symbol hid a truth in it, but he must not manifest it, or else why symbolize it?" For fear this message might not be seen as a direct reply to the *Narcisse*, Louÿs dedicated it: "To my friend André Gide." Yet Gide never referred to it in any of his published writings.

Contemporary readers, however, could not know that the *Traité du Narcisse* represented one stage in a prolonged meditation on the sincerity of the artist. For instance, Gide noted in his *Journals* for 31 December 1891: "When one has begun to write, the hardest thing is to be sincere. Essential to mull over that idea and to define artistic sincerity. Meanwhile, I hit upon this: the word must never precede the idea. Or else: the word must always be necessitated by the idea. It must be irresistible and inevitable; and the same is true of the sentence, of the whole work of art. And for the artist's whole life, for his vocation must be irresistible." Nor could his first readers have foreseen that the idea of renunciation, the theory of losing oneself to find oneself, would continue to haunt André Gide for the next sixty years.

If the *Traité du Narcisse* is an impersonal treatise on symbolism, Gide's third book, *Le Voyage d'Urien (Urien's Travels)*, is an allegory which could be said to expand the long footnote to *Narcisse*, for it concerns the manifesting of an essence. Written at La Roque during the summer of 1892, it was published in 1893 with illustrations by Maurice Denis. When the author presented a copy to Mallarmé, the poet of vision and inactivity was alarmed, fearing that the book related a real voyage. But the master must have been reassured at once upon noting that the title might have been spelled *Le Voyage du rien*—the voyage of nothing, or of nothingness. Indeed, this work belongs in the tradition of the imaginary or spiritual voyage which Baudelaire, Rimbaud, Camille Mauclair, and Mallarmé himself had enriched. Somewhat later, that exceptional Symbolist and precursor of Surrealism, Alfred Jarry, wrote a series of poems for which he rejected Lewis Carroll's title *Through the Looking Glass* in favor of his own *Navigations in the Mirror*; this title would exactly fit *Le Voyage d'Urien*. For here André Gide has carried to its logical, and perhaps absurd, conclusion his theory of the reversibility of landscape and emotion by consistently implying his characters' emotions solely through minute descriptions of the landscape.

Probably none of Gide's works has been given less attention by his commentators than this "symbolic novel," as he calls it. In one of the very few references he later made to it, however, he noted in his *Journals* in 1910: "I have not written a single work without having felt a profound need to write it, with the sole exception of *Le Voyage d'Urien*, and yet it seems to me that I put into it a large share of myself and that, for him who knows how to read, it too is revelatory."

A Prelude, three parts of unequal length, and a verse Envoi make up the novel or prose-poem. The Prelude begins:

"When the bitter night of thought, of study, and of theological ecstasy was over, my soul, which since evening had been burning solitary and faithful, feeling dawn coming at last, awoke listless and tired. Without my being aware, my lamp had gone out and my window had opened on daybreak. I moistened my forehead in the dew on the panes, and thrusting into the past my spent musing, my eyes fixed on the dawn, I ventured forth into the narrow vale of metempsychoses." After walking at length in that tragic valley, Urien finds the rocks opening wider and sees an azure sea. "On the beach awaited me the companions of my pilgrimage. I recognized them all though not knowing whether I had ever seen them; but our virtues were similar."

In a nearby harbor they see a ship recently arrived from the West Indies with a shipment of rare woods, vari-colored birds, and shells that "sang of the wash of waves on those happy shores," another from Norway loaded with green, diaphanous ice, and a third from Syria with slaves, bales of purple, and gold nuggets. "Then, having tasted this day promises of all future encounters, ceasing to look toward the past, we shall turn

our eyes toward the future." And their marvelous ship sets out
toward a new dawn, though none knows its destination.

From the four-page prelude alone a double—allegorical
and ironic—intent should be apparent. The setting forth at dawn
after a night of theological ecstasy, the wandering through the
vale of metempsychoses, the pilgrimage companions—all suggest John Bunyan, as do the references to valiance and virtues,
to which will soon be added "our courages," "our glorious
destinies," and "our joyous wills." Indeed, the traditional allegorical implications become clearer as the journey progresses
and the reader meets Urien's twenty companions, sometimes
referred to as "chevaliers," who bear such exceptional names
as Agloval, Aguisel, Alain, Alfasar, Angaire, Axel, Cabilor,
Clarion, Eric, Hector, Hélain, Lambègue, Mélian, Morgain, Nathanaël, Odinel, Paride, Tradelineau, Ydier, and Yvon. Curiously, it has never been pointed out that the majority of these
names—including that of Urien himself—had figured in the
Arthurian legend, which was accessible to Gide in the work of
Paulin Paris.

The first part, entitled *"L'Océan pathétique"* ("The Sea of
Emotion"), recounts exotic lands and fantastic adventures; it
owes something to Rimbaud's *Bateau ivre*, to the *Odyssey*, and
to *The Arabian Nights*, which Gide had enthusiastically read as
a child and from which he has borrowed such names as Haiatalnefous and Camaralzaman. On their ship *Orion*, the twenty-
one companions sail past islands and sharp promontories and
become familiar with the creatures of the sea. None knows how
he came there, but none regrets "the bitter night of thought."
Nathanaël suggests that they are living their dream while still
sleeping in their room.

They pass floating islands heavy with vegetation and exhal-
ing suffocating perfumes. They bathe in pink and green water.
On the seventh day four of the companions, exploring a sandy
shore, discover a prodigious city: "It was dawn-colored and
Moslem, with odd, rising minarets; flights of stairs led to hang-

ing gardens, and from the terraces leaned mauve palm-trees. Above the city floated clouds of fog torn by the pointed minarets. The minarets were so lofty that the clouds caught on them and looked like oriflammes stretched taut despite the fluid air in which no breeze stirred." It proves to be a mirage, and its disappearance, after each minaret has sung in turn, reveals sleeping sirens on the water's edge. The adventurers flee back to the ship and each one describes the sirens differently. But whatever they were, no one bathed that day, for fear of them.

After visiting a dead city on another shore, witnessing a dance by whirling dervishes, and severely repulsing the voluptuous suggestions of the hot night, the group is divided by the experience of a few who go ashore on the twenty-first day and spend the night with the women in a strange city, returning with dazzlingly beautiful fruit.

Morgain having fallen ill, five companions go ashore on a mountainous island to get fresh snow to cool his fever. On the beach they encounter a mysterious blond child straight out of Novalis, as Gide loyally indicates in a footnote, trying to understand words he has written in the sand.

Finally, on their seventh stop, the travelers enter the royal city of Queen Haiatalnefous, peopled solely by beautiful women, to whom all the sailors and all but twelve of the companions succumb. Prisoners of the Queen, those twelve, intent on their proud destinies, glory in their austere resistance to her blandishments, her city of calm canals and terraced gardens, her blue grotto, her parties and celebrations. Eventually a plague descends upon the city at the height of its orgy, killing all but the twelve pure knights, who are ultimately driven away by the stench of the dead.

Throughout *"L'Océan pathétique"* the twenty-one uncharacterized companions remain strangely undifferentiated; they are obviously but varied aspects of one person. Their adventures, treated with a sumptuous seriousness, suggest those of the figures satirized in the poem "The Abstainers." The distinc-

tion of the twelve virtuous pilgrims spared at the end lies precisely in their resisting temptation, symbolized by women, exotic
fruit, and bathing. Often they have simply been afraid to dip
into life, as into the alluring waters of the sea. Timorous despite
their lofty ambitions, they are yet haunted by a vague regret for
lost opportunities.

Part two, entitled *"La Mer des Sargasses"* ("The Sargasso
Sea"), is the canticle of boredom—the mystic's dark night of
the soul—and is mercifully shorter. To be sure, everything is
reduced in scale because of the pettiness of boredom. Now all
stimulus is lost, and obvious temptations have ceased to beset
the travelers. With all collective purpose dissipated, Urien
stands out alone and speaks in his own name.

The *Orion* navigates slowly in a narrow canal between ex-
panses of seaweed which soon become thicker and more stationary, until they eventually rise out of the water in low, muddy
banks. Gradually the ship becomes a small boat manned by oars
and the canal, a river. On the seventh day they meet the girl
Ellis, who, come overland, had been waiting fourteen days for
them. Dressed in a polka-dot dress and carrying a cerise para-
sol, she has an overnight bag loaded with toilet articles and
books: *Prolegomena to all Future Metaphysics*, the *Theodicea*,
Treatise of Contingency, a *Life of Franklin*, a *Flora of Temperate Zones*, Paul Desjardins's *Devoir présent* (*Our Present
Duty*, which had played a part in inspiring the *Cahiers d'André
Walter*), three engagement-books, and a supply of moral bro-
chures.

Ellis, a dimmer version of the already shadowy Emmanuèle, obviously represents the distortion of an ideal of the past.
With her bad taste in clothes and books and her constant mute
recall of the past Urien is fleeing, she becomes increasingly un-
congenial to him, who soon doubts that she is the true Ellis.

After the water of the river has become painfully stagnant,
it begins to move again, but in the opposite direction. "And as
in a story read backward, or as in the reflection of the past, we

resumed our voyage; we found the same old banks again; we relived our boredom. [. . .] I shall not repeat that monotony; it already cost me too much to tell it once."

Eventually out at sea again, they encounter icebergs as they move toward ever colder regions, and the *Orion* again becomes a ship. While Ellis is fading visibly away and becoming ever less real, Urien abandons her, together with four of the companions who are ill of boredom, on a shore dotted with Eskimo huts, and sails off calmly toward the pole.

The third part, *"Voyage vers une mer glaciale"* ("Voyage Toward an Arctic Sea"), has a chill, invigorating air. The remaining eight, purified by their passage through the mud flats, or Slough of Despond, are animated by a spirit of resistance and the desire to push onward. At last they seem to have a goal; Urien tells them: "Toward the loftiest cities lead the most painful roads; we are going toward the City of God."

They encounter flocks of whales, huge icebergs with strange objects caught in their transparent mass, eiders and guillemots perched on steep cliffs, and Eskimos. If part two is a triumph of the preposterous (*le saugrenu*) handled with cold irony, nothing could surpass in this regard the delightfully comic description of the Eskimos in part three.

The eight knights, having now definitively won joy through renunciation and effort, even glory in the scurvy that lays them low and kills Paride; without regret they burn their ice-locked ship and take to a reindeer-drawn sled. Suddenly a black-haired Ellis (the earlier apparition had been pale blond) appears seated on a rock in a snow-colored dress. Urien calls on her to guide him but, taking him to a pinnacle and showing him the aurora borealis, she chides him for not continuing to dream her and for conjuring up a false Ellis. She tells him that his long voyage is about to end and that he must cease looking toward the past; and she adds sententiously: "For each the way is unique and each way leads to God." Thereupon Urien sees her drawn up to Heaven among the angels.

The seven advance toward the pole through snow storms, cutting their way over ice-mountains. In a wall of ice beside which they take refuge, they find cut as with a diamond: HIC DESPERATUS. Under these words, in the ice, lies the corpse of a man with a paper in his hand. Over the wall they find a gentle slope, a line of grass, and a calm, unfrozen lake. They go back to get the cadaver in order to bury it on the shore of the lake and, on breaking the ice, discover the paper in his hand to be absolutely blank. The voyage ends with the following words:

"We felt no further desires to return and revisit more luxurious lands; that would have been the past without surprises; one does not go back down toward life. If we had known at first that this was what we had come to see, perhaps we should never have set out; accordingly we thanked God for having hidden the goal from us and for having made it so remote that our efforts to achieve it already caused us some joy, the only sure one; and we thanked God for the fact that such great tribulations had made us hope for a more glorious end.

"We should have liked to invent anew some frail and more pious hope; having satisfied our pride, and feeling that the fulfilment of our destinies no longer depended on us, we now waited for things, around us, to become a bit more faithful to us.

"And having knelt down again, we sought in the black water the reflection of the heaven that *I* dream."

The rather unnecessary Envoi tells us, in most prosaic verse, what any reader should have guessed: that the journey was a dream and the exploits, mirages; for—

"We never went out
Of the chamber of our thoughts,
And we went through life
Without seeing it. We were reading."

Vastly more helpful than the Envoi in understanding the author's intention is the preface he wrote for a second edition of *Le Voyage d'Urien*. I have already referred to those three pages for their statement of the "aesthetic algebra" by which emotion and landscape form an equation. By the way, it should be noted that the landscapes in this work, which reflect the author's moods, are altogether imaginary. Whether lush or desolate, oriental, tropical, or arctic, they correspond to nothing he had ever seen. Many of those in the first part hark back, doubtless, to his early impressions of *The Arabian Nights*. Most of the others could have resulted from conversations with a much older cousin, then professor of comparative anatomy at the Museum of Natural History. The clue to this assumption lies in a single sentence of the memoirs: "I had made up my mind to set out, but had long hesitated as to whether or not I should accompany my cousin, Georges Pouchet, as he invited me to do, on a scientific cruise to Iceland." Now, Georges Pouchet (1833–94), the son of that Félix-Archimède whose collection of coleoptera the boy André Gide had inherited, had indeed spent the month of August 1890 among the Faroe Islands and the summer of 1891 in the fjords of Iceland on just such expeditions, as we learn from his reports to the Academy of Sciences. In his account of an expedition off the shores of Newfoundland aboard the Prince of Monaco's yacht-laboratory in the summer of 1887, he wrote most learnedly of climate and icebergs, with certain details paralleled in *Le Voyage d'Urien*. For more popular consumption, he wrote in 1888 a lively article on the cachalot or sperm whale. Doubtless Dr. Pouchet, who held both the M.D. and the Sc.D., could talk as fascinatingly to his young cousin of Eskimos and guillemots as of his specialty, pelagic flora and fauna. This assumption finds confirmation in the original dedication of the third part or *"Voyage vers une mer glaciale"* to Georges Pouchet—a mark of gratitude which was suppressed in later editions, after the marine biologist's death. To be sure, Gide could have drawn some of his information about Eskimos and arctic fauna from the famous *Tierleben* of Alfred Edmund Brehm, which was accessible to him in a ten-volume translation entitled *Les Merveilles de la Nature*. Throughout life André Gide regularly consulted that fascinating mine of information, sometimes using the French edition and sometimes the original German.

To return to the preface, however, Gide explicitly says there: "But the central emotion in this book is not a particular emotion; it is the very one communicated to us by our dream of life, from astonished birth to unconvinced death; and my characterless travelers become in turn either the whole of humanity or else are reduced to myself.

"Everything else I might say Urien says or relates. If we speak eloquently of such things, this is because we suffered deeply from them—poor generation that would like heroism in an age that does not overwhelm it with beauties. . ."

Whether Urien and his colorless companions represent the whole of humanity, a single unhappy generation, or the author's various selves, Gide himself claims not to be certain. The interchangeable use of the first person singular and the first person plural in the opening and closing passages suggests rather the last alternative. After all, the voyage is a dream, we are told, and it is quite normal for the dreamer to share his personality, his impulses, and his fears among several actors. The allegory consists in the pursuit of the ideal *à la* Novalis; Renée Lang has traced this influence most adequately and made the most of Gide's announced but unfulfilled intention of translating *Heinrich von Ofterdingen* at just this time. That ideal ultimately becomes a chill, ascetic ideal, an anticlimax to the glorious affirmation of self for which the knights set sail. Throughout, their odyssey is marked by an overtone of mockery for those who flee life while purporting to seek it. This was indeed the peculiar malady of the nineties in France, and none was more keenly aware of its symptoms than the young André Gide. Are not the frustrated themes of *Urien* the same as those of the poems? Gide himself was ready for action and a complete break with his surroundings.

But first he felt he had to liquidate his past. It is impossible to read this work without noting its insistence on the future, the

forward direction and view, and also the persistence with which
the past keeps interjecting itself into Urien's thoughts. He constantly struggles to stifle the past as it inevitably wells up each
time he weakens or relaxes. It lies in the repetition of experience and thoughts, in his boredom, in the backward-flowing
stream, and especially in the false Ellis and her books. In fact,
books and study and reading (as in the Envoi) appear to be
the author's chief vice; he is fleeing nothing so studiously as his
studious habits. Yet we have noted what a bookish flavor the
work has, and how many erudite sources it reveals.

To them must be added another, perhaps the central, influence. It is but natural that, writing an allegory in the form of
an imaginary voyage, the modern author should turn to that
great model, the *Divina Commedia*. The division of *Le Voyage
d'Urien* into three parts that progress from a sort of Hell,
through Purgatory, to Paradise suggests that Gide had Dante in
mind, as does his precise indication, at least in the beginning,
of the day-by-day events of the journey and, in general, his insistence on the numbers three, seven, twelve, and twenty-one.
Like Dante entering Paradise, Urien recognizes as he ap-
proaches the polar region that his trials are over and he is advancing toward the City of God. On the threshold of that region,
he encounters the true Ellis as Dante finds his lost Beatrice in
the Earthly Paradise. Both figures of love and of the past are
now pure spirit and dwell among the angels; both bid the poet
forget the past. Like Beatrice, Ellis addresses her poet as
"brother" and chides him for following false imaginings, with
which he had thought to supplant his true guide. It is most significant that Urien at once expects her to serve as a guide and
that she, in fact, does give him sober and definitive advice and
marks out his way for him. Later she again appears momentarily before him, allusive and dreamlike.

The even younger André Walter, he of the *Cahiers*, had already turned to Beatrice as an ideal, and, interestingly enough,
it was just this Beatrice from Canto XXX of the *Purgatorio* who

attracted him: ". . . a cloudy Beatrice, *fior gittando sopra e d'intorno,* like a Blessed Lady, immaterially pure, wearing a long gown, sappharine in its highlights and azure in the recesses of its folds. . ."

There is, however, nothing Dantesque about Gide's next work, *La Tentative amoureuse ou le Traité du vain désir (The Attempt at Love or the Treatise of Vain Desire).* Rather, it reveals the author's half-conscious dissatisfaction with the immaterial or, viewed from another angle, his but half-convinced rationalization for not indulging in physical love. Composed in the summer of 1893 in Normandy, it was published that same year. Although much shorter than *Urien,* it is no less complex and revealing. Like the preceding works, this treatise presents a world of complete subjectivity. Against a stylized and conventional background of nature, it tells the story of a stylized and conventional love that blossoms vigorously in the Spring, is consummated in Summer, and wistfully fades out in Autumn. One of Gide's express intentions was "to recount a relationship of seasons with the soul"; hence the poetic tale is dominated by the rhythms of the seasons.

An ironic summary of the action is inserted in the midst of its unfolding: "Two souls meet one day and, because they were gathering flowers, both thought they were similar. They took one another by the hand, thinking to continue their way. The continuation of the past separates them. The hands let one another drop and, behold, by virtue of the past each will continue the way alone. It is a necessary separation, for solely a like past can make souls alike. Everything is continuous for souls." Luc and Rachel do nothing but pick flowers, love one another, sit in the grass, walk over the hills and along the beach. "Alas for them, Luc and Rachel loved one another," says Gide; "for the unity of my tale, indeed, they did nothing else; of boredom they knew only that of happiness." Gradually Luc becomes surfeited with uneventful happiness and begins to feel unrest and a thirst for adventure; in answer to Rachel's statement that he is her whole life, he points out that she is not all of *his*. Eventually his boredom is communicated to her too, and by common agreement they separate.

Gide's favorite composition in depth appears here as in the *Cahiers*: the author is relating the story of Luc and Rachel to an unidentified woman with whom he maintains a Platonic relationship and whom he addresses frequently as "Madame" and, once toward the end, as "sister." Luc's boredom with happiness thus communicates itself to the narrator himself, and through him to the audience for which he is writing. At the end, having reached Autumn and the separation of the lovers in his story, the narrator tells "Madame" that it is Autumn where he is too, and raining; he is alone by his fireside, among his books, and "I have finished telling you this story that bores us; great tasks call us now. I know that on the sea, the ocean of life, glorious shipwrecks await—and lost sailors, and islands to be discovered. But we remain poring over our books, and our desires go off toward more certain deeds. That is what makes us, I know, more joyous than other men."

The little tale involves even a third level of narration, for Luc in turn tells Rachel stories that have the value of exteriorizing his moods. Each of *his* three prose-poems corresponds to one of the seasons through which his love evolves. Rachel is not a good listener: during the first one she falls asleep; the second one she interrupts twice; and the third one she definitively stops in the middle by saying it is stupid.

Obviously Luc stands for the author as he has momentarily thought he would like to be. But as Luc's contentment breeds ever more deadly boredom, the author begins to congratulate himself that he is not thus. Hence there is at one and the same time a self-conscious identification between creature and creator and an equally artificial opposition between the two. Early in the work we are told: "Luc longed for love but was afraid of carnal possession as of something bruised. Sorry upbringing we had which made us foresee as sobbing and heart-broken or else

morose and solitary all sensual pleasure, glorious and serene
though it really be. We shall no longer ask God to lift us up to
happiness.—Yet no! Luc was not like that, for it is a ridiculous
mania always to make like oneself whomever one invents.—
Hence Luc possessed that woman." Later in the idyll of the lovers the author bursts out: "Happy are those who like them can
love without conscience! They were scarcely tired by it—for it
is not so much love, and it is not so much sin as repenting of it
that tires."

Thus the love of Luc and Rachel is in direct opposition to
the incomplete, thwarted experience of the narrator with his
"Madame." In order to understand the purpose of this opposition, we must turn to the Foreword to the *Tentative amoureuse*,
which reads:

"Our books will prove not to have been very veracious accounts of ourselves, but rather our plaintive desires, a longing
for other, forever forbidden, lives, for all the impossible deeds.
Here I am writing down a dream that troubled my mind excessively and demanded existence. [. . .] And each book is but
the deferring of a temptation." The temptation for Gide at this
time invited him to turn from his path and seek happiness in
sensual delights, but he purged himself of his urgent desires by
writing a book to prove to himself that their satisfaction would
be empty and futile. Since abstract knowledge cannot convince
feelings, the *Treatise of Vain Desire* is an imaginative evoca-
tion. Nowhere does Gide pass a moral judgment on Luc, leaving
it rather to time to prove the futility of his love. Yet the author
sees himself, as well as his character, in perspective: for every
shaft of irony directed at Luc there are two for the author. Imagining Luc's experience of consummated love and especially
his subsequent attitude has taken the place, for Gide, of direct
personal experience; thus he calms, without satisfying, his desires. In his *Journals* for late August or early September 1893
(that is, just after finishing this treatise), he makes even clearer
the meaning of his Foreword:

"I wanted to suggest, in the *Tentative amoureuse*, the influence of the book upon the one who is writing it, and during that very writing. As the book issues from us it changes us, modifying the course of our life, just as in physics those free-hanging vases, full of liquid, are seen, as they empty, to receive an impulse in the opposite direction from that of the liquid's flow. Our acts exercise a retroaction upon us. 'Our deeds act upon us as much as we act upon them,' said George Eliot.

"In my case I was sad because a dream of irrealizable joy was tormenting me. I relate that dream and, isolating the joy from the dream, I make it mine; my dream has broken the spell and I am full of joy.

"No action upon an object without retroaction of that object upon the subject. I wanted to indicate that reciprocity, not in one's relations with others, but with oneself."

Literature, then, can become a substitute for experience—for him who writes it. By the same token, it can provide an all but automatic safety-valve in moments of stress and temptation. The writer has but to objectify his conflict to be rid of it; this is just what Gide had done with André Walter and what Walter had tried to do with his Allain. The Foreword to the *Tentative* is a capital document because it offers the first statement of this theory of personal catharsis which was to find such frequent restatement throughout Gide's work. Certainly no other theory contributes more to the understanding of his fiction and drama or dispels more accumulated errors in interpretation. Yet simple as it is, Gide had to repeat it again and again. The clearest statement is doubtless contained in a letter of 1902 to a critic who, in reviewing *L'Immoraliste*, had too readily identified Michel with his creator. "That a germ of Michel exists in me goes without saying," Gide admitted and then added: "How many buds we bear in us, Scheffer, that will never blossom save in our books! They are 'dormant eyes' as the botanists call them. But if intentionally you suppress all of them *but one*, how it grows at once! How it enlarges, immediately monopolizing all the sap! My recipe for creating a fictional hero is very simple: take one of those buds and put it in a pot *all alone;* you soon achieve a wonderful individual. Advice: choose preferably (if it is true that you can choose) the bud that bothers you the most. You get rid of it at the same time. This is perhaps what Aristotle called the purging of passions." Gide knew at least as well as we that Aristotle meant no such thing, but it pleased him to suggest a confusing analogy. Others, however, have expressed the same theory, even going so far as to see works of imagination serving to prevent the writer from indulging in the excesses that symbolize his characters. Bergson, for instance, remarked that "Shakespeare was not Macbeth nor Hamlet nor Othello, but he would have been those various characters if circumstances and the consent of his will had brought to a state of eruption what was but an inner urge."

André Gide has found the same kind of subjective objectivity in Shakespeare, Browning, *Wuthering Heights,* and especially in Dostoevsky. In his penetrating and self-revealing study of the Russian novelist, he states that Dostoevsky is to be found in each of his characters because he lost himself in each of them and that the first result of such a depersonalization is to protect his own incoherences. Often he speaks of abnegation in this regard, and once he refers to a letter in which Keats denies the poet any identity because he is continually "filling some other body."

For Gide the words "objective" and "subjective" lose all meaning, for if he most frequently uses himself as a model this is possible because he had already *become* the person he wanted to portray. Obviously the danger of such a method of characterization is that of the author's being blamed for never having portrayed anyone but himself. Most of Gide's critics, in fact, have at some time made this accusation, even denying him creative imagination and seeing in his books a succession of personal confessions. His consistent use of narration in the first person has regularly misled those who read hastily or approach him with a prejudice; very few of the many who have written on Gide have avoided taking out of context a statement made by such a character as Michel, Saül, or Édouard and attributing it to the author.

To identify Gide closely with each of his characters in turn, however, became increasingly difficult as his works multiplied, for those characters differ so widely from one another. It is not easy to find the common denominator in the principal protagonists of *L'Immoraliste* (*The Immoralist*), *La Porte étroite* (*Strait is the Gate*), *Isabelle*, and *Les Caves du Vatican* (*Lafcadio's Adventures*)—to mention only the important fictions published between 1902 and 1914. Yet that common denominator lies in the author, for as Gide noted in his *Journals* for 8 February 1927: "The resources of the author, his complexity, the antagonism of his too diverse possibilities, will permit the greatest diversity of his creations. But everything derives from him. He is the only one to vouch for the truth he reveals, and the only judge. All the heaven and hell of his characters is in him. It is not himself that he depicts, but he could have become what he depicts if he had not become everything himself. It was in order to be able to write *Hamlet* that Shakespeare did not let himself become Othello."

Consequently we see that Gide's personal theory of catharsis results from, and in turn permits, his cherished complexity. In his own view of himself, no concepts are more essential than these two to an understanding of his work. We have noted that he attributed his multiple potentialities to his conflicts and contradictions. On the other hand, as he progressed in life and cultivated the unrest that he first glorified in the *Nourritures terrestres* of 1897, that Protean nature, evident in the diversity of his works, seemed to contribute to his conflicts and his restlessness. But eventually the eternal association of him with unrest came to bore him, and it is interesting to see him defending himself on that score, in a letter of 1924, by reference to his method of purgation: "I was restless in the past; but it so happens that the diversity of my books is misleading, for I owe to it the fact that I am no longer restless today. I should probably still be so if I had not managed to liberate my various possibilities in my books and project outside myself the contradictory characters that inhabited me. The result of that moral purgation is a great calm and, if I dare say so, a certain serenity."

Such serenity was certainly not evident in 1893, nor would it have been becoming in one so young; to grasp the importance of this personal catharsis one must anticipate the later career. Yet the theory, as we have seen, was first voiced in connection with the *Tentative amoureuse,* and had even been practiced earlier in the initial *Cahiers d'André Walter.* The idea thus had its inception during the period of Gide's greatest narcissism, when he indulged in the most intense self-scrutiny. Later, it served to justify and excuse, at least in the author's eyes, a continuing concern with self.

Whether the mature André Gide modeled his characters on himself or on his latent potentialities mattered little to his critics; it sufficed that each of his protagonists was in some way closely related to him, that a germ of Gide could be found in each of them. Frequently the accusation of narcissism was directed against his entire work, just as Barbey d'Aurevilly had characterized Goethe as "An aged Narcissus contemplating himself all life long in every rut and all the puddles of his work." And Gide, like Goethe, had furnished grounds for such a theory by the scrupulous keeping of a private journal throughout sixty years, by his predilection for first-person narration in his works of imagination, by his self-justification in *Si le grain ne meurt . . .* and *Corydon,* by his lifelong preoccupation with sincerity, and finally by the subtle play of mirrors involved in regularly composing a book within a book. On the other hand, such dominant traits as his desire to teach and influence others, his horror of the static and obsession with the idea of progress, his productive cult of unrest, and his growing concern for social problems emphatically belie the myth of the handsome youth studiously bent over his own beloved image. In so far as Gide maintained an astonishingly youthful attitude down to his death in his eighty-second year, it might be said that he instinctively preserved, as part of a strange fidelity to his own youth, a certain narcissism—but transfused, sublimated, restless, and rendered effectively creative. To reduce the figure of Gide, however, to terms of this single myth amounts to substituting the caricature for the portrait.

Yet no myth better corresponds to the period of his adolescence. It is but natural, during that transitional period of awakening, to strive to know oneself and define one's possibilities and limitations. The more perceptive and articulate the youth is, the more searching and productive will be his self-scrutiny. "At that time," Gide records in his memoirs, "I had to discover everything, to invent at one and the same time both the torment and the remedy, and I know not which of the two seemed to me the more monstrous." That André Gide knew what he was doing is apparent from his technique of a book within the book in both the *Cahiers* and the *Tentative*, from his choice of the legend of Narcissus, and from the Envoi of *Urien*. He was conscious, indeed, even to the point of making fun of himself, as can be seen from the ironic element in those first works. For instance, at the low point of his adventure, when all but becalmed in the canal of boredom, Urien indulges in a narcissism that the author intends to render ridiculous: ". . . leaning over toward what the water reflected of myself, which I did not know, I sought in my sad eyes to better understand my thoughts and to read in the curve of my lips the bitterness of the regret that curves them."

Despite the light that Gide's first five works cast upon their author's formative period, they hold a decidedly minor place within his total literary production. If he had not gone on to achieve a particularly brilliant position in modern letters, they would justly be quite ignored today. They have an artificial, stilted, *fin-de-siècle* flavor curiously at variance with the vigor, forthrightness, and simplicity of his mature writings. When planning a reprinting of some of them in 1910, he noted in his *Journals* that, though he did not feel like disavowing his youthful works, he hoped they would not be looked upon with the same eye as the products of a more mature age. Did we not examine them most closely with the advantage of hindsight, they might readily, in fact, be confused with works written at the same time by permanently obscure contemporaries. As Logan Pearsall Smith has said, ". . . the youth of every generation paints the same picture or writes the same kind of prose or poetry. Then, little by little, or sometimes suddenly, those few who are fated to do so find their originality, their special note or vision—their 'virtue' as we say of a herb or jewel, the thing that they, and they alone, can do. A secret door seems to open for them into a realm of imagination which is theirs alone."

The secret door was to open for Gide with his first trip to Africa in October 1893. This was not the first time he crossed the frontiers of France, for he had already briefly visited Belgium, a part of Germany, and Spain; but this was to be the first time he would get far away from home and mother and be entirely on his own. He was obscurely aware before he set out—as is evident from his leaving behind for the first time his familiar Bible—that this voyage was to effect more than his conscious break with the literary milieus of Symbolism, that it was to mark the great turning-point in his life. For three years he had been trying to say farewell to his adolescent conflicts, and now suddenly he was offered an exceptional opportunity to cast off the dead skin of the past. At that time he would have been quite unable to define the problem that beset him, but looking back in his memoirs he saw it thus:

"In the name of what God, of what ideal do you forbid me to live according to my nature? And where would that nature lead me if I simply followed it? Until now I had followed the rule of Christ or at least a certain puritanism that had

been taught me as the rule of Christ. My only reward for having striven to submit to it had been a complete physical and
spiritual upset. I could not agree to live without a code, and the
demands of my flesh required the consent of my mind. If those
demands had been more banal, I doubt if the anxiety they caused
me would have been any less great. For it did not matter what
my desire called for so long as I thought I had to refuse it
everything. [. . .] Eventually I sensed that this discordant
dualism might well perhaps resolve into harmony. At once it
appeared to me that such harmony was to be my sovereign aim
and seeking to achieve it the evident purpose of my life. When,
in October 93, I sailed for Algeria, it was less toward a new
land than toward *that*, toward that golden fleece, that my enthusiasm drove me."

But this passage, persuasive and memorable as it is, was
written by a man of fifty who knew what a total awakening he
had experienced nearly thirty years earlier in North Africa
and who dated his mature life from that revelation of his true
self. More convincing as a testimony of his state of mind *then*
is a page of his *Journals* written just after the start of his southward journey and dated at Montpellier, 10 October 1893:

"Whereupon, ceasing to call my desires temptations, ceasing to resist them, I strove on the contrary to follow them. Pride
seemed to me a less desirable thing. In that splendid egoism
full of religion, I now saw, perhaps wrongly, only restrictions
and limitations. Self-abandon struck me as a superior wisdom;
it seemed to me that I would find in it greater profit for my soul.
This was, I am well aware, still a form of egoism, but a newer,
more curious form, and one that satisfied in me more potential
powers."

He was obviously ripe for his encounter with Dionysus.
Accordingly, before setting out for the unknown, he took leave
of Narcissus by rereading all of his journal with "inexpressible
disgust" and finding it pretentious and tiresome. "I have come,"
he noted, "to wish not to be concerned with myself at all." Then

it was also that, symbolically as it were, he added to his imper-sonal *Traité du Narcisse* the startling, not to say jarring, con-clusion we now know, which suddenly adopts the first person singular:

"Indeed, nor the importunate laws of men, nor fears, nor decency, nor remorse, nor respect for myself or for my dreams, nor you, melancholy death, nor terror of the beyond will pre-vent me from achieving what I desire, nor anything—anything but the pride, knowing a thing to be so powerful, of feeling even more powerful myself and of overcoming it. But the joy of so lofty a victory is still not so sweet, not so good, as yielding to you, desires, and being conquered without a struggle." None of Gide's contemporaries could have signed this unashamed glorification of desire at the time—nor could even he himself have done so in 1891 when the *Narcisse* first appeared.

V. THE FRENZY OF DIONYSUS

"Life for us was savage and sudden in savor."

"For I was not satisfied to emancipate myself from the rule; I aimed to legitimize my frenzy, to justify my folly."

A FRICA was to play a capital rôle in André Gide's life. On its soil he discovered himself and life in 1893. Returning a year later, he spent a few crucial weeks with Oscar Wilde and Lord Alfred Douglas at Blida, Algiers, and Biskra. His third voyage across the Mediterranean was his wedding-trip, and thenceforth he was to seek the desert and its oases almost periodically as a refuge from the contacts of civilization and as a self-renewal. In 1925, pushing into the remote Congo, he was to awake fully to the urgency of social problems and thus give his life a new direction. During the Second World War he was to spend his exile from home and friends in Tunisia, and finally, on the eve of his death in 1951, he was projecting a sojourn in southern Morocco.

Yet the choice of French North Africa as his destination in 1893 was the result of chance. He longed to get far away, and had even thought of going to Iceland, when suddenly a friend, the young painter Paul-Albert Laurens, won a traveling fellowship and urged Gide to accompany him on his year abroad. The elder son of the academic painter, Jean-Paul Laurens, whose frescoes of Sainte Geneviève in the Panthéon and ceiling for the Théâtre de l'Odéon had won him a place in the Institut de France, Laurens had been Gide's classmate for a year in childhood. The two young men were of the same age, the same height and build, and shared the same intellectual and artistic tastes. In his memoirs Gide stresses the point that both were virgins—an unusual condition for Frenchmen of twenty-three—and implies that they resolved in advance not to return so. Tired of adolescent doubts, indecision, and morbid melancholy, they longed for fulfillment, health, and equilibrium. "This marked, I daresay, my first aspiration," Gide adds, "toward what is today called 'classicism'; to what a degree it was opposed to my original Christian ideal, I could never over-emphasize." It was doubtless more of a wrench for him to bid farewell to Christ in the pursuit of his new ideal than to forget his love for his cousin. In fact, he did not even need to do so, for his love was so pure and almost mystical that the admixture of anything carnal with it was unthinkable. He had already made up his mind to dissociate love and sexual pleasure, as André Walter had dreamed of doing, convincing himself that both would be purer and more intense if the heart and the body went their separate ways.

Crossing from Marseille to Tunis, the young travelers planned to reach Biskra by the southern route, across the desert. Having accordingly hired a huge landau drawn by four horses and driven by a swarthy coachman, they wrapped themselves in burnouses and plunged into the desert. Via Zaghouan and Kairouan they reached Susa on the east coast of Tunisia, and would have pushed on to Sfax and Gabès had it not been for Gide's health.

He had always been delicate, and the army recruiting board had declared him unfit for service, writing the dread word "tuberculosis" on his record. Furthermore, his father had died of intestinal tuberculosis at the age of forty-eight. Consequently when André Gide caught cold on the eve of leaving France, he almost abandoned the trip. Then the sudden changes of temperature in the desert, its stifling heat followed by chilling winds, irritated and congested his lungs until he could hardly breathe. A doctor whom Laurens called at Susa frightened both the patient and his companion and put an end to their glorious adventure. Paul Laurens would not go on without his friend, and Biskra still seemed an attractive place to spend the winter; so they simply returned to Tunis and went there prosaically by train.

In Biskra, Gide underwent a regular treatment of thermo-cautery, the doctor puncturing alternately his chest and his back and then bathing the spots with turpentine. But as soon as the congestion became localized, it moved from one lung to the other. Periodic fevers and a constant difficulty in breathing made it impossible for him to work or even to enjoy the piano he had had sent out from Algiers. Aimlessly dawdling through-out the day—for his condition did not condemn him to bed or even to remain indoors—he found his sole distraction in watch-ing the Arab children play in the public garden that began at his door or on the terraces that ringed his apartment. Years later that almost royal suite of rooms in the Hôtel de l'Oasis, which he shared with Paul Laurens and their fourteen-year-old servant Athman, entered *L'Immoraliste* almost unchanged, as did the invalid's preoccupation with the health and beauty of the dark-skinned youngsters. But if the Michel of that novel resembles the André Gide of 1893–4 so strongly that it is al-most impossible to resist drawing upon his experiences in recording Gide's, yet he differs from his creator in at least one important respect.

Whereas Michel is depicted as a latent homosexual not fully aware of his penchant, André Gide had already enjoyed his first liberating encounter. It had taken place at the provocation of an Arab youth named Ali on the dunes outside Susa, just after he had heard from the local doctor what seemed his death-sentence. Having thus been forced to recognize his natural inclination, he strengthened it by struggling against it. Failing to overcome it otherwise, and not admitting its exclusiveness, he even tried in vain to emulate Laurens's desires for the beautiful Ouled Naïl girls, who traditionally earn their dowry through prostitution. If anyone might have reconciled him to normal relations, surely it was the sixteen-year-old Mériem, on whose amber skin the sun had left its trace. His single night with her gave him an impression of extraordinary well-being and, he felt, did him more good than all the doctor's counter-irritants. But the two youths had hardly begun sharing her favors when their comfortable and frank *ménage à trois* was broken up by the untimely arrival of Mme Paul Gide, come to nurse her ailing son.

Unlike Michel, then, Gide fully appreciated the mingled reasons for his interest in the children at play. Later he could write in the only account he has left of this period (for the *Journals* omit this climactic voyage as if to concentrate it in *Si le grain ne meurt . . .*): "And I was not enamoured of any one among them but rather, indistinctly, of their youth. The sight of their health sustained me, and I wished no other company than theirs. Perhaps the tacit counsel of their naïve gestures and childish talk urged me to surrender more to life. With the help of the climate and my illness, I felt my austerity melting and my frown relaxing."

As Spring warmed the oasis and brought new life in the shade of the palms, the invalid felt progressively better. Little by little he lengthened his walks and shared in the life around him. Now he felt that he had narrowly escaped death, and, a convalescent, prized every aspect of life, looking upon it with new eyes. Receptive to all impulses, he suddenly felt like yielding to them all. As he wrote in his *Nourritures terrestres* (*The Fruits of the Earth*): ". . . my marvelous convalescence was a palingenesis. I was reborn with a new nature, under a new sky and amidst things completely renewed."

It would be impossible to exaggerate the importance of the reversal of values that André Gide experienced during the winter of 1893–4, which indeed was to furnish the subject of his writings for many years to come. Doubtless this crisis in his life would not have occurred as it did had not all the circumstances contributed to it. His previous restraint, the austerity of his background and his sheltered childhood, intensified the joy of his release. His uprooting from home and tradition, the sense of being delightfully out of his element (*dépaysé* as the French succinctly say) in a strange and intoxicating Orient, facilitated his forgetting of "past, future, laws, religion, morals, and literature, and constraint" in order to live solely in the present moment. Finally, his illness was providential in that it forced him, who had until now lived in and for the mind, to a constant and all but exclusive preoccupation with the body. The discovery of his sexual orientation in a land which, if it did not actually encourage such tastes, looked upon them as natural and did nothing to discourage them, thus fused with the larger revelation of the value and beauty of life. Years later he was to apply specifically to himself, as Goethe had done before him, Lessing's suggestive line: *"Es wandelt niemand unbestraft unter Palmen"*—"No one walks with impunity under palms."

It seems reasonable that the crisis of puberty in the life of a homosexual should take place under different circumstances from those in which it normally occurs among adolescents of heterosexual instincts. Like a duckling hatched in a brood of chickens, he can have no recourse either to the example of his comrades or to the advice of his elders. When he begins to experience desires and to sense their unorthodox character, the resulting spiritual conflict surpasses in intensity and duration anything that the normal youth knows. Whether Gide's austere religious upbringing or his sexual anomaly played a larger part in prolonging his chastity and retarding his awakening is impossible to say. Both certainly tended to delay and intensify the crisis. When he doubts, in his memoirs, if his perturbation would have been any less great had his desires been more normal (he had been taught to resist all his desires), he is indulging in an idle supposition. In shying away from the street-walkers of the Latin Quarter, the youth had simply expressed a natural aversion, flattered and cloaked by his puritanical education. But as soon as the provocations became those to which he was susceptible—that is to say, in Africa—nothing withheld him from responding to them.

Not until the experience of Susa at the age of twenty-four did he leave behind his adolescence and put on the *toga virilis*. It is only natural, then, that the formative period of life with its restless indecision and tormented questionings should have left upon him an indelible mark. In his case not only was adolescence prolonged beyond its usual span, but also the awakening of puberty was rendered more violent and more memorable by its extraordinary delay—just as an innocuous childhood malady often assumes frightening proportions when it attacks a mature organism that is not already immune. "I lived until the age of twenty-three," Gide wrote in his *Journals*, "completely virgin and utterly depraved; crazed to such a point that eventually I came to seek everywhere some bit of flesh on which to press my lips."

Few things remain more impenetrable to us than our own adolescence, for we pass through it at a time when we are least conscious of what we are experiencing. André Gide had an advantage over the rest of the world in this regard, for his spiritual growth occurred at an age when he had already developed the habit of self-observation. For many years he had been keeping a diary, of which the version we know presents but fragments, and he had already written that profound self-portrait, *Les Cahiers d'André Walter*. It is a truism that in an adolescent the sexual urge, more precisely the figure he cuts with the opposite sex, powerfully pushes him to emulate his elders and become a man. But the pederast lacks this impulse, feeling no incentive to force his development. Even after he reaches maturity he is likely not only to preserve better the memory of his youth but actually to remain young in spirit, for, by the time he is himself mature, he has become specifically interested in youth, not so much his own as that of others.

For these reasons André Gide was to give a special and permanent place in his writing to the adolescent. In this regard he was ahead of his time. From the tortured André Walter of 1891 to the self-assured Thésée of 1946, by way of the prodigal son, Lafcadio, and the Bernard, Olivier, and Georges of *Les Faux-Monnayeurs*, he has viewed the formative period of life from almost every angle. And what is Michel of *L'Immoraliste*, despite his twenty-seven years at the novel's end, but an adolescent in the act of self-discovery?

To limit the crisis in the young writer's life to his belated sexual initiation, however, would be a grave mistake. The important fact is that that initiation occurred when and where it did, that it coincided with a severe illness in a strange country and was followed by a slow convalescence that partook of a veritable rebirth or return from the dead.

During that first winter in Tunisia and Algeria, André Gide had met and embraced Apollo and Dionysus, temporarily substituting for his former Christian outlook a confused pagan ideal of classic harmony and dithyrambic frenzy. Throughout the rest of his life he was to strive to reconcile these ideals. In more ways than one he had emancipated himself and, though he knew only too well from what he was free, he did not yet know *for* what. At this point in his career another nature than his might have sunk into self-indulgence or succumbed, like his Saül, to his familiar demons. But a certain innate self-respect and rigid sense of duty steadied Gide at all times. As he was to make the protagonist of *L'Immoraliste* say in 1902: "Knowing how to free oneself is nothing; it's being free that is hard." To be sure, from 1894 onward the concern for personal freedom and the problems it raises will be one of the dominants of his work.

But in the Spring and Summer of 1894 the chief problem for him was to keep alive and build up his health. The homeward journey through Italy with Paul Laurens strained and

fatigued him, and from Florence he went directly to Geneva
to consult Dr. Andreæ. To that sensible man, who convinced
him that solely his nerves were ill, Gide later felt that he owed
his life, for he followed to the letter the doctor's prescription
of the baths at Champel and a winter in the mountains as well
as the advice to plunge into any water he saw. "O frothy tor-
rents!" Gide bursts out in the tone he was to adopt for his *Nourritures terrestres*, "waterfalls, icy lakes, shady brooks, limpid
springs, transparent palaces of the sea, your coolness draws me;
then, on the pale sand, the sweet repose beside the ebbing
wave. [. . .] With my clothing I cast off all torments, compul-
sions, anxieties, and, as all will volatilized, I let my sensations
secretly distill in me, porous like a bee-hive, that honey which
flowed into my *Nourritures*."

Already he had the conception of that book, but felt that it
had to write itself slowly. Somewhere on his travels, however,
he had written, as an exercise in "more supple obedience to
inner rhythm," *La Ronde de la Grenade* (*The Round of the
Pomegranate*), which was to form a part of that book. While
he was taking the cure at Champel, Pierre Louÿs and Ferdinand
Hérold visited him to hear of his journey. Before his enthusiastic account sent them off to Biskra and Mériem, in whose
company Louÿs wrote most of his voluptuous *Chansons de
Bilitis*, he read his poem to the two uncomprehending Parnassian poets. Small wonder it is that they failed to appreciate
Gide's new lyricism; to do so they would have to have shared
his African awakening. For the poem, written in the freest possible form, had none of the pictorial impassivity they admired
or of the obscure symbolism then coming into vogue. Clear in
its allusions and frank in its glorification of the senses, it perfectly prefigures the book to come, the book we should expect
to emerge from its author's new scale of values. The poem
begins by singing the joys of the senses as opposed to those
of the mind and heart; then it urges Nathanaël, to whom it is
addressed, to beware the distressing sense of sight and to de-

sire only what he can touch. Associating the glorification of
thirsts of all kinds with thirst-quenching fruits, the poet next
sings various exotic fruits in terms reminiscent of the "wonderful scarlet fruit, bleeding like wounds" which Urien's companions brought back from the shore where they first lay with
strange women. At that time the pure knights spurned it as
vicious and venomous; here, as before, the fruit is symbolic,
but by now it is eagerly welcomed and even sought after:

"Where, O Nathanaël, in our travels
      Are new fruits to give us other desires?"

Finally the poet comes to the pomegranate, which will always
figure for him the lure of the remote and savage as it is later
to do for his prodigal son:

"Hoarded treasure, honeycomb compartments,
    Abundance of savor,
    Pentagonal architecture.
    The rind splits; out fall the seeds,
    Seeds of blood in azure cups;
    And others, golden drops in bowls of enameled bronze."

But such a mingling of enthusiastic exoticism and unashamed sensuality was too heady for Gide's friends. It must
have surprised them especially coming from the rigid young
Calvinist whose scruples Louÿs had been accustomed to mock.
None of those he encountered was, in fact, able to grasp the
extent of the change that had taken place in him. "Upon returning to France," the memoirs record, "I brought back the secret
of one resuscitated and came to know, in the early days, that
sort of abominable anguish which Lazarus must have felt on
his escape from the tomb. Nothing of what had previously concerned me any longer seemed important to me." As he resumed
contact with the groups in which he had formerly lived, he
wondered how he could have breathed in their stifling atmosphere pervaded by an odor of death. He felt that others had
stood still while he had developed and was shocked that they
did not sense his secret revelation. "I should have wished to

persuade them," he says, "and deliver my message to them, but none of them leaned forward to listen to me. They continued to live; they went heedlessly on, and what satisfied them seemed to me so wretched that I could have cried out in despair not to convince them of this."

It was this feeling of estrangement, surely, that turned Gide temporarily away from the dithyrambic singing of the senses that he had begun in *La Ronde de la Grenade*. After all, if the public, even in its best elements, was not ready for such a work, he could return to his ironic vein and mock them for not being so while also mocking himself for taking their indifference so seriously. This is just what he did in *Paludes*—which has recently been translated into English as *Marshlands*. The book was written during three months in the winter of 1894–5 at La Brévine, a Swiss village high in the Jura Mountains, to which Gide had gone at Dr. Andreæ's recommendation. Years later he was to describe that snowbound, inhospitable village, where the temperature often drops to twenty below zero, as the setting for his *Symphonie pastorale (Pastoral Symphony)*. There, loathing Switzerland and dreaming of Biskra, strengthening his body by long walks and sleeping with his window open, he stayed just long enough to finish his masterpiece of delicate, involved irony.

Everything in *Paludes* is ironic—from the pseudo-Virgilian epigraph *"Dic cur hic"* (doubtless to balance the genuine *"Dic quibus in terris . . ."* of *Le Voyage d'Urien*) and the dedication "For my friend Eugène Rouart I wrote this satire of what?" to the Envoi, the alternative Envoi, and the "Table of the most remarkable sentences in *Paludes*." Not the least ironic touch, coming from so conscious and even self-conscious an author, is the foreword inviting us to read anything we wish into his book: "Before explaining my book to others, I am waiting for others to explain it to me. Wanting to explain it at the outset amounts to limiting its meaning at once; for if we know what we meant to say, we do not know whether or not we said only that. One always says more than THAT." To believe this would be tantamount to taking Laurence Sterne quite literally; yet there is just enough sense in it to tempt our credibility. Gide has regularly asked to be read with the most profound and sustained attention and even stated that he wrote to be reread; consistently he has called for the reader's collaboration. Whoever reads more into Gide than there is there can find his justification here. The fact is that, intentionally or unintentionally, he put into this little book as many provocative elements as into any of his later and longer works.

Let it be said at once, in reply to the dedication, that Gide has here satirized stagnation and acceptance, which are really but two facets of the same thing. But at the same time he ridicules the one who would spread dissatisfaction, the sower of unrest that he himself then was and long continued to be, who succeeds here only in exacerbating himself. Reflecting the author and speaking in the first person, that young man has no name; for convenience he might be called André. André recounts in these pages six days in his monotonous life, his talks with the active, extrovert Hubert and the virtuous, self-effacing Richard, a visit to the Botanical Gardens, an evening gathering of literary people in Angèle's salon, a day's trip with Angèle, his dreams, and his efforts to outwit his agenda. But above all, as we learn on the first page, he is writing a book called *Paludes*; this is, in fact, his sole occupation and justification. Thus Gide has again given us a book within a book, using the device in almost precisely the same way as he was to do thirty years later in *Les Faux-Monnayeurs*. For, here too, subject and title of both books are the same, and the implied criticism of the book we are reading is contained in the book we are reading about. One can go a step further and say that Gide's *Paludes* is the journal or logbook of the writing of André's *Paludes*.

As a start for *his* book, André is inspired by the lines from

the first of Virgil's *Bucolics* in which Meliboeus congratulates
the shepherd Tityrus for having got back his farm and being
satisfied with it, though it is small and stony and marshy—

> *et tibi magna satis, quamvis lapis omnia nudus*
> *limosoque palus obducat pascua junco.*

In that poem, incidentally, Virgil was using Tityrus as a per-
sonification of himself rejoicing over the return of his farm by
Octavian, and he introduced the same shepherd into the end of
the *Georgics* as a kind of signature; hence there is an erudite
sort of justification for André's use of Tityrus as a symbol for
himself. Most of André's friends are intrigued by his title; they
have heard from Hubert that the new book is to be quite different from his latest one, and, though they have not read the
latest one, they would like to know in advance about the work
now in progress. Unable to believe that it really concerns a
bachelor living in a tower surrounded by swamps who fishes
in his moat, and who then, impatient, eats the earthworm-bait
and hence catches nothing, they surround and beseech the
author. Embarrassed because he is talking to so many at once,
he tells them that it is "the story of the neutral ground that belongs to everyone . . . better, of the normal man, from whom
we all spring—the story of the third person, the one we talk
about, who lives in each of us and does not die with us." Finally,
he bursts out: "But understand, I beg you, that the only way
to relate the same thing to each—the same thing, you understand—is to change its form to fit each new mind."

Because his book concerns the morasses of the mind and
the sloughs of resignation, André shows an understandable preoccupation with the mud and slime of stagnation. The world
he sees is all in *grisaille*, made up of spongy mosses, rank
rushes, glaucous algae, worms, and "delicate gray things."
Like Tityrus placing a mud-filled aquarium in his room to reflect the world outside, he can say: "I like a landscape, as I
like a book, which does not distract me from my thought." When
André visits the Botanical Gardens it is to study the new varie-

ties of potamogeton or pondweeds. Indeed, he combines, like his creator, an interest in literature with an interest in biology, using such unfamiliar terms as *lycopodium* (club-moss), *carex* (sedge), *guimauves efficaces* (marsh-mallows), *centaurées* (centauries of the gentian family), all of which significantly refer to marsh plants. On two occasions he spends some time collecting epithets to use with unusual nouns. One of those substantives is *fungosities* which, like the irridescent surface of stagnant pools more beautiful than any butterfly's wings, reflects his attention to the beauty of decay. The other is *blastoderm*—the germinal membrane in the impregnated living ovum.

But this unexpected term belongs to another series of symbols: that of the prison rather than that of the swamp. The message André wants to impress upon his friends is that they are "terribly shut in." Hence he insists upon their narrow rooms, the airless inner courts on which they look, Angèle's crowded salon, for which he would reserve the word "exiguous"—and, as Gide said in a later preface, "that myopia of windows, that regulation of pleasure, that intercepting of sunlight, that stifling of people who insist on breathing only through cigarettes." Even the little trip taken by André and Angèle, from which he had expected a change of horizon which would give a new direction to his talent, takes them no farther than Montmorency and fails to liberate them, for "one can get out of cities only by energetic means such as express trains; the hard thing is to get beyond the suburbs." The blastoderm suggests such imprisonment, while at the same time symbolizing André's germinal idea that should eventually burst the egg and emerge into the light of day.

Another allusion to claustrophobia is even more subtle. The memoirs record that *Paludes* took shape in Gide's mind around two phrases that came to him in Milan on his way from Africa to Switzerland. One of those phrases was simply "*chemin bordé d'aristoloches*" and it appears in *Paludes* without any further development. What is there about a path bordered with aristolochia, aside from the balanced rhythm of its eight syllables in French, the interrelation of its vowel sounds and the suggestion of aristocrats, that should have held the attention even of an experienced botanist like André Gide? It happens that since the late eighteenth century this flower has been known as an example of protogyny or the favoring of cross-pollination and prevention of self-pollination through the maturing of the female element while the male element remains immature. The flower has a tubular calyx with a dilated lower portion; in its first, or female, stage the erect tube is lined with stiff hairs pointing downward. Fertilization is effected by small flies that creep down into the wider part, where they find mature stigmas. Unable to escape through the barrier of rigid hairs, they wander about in the floral trap and thus fertilize the stigmas with pollen brought from previously visited flowers. After some hours, the stigmas wilt, the anthers open and dust the flies with fresh pollen, and, as the calyx tube bends downward and the hairs wither, the prisoners are released to carry their pollen to the receptive stigmas of younger flowers. Like the other symbols cited by André—the caged beasts in the zoo, the tubercular in his tiny room, the miner underground longing for the light of day, the pearl-diver oppressed by the weight of the sea's dark depths—the midge prisoners in the pipe-shaped flower stand for frustrated, stifling humanity trapped by blind routine. The aristolochia, then, which was long the only known example of a temporary prison for insects, offers a perfect parallel to the closed literary circles in which André and his friends move.

In fact, if any of the symbols is more frequent in *Paludes* than those of the swamp and the prison, it is the figure of the circle. The riding-ring appears on the very first page, and in the description of the literary evening the stationary whirling of the ventilator all but drowns out all conversation. The suburbs ringing the city, old age turning into second childhood, the normal that is achieved by crossing rare species and thus canceling out their individuality, and Tityrus adapting his blood to the malaria of the swamps—*similia similibus*, as the doctor says—by eating mud-worms are striking examples of the image. André sees all life as a vicious circle: "All careers without self-enrichment," he says, "are horrible—those which merely bring in money, and so little that one has constantly to begin over again. What stagnations! At the moment of death, what will they have accomplished? They will have fulfilled their mission in life. I should think so! They chose it as small as they!" But in his efforts to liberate others from the grindstone (which image, incidentally, *might* have figured here), he meets circular arguments from his friends, such as the cryptic notes exchanged with Martin. Elsewhere Barnabé points out that by trying to force others to action André is paradoxically increasing their passivity and his own responsibility. Another acquaintance interjects: "In short, Sir, you are blaming people for living as they do, and yet you deny that they can live otherwise and you criticize them for being happy living as they do. But if that's what they want?"

In an effort to vary the monotony of his own life, André keeps an agenda in which he writes his day's program a week in advance, thus giving himself time to forget and enjoy the pleasure of surprise. Consequently, though already decided in advance by him, the morrow is always unknown to him. Because each evening he notes down what he has actually done, he can subtract what he has done from what he planned to do, and the remainder, what he should have done, can be copied down for the month of December, thus providing him moral reflections. On other occasions he rejoices at not having done what he ought to have done—which he might have forgotten without the agenda. This is what he calls the negative unforeseen.

It is not enough, however, for the book to abound in circular images, arguments, and anecdotes; after all, the entire central theme of the "agitated agitator" (as Gide called him in 1935) is circular. Merely through describing other's maladies to make the victims conscious of them, André feels that he is catching them himself and suffers all the torments that he fails to arouse in others. Then he comes to wonder if his consciousness of these sufferings does not increase them. In short the whole book is summed up in a single reply that André makes when asked of what he is complaining: "I am complaining of the fact that no one complains."

Even the form of *Paludes* is a perfect circle, for André at the end stands exactly where he was in the beginning—except that, having finished his book, in which Tityrus gets nowhere, he is now working on another, very similar one entitled *Polders* —which means low land reclaimed from the sea.

André is not the only writer in *Paludes*; almost all of his friends are also men of letters, and he intends for them the book he is writing. Likewise the book in which he figures, Gide's book, is addressed to an alert, sophisticated audience. Hence the timely literary allusions that punctuate the work. Because the young purists of Mallarmé's camp rather resented the literary reputation of the slightly older Maurice Barrès and his successful political activity, André upon quoting him identifies him as "Barrès, you know, the Député, my dear!" The air-gun with which André hunted ducks "made no other sound than that of a roman candle bursting in the air—or rather the sound of the word *'Palmes!'* in one of Monsieur Mallarmé's lines." Many of Gide's readers would have recognized the false alexandrine (*Les capitaines vainqueurs ont une odeur forte!*) which he attributes to "my young friend Tancrède"; for these words had appeared in January–February 1894 as the opening of a prose-poem in *L'Art Littéraire* by the sixteen-year-old Léon-Paul Fargue, who was even then writing a book to be called *Tancrède*. The line has its own amusing history. Guillaume Apollinaire relates that the young Fargue's reputation was made by Gide's quoting one of his verses, always this same one; yet when *Tancrède* appeared, it opened with this line as an epigraph attributed to Gide! The usually so sophisticated Apollinaire, apologist of cubism, discoverer of the Douanier Rousseau and inventor of the term *"surréalisme,"* reported that Fargue owed his first fame to a line by Gide, whereas in reality he had simply recognized Gide's adoption of his own words. In this literary volleying of the simple statement that "victorious captains smell strong" there is a circular irony altogether worthy of Angèle's *salon.*

Perhaps it would be possible to identify others among the many names appearing in *Paludes,* some of them quite ordinary, others—like Ildevert, Madruce, Hildebrant—medieval, and still others—such as Urbain, Ponce, Philoxène—classical in inspiration. Probably Valentin Knox, who so eloquently defends the abnormal and the positive value of malady, echoes Oscar Wilde. And certainly "Walter whom I cannot endure" stands for the already dead André Walter, or twenty-year-old Gide.

Surely the reader who was capable of catching such allusions would have delighted in the ironic description of the writer's calm existence, which one never bothers because, though always busy, he is working solely for us and would rather talk to us. And the same reader would have especially appreciated André's outburst when told that he ought to put a certain thing into his book: "Will you never understand anything, poor friend, about the *raison d'être* of a poem? About its nature and genesis? A book . . . but a book is closed, full, smooth like an egg. One cannot put anything into it, not even a needle, except by using force, and its form would be broken." "Then your egg is full?" his interlocutor asks, and he shouts back: "But, my friend, eggs are not filled; eggs are born full." Certain developments, also, about the general application of the particular subject express the attitude that was Gide's throughout his career and might have been consigned to his *Journals* at the age of sixty or seventy.

But the remarkable thing is that this little *Treatise on Contingency* (as *Paludes* was originally sub-titled), with all its mature wisdom thinly disguised in the trappings of paradoxical folly, was the work of a writer of but twenty-five. The first edition, consisting of fewer than four hundred copies, appeared in the Spring of 1895, and only a few months later, in November, the *Mercure de France* published Gide's "Preface for a Second Edition of *Paludes*." Fearing that readers, submerged under his accumulated irony, had failed to understand, he could not resist the temptation, which he had foreseen and repulsed in the original Foreword, to explain his book. Those few explanatory pages —the chief indication of the author's immaturity—appeared in the collective edition of *Le Voyage d'Urien* and *Paludes* in 1896, after which Gide must have recognized his error, for they were never reproduced again. Yet the critic cannot ignore them, for they do throw additional light upon the writer's intentions and state of mind. They begin by defending the author, who claims to be happy and complaining of nothing, against identification with his hero. Whoever sees the mediocre lacks perspective and breadth of vision; "do not artificially isolate something so that it will appear mediocre—gray in a painting which a touch of yellow nearby will turn to mauve." By telling us in advance that *Paludes* is the story of a warped mind, Gide might have saved appearances, he now thinks. André has but one shortcoming: that he will not leave well enough alone; hence he wants to reform everyone. At this point Gide mischievously suggests, with dashes and suspension points, a certain parallel between intellectual shortcomings and Christian virtues.

The most helpful comment in the Preface concerns the Shandyan "Table of the Most Remarkable Sentences in *Paludes*" following the last page of the book. The Table contains but two sentences at the top of an otherwise blank page followed by this footnote: "In order to respect everyone's idiosyncracy, we are leaving it to each reader to fill out this page." The two sentences —"He said: 'What! You are working!' " and "One must carry out to their conclusion all the ideas one brings up"—might not seem remarkable to most readers. But according to the preface, there is an intimate relationship between them, and together they sum up the subject of the book. To understand this, one must recall that the reply to the first remark is: "I am writing *Paludes*," and there, says the preface, is an idea brought up which must be carried to its logical conclusion. For the book "is the story of an idea rather than the story of anything else. It is the story of the sickness it brings to a certain mind. Any idea can become a corrupting element in a mind. Element of life? No, of fever—of a semblance of life. It is all-consuming and lives on us; we are here only to allow it to live."

Furthermore, Gide confesses here that he likes a book to contain, hidden within it, its own refutation, the wherewithal to negate and suppress it altogether. The book must be such a closed entity that it can be suppressed only as a whole, leaving no residue or ashes, just as a chemical composition in perfect balance can be instantly suppressed by a spark "in a volatile disappearance, in a subtle gas—a laughing gas."

This *Paludes* decidedly does, for in this way also the book is circular, turning back upon itself to destroy itself. Years later, when Gide was undergoing a crisis similar to the one that produced *Paludes*, he wrote to the poet Francis Jammes: "Why will you not realize that I detest *my thought*? I am wearing myself out struggling against it, but can negate it only through it, as a demon is driven out by Beelzebub the prince of demons. What else did I try to show in *Paludes*?" Even though they may often cost him torment, Gide, we have seen, cherishes his contradictions. *Paludes* is a milestone in this sense, for in it its author gives free rein for the first time to his sense of the *saugrenu*, the absurd, already so apparent in *Urien*. Its satire of unrest cancels out its satire of smugness. By a further contradiction, the belated preface, denying that anything in life is mediocre to him who knows how to view it, annihilates the poor André.

In November 1895, as soon as the preface appeared in the *Mercure*, Jammes wrote to Gide: "Why did you explain *Paludes*? Régnier must have understood, Griffin and Mallarmé also, and I." Those poets probably did understand, though there is no proof left that they did. Another poet most certainly did, as we

know from Paul Claudel's letter to Gide in which he speaks of
"those recitatives of *Paludes*, which resemble those little vials
the Chinese seem to have cut out of translucid agate to hold sam-
ples of all varieties of fog: river-fog, sea-fog, morning fog half
saturated with sunlight. *Paludes* is the most complete document
we have as to that special atmosphere of stifling and stagnation
which we breathed from 1885 to 1890." Claudel rather shortens
the dates of that period, doubtless because his own escape to the
Orient kept him from being painfully aware of what was going
on in the Paris of 1895. Among contemporary reviewers the one
who most keenly appreciated the little work was Léon Blum—
for, before entering politics, the future leader of the Socialist
Party and many times Premier of France devoted himself to
letters and particularly to the rubric of literary criticism in *La
Revue Blanche*. His review in early 1897 opened: "M. André
Gide is an excellent writer. He possesses to the highest degree
the gift and science of language. [. . .] How can one doubt that
he must one day be one of those whose thought will influence
universal thought?" With the double advantage of having read
the preface and talked with the author, whom he already knew
rather well, Blum saw that never had there been a gayer novel of
boredom or one richer in its monotony because "the uniformity
of the narrative and the thought is varied by an unbelievable
wealth of observation and psychological imagination." He was
also aware that the author had lived *Paludes* and had to go
through that transitional state in order to achieve his future
work, making a clean sweep of the past according to the Carte-
sian method.

In this Léon Blum was right: the *Journals* refer to *Paludes*
as the work of an invalid and the memoirs record that Gide's
feeling of estrangement (for which he uses the English word)
was such that it might have led him to suicide had it not been
for the release he found in describing it ironically in *Paludes*.
Thus, once again, André Gide effected a catharsis through his

writing. Yet *Paludes* has proved to be of more than a personal therapeutic value. To some in 1895 it doubtless seemed an extremely clever sort of private joke for the author and his friends; now, more than half a century after its original appearance, it has become a message applicable to all frustrated intellectuals of whatever time or place, a more accessible *Wasteland*. Many admirers of Gide place it very high among his works; in fact, certain sophisticated readers of today prefer its cool irony and impeccable form to the more widely known later novels. Twenty years ago Jean Giraudoux could state, with tacit reference to *Paludes*, that *aristoloche* was one of the secret pass-words by which cultivated Frenchmen of the twentieth century could recognize one another.

Paludes is a negative book reflecting the dejection of the traveler who has returned from far-off fascinating places and varied enriching experiences to find the same humdrum existence he had half forgotten. "I am better aware now of all I should have liked to leave behind when I see all that comes back to me on my return," says André after his day's journey to the suburbs. But Gide had to write that negative work before returning to the elaboration of his positive message. What was to others their "literary career" he insisted upon considering as his life. His life and his work, in other words, are one, since he lived solely for his work; and from 1897 onward the biography of André Gide lies in the history of his ideas and the succession of his literary accomplishments. But before he could complete his revolutionary *Nourritures terrestres*, three events of major importance were to occur in his life: his decisive and liberating encounter with Oscar Wilde in Africa, the death of his mother, and his marriage.

The moment *Paludes* was finished, he was once again free to seek peace and fulfillment in the desert. Biskra had been so much in his mind during the winter in the frigid mountains that it had even crept into his book, where André, striving to move his

friends to action and change, talks enthusiastically of the oasis
he has never seen but has chosen at random as a symbol of the
remote and romantic.

Upon sailing from Marseille in January 1895, Gide had expected to find a precocious Spring in Algiers. But, disappointed,
he had taken his melancholy to the resort town of Blida, between
Algiers and Oran, and was about to leave there in turn. In fact,
he had already sent his luggage to the station and was paying
his bill when he noticed on the list of hotel guests, close to his
own, the names of Oscar Wilde and Lord Alfred Douglas. Eager
only for solitude, he quickly expunged his name from the slate
and started out on foot for the station. On the way he reflected
that perhaps a certain cowardice had dictated his gesture; for
the company of Wilde, whom he had frequented in Paris in
1891–2, had recently become compromising. Though the English writer had always observed complete discretion in his relations with Gide, the latter had heard of his growing notoriety.
The cynicism with which he made no attempt to hide his tastes
caused former friends to desert him. It was characteristic of Gide
that, fleeing what might have seemed a cowardly act and perhaps yielding to a certain curiosity about Wilde and about himself, he with his luggage promptly returned from the station to
the hotel, where he again wrote his name on the slate.

Gide has left two accounts of that meeting and the ensuing
weeks. The first one, full of pious admiration for the man Wilde,
is in the memorial essay written on the first anniversary of the
dramatist's death, and the other, more detailed and confessional
in tone, in *Si le grain ne meurt . . .*, written almost twenty
years later. The two records corroborate and complement one
another. Wilde had changed greatly in manner, his laugh now
grown harsh and his affectations more brazen. He no longer
talked in delicate parables such as he had related three years
earlier, before writing them down as his *Poems in Prose*. He
talked of pleasure as his duty, boasted of his rôle as a demoral-
izer, and admitted that in returning to London and the Marquess

of Queensbury's attacks, as he was shortly to do, he was following his tragic destiny. Something had to happen, as he said, because he could go no farther in his direction. Gide listened to him with a mingling of amazement, admiration, and fear.

But above all, Wilde and Douglas boldly—even cynically—revealed at once their interest in young boys, so easy to satisfy in Arab lands, as if to warn Gide that he must accept them on their own terms. Wilde was then thirty-nine; and Gide, twenty-five, would accompany this experienced companion in his round of Moorish cafés. Although the young writer had never consciously let any friend suspect his inclinations, on one such excursion the older man risked the assumption that Gide shared his tastes and exulted upon learning that he had guessed the truth. Since Gide's adventure at Susa over a year before, he had overcome all his scruples but was not yet aware of this. It was probably only as he instinctively replied a choking, muffled "Yes" to Wilde's indiscreet, yet welcome question that he consciously admitted to himself and accepted the change that had come over him. The recognition that there were others of similar inclination and that he could disclose his secret nature to them marked an important step in Gide's moral liberation. He was now suddenly forced to recognize that his mind condoned and even contributed to encourage a native penchant whose expression at Susa might have seemed merely accidental.

Without knowing it, he had returned to North Africa, sensing the facility and indulgence it offered, doubtless for the same reason that Wilde and Douglas were there. Had he never known Wilde, some other friend or acquaintance would sooner or later have played the same rôle in his life; the debauchee likes nothing so much as leading others to debauch, he says. But the fact that his early guide was the scintillating Oscar Wilde, a literary legend in at least two countries already, is appropriate. And who can say what an influence upon his own life may have had Wilde's leaving him in Algiers to return directly to London, the most scandalous trial of the epoch, and a sentence of two years at hard labor? The space devoted to the English writer in the memoirs and the tone of the essay, as well as the great importance given to Ménalque in both the *Nourritures terrestres* and the *Immoraliste,* suggest that the thought of Oscar Wilde was ever-present in Gide's mind between 1895 and 1900—crucial years of full productivity.

Apart from their one basic similarity, the two men are about as different as men can be. Yet the writers have much in common, as a juxtaposition of *Intentions* with Gide's critical writings and a comparison of *The Picture of Dorian Gray* with *L'Immoraliste* would reveal. As the memorial essay tells us, Gide was one of the first to visit the paroled and chastened Sebastian Melmoth at Berneval, as he was one of the last to sit on a Parisian café terrace with the pitiable, soft Wilde who stares out at us from Toulouse-Lautrec's painting. The thought may never have crossed his mind on those occasions, so different did he recognize his own ethic and force of will to be, to contrast himself with his interlocutor. Yet Wilde's example had assuredly taught him a double lesson and, thanks in part to it, he was eventually to attempt a justification of his own way of life in *Corydon* and again in *Si le grain ne meurt.* . .

Meanwhile Gide stayed on in Algeria, spending several weeks in his beloved Biskra, even buying a small plot there for an eventual house and making plans, which his mother categorically and successfully opposed, to take his guide Athman back to Paris with him. He was so reluctant to leave Africa that the solicitous Mme Gide came to suspect a *liaison* and urged him to "break off." "The truth, if she could have known," he comments, "would have frightened her much more, for it is easier to break with another than to escape oneself. And, to succeed in doing so, one must first want this. But at the moment of beginning to discover myself I could hardly long to quit myself, on the point of discovering in me the tables of my new law." Finally, however, he did return in time to spend a fortnight with his mother in Paris before she left for La Roque. Fortunately those two weeks were a period of truce with the mother whose exclusive affection and insistent intervention in his acts, thoughts, expenditures, choice of clothing, and even the titles of his books exasperated him beyond endurance. As if through a presentiment that they were spending their last days together, the brief period following his return was so free of clashes that the son intended to spend the entire summer with his mother in Normandy. Before the time came when he had planned to join her, however, a telegram called him to her deathbed.

The authoritative genealogical study of the Rondeaux family by Pierre Le Verdier records that "Mme Paul Gide, Juliette Rondeaux, died at the château of La Roque-Baignard on 31 March 1895 at the age of sixty years." But Gide's own records, together with the date of Jammes's letter of condolence, indicate that this date is a misprint for 31 May.

On this occasion Gide's memory had not betrayed him, as he was aware that it so often did in matters of mere chronology. On the other hand, it was always extraordinarily sure whenever sensation or emotion was involved. Hence we can credit his description of his feelings after his mother's death: "Then it was," he says, "that I experienced my mind's peculiar readiness to be intoxicated by the sublime. During the first period of my mourning, I recall, I lived in a sort of moral intoxication that urged me to the most rash acts. It was enough for them to seem noble in order to win the approval of my mind and heart. I began by distributing as remembrances to even distant relatives, some of whom had hardly known my mother, the little jewels and trinkets which, having belonged to her, might have the greatest value for me. Through exaltation, love, and a strange thirst for poverty I could have given away, at the very moment of coming into possession of it, my whole fortune; I could have given myself away. [. . .] That very freedom for which I panted while my mother was alive stunned and choked me like a gush of fresh air, perhaps even frightened me."

The one fixed point in his life remained his love for his

cousin Madeleine. Her father, Émile Rondeaux, having died in early 1890, she and her sisters had become the responsibility of their aunts, particularly of Mme Gide. As family concern about André's way of life grew during his early literary career and his first trips to Africa, the relatives in general gradually came to look upon his eventual marriage with his orphaned first cousin as a possible steadying influence. While doubting that such a union would be happy, his uncle, Charles Gide, wrote the youth's mother with a scholar's instinctive caution: "Yet, if it does not take place, probably both of them will be surely unhappy, so that there remains only a choice between a certain evil and a possible one." Finally, during their last hours together, Mme Gide, foreseeing her death and perhaps fearing to leave him alone, admitted to her son that she wished to see him marry the niece whom she had long considered as her daughter-in-law. André himself was convinced that his cousin needed him to be happy, and when, shortly after his loss, he asked for her hand, he was thinking less of himself than of her. As the mature Gide says most meaningfully in the last lines of his memoirs: "Our most sincere acts are also the least calculated; the explanation one looks for later on is useless. Fate was leading me, perhaps also a secret need to challenge my nature; for was it not virtue itself that I loved in her? It was heaven that my insatiable hell was marrying; but at the moment I was omitting that hell; the tears of my grief had extinguished all its fires; I was as if dazzled with azure, and what I refused to see had ceased to exist for me. I believed that I could give myself to her wholly, and I did so without withholding anything."

On the eighth of October 1895 the young cousins were married at Étretat, a few miles from Madeleine's estate of Cuverville, with a Protestant minister named Roberty from Rouen officiating; the best man was Élie Allégret, himself a minister and missionary, who later became director of all French Protestant missions. It was not until 1951—thirteen years after the death of Mme André Gide and a few months after the writer's death—

that Gide's little memoir entitled *Et nunc manet in te* (which has been entitled *Madeleine* in translation) penetrated the mystery of that union between two such dissimilar people and revealed to the world their tragic relationship. The very conception of a "marriage of Heaven and Hell" (which must have been suggested to Gide by his translation in 1922 of William Blake's prophetic work with that title) already divulges much of the truth, while surely explaining the name that Gide consistently gave his wife in his writings. As early as *Les Cahiers d'André Walter*, his first work, he had adopted for his heroine the euphonious name of "Emmanuèle," which was later to designate his cousin and wife in both his memoirs and *Journals*. He might have satisfied her natural discretion and fear of the limelight by adopting one of the unused given names of Louise-Mathilde-Madeleine Rondeaux. It would be quite unlike Gide ever to have explained, yet it is strange that no one else has ever pointed out, that the name Emmanuel is interpreted in the Bible as "God with us." Throughout life his wife appeared to André Gide as his refuge, his anchor to windward, his link with tradition and the past, his protection against everything in himself that he feared, and his possible salvation. It is for this reason that her headstone in the little cemetery at Cuverville-en-Caux bears a verse from the beatitudes: "Blessed are the peacemakers: for they shall be called the children of God." In the French version by Ostervald, which Gide chose for the stone-carver, the wording is even more appropriate, for it reads: "Heureux ceux qui procurent la paix. . ."

Immediately after the marriage, the young couple set out on a protracted journey that was to last until May of the following year. After two months in Switzerland and another two in Italy, they reached North Africa in February 1896, where they visited Tunis, El Kantara, Biskra, and Touggourt. This was André Gide's third sojourn in the desert and its oases; it seems as if a fatal attraction, which he will later attribute to the Michel of his *Immoraliste*, drew him back to the scene of his awakening. Instead of tying him down to Paris or the two Norman estates that he and his wife had now inherited, marriage was not to influence his restless roving. From Neuchâtel a fortnight after the wedding he wrote a friend: "Now I am beginning an indefatigable rest beside the calmest of wives." But only three months later he wrote from Rome: "Here it is madly beautiful weather and my senses and soul are stampeding; I am drinking in the sunlight like an over-warm wine and my wisdom is confounded."

It was in this state of mind that he continued to write *Les Nourritures terrestres* which had begun with *La Ronde de la Grenade*. Doubtless the travels and their attendant self-renewal were necessary to the continuation of that work; certainly it owed little if anything to the marriage. While he was in southern Italy and Africa, the poem he had read to Louÿs and Hérold at Champel appeared in the first issue of Louÿs's new and luxurious periodical in Paris. At roughly the same time, in January 1896, another Parisian review devoted its first seven pages to another fragment of the forthcoming book. *L'Ermitage*, founded as a monthly in 1890, had just undergone a reorganization, and the new editor, Édouard Ducoté, wrote to Gide asking him to open the initial number of the new series. The letter reached Gide in Switzerland, where he immediately and rapidly put together some of the notes jotted down for the *Nourritures*. The result was *"Ménalque"*—a coherent, first-person account of the life of a hedonist. Unashamedly, even cynically, Ménalque boasts of his joy in living, his sensuality and cultivation of the ego, his receptivity to all ideas and emotions, his pantheism and scorn for tradition. He tells how at the age of twenty-five he finally settled down to accumulate art objects and erudition and friends, and how at the age of fifty he turned his then vast fortune into liquid assets, rid himself of everything personal, and set out for a life of adventure and change. His subsequent years have been a round of varied pleasures in many of the most beautiful spots on earth. In his nomadic life he has known the caresses of cabin-boys and courtesans as well as those of patrician beauties. "Do not think," he concludes, "that my happiness has been bought with wealth; my heart, devoid of earthly attachment, has remained poor, and I shall die with ease. My happiness is made of fervor. Through everything indiscriminately, I have madly adored."

As soon as *"Ménalque"* appeared in *L'Ermitage*, Gide rather regretted having revealed his notes to the public and having, through modesty, attributed those notes to an imaginary character. He worried as to how his friends would take this sample of the work to come. And when Francis Jammes, the bucolic poet of the Pyrenees with whom Gide had been corresponding since 1893, wrote a smug and silly "Reply to Ménalque," Gide was sincerely delighted; the puritan in him enjoyed hearing his cynical Ménalque lectured in the name of humility and resignation. To Jammes and others he protested that *"Ménalque"* did not give a fair foretaste of the book, which would be better and which, in fact, would not even include that fragment.

Yet when the volume came out, over a year later, it did contain that piece of bravura. Since Ménalque's autobiography included all the principal themes of the *Nourritures*, Gide could not resist the desire once more to achieve composition in depth by incorporating those seven pages in the middle of his manuscript. As always when he created a book within a book, Ménalque's story provides a salutary element of self-criticism, for there the doctrine is exemplified with enough crude objectivity and complacent boldness to imply and invoke an unfavorable judgment. This, then, probably explains why the author changed his mind in the matter and preserved the fragment verbatim as *L'Ermitage* had printed it. Furthermore, to Gide the unpopular attitude always seemed the more sincere, and the fact that his friends did not like Ménalque doubtless spurred him to greater loyalty to that fiction of his own mind.

Soon after the young Gide couple returned to Paris from

their wedding-trip in May 1896, the poet of the nomadic life who was engaged in glorifying the carefree and spontaneous learned that he had just been elected mayor of La Roque-Baignard in Normandy. Oblivious to the distinction of being the youngest mayor in France, he saw only the responsibilities and administrative chores attached to that post, to which he would now be tied for years. His little tale of 1931 entitled *Jeunesse (Youth)* reveals how conscientiously he fulfilled the numerous functions of mayor. For instance, the ever-sober Gide, as he strove to check the ravages of alcoholism for which that region of Calvados is notorious, found it increasingly difficult to sing in his book the joys of intoxication, both physical and spiritual. Yet he continued to assemble his notes and to compose his daring work of lyricism. And in writing to his friends, as if in the spirit of challenge, he frequently referred to the forthcoming book, the present title of which he had definitively decided upon even before his mother's death, as *Ménalque*. The moment he was able to get away from his duties at La Roque, he fled Normandy for Paris, where he spent the winter of 1896–7 putting the finishing touches to the *Nourritures*.

In April 1897 *Les Nourritures terrestres (The Fruits of the Earth)* finally appeared in a volume of 213 pages. A longer book than any of Gide's so far, except for the *Cahiers d'André Walter*, it was still a short work by today's standards. Its eight books of vehemently sincere exaltation sing the joys of sensations of all kinds in a rhythmic prose that frequently breaks into a free form of verse. The whole is preceded by a single page of Foreword, essential to our understanding:

"Be not misled, Nathanael, by the brutal title I have been pleased to give this book; I might have called it *Ménalque*, but Ménalque never, any more than you, existed. The only man's name that could have been put on this book is my own; but then how could I have dared sign it?

"I put myself into it without affectation and without modesty; and if sometimes I speak here of countries I have not seen, of perfumes I have not breathed, of deeds I have not done—or of you, my Nathanael, whom I have not yet met— this is not hypocrisy and these things are no more falsehoods than this name, Nathanael who will read me, that I give you, not knowing yours to come.

"And when you have read me, throw away this book—and go out. I should like it to have given you a desire to get away —get away from anywhere, from your town, from your family, from your room, from your thought. Do not take my book with you. If I were Ménalque, in order to lead you I should have taken your right hand but your left hand would have known it not, and I should have dropped that clasped hand at the earliest opportunity, as soon as we were far from towns, and said to you: forget me.

"May my book teach you to be more interested in yourself than in it—then in all the rest more than in yourself."

The volume might well have borne the author's name in the place of a title, so completely has he put himself, both as he then was and as he wanted to be, into his book. In fact, the book *is* the André Gide of 1895–7, whence its evident contradictions and confusion. It might just as well have been entitled *Ménalque*; for that strange figure, who tells the story of his life in Book IV and reappears elsewhere as a model or as a subject of regret and nostalgia, did effectively exist. Some would say that—with his cosmopolitanism, sybaritic tastes, selfishness, pantheism, receptivity, indulgence in debauch, sexual preferences, cynicism, and "hard, gem-like" fervor—he represents Oscar Wilde as Gide knew him in Paris and later saw him in Florence and Blida. Most certainly Wilde contributed elements to his portrait, but the very name, borrowed from the shepherd Menalcas of Virgil's *Bucolics*, should provide another clue. Generations of critics, armed with irrefutable internal evidence, have recognized Virgil himself in Menalcas. Even though the author speaks elsewhere in the first person, is it not possible that Gide has projected himself, or certain facets of himself, into Ménalque precisely as Virgil did? Ménalque is the author's master as Nathanael is the author's disciple, one a projection into the past and the other an anticipation of the future in the person of that coming adolescent, similar to what Gide himself was at sixteen, but freer and more resourceful, to whom he was henceforth to address himself. The hypothetical and desired disciple is obviously "God-given," he of whom Jesus said: "Behold an Israelite indeed, in whom is no guile!"—hence his name, Nathanael. Thus at the very outset of his book Gide has discreetly confessed his double inspiration, at once pagan and Christian. Accordingly Ménalque represents a certain André Gide as he saw himself at the age of twenty-five, distorted as in a mirror. Similarly Milton mingled in *Lycidas* (his pastoral inspired by Virgil's fifth *Eclogue*) shepherds, nymphs, Old Testament figures, and Christ. And, like Milton, Gide fits even the New Testament Nathanael into the pastoral mold, calling him "little shepherd."

No less essential and memorable than the Foreword, the Envoi with which the volume closes further enlightens us as to the author's seriousness and the urgency of his message:

"And now, Nathanael, throw away my book. Emancipate yourself from it. Leave me. Leave me; you stand in my way now; you are holding me back; my love for you, which I overrated, has taken too great a hold on me. I am tired of pretending to educate someone. When did I say that I wanted you to be like me? It is because you differ from me that I love you; I love in you only what differs from me. Educate? Whom should I educate, after all, but myself? Shall I tell you, Nathanael? I have educated myself interminably. I am continuing to do so. I never value myself save in what I might do.

"Nathanael, throw away my book; be not satisfied with it. Do not think that *your* truth can be found by someone else; more than of anything, be ashamed of that. If I fetched you food, you would not be hungry for it; if I made your bed, you would not be sleepy.

"Throw away my book; tell yourself that it is but *one* of the thousand possible postures for confronting life. Seek your own. What another might have done as well as you, do not do. What another might have said or written as well as you, do not say or write. In yourself cleave only to what you feel to be nowhere but in you, and make of yourself, impatiently or patiently, ah! the most irreplaceable of men."

Nowhere does the didactic intent of the *Nourritures* become so apparent as in the Foreword and the Envoi. To be sure, the poetic prose abounds with vocatives and imperatives; the poet constantly tells Nathanael how to face and embrace life. His message is one of the necessity of finding and asserting oneself. And what message could be more universally appropriate— for the artist, the thinker, the filing clerk, the lover, husband, or son—than to make of himself the most irreplaceable of men?

The four cardinal points of the doctrine are *l'inquiétude, le déracinement, la disponibilité,* and *la ferveur.* The most fundamental is the first, for without restlessness and dissatisfaction it is impossible to achieve anything in life or to attain the divine fervor that gives life its zest. Already the hero of *Paludes* is ineffectually aware of this, but fails to get beyond the initial unrest; and throughout his career Gide will not cease to proclaim that his function is to disturb.

Uprooting, the second point, is a necessary corollary of unrest: to launch out into the unknown one must break with tradition, getting away from the restrictive influences of family, heredity, conventions, and the patterns of one's own thought. Man is ever attached to his comforting and convenient habits; as soon as he settles somewhere, he begins to secrete a shell that exactly resembles him. But here Gide teaches that one must resist that natural tendency and flee whatever has taken on one's resemblance.

This element in the *Nourritures* inevitably pitted Gide squarely against the powerful and popular Maurice Barrès. In his review of Barrès's first thesis novel upholding nationalism and federalism (which appeared in the same year as the *Nourritures*) he claimed that uprooting may be a school of virtue as well, since all education is an intellectual uprooting that harms only the weak, strengthening the strong. "One rarely acquires the virtues one can do without," he quotes Laclos as saying. Meanwhile, Charles Maurras, the future founder of the nationalist movement known as *Action Française* and eventual ideologist of the Vichy government, came to the defense of Barrès. Gide debated with him at some length about the strengthening of trees and plants through uprooting and transplantation, for Maurras had ventured to speak of poplars without foreseeing that the Norman landowner and gentleman farmer in Gide would worst him in a most amusing argument.

Through initial uprooting and permanently cultivated unrest one should maintain oneself unattached, ready and receptive for whatever comes; this is the meaning of the untranslatable *disponibilité*. Nathanael is taught not to prepare any of his joys, for *another* joy, in its place, will surprise him. Taking nothing for granted and maintaining a constantly fresh vision, the wise man finds everything a source of wonder and amazement.

Fervor, the fourth point of the doctrine, means nothing less than the magic glow from within, that spontaneous and unalterable flame with which Walter Pater's disciples burned after reading the conclusion to his *Renaissance*, which later seemed to its author so subtly subversive that he suppressed it. Pater's essays appeared in the year of André Gide's birth, and it is tempting to think of the most notorious of Pater's students passing on his lighted brand to the eminently receptive young French writer in the dark alleyways of Algiers. Did not Oscar Wilde confess to him that he had put his genius into his life, giving but his talent to his books? Gidian fervor, in any case, is simply the recognition that merely being alive is a voluptuous pleasure.

The doctrine contained in the *Nourritures* was so new, so

startling in French letters in the mid-nineties that few readers realized how almost incidentally it grew, as things in nature grow, from the dithyrambic, lyrical tone of the book. Certainly the original intention was to celebrate the five senses and the manifold joys they bring. The title is, after all, *The Fruits of the Earth*—which enter the body through the senses; consequently Gide emphasizes hunger and thirst, symbolic of all desires. *Paludes*, we have seen, reeks appropriately of stagnant, scummy water. The *Nourritures*, on the contrary, flows with living water, trickling, bubbling, lapping, dripping, cascading through its pages. Fresh water for bathing or drinking wells up even in the desert, and elsewhere rushes down from the mountain; it falls from heaven on the rain-soaked Norman countryside. Gide seems to be passing on to us Dr. Andreæ's advice to plunge into every body of refreshing water, so frequently do he and his companions bathe. The timid knights of *Le Voyage d'Urien*, who abstained from dipping into the sea of life, are far in the past; yet, by a characteristic irony, Gide has given to some of his new characters names he had previously used in *Urien*.

While working on the *Nourritures*, Gide called it his volume of "pure lyricism"; and so it originally was. In the book itself he says: "I should like to have been born in a period when, as a poet, I might have sung all things merely by naming them. My admiration would have centered successively on each one, and my praise of it would have revealed it; that would have been its sufficient reason." Thus he justifies the many simple enumerations, Virgilian or Whitmanesque, of so many passages in prose or verse. Elsewhere he defines the poet's special gift as that of being excited by mere plums—that is, by anything at all or nothing at all; hence he claims there is no need to exercise any choice or to compose his work at all.

Now, Nathanael becomes necessary and the poet's attitude becomes doctrine simply because his joy reaches such a paroxysm that he *must* communicate it. Furthermore, Gide was a born teacher and belonged to the French tradition of the *moral-*

istes, of those concerned with analyzing and judging human behavior. Whether his own prescriptions, in this book or elsewhere, would be called moral, amoral, or immoral—and it
would be unfair to judge them on this single early work—he
could not resist expressing them.

As a work of pure lyricism, the *Nourritures* suggests parallels with Virgil's *Bucolics* and with Walt Whitman's *Leaves of
Grass.* Already both *Le Voyage d'Urien* and *Paludes* had borne
Virgilian epigraphs, and the recumbent Tityrus of the first
Bucolic had served as the protagonist of the book-within-a-book
of *Paludes.* Besides Menalcas, Amyntas, Meliboeus, Mopsus,
and Tityrus all figure in the *Nourritures,* which, as a song of
love, of the beauty of nature, and of the joys of the senses, bears
distinct relation to the pastoral tradition. Its frequent breaking
into lyric strophes to give a song within a song and its use of
amoebean verse (in which two or more singers in turn celebrate
the same subject or ring extemporaneous changes on a theme)
reveal further Virgilian inspiration, as do certain telling details of style. There is less evidence that Gide knew at all well
the American *Leaves of Grass,* of which but seventeen poems,
not always the most characteristic, had been published in French
translation prior to 1897. Yet Marcel Schwob, who frequently
read extempore translations from Whitman to his friends, may
possibly have included Gide among his auditors and thus introduced him to such poems as "Song of Myself," "Song of the
Open Road," and "Salut au monde."

Both the Roman and the American poets, whatever their
differences, must have delighted the young writer by their frequently pederastic inspiration and their like treatment of homosexual and heterosexual love on a plane of moral and aesthetic
equality. In them he must have heard an echo of his own emotions and a self-justification, as it were, in the eyes of a society
that seemed to have no place for such as he.

As for its doctrine of self-expression and self-fulfillment, the
Nourritures most strongly suggests Goethe and Nietzsche. The

influence of those two German giants upon André Gide has been exhaustively studied by my pupil Renée Lang and, in so far as this single book is concerned, by Yvonne Davet. Before 1897 Gide had read of Goethe at least *Wilhelm Meister, Werther, Faust, Part II*, the *Roman Elegies* and *Prometheus*, and had noted in his *Journals*: "Nothing has ever served to calm me in life so much as the contemplation of that great figure." By nature, André Gide shared with the sage of Weimar a basic optimism and love of life, an innate inclination toward the natural sciences and an insatiable curiosity, an anti-mysticism and a preference for everything involving effort. Small wonder it is, then, that, playing on the word, he could speak of *recognizing* his debt to Goethe because he constantly *recognized* himself in Goethe, who informed him of his own true nature. As for Nietzsche, Gide was less willing to acknowledge his early influence; and to those who would insist upon Zarathustra's ample contribution to the *Nourritures*, this attitude seems ungracious on the part of one who was shortly to pronounce an eloquent apology of all influences. To be sure, Gide was not so ignorant of Nietzsche as his published writings imply. From his close friend and future brother-in-law, the Germanist Marcel Drouin, he had absorbed more of the revolutionary doctrine than he was himself aware. To Drouin he wrote at the end of 1895 that he was somewhat afraid of Nietzsche, who drew him with the dizzying and fatal attraction of great heights. In March 1898 he wrote to the same friend and initiator that Nietzsche's entire achievement was merely a preface to works that Nietzsche himself was incapable of creating. "The amazing thing," Gide wrote, "is that, because of his Protestant past, his wonderful philological education, and his very sickly nature (which made it impossible for him to *practice* what he preached), that youthful crisis lasted. Thus it is, because he analyzes it and allows us to examine it with great care, that it takes on such importance and seems a revelation—like any new explanation of anything familiar. [. . .] For an artist to be surprised at finding within him, almost unsuspected, the thoughts that Nietzsche reveals openly is tantamount to his being surprised at having an artistic vision of the world. Nietzsche's books form the invisible and often unconscious framework of many great works of art and of many actions, both great and small." In other words, Gide found in Nietzsche, much as he had found in Goethe, Wilde, and so many others, an anticipation of his own most cherished and most secret thoughts.

Rarely has a book had a stranger history than that of *Les Nourritures terrestres*. Published in early 1897 in an edition of 1650 copies, the first printing was not completely sold out until 1915—that is, eighteen years after its appearance! When, in 1917, the publishing house of *La Nouvelle Revue Française*, which Gide and his friends had founded as an adjunct to their monthly review of the same name, acquired the rights to this book from the original publisher, *Le Mercure de France*, there was no question of payment involved, so unpleasant was the *Mercure*'s memory of the piles of stock filling its shelves for twenty years. Yet, only ten years later, in 1927, Gide already felt the need of protesting against the popularity of the book.

The story of the gradual conquest of the public by the *Nourritures* offers a parallel and a key to that of Gide's literary fortune. As early as 1892, Oscar Wilde had prophetically said to Gide, as the latter reported in his memorial essay on the English writer: "There are two kinds of artists: some provide replies and the others, questions. It is essential to know whether one is among those who reply or among those who question, for he who questions is never he who replies. There are works that wait and are not understood for a long time; this is because they provided replies to questions that had not yet been asked; for the question often comes dreadfully long after the reply." No better explanation for Gide's tardy success could be given even today; like so many writers of importance, he was in advance of his time; it required more than twenty years for the public to become his contemporaries. And, even then, the Gide whom the public assimilated had long ago been outdistanced and, as we shall see, repudiated by Gide himself.

Upon its publication, the little volume was not noticed by any of the large newspapers. During the first year it was reviewed in but seven literary reviews—in most cases the article being written by such old friends as Léon Blum or by new acquaintances like the future dramatist Henri Ghéon and the poet Emmanuel Signoret. One newspaper, *L'Indépendance Républicaine* of Marseille, devoted an article to the *Nourritures*; it was written by a nineteen-year-old local poet named Edmond Jaloux, who was later to distinguish himself as critic and novelist and to win election to the French Academy. That young Marseillais was, in fact, one of the very first to recognize himself in Nathanael and to sense the book's importance: "It brings something absolutely new in thought," he wrote under the date of 26 June 1897, "and it may be that the literature of the coming century will be marked by the influence of Ménalque, the hero of the *Nourritures*, as the literature of this century has been marked by that of Werther and René. [. . .] I know of numerous minds that have been profoundly shaken by the *Nourritures terrestres*, and I myself have made it my gospel."

Little by little, over the years, the book reached other Nathanaels in the depths of their provinces, forming the very kind of disciples of whom Gide had dreamed and to whom he had addressed himself. In 1901 the twenty-two-year-old Jacques Copeau, who was later to become the Stanislavski of France by renewing the entire art of the theater through his Vieux-Colombier, discovered the *Nourritures*: "When I was closed in my room and in a fierce idleness, rejecting everything, consumed by desires, parched with waiting, this book had come to quench my thirst. Together with Rimbaud, it marked my adolescence more deeply than anything else. Gide never left my side. I used to employ the intimate form when addressing him in my 'diary.' I was awaiting him. 'I should like you to be my friend,' I told him. . ." Five years later, in 1906, the twenty-year-old

Jacques Rivière, destined to become the keenest literary critic
of his generation, wrote a friend enthusiastically and impres-
sionistically summing up the *Nourritures*, declaring that Gide
would surely influence him, and urging his friend, Alain-Fournier, to live sensually rather than intellectually by becoming a
disciple of André Gide.

In this manner the lyrical gospel of escape made its way,
finding fervent readers among the very young. André Gide was
not the first writer to address himself specifically to adolescents,
but his eloquence was less oratorical, and therefore more subtly
persuasive, than that of Maurice Barrès, for instance. Between
them there is all the difference that lies between the pronoun
of the first person singular and the *tutoiement* of intimacy. In an
unforgettable page of his voluminous novel, *Les Thibault* (*The
World of the Thibaults*), Roger Martin du Gard has one of his
young protagonists, Daniel de Fontanin, discover the *Nourritures* at the age of twenty. The episode takes place some time
before 1914. Over the shoulder of a stranger in a train, Daniel
reads sentences that keenly arouse his curiosity and just has
time to make out the running title at the top of the pages. None
of the booksellers he visits recognizes *Les Nourritures terrestres*,
and, without the author's name, he spends two days finding the
book. Immediately he reads it through twice with the feeling
that it is giving him a new vision of life and upsetting his out-
worn scale of values. Suddenly rejecting what he had previously
considered immutable, for the first time he achieves a calm
equilibrium among the forces that had been dividing him. According to the Aristotelian dictum that the work of the artist
is often truer than fact, Roger Martin du Gard's testimony, just
because it is fictional and hence a summary of many actual
cases, should bear more weight than that of any number of
real witnesses. Gide must particularly have enjoyed this passage
because of the semi-clandestine way in which Daniel made his
discovery and the effort he had to put forth before confirming
it and acquiring the little-known book.

Martin du Gard's novel containing this very direct homage to Gide appeared in 1923, just when the *Nourritures*, thanks to a third and unlimited edition, was reaching a new generation of adolescents. Despite the fact that he had been writing for over thirty years, Gide struck them with all the novelty of a discovery. The author of five novels which differed greatly from one another, the perceptive literary critic who had anticipated their tastes and even then, though middle-aged, was receptive to the most *avant-garde* manifestations in the arts, the gray eminence behind the youngest and yet most powerful of the literary periodicals, he assumed the proportions of a gigantic figure, not on their horizon, but in their very midst. Yet he also had the added prestige of remaining elusive, unpredictable, and somewhat mysterious, forever fleeing Paris for London, Berlin, Florence, or remote Biskra, and suddenly reappearing as sponsor of a new writer, translator of an unknown work, or author of another volume totally different from anything he had previously written. During the twenties the young read simultaneously the Gide in the latest issue of *La Nouvelle Revue Française* and the Gide of twenty-five years earlier, equally delighted to recognize themselves in the Lafcadio of 1914 as to discover a premonition of his gratuitous act in the Prometheus of 1899. Few readers stopped to reflect that *Les Nourritures terrestres* had originally appeared years before they were born, so appropriate did the book seem to the atmosphere of permanent unrest and feverish exaltation, of spiritual anarchy and emotional inflation, which marked that post-war decade. For the first time, in that frantic and troubled climate, the book found a large public receptive to it, and readily it became a breviary.

André Gide, however, had always fled success, firmly convinced that there was an element of misunderstanding in any popular acclaim of the artist. The sudden though tardy success of the *Nourritures* alarmed him, and in July 1926 he wrote a four-page preface for the fourth edition. Protesting that it had

become customary to imprison him in that manual of escape,
he proceeded to give six reasons for limiting its importance by
situating it in the chronology of his life and in the whole of his
work. First, the *Nourritures* is the work of a convalescent; hence
its lyricism has that excessive quality one would expect from
a poet who embraces life eagerly as something he had almost
lost. Already in his *Renoncement au voyage* (*Renouncing
Travel*) of 1906 he had written: "It seems that in susceptibility to sensations a weakened organism is more porous, more
transparent, softer, and more completely receptive. Despite my
illness, or perhaps because of it, I was all receptivity and joy.
Perhaps my recollection of that period is somewhat confused
in details, for I have a bad memory, but the bouquets of sensations I brought back from that first trip to Africa still give off
a scent so vivid that sometimes it hinders me from savoring the
present moment." Secondly, he wrote the book at a time when
literature reeked of artifice and mustiness, and consequently he
felt a duty to bring it back to earth. Even without having read
the satire of *Paludes*, we know this to have been true. In September 1896, in fact, Gide had written to his friend André
Ruyters: "Literature must be hurled into an abyss of sensualism from which it will later emerge altogether regenerated."
Thirdly, he wrote the *Nourritures* just as he had relinquished
his freedom in marriage; for this reason the work of art could,
and did, call all the more vigorously for freedom. Thus the young
Gide had spontaneously done what he could to re-establish the
equilibrium. Fourthly, he intended at the time not to end his
career with that book. In fact, he depicted his indecisive condition of 1895–7 in order to make it a thing of the past, to rid
himself of it. In other words, he was again indulging, as he was
so often to do later on, in a personal form of catharsis. In the
fifth place, he objects to being judged on the basis of this single
youthful work—as if he had not been the first to follow his own
advice and throw away the book. In the sixth and last place, he
claims that he now sees in his book, when he turns back to it,

less the glorification of desire so apparent to most readers than an apology for *dénuement* or destitution and austerity. This is all that he has retained, he says, of that youthful state of mind, and this is what has allowed him to return to the Gospel and find in self-renunciation the most complete self-realization.

Although the *Nourritures* does teach the value of maintaining one's hunger and of fleeing all earthly possessions, though it does glorify the primitive nudity of the man who has systematically burned his books, shedding his veneer of education and his old moral code, "which was good only for winter," nonetheless there is something specious about the final argument in Gide's preface to the 1927 edition. For so dithyrambic is the paean to instinct, freedom, and fulfillment that the charmed reader must make an effort to be aware of the minor theme, with its relatively muted hymn to austerity. When he does so, he notes the author's enjoyment of "excessive frugalities" and of the "voluptuous pleasure of renunciation" and is struck by the praise of travel for taking us away from all that is not indispensable: "Ah, how much else, Nathanael, one could have done without! Souls never sufficiently destitute to be at last sufficiently filled with love—with love, expectation, and hope, which are our only true possessions."

This note is, indeed, a constant in Gide's mind. Throughout life he enjoyed quoting Christ's injunctions to sell all one's goods and to forsake home and family; he recognized that it was impossible to follow Christ without abandoning everything one has. In the uprooting from all possessions, whether physical or spiritual, and in the readiness and receptivity of one who travels light, there *is* an evangelical exhortation to poverty and simplicity.

One cannot fail to note, however, the sophistry of Gide's 1927 preface, in which the final point emphasizes this Christian ethic after the five preceding points have explained and apologized for the book's Dionysiac frenzy. If the work's basic doctrine was really so estimable, one might ask, why did the author boast of having been the first to cast the book from him? The answer is doubtless that in the 1920's Gide was particularly uneasy about the accusations of amoralism so frequently directed at him, and consequently had recourse to any and every defence. Despite any later rationalization, the truth is that even in 1897 he was aware of the possible danger in the message of the *Nourritures* and hastened to react against his own creation.

Just as it was characteristic of Gide to flee success, it was natural for him to withdraw from, and even to contradict, the book he had just written. For this reason almost every one of his writings marks a distinct break with the preceding writing, and, just as his readers thought they could detect his true physiognomy and his current preoccupations in his latest work, he regularly felt more remote from that recent production than from anything else in his nature and career. The very systole and diastole of his creative impulse consistently produced such contrasts; his personal theory of catharsis is intimately related to this characteristic movement from one extreme to another of his latent possibilities. Thus, the moment he had extolled the intoxication of self-indulgence in the *Nourritures,* he rapidly withdrew to the rigorous austerity of his pre-African puritanism. During the composition of the work, Francis Jammes referred to him as a Protestant minister and a poet rolled into one; and years later Gide was to say of himself: "I am merely a little boy having a good time—compounded with a Protestant minister who bores him."

As soon as Jammes had read the whole book in June 1897, he wrote the author: "I feel very clearly that the only way I can read it is in reverse, as if I were turning each page to a mirror in order to read from right to left. It is odd. I am reading *another book,* and that is it. And the only real sensual pleasure you have made me desire is that of *drinking water.* [. . .] If this book may console a few people who indulge in excesses and still have scruples about it, it will scarcely *deprave* any but schoolboys who would not understand it." To this Gide replied with delighted gratitude that "under the mask of Ménalque the little Huguenot Walter is proud of having been recognized by you." Similarly when André Ruyters had too enthusiastically endorsed Gide's recommendation to plunge literature into an abyss of sensualism, Gide noted with remarkable foresight: "O my deplorable and beloved posterity!" And now, perhaps remembering this at the end of October 1897, he wrote to the same Ruyters: "I seem to be preaching hedonism, but great souls cannot stop there; they must be used up by the Idea and not by pleasure."

One may be sure, knowing André Gide, that the *Nourritures* did not result simply from the surrender to his instincts which marked the African phase of his young life. Nor was the book a mere justification of his own behavior. On the contrary, as soon as he recognized his unorthodox nature, he flung himself into the most orthodox marriage he could imagine, willingly accepted the onerous responsibilities of the highest administrative post in his town, and consigned to his *Journals* his dominant love of duty. *The Fruits of the Earth* grew out of an idea rather than from an irresistible impulse and, according to Gide's early discovery that "the work of art is the exaggeration of an idea," he carried that idea to its extreme development in his little handbook of escape, at the risk of appearing a preacher of immoralism.

Even while writing the *Nourritures* and devoting himself wholeheartedly, one might think, to exaggerating its basic idea, André Gide was already reacting against the intellectual excess in which he was indulging. During August 1896, back at La Roque after his third stay in North Africa and just entering upon his duties as mayor, he wrote a short tale, as he said, "about nothing but the desert." He expected it to be boring to read because it had been most boring to write. He entitled it *El Hadj—or The Treatise of the False Prophet*, and, despite his dissatisfaction with Louÿs's rather lush review, allowed *Le Centaure* to publish it in the second issue in late 1896. Briefly

El Hadj recounts in the first person the story of a singer by that name who, with an entire nation, followed a mysterious prince into the desert without purpose or destination. Eventually El Hadj, by singing of the Prince's divinely inspired pilgrimage to marry a beautiful princess on the other side of the ocean, succeeds in seeing the prince and becoming his sole confidant. And just as the nomadic people, with the prince's closed tent in the van, encamps on the shore of a vast sea that El Hadj knows to be but a mud lake encrusted with salt deposits, the prince dies. Thenceforth the singer, now become a prophet who has long voiced the prince's will to the following caravan, must lead the people back out of the desert without revealing that their prince has died. Had not André Gide, like El Hadj the singer unwillingly become a prophet, begun his *Nourritures* as a work of pure lyricism and then been drawn into preaching a doctrine? Just as El Hadj—whose name in Arabic means simply "pilgrim to Mecca"—had invented the invisible prince and spoken in his name, so Gide had created Ménalque and made him speak in parables.

This little tale is itself a parable for Gide's own experience. Written during his disappointment over his friends' reception of the sampling of the *Nourritures* which he had offered in *"Ménalque"* (published in January 1896), *El Hadj* is Gide's first attempt to view objectively his own infatuation with a new experience and a new doctrine. At the same time it explains dispassionately how a lyrical poet becomes a teacher and leader without yet knowing where he is leading his followers. That, beyond two or three letters dated during the composition of *El Hadj*, Gide never mentioned that brief work may be explained by the fact that he provided in so many later and more important writings what he considered the necessary corrective to the *Nourritures*. Yet the tale may be taken as his first apology for the excesses of the *Nourritures*, valuable chiefly for its indication of the ease with which his contradictory nature reacted against a new ethic even while he was elaborating it.

"My writings are comparable to Achilles's spear," he confided to his *Journals* in 1928, "with which a second contact cured those it had first wounded. If one of my books disconcerts you, reread it; under the apparent poison, I took care to hide the antidote; each one of them does not so much disturb as it warns." In eventually insisting upon the undercurrent of austerity in the *Nourritures*, he tried to persuade himself and his readers that the antidote to that book's sensual frenzy was clearly indicated and accessible in the book itself. At the time, however, he must not have been so sure of this, for during the years immediately following he made every effort to multiply the antidotes and make them ever more efficacious. The two plays, *Le Roi Candaule* and *Saül*, and the novel *L'Immoraliste*, as well as the moral farce of *Le Prométhée mal enchaîné*, were all written as correctives to *Les Nourritures terrestres*.

Through his African experiences of 1893 to 1896, André Gide had embraced Dionysus and, in his momentary intoxication, had generalized his experience for a world bound by false traditions and vitiated ideals. Immediately the pendulum began to swing backward and he then proceeded to criticize his attitude of 1897 in his subsequent works. But the experience had taught him to be concerned thenceforth with the problems of freedom and self-fulfillment on a most serious and permanent plane of interest.

As he had done with Narcissus, he absorbed and went beyond Dionysus—for, though he had not yet adopted the archaic expression of *"passer outre,"* which was to appear so frequently in his *Thésée* of 1946, the impulse to go forward to the next step was already a characteristic of his nature.

VI. PHILOCTETES: THE ANOMALY
AND THE ART

> "In any case, the eagle consumes us, vice
> or virtue, duty or passion; cease being nonde-
> script and you cannot escape this."

> "The only drama that really interests me
> and that I should always be willing to depict
> anew is the debate of the individual with what-
> ever keeps him from being authentic, with
> whatever is opposed to his integrity, to his in-
> tegration. Most often the obstacle is within
> him. And all the rest is merely accidental."

PHILOCTETES is somewhat less widely known today than
his companions in arms at the siege of Troy. To some his
name evokes but a noisome wound, to others solely a fabulous
bow. The tragedies devoted to his story by Aeschylus and Eu-
ripides have been lost, but the play by Sophocles survives. It
concentrates on the rape of the precious bow and arrows by wily
Odysseus and the youthful Neoptolemus, son of Achilles, on the
deserted island of Lemnos, where he had long before been abandoned by the Greek host, unable to endure his piercing screams.
Odysseus's deceitful scheme almost fails because of the remorse-
ful pity of Neoptolemus; but all is saved when Heracles, appearing in a vision, bids Philoctetes proceed to Troy, where he will
be cured in time to shoot Paris and raise the siege.

Directly inspired by Sophocles, Gide's brief *Philoctète* originally appeared in the issue of *La Revue Blanche* for December 1898. The following year it came out in a volume which also contained *Le Traité du Narcisse, El Hadj,* and *La Tentative amoureuse*. Clearly, despite its traditional five acts, it belongs among the symbolist treatises, and indeed it bears the subtitle of "Treatise of the Three Ethics." Until very recent years, it was never published among Gide's dramatic works; presented but once by a group of friends in a private theater, it was never intended for the stage. Its beautiful prose style remains just this side of verse, and many lines form perfect alexandrines, such as

Les dieux que je sers ne servent que la Grèce
of Neoptolemus, or the last speech of Philoctetes:

Ils ne reviendront plus; ils n'ont plus d'arc à prendre.

Suppressing the chorus of mariners, the messenger, and the divine apparition of Heracles, all of which appear in Sophocles, Gide has written a philosophic dialogue on the nature of virtue. Isolated from men, Philoctetes has developed his virtue in solitude; his lamentations have become a song; and nothing joins him to the outside world but his bow, essential for securing nourishment by shooting birds. Alone on his desert island, he insists, he has gradually become less Greek and more human. Here he is summing up a reflection that Gide consigned to his *Journals* at just this time: "Individual characteristics are more general (I mean more human) than ethnical characteristics. To restate this: the individual man tries to escape the race. And as soon as he ceases to represent the race, he represents man; the idiosyncrasy is a pretext for generalities." Each of Gide's three characters stands for a different rule of conduct, a specific conception of virtue; hence the sub-title. Ulysses, whose every other word is "Greece" or "the Fatherland," represents the Welfare of the State. Opposite him, Philoctetes embodies an aesthetic and Nietzschean virtue, the integral virtue that no one practices. And between them is the bewildered adolescent, Neoptolemus, questioning both, seeking a definition, and devoting himself to Philoctetes through sympathy and pity.

Ulysses obviously has no respect for virtue exercised in solitude, but Philoctetes, cut off from the world, has solved the conflict which tormented the young Gide: that between *being* and *appearing*; because there is no one there before whom to make an appearance, he can be concerned solely with *being*. Deriving nothing from others, he is forced to obtain everything from himself. Consequently, his aim is one of *dépassement*, of surpassing himself, and he answers the youth's urgent question with the statement: "What one undertakes beyond one's strength, Neoptolemus, that is what is called virtue." Manifestly dominated by the *amor fati* of Nietzsche, he is cultivating the ideal of the Superman. When asked what stands above the gods, to which one might consecrate oneself, he seizes his head in his hands, gasps, and finally blurts out: "Ah! ah! Oneself!"

Spurning the Sophoclean *deus ex machina*, Gide makes Philoctetes transcend himself by *willingly* giving up his arms to Neoptolemus. Although stating that "Of all sacrifices the maddest is that performed for others, for then one becomes superior to them," still he surrenders his life-sustaining bow and, unlike his Sophoclean model, remains behind as the others set out again for Troy. The last words we hear him speak are: "I am happy." His voice has become exceptionally beautiful; flowers pierce the snow about him, and "birds from Heaven come down to feed him"—as they once fed the prophet Elijah. Now, in a lecture of March 1904 on the theater Gide quotes Machiavelli to the effect that, whereas ancient religion beatified men of action such as military leaders and founders of states, our religion glorifies rather the humble and contemplative men. Later, in his own words, he clarifies this thought, saying: "The soul demands heroism; but our present society barely leaves room for one form of heroism (if it even is heroism)—that of resignation, acceptance."

In this, Gide's Philoctetes is more Christian than pagan. Perhaps this explains why the author has transferred the Greek island of Lemnos to that same polar region of snow and ice, beyond the distinction of night and day, in which is laid the last part of *Le Voyage d'Urien*. For Gide that frigid zone, where everything is and remains eternally, and nothing ever becomes, clearly represents the metaphysical realm.

Many a critic has followed the lead of Louis Martin-Chauffier and seen in *Philoctète* a distant echo of the Dreyfus Affair. The date of the work (just after Zola's famous accusatory letter), the hero's exile on a deserted island, and the sharp opposition between patriotic arguments and individual virtue make this theory most appealing. Without straining a word, one can readily see in Ulysses the anti-revisionist and in Neoptolemus the ardent revisionist or *dreyfusard*. We know that, despite the example of numerous friends on the side of the Army, André Gide himself shared the *dreyfusard* views. But he never wrote anything significant on the subject for publication; his clearest statements regarding the Affair can be found in a few letters to friends, notably one of January 1898 to Eugène Rouart and one to Francis Jammes in April of the same year. In the latter he stated that, though he had convictions, he had no opinion and that, when he revolted against the oppression of a single man with the pretext of saving the community, his friends considered him a deplorable Protestant. This hardly suggests that he would have made of *Philoctète* a parable of the Affair, as Anatole France (then far more socially minded than Gide) was to do in the story of *Crainquebille*.

If one must seek a topical allusion in the work of a writer not much given to such inspirations, it is worth considering, as a young American scholar has recently suggested, another *cause célèbre* of that time—one that doubtless touched Gide more intimately. In 1897 his friend Oscar Wilde had emerged from two years of hard labor and Gide had visited him at Berneval on the Channel coast. Chastened by his solitary confinement, Wilde had written *The Ballad of Reading Gaol* and *De Profundis* during his imprisonment, and now entertained many plans for future works. Living in solitude, he gave promise of overcoming his weaknesses and fulfilling his artistic mission. Like Philoctetes at the time he had been bitten by a snake on the island of Tenedos, Wilde had once deserved admiration and renown; he had been "one of the nobles among us," as Ulysses says of Philoctetes. But soon the Greek warrior's festering wound, the stench of it, and his constant lamentations had caused his companions to cast him off on Lemnos. Similarly society had rejected Oscar Wilde when the wound that distinguished him from other men became fully apparent. While Gide was writing *Philoctète*, the work significantly bore a different sub-title, which appeared in at least one periodical announcement: *"Traité de l'immonde blessure"* ("Treatise of the Foul Wound").

It is interesting that André Gide should have begun with the wound rather than with the bow or the exile. For several years already he had shown a special concern for the individual, the exceptional. Physical and psychological abnormality had come to be equated in his mind with uniqueness. Already in *Paludes*, a strange character with an English name, Valentin Knox, had expressed this Wildian paradox: "Health does not seem to me such an enviable possession. It is merely an equilibrium, a state of mediocrity in everything; it is an absence of hypertrophies. Our value lies solely in what distinguishes us from others; idiosyncrasy is the disease that gives us that value;—or in other words, what matters in us is what we alone possess, what can be found in no other, what your *normal man* lacks—hence what you call disease. So, cease looking upon disease as a deficiency; rather, it is something additional. A humpback is a man plus a hump, and I prefer that you should look on health as a deficiency of disease."

Shortly before writing *Paludes*, Gide had discovered his

own hump, his distinguishing wound. It was quite natural that he should begin by trying to believe in some system of compensations, and indeed, hastening to the defense of the bizarre and idiosyncratic, should seek to legitimize his own anomaly. Among the "Detached Pages" of his *Journals* written shortly after 1896 is a capital meditation, inspired by Pascal, on the value of ill-health, which reads: "The vast sickly unrest of ancient heroes: Prometheus, Orestes, Ajax, Phaedra, Pentheus, Oedipus. [. . .] Ill health offers man a new restlessness that he is called on to legitimize. Whence the value of Rousseau, as well as of Nietzsche."

In an essay on the Sophoclean Philoctetes, Edmund Wilson points out a striking similarity between that hero and the fallen Oedipus at Colonus, both humbled, outlawed, and crushed by hardship. He sees Philoctetes's ulcer as the equivalent for the abhorrent sins of Oedipus, which have made him a pariah. Later, in an oblique but sharp glance at Gide's play, he suggests that the modern French author may have wanted to imply "the idea that genius and disease, like strength and mutilation, may be inextricably bound up together." It might be argued that for somewhat similar reasons Sophocles and Gide were drawn to a legendary hero who combined in his person a suppurating sore and the unequalled mastery of an art that made his fellow-men beat a path through the wilderness to his cave.

The author himself characterized *Paludes* as the work of an invalid and the *Nourritures* as the work of a convalescent. Must we take those words in their most literal sense as referring to a purely physical ailment? That Gide was not so readily cured of his intimate disorder is indicated by the fact that, for the next several years after his marriage and the lyricism of the *Nourritures*, he devoted himself to creating a series of diseased heroes: Philoctetes, Prometheus, Candaules, Saul, and finally Michel of *L'Immoraliste*. For a time at least the young writer must have wondered about the relationship between his abnormality and his literary talent. For this reason, doubtless, the

Envoi of the *Nourritures* recommended the cultivation of one's uniqueness.

Furthermore, at the same time that, in *Philoctète*, he was earnestly glorifying the individual who transcends himself in a solitary quest for virtue and in eventual self-immolation, he was also dealing, in *Le Prométhée mal enchaîné* (*Prometheus Misbound*), with the same problem of personality in a playful, bantering tone.

No one has yet done justice to Gide's lively sense of humor. Doubtless his high seriousness, the profundity of so much of his thought, and the outward austerity of the man combined to keep critics from appreciating the ever-present comic element in his work. His intimate friends, at least, were aware of the contradiction in his nature between the little boy having fun and the kill-joy Protestant minister. Various accounts record, for instance, his delight in parlor games, charades, and family jokes which made him the life of the summer gatherings at the Abbaye de Pontigny. Since his death, his nephew, M. Dominique Drouin, has told how he used to amuse nieces and nephews at Cuverville by galloping over the lawn at dusk and emitting owlish cries, which they attributed to a legendary *"Bête Noire."*

The same youthful spirit of fun circulates through his writings. One of his closest friends and most enlightened readers, Mme Maria Théo Van Rysselberghe, writing under the penname of M. Saint-Clair, states that "Gide's comic sense has its own intimate chemistry that obeys undiscernable laws." This is just what Gide himself set down in the late nineties as a desideratum of the artist, after saying that he must bring to us "a special world of which he alone has the key": "He must have a personal philosophy, aesthetics, and ethics; his entire work tends only to reveal it. And that is what makes his style. I have discovered too, and this is very important, that he must have a personal manner of joking, his own form of humor."

We have already noted a keen sense of irony, unusual in

so young a writer, in the first published work and again in *La Tentative amoureuse*. The second part of *Le Voyage d'Urien*—"The Sargasso Sea"—whose suppression friends urged at the time—is generally looked upon as marking the first appearance in Gide's work of the *saugrenu,* or exploitation of the ridiculous, which was to flower in the three *soties* and in such minor pieces as the farce of 1935 entitled *Le Treizième Arbre* (*The Thirteenth Tree*) and the almost surrealistically silly *Art bitraire* (*The Arbitrary*) written on April Fool's day 1947. In addition, a comic of situation and of character, verbal humor and the play of ideas, sharp-pointed irony and coarse farce—in fact almost all the forms of humor—can be found in other, ostensibly serious works. And in all its variety, addressed as it is to a cultivated and alert reader and inseparable from its context, that humor preserves a personal character. It is significant that the note on the necessity of the artist's having his own individual form of humor was first published among the "Reflections" following *Le Prométhée* in the first edition of 1899.

For whatever else that book may be—a subtle disquisition on the origin of personality, an exhortation to be oneself, a summary of the history of humanity, or an allegory of man's fate, it is first of all a very funny product of an intellectual sense of humor. Consequently, while writing it, Gide most appropriately reflected on the nature of his own comic sense.

Others had written of "Prometheus Bound" and of "Prometheus Unbound" but it remained for André Gide to write a "Prometheus Ill-Bound." This brief ironic treatise belongs in the specifically Gidian tradition of *Paludes*. Originally published without sub-title or indication as to *genre*, it eventually was classified by the author as a *sotie* together with *Paludes* and *Les Caves du Vatican* of 1914. In the French theatre of the Middle Ages a *sotie* was a sort of satirical farce embodying a moral or political lesson. Midway between the morality play and the non-didactic farce, that comic form was invented by the

"*Enfants sans souci*" or Brotherhood of Fools governed by a "*Prince des Sots*." Students and young idlers, they were often highly educated clerks similar to the colorful François Villon; and their productions seem to have been distinguished from others chiefly by the presence of the long-eared cap and symbolic bauble. Commonly the *sotie* mocked the follies of the age or served as a political weapon, as did Pierre Gringore's famous attack on Pope Julius II in 1511.

It was doubtless a recollection of that piece of anti-clericalism which caused Gide to revive the term *sotie* in 1914 for his gay imbroglio revolving around the august but invisible Leo XIII. And, once he had resurrected the all-but-forgotten designation, he naturally applied it in retrospect to his two earlier works in the same vein. Like their medieval antecedents, all three works cloak fundamental wisdom in the motley garb of folly, and the last two of them are decidedly irreverent.

Le Prométhée is divided into three parts, of five chapters each, entitled respectively: "Chronicle of Private Morality," "The Imprisonment of Prometheus," and "The Illness of Damocles." The first introduces the five characters and poses the problem; the second offers a solution; and the third depicts the results ensuing from such a solution.

With a flat, journalistic account of an incident in the daily life of Paris the action begins:

"In the month of May 189 . . . at two in the afternoon this was seen which might have seemed strange:

"On the boulevard leading from the Madeleine to the Opéra, a fat middle-aged gentleman, distinctive solely because of his unusual corpulence, was accosted by a thin gentleman who, smiling and without evil intention, I beg you to believe, handed the former a handkerchief he had just dropped. The corpulent gentleman thanked him briefly and was about to continue on his way when, changing his mind, he leaned toward the thin man and must have asked him a question that must have been answered, for, immediately taking out of his pocket a portable inkwell and pens, the fat gentleman unceremoniously handed them to the thin gentleman, together with an envelope that he had until then been holding in his hand. And the passers-by might have seen the thin man write an address on it without hesitating. But this is where the oddness of the story begins, which nevertheless no newspaper recorded: after having returned the pen and the envelope, the thin gentleman had not had time to smile a farewell before the fat gentleman, by way of thanks, suddenly slapped him on the cheek, then jumped into a cab and disappeared before any of the idlers attracted by the scene (I was one of them) had got over his surprise and thought of stopping him.

"I learned later that he was Zeus, the Banker."

And thus we have met two of the characters: Zeus the Miglionaire (to be compared with Nietzsche's Banker), a deity of Mediterranean origin as the *gl* in his title indicates, a gambler of unlimited means who enjoys lending to men without security for the pleasure of watching his gratuitous loan grow; and Cocles, as we later identify the thin man,—that is, that famous one-eyed Horatius who held back the Etruscans from the Sublician bridge until it could be destroyed, and then, despite his wounds, swam across the Tiber to safety. Now, it happens that the envelope Zeus handed him contained a 500-franc banknote (about one hundred dollars in those days), and that he wrote on it the address of an unknown Damocles—that is, the mythological courtier of Dionysius I, who was feasted with a symbolical sword hung by a hair over his head so that he might taste the joys of the tyrant's life.

But before we learn their identity—and aside from their names Gide never gives a clue as to their legendary models— Prometheus has cast off the "chains, lugs, strait-jackets, breastworks, and other scruples" that bound him to the Caucasus and sat down in a café on the Paris boulevard. There he is served by a waiter who, interested solely in the interplay of personalities or relations among people, places him at a table with two strangers. By a marvelous coincidence, they prove to be none other than Cocles and Damocles, strangers to one another as well. As each tells his story, the full truth emerges. Damocles aimed to resemble the commonest of men, striving for perfect moderation in everything until one day he mysteriously received 500 francs apparently not intended for him. "Before, I was banal but free," he says. "Now I belong to my banknote. That adventure has determined my fate: I was nondescript; now I am someone." Zeus's unconsidered act has thrown him into unrest and anguish, from which he eventually dies, vainly trying to learn who his benefactor is. Cocles, on the other hand, had originally been restless and at the mercy of events: "I went down into the street soliciting a determination from the outside," he admits. Zeus's act, in his case, by making him pay for a benefaction to someone else has given him a *raison d'être* that he calmly accepts; as a positive man of action, he makes the best of it. He does likewise when, after losing his eye by a second slap, he takes advantage of a charitable collection, founds a home for one-eyed men (of which he naturally becomes director), and calmly comments on Damocles's suffering.

In this way the double act of Zeus has conferred a personality on two very different individuals. They should be happy because, as the waiter says, all the people passing down the boulevard are seeking a personality. But, of those two, Damocles is the spiritual man who cannot endure the anguish and responsibility that have come to him, whereas Cocles is an all-too-healthy extrovert on whom experiences make no deep impression. Looking back to *Paludes*, one might say that Damocles parallels André, the agitated agitator, while Cocles corresponds to Hubert, the man of action. Looking forward to the *Thésée* of 1946, one might see Damocles as the tormented Oedipus who punishes himself for his former happiness, and Cocles as the forthright, self-satisfied Theseus, who makes the best of what comes his way. With Damocles at the height of his spiritual torment, Cocles callously refers to the fate of one who profited from another's suffering. And he admits that he has ceased to feel his slap, though he would not wish never to have received it. "It revealed to me my kindness," he says, "which honors and pleases me greatly. I never cease reflecting that my suffering served as provender for my neighbor by bringing him 500 francs." One can hear the voice of Gide's Theseus.

After each of Zeus's victims has told his story, they together turn to the silent Prometheus, asking him to reveal his distinctive feature, whatever he has that no one else possesses. Rising, he utters a wild cry and a huge bird swoops down from heaven breaking the plate-glass window of the café and putting out Cocles's eye with its flapping wings (like that winged black horse in the *Arabian Nights* which Gide had mentioned in a review). Calmly Prometheus opens his waistcoat and the bird begins voraciously to peck at its master's liver.

From this point in the story, the bird plays a major rôle. Indeed, that rôle is so important that the title-page of the first edition bears an epigraph from Victor Hugo, unaccountably dropped from later editions, reading: "Eagle, vulture, or dove." Though the agent of God's vengeance is an eagle in Aeschylus, it has become a vulture in Byron and Shelley; Gide, through a knowledge of literature rather than an ignorance of ornithology, wavers between the two, calling it an eagle when it is thriving and beautiful and a vulture when it is puny and mean. On its first appearance, at any rate, Prometheus himself refers to it as an eagle; whereupon some of the people in the café exclaim with remarkable clairvoyance: "That an eagle! . . . at most a conscience!" And they proceed to point out that we all have them but don't wear them in Paris; some stifle theirs and others sell theirs.

The most obvious identification of the eagle is with the conscience. Thus Prometheus, in his strangely circular public speech, which postulates that everyone must have an eagle and then goes on to prove that everyone does have one, makes his oft-quoted statement: "I care less for men than for what consumes them." But the word *conscience* in French does double duty for moral conscience and intellectual awareness or consciousness. Therefore Prometheus can make this point: "Gentlemen, I loved men passionately, wildly, deplorably. And I did so much for them that you might as well say I made them myself, for what were they before? They existed, but had no awareness of existing. Like a fire to light them, Gentlemen, I created that awareness out of my great love for them." But men needed more than mere consciousness; according to the titan who has defined his profession as a manufacturer of matches, they also needed hope in the future. And in his stirring and urgent speech —which is understood, and but half understood at that, solely by the anguished Damocles—he says: "Moreover, having created man in my own image, I realize now that something as yet undeveloped, as yet unhatched, was waiting in each man; in each of them was an eagle-egg. [. . .] All I know is that, not satisfied with giving them an awareness of existing, I wanted to give them also a *raison d'être.* I gave them fire, flame, and all the arts fed by flame. Warming their minds, I hatched out in them the devouring belief in progress. [. . .] No longer belief in the good, but an unhealthy hope of something better. The belief in progress, Gentlemen, was their eagle. Our eagle is our *raison d'être,* Gentlemen."

Conscience, consciousness, and consuming belief in progress—the eagle is all of these. For the eagle to become strong and beautiful, one must love it and sacrifice oneself to it. Prometheus gives an example of such attachment to the eagle when he is imprisoned through the waiter's denunciation (for the waiter is but an observer and agent of Zeus). As he languishes behind bars, he daily receives and nourishes his eagle, who waxes strong and sleek as its victim grows ever weaker. In this connection Prometheus even quotes John the Baptist as recorded in John III, 30: "He must increase but I must decrease." The secret of Cocles's and Damocles's lives should likewise lie in their attachment to their debt: in one case a slap and in the other a banknote, for that is their eagle. But whereas Cocles remains impervious, making capital of apparent disadvantage, Damocles sacrifices himself until he is wholly consumed.

Prometheus, on the other hand, reacts vigorously. When he has become so weak and the eagle so strong that the latter can carry him out of prison, he makes his speech of desperate exhortation. And after he has vainly questioned the eagle before an audience, he kills and eats the bird, thus absorbing and making it an integral part of himself. As soon as the eagle is dead, Prometheus recovers health and equilibrium.

Like that dynamic tycoon who, when asked how he could keep such a frantic pace without getting ulcers, said: "I'm not the type that gets ulcers; I *give* them!"—So Zeus admits that he has no eagle though he confers them on others. The Miglionaire stands outside the action giving merely the original flick of the finger, or initial impulse, to that action. Consequently his deed is related first so that the story can get under way. And significantly, his complex act is described no fewer than four times throughout the *sotie:* first, flatly by the author; second, enthusiastically by the waiter; third, by Damocles and Cocles from their separate points of view; and fourth, as an illustration of his gambling, by the Miglionaire himself, who is interrupted by Prometheus. Is this not an anticipation of the technique to be adopted a quarter of a century later in *Les Faux-Monnayeurs* (*The Counterfeiters* or *The Coiners*)? While writing that later novel, Gide defined his narrative form thus: "I should like events never to be related directly by the author, but instead exposed (and several times from different vantages) by those actors who will be influenced by those events. In their account of the action I should like the events to appear slightly warped; the reader will take a sort of interest from the mere fact of having to *reconstruct*."

"But this reminds me of an anecdote . . ." is the deceptive refrain of *Le Prométhée mal enchaîné.* First said by the author as he introduces Prometheus, it is repeated by the waiter be-

fore he tells the story of Zeus's strange deed, and finally by
Prometheus himself to introduce the story of Tityrus into his
speech at the grave of Damocles. Everything in the little book,
in other words, is anecdotal; in fact, the whole book is itself
an anecdote, as if this were the only form appropriate for dealing with a most serious subject. When Prometheus speaks at the
grave, he is healthy, smiling, and flippant in his manner. He
has already killed his eagle, which he will eat after the cere-
mony. He begins his illustrative tale with an irreverent parody
of the first chapter of the Gospel according to St. John: "In the
beginning was Tityrus. And Tityrus being alone was bored,
completely surrounded by swamps.—Now, Ménalque happened
by who put an idea into Tityrus's brain, a seed into the swamp
before him. And that idea was the seed, and that seed was the
Idea."

The plant grows, its strong roots drying up the surrounding
swamplands, until it becomes a great oak. And Tityrus alone
cannot "weed and hoe around it, water it, prune it, polish it,
depilate it, strip it of caterpillars, and take care in season of
the harvest of its fruits both numerous and various"; accordingly he hires others, and they in turn lead to others: an ac-
countant, a judge and two lawyers, a secretary, a keeper of the
archives, etc., until a town grows up around the oak. As his
life becomes more complicated and more industrious, Tityrus
waxes fully happy, feeling his excessively busy life to be useful to others.

Angèle, who runs the circulating library that he has brought
into the community, suggests their going away together, but he
objects that he is attached to his oak. "And soon thereafter, having recognized that after all neither the occupations, responsibilities and various scruples nor the oak held him, Tityrus
smiled, checked the weather, set out, taking the receipts and
Angèle, and in the late afternoon walked with her down the
boulevard leading from the Madeleine to the Opéra." This is
the same boulevard, by the way, on which Zeus had walked

one May afternoon and on which Prometheus, liberated from
the Caucasus, had sat in a café in October.

As they mingle with the waiting crowd, Prometheus continues, naked Meliboeus walks down the boulevard playing his
flute—as in Virgil's first *Bucolic*, which indeed he quotes in
Latin. Charmed by him, Angèle takes his arm and together, as
in the comic films that were to delight Gide many years later,
they "disappear into the definitive twilight." As in the beginning, Tityrus finds himself alone surrounded by swamps.

When Cocles, laughing heartily at the anecdote, asks how it
is appropriate to the occasion, Prometheus simply replies that,
had it been more apropos, Cocles would have enjoyed it less.
It could, in fact, hardly be more so: Tityrus's seed, Idea, oak
is his eagle, which comes to possess him as Damocles was possessed; then, thanks to Angèle, he casts it off as Cocles does;
and finally Meliboeus takes her from him, leaving him precisely
where he was in the beginning. There is no enrichment because
everything—both initial germ and eventual liberation—comes
from the outside. Again André Gide has retold his story in
miniature, reducing it to the scale of the characters, to serve as
a book within the book. And, by way of further complication,
the characters of that inner anecdote are all borrowed from
Gide's earlier works—Angèle from the outer *Paludes*, Tityrus
from the inner *Paludes*, and Ménalque from the *Nourritures
terrestres*—in a little innocent play of mirrors and ironic homage to Narcissus.

Although Gide's Prometheus incidentally embodies qualities that we traditionally think of as Promethean, he first and
most obviously appears here as the symbol of man's unrest, resulting from a powerfully distinguishing individuality. Each
of the characters in this moral tale—and Prometheus most consciously—has escaped the nondescript through nourishing a
consuming eagle: vice or virtue, duty or passion. Each has his
cross to bear, which, in another sense of the word, his entourage
has to bear also, as Cocles learned after losing an eye to his

neighbor's eagle. True personality, and this is the moral of the *sotie*, comes only from accepting one's idiosyncrasy or anomaly and making it a part of oneself.

This Philoctetes had learned to do in his solitary exile. Candaules was to force his upon those closest to him at the expense of their happiness and his life; and Saul was to allow his to suppress him completely. Although *Le Prométhée* maintains a jocular tone, whereas *Philoctète*, *Le Roi Candaule* (*King Candaules*), and *Saül* are eminently serious, all four works belong to the same cycle, as it were, to which must also be added the novel, *L'Immoraliste*. André Gide admitted this when he wrote to Francis Jammes in 1902 that without having written *Paludes*, he could not have written *Saül*, that he had to write *Le Prométhée* to keep that material out of his *Roi Candaule*.

His verse-drama in three acts about the Lydian king first appeared in the monthly *Ermitage* during September, November, and December 1899. In 1901 it came out as a book issued by the publishing house of the *Revue Blanche*, and on the ninth of May of the same year it was presented in a single performance at the Théâtre de l'Œuvre by Lugné-Poe, who played the title rôle.

In retelling the legend in his *Contes*, the seventeenth-century poet La Fontaine had already referred to it as sufficiently well known. Discussing the new version in Théophile Gautier's *Nouvelles*, Baudelaire had said that it would be hard to find a more familiar theme, adding: "but real writers like such difficulties." Yet Gide completely renewed the myth, giving it a value it had never had before.

Starting with the flat but suggestive story as told by Herodotus at the beginning of his "Clio" or Book I, he added the element of a magic ring which appears in the tale as told by Glaucon in Plato's *Republic*, Book II. There Gyges is a shepherd, rather than the palace guard and king's confidant that Herodotus depicts, and he finds the ring on the finger of a dead giant in a mysterious cave. Invisible so long as he wears the

ring, he can readily seduce the queen and slay the king. Thus
Plato's account explains, by the magic invisibility, how the substitution took place, but at the same time loses the essential fact
of the historian's version: the positive rôle of Candaules in his
own undoing. But elsewhere in Herodotus Gide found a tale,
quite unrelated to that of the Lydian king, which permitted him
to fuse the two legends. Neither La Fontaine nor Fontenelle,
neither Théophile Gautier nor Friedrich Hebbel, had thought
of that other ring which the over-fortunate Polycrates, of whom
the gods were jealous, threw into the deep sea on the recommendation of a wise friend and then miraculously recovered
when a poor fisherman brought to his table a beautiful fish that
had swallowed it.

Now the ring of Polycrates possessed no magic power, but
the French writer had already found that in Plato. What, then,
was more natural than to transform the Platonic Gyges from a
poor shepherd into a poor fisherman, and have King Candaules,
inviting him to sup in the palace as Polycrates did with his
fisherman, *give* him the powerful talisman he had unwittingly
fished up? Such an innovation returned to Candaules the central rôle in the action; for the first time, in the many versions
of this strange legend, motivation and means were effectively
combined in the modern play.

In his preface to the first edition of *Le Roi Candaule*, while
quoting the appropriate passage from "Clio" and acknowledging Plato's Gyges and his ring, Gide apologizes for deviating
from both history and legend, inasmuch as the traditional ring
was not found in a fish and Gyges was actually a shepherd and
not a fisherman. In other words, the French dramatist fails to
mention Polycrates and his ring; but the writer is under no ob-
ligation to publish *all* his sources.

The courtiers simply supply background, contrast, and
comic relief. But slightly differentiated from one another, they
epitomize parasites and flatterers. Neither Nyssia nor even
Gyges is portrayed in detail. Whereas Gautier had provided a

fuller psychological portrait of Nyssia than of Candaules, in an effort to explain her exceptional modesty, and had carefully depicted Gyges as a very handsome guard and renowned lover, Gide limits her to her beauty and him to his poverty. As in a sharply focussed photograph, he has purposely blurred all but the central figure of Candaules.

Like Herodotus and Hebbel, Gautier restricted the action to what he calls a "visual adultery." But he took an important step forward when he made Candaules an artist whose enthusiastic admiration for his wife's beauty has stifled the natural jealousy of the lover. Baudelaire particularly admired this, speaking of the King as the victim of an imperious and bizarre urge in revealing the naked Queen to a potential rival. Gide goes still farther when he insists upon Candaules as pathologically unable to enjoy anything in secrecy—Fontenelle had already suggested this in his subtle *Dialogues des morts* (*Dialogues of the Dead*) in 1683—and consequently has him intentionally close the invisible Gyges in the bed-chamber with Nyssia. It was surely this daring innovation which caused one German critic, when the play was produced in Berlin in January 1908, to place Hebbel's interpretation as far above Gide's as Kleist's handling of the Amphitryon legend stood above Molière's, and made another Berlin paper call it "such a *Schweinerei*"!

Incidentally, *Le Roi Candaule* treats the same opposition between *being* and *appearing* which underlies the argument of *Philoctète*. Two of the sycophants, for instance, discuss whether the King is really happy or simply seems to be, and one of them states that it requires more wisdom to seem to be so. At another point, Candaules himself admits that his happiness "exists only in the knowledge others have of it."

The chief originality of Gide's drama, however, lies in the powerful realization of the protagonist's extraordinary impulse to share his beautiful wife. That he treats her as a mere object, the rarest of his many possessions, disposing of her as he does of material things, is his unforgivable crime. But Gide makes little of this element in the tragedy, leaving it rather to Nyssia to avenge herself; in none of the other versions of the story has she had equal cause to do so. The modern dramatist's interest centers rather on Candaules in an effort to make his strange psychology credible. At this period in his life, we have seen, Gide had discovered Nietzsche and was reading him voraciously. In *Thus Spake Zarathustra, Beyond Good and Evil*, and the yet untranslated *Birth of Tragedy* (which he doubtless knew through Marcel Drouin) he found an echo and an affirmation of his own thought. Those are precisely the works of the German philosopher which Gide recommended particularly in his monthly *"Lettre à Angèle"* of September 1899, after complaining of the absence of real characters in the theatre and stating : "I believe that to have a new drama will require a new ethic. Do we have it? I think so. [. . .] Nietzsche has given us that ethic." Accordingly, he made his Candaules exemplify that "bestowing virtue" of Zarathustra, which goes so far as to lose all sense of shame. In his original preface, the author speaks of Candaules as "too great, too generous, and driving himself to extremities" and cites in a footnote Nietzsche's "generous to the point of vice." Indeed, the version of the play published in the periodical *Ermitage* contains, among the few lines cut from the definitive text, this exchange:

Simmias: "The generosity you were just describing is merely vice."

Candaules: "You are right, Simmias. It requires that
For one to take so much pleasure in it."

A true Superman, Candaules surpasses himself—as the Gidian Philoctetes does also—by giving away his most precious possession and victimizing himself. Embarrassed by his universal good-fortune, "ashamed when the dice fall in his favor," as Nietzsche says, he deliberately risks his happiness, willing to succumb if need be to his rash experiment. Beyond good and evil, he ignores traditional restraints and casts away his advantage in a startlingly novel gamble.

Though led by an irresistible urge, Candaules by no means acts as in a dream. On the contrary, he is fully conscious of the originality and boldness of his deed. When the idea first occurs to him, he mutters to himself: "What art thou proposing, O my restless thought?" And again, still before he has voiced that idea to the audience:

"Louder! Speak louder, O newest thought of mine!
Where willst thou lead me? Amazing Candaules!"

He admires himself for daring to harbor such an idea and for being about to realize what he characterizes as "sheer madness"; "Who else would ever do it, if not thou?" he asks himself. Thus he carries what is originally a virtue to the point where, in the eyes of the world, it becomes a vice. And in developing his swift evolution Gide achieves a powerful characterization and a truly tragic figure, brought to his doom through fulfilling his nature.

Gide's Saul likewise goes to his doom through following his bent. In his case, too, the obstacle between him and happiness is within him. The great difference between the two protagonists, however, lies in Saul's lack of will: rather than surpassing himself, he surrenders to his instincts. The five-act drama in prose on the Old Testament king of Israel was written shortly before *Le Roi Candaule*. In a letter of July 1897 Gide says that he is writing "the terrible drama" of *King Saul*, and another letter shows that he was still working on it at Assisi in March 1898. Fragments of the last three acts were published in the *Revue Blanche* for 15 June of that year, at which time the play must have been finished. Yet the first edition did not appear until 1903. Such a delay, together with the date of 1902 appearing on the front cover, as if publication had been deliberately held up, suggests that the author postponed publication in the hope of a stage performance. And indeed, Roger Martin du Gard has recently recorded that André Antoine had promised Gide to put on the somber tragedy if he made money with his new production. The young author naturally rushed to the opening of the new offering, which was Brieux's *Résultat des courses,* and by the second act recognized that it was a miserable flop. Accordingly, *Saül* had to wait twenty years; it was staged by Copeau at the Vieux-Colombier in June 1922. Even then it was given but nine performances.

Yet, as late as 1931, Gide spoke of it as one of the best things he had ever written, "and perhaps the most surprising"; Martin du Gard confessed that if he could take only one of his friend's works with him to a desert island, he would choose *Saül.* As in *Le Roi Candaule,* Gide has taken as subject the end of a proud reign, the downfall of a mighty king; but Saul knows in advance that he is rapidly approaching ruin and that his son will not succeed him. Obviously the subject comes from the first book of Samuel, where Gide must have been struck by the "evil spirit from God" that descended upon Saul, which David alone was able to quiet. This was enough to suggest the dangers of the receptivity that Gide had just advocated in the *Nourritures.* The entire play may be regarded as a critique of that doctrine; for Saul welcomes with open arms what harms him— not only his familiar demons, but also, and especially, David who will succeed him on the throne. The opening scene in which the demons rush into the throne-room while Saul is praying and, having decided to inhabit him, take up their various assignments (one his wine-cup, another his couch, another his scepter, another the purple, and another his crown) sets the tone for the entire action.

As early as 1895 from Rome Gide had written Marcel Drouin: "I shall write a poem in which I shall compare my desires to the daughters of King Lear, for I feel like unto the dispossessed king for having listened to the passions that charm me." An echo of the mad Lear remained in the finished play, especially in the scene in the desert, just as the scene with the

Witch of Endor inevitably recalls *Macbeth* and the final lines
echo the ending of *Hamlet*; but the daughters of Lear were to
become lithe demons. One stage in the transition can be seen in
the *Nourritures*, where the germ of *Saül* hides in these lines:
"And each of my senses had its desires. When I wanted to
return within myself, I found my servants and my handmaidens
at my table; I no longer had the slightest place to sit. The place
of honor was occupied by Thirst; other thirsts were disputing
the best place with him. The whole table was quarrelsome, but
they were all banded together against me." Yet the final crys-
talization of the subject was brought about, as the author confided in a letter of February 1907 to Christian Beck, and again
in his *Journals* for 1943, by an entomological observation: "It
is because of having found in my garden a bombyx chrysalis
completely occupied by small cocoons of ichneumon that I had
the idea of writing my *Saül* dispossessed of himself by his
demons."

Gide's sensual curiosity was the trait against which he had
to struggle most vigorously throughout his life. What was more
natural than for him, while writing the first antidote to the poison contained in his *Nourritures*, to attribute to Saul the same
form of irresistible curiosity from which he was then suffering
himself? In the first book of Samuel he found the mutual love
of David and Jonathan, "passing the love of women"; he also
must have noted Saul's obvious obsession with the thought of
David, the humble shepherd who reminded him of his own
youth. To be sure, that obsession expresses itself in the Old
Testament in the form of an armed pursuit with attempt to
slaughter a potential successor. But even then André Gide must
have already noted the close similarity between love and hate
or love and fear; and he must have been intrigued by David's
devotion to his king and master, whose life he saves twice because Saul had originally welcomed him as a soothing harpist.

It required but a step, then, to see Saul as a previously unconscious homosexual, passionately attracted to the naïve David,

who repulses him, slowly awakening to his abnormality though he knows he should fear the youth. Once Gide had envisaged this interpretation of the king's behavior, it became necessary to depict Jonathan as a feeble replica of his father, weak and inapt for ruling. Like Phèdre in Racine's tragedy, Saul is jealous of the young couple formed of David and Jonathan, who indulge in a legitimate, pure love, the counterpart of his guilty passion. In April 1896 at Touggourt Gide had learned from his guide Athman the Arab diminutive for David— "Daoud"—and this provided a convenient key to the relationships in his play: whereas the Gidian David asks Jonathan to call him thus, he refuses both Saul and the Queen the right to use the familiar form.

Thus André Gide dared to take the same liberties with the Bible as he regularly took with the ancients. In a letter of 1922 thanking François Mauriac for a perceptive article on the Copeau production of the play (than which he claimed never to have written anything "more monitory"), he flatly stated: "I consider the Scriptures, just like Greek mythology (and even more so), inexhaustibly, infinitely resourceful and destined to enrich themselves with each interpretation suggested by a new intellectual orientation. In order not to cease interrogating them, I do not confine myself to their first reply."

Saul's sole preoccupation, his passion for David, makes him incapable both for war and for the throne. The black demons exteriorize his thought and figure his vices; as the play progresses their relationship to him assumes an increasingly homosexual character. Finally, all will evaporated, the king, "deplorably disposed" to passive acceptance of all external influences, can truthfully say: "I am utterly dispossessed." There is nothing heroic about Saul save the extent of his collapse and the remorseless lucidity that marks him, for he is able to foresee his ruin and sum it up in a maxim: "With what shall man console himself for a fall, unless with what felled him?"

There is assuredly nothing of the superman in Saul either, though like Candaules, Philoctetes, and the characters of *Le Prométhée mal enchaîné*, he bears deep within him an incurable wound and a consuming eagle. In a letter written from Orvieto in March 1898 just before he completed the play, Gide wrote: "The fact is that of the three relationships taught by the catechism—with others, with God, and with oneself—the first seems to me reducible to the second, which seems to me reducible to the third. . ." The relationship with oneself was precisely what he was treating in all the works of that period.

During the first ten years of his literary career, in fact, André Gide grappled constantly and almost exclusively with that problem. Like all the young, he ardently desired to know his true nature; but (and here he is typical rather of the best among them) he recognized that this was not enough: among the multiple possibilities that life offers to each, he saw the necessity of choosing. As early as June 1891, at twenty-one, he noted in his *Journals*: *"Dare to be yourself.* I must underline that in my head too." Not yet knowing what he wanted to be while still knowing that he must choose and limit himself in order to shape his life constituted his youthful torment. And, early in life, this raised the whole annoying question of sincerity. In January 1892 he reflected: "I am torn by a conflict between the rules of morality and the rules of sincerity. Morality consists in substituting for the natural creature (the old Adam) a fiction that you prefer. But then you are no longer sincere. The old Adam is the sincere man. This occurs to me: the old Adam is the poet. The new man, whom you prefer, is the artist. The artist must take the place of the poet. From the struggle between the two is born the work of art." In Gide's personal terminology at that time, the poet was wholly subject to inspiration, whereas the artist was dominated by discipline. By the end of April of the following year, the new man in him was rebelling against his puritanical upbringing and he was praying to God to help burst his narrow ethic and let him live fully. The habit of resistance and privation had become so much a part of him that he had to struggle to cast off the thought of sin and suppress his scruples.

It was in such a state of mind that he set out for Africa, where an indulgent sun, a strange civilization, and the necessity of pampering his weakened body combined to make his former conception of good and evil seem remote and academic. On his return, he stated: "I am unwilling to understand a rule of conduct which does not permit and even teach the greatest, the finest, and the freest use and development of all our powers." Stifling his earlier impulse to encourage his inner antagonism, he then decided that following "the direction of oneself" was much more difficult than resisting the current. Education, based on rules of conduct, should raise man to the point where he can do without such rules: "The wise man lives without a rule of conduct, according to his wisdom. We must try to reach a higher immorality."

These reflections—which led to the creation of such characters as Ménalque, Philoctetes, Candaules, and Saul, to the intense satire of *Paludes*, the lyricism of the *Nourritures*, and the powerful symbol of Prometheus—found their most urgent and most personal expression in Gide's first novel. Finished on 25 October 1901, *L'Immoraliste* (*The Immoralist*) was published in May 1902 in an edition of 300 copies, the number at which the young author then estimated his potential public. On sending the book to Francis Jammes, he said: "I have lived it for four years and have written it to put it behind me. I suffer a book as one suffers an illness. I now respect only the books that all but kill their authors." The torment of Michel, the protagonist of the novel, is the very torment Gide had been experiencing. Having undergone a physical and spiritual awakening, Michel returns to civilization bearing the secret of a resuscitated Lazarus. After catching a glimpse, during his convalescence, of another and neglected self, he deliberately sets out to discover "the authentic creature, the 'old Adam', that the

Gospel cast off." A scholar himself, he compares himself to a palimpsest on which recent writings cover and obscure a very ancient, infinitely more valuable, text. He begins by using his accumulated learning as a means to efface the deposit formed by centuries of learning and get back to the crude original. Eventually, enamored of what he finds, he would identify himself with it, rejecting what now seems to him the encrusted veneer of his own culture. Candaules and Gyges personified a dramatic conflict between refined culture and brute instinct; but in Michel culture and instinct are bitterly opposed in one person, as they were in the writer himself.

Now, on the most elementary plane, the conflict between culture and instinct can be translated into an opposition between mind and body, and the novel treats also of their necessary equilibrium. The young historian who marries Marceline seems pure intellect, but his nearly fatal attack of tuberculosis can be cured solely by an exclusive concern with the physical. Telling his own story, he apologizes thus: "I am going to speak at length of my body. I am going to speak of it so much that it will seem to you at first that I am forgetting the mind's share. [. . .] I did not have enough strength to maintain a double life; as for the mind and the rest, I told myself, I shall think of them later on when I am better." Of the three parts of the novel, the first reveals his transformation, the second describes his momentary balance between the intellectual and the physical (while he is preparing his course and governing his estate during the first summer in Normandy), followed by a gradual leaning toward the purely physical, and the third reports his vertiginous descent to a life of sheer sensation. The germ of this aspect of the novel, like that of so many later developments in Gide's thought, can be found in the *Nourritures*: "Then I wrote: 'I owed the salvation of my flesh only to the irremediable poisoning of my soul.' Later, I ceased to understand at all what I had meant by that." Michel's entire evolution is contained in those two sentences.

In the course of his "palpitating discovery" of life and of himself, Michel concludes, as Ménalque of the *Nourritures* had done before him and as Nathanael had been taught, that his individual value lies in what distinguishes him from others. At the mid-point of the novel, in fact, just where the relationship between Michel and Marceline is reversed and (as in the device of the backward-flowing stream of the *Voyage d'Urien*) the action begins to repeat itself in the opposite direction, Michel encounters his former acquaintance Ménalque.

In later years Gide felt that the figure of Ménalque was better drawn in *L'Immoraliste* than in the *Nourritures*; in any case he serves here the specific purpose of precipitating Michel's evolution. Before the novel was finished, Oscar Wilde had died; and Gide could safely attribute to his creature more of the Irishman's features. In addition to the cosmopolitanism, hedonism, homosexuality, scorn of principles, and love of danger he had revealed in the earlier work, he now has been the victim of "an absurd, a shameful, scandalous trial" resulting in public ostracism. Insolent in his manner, he indulges in frequent Wildian epigrams, such as: "I cannot expect my virtues of everyone; it is remarkable enough if I find in them my vices" and "Regrets, remorse, repentance are but erstwhile joys seen from the back." At some length, he even discourses in a way that momentarily makes him indistinguishable from the Gilbert of "The Critic as Artist." The non-Wildian features—his sobriety, courage, abnegation, piratical appearance, and positive discoveries—are there partly to keep him from seeming a portrait, and even more to enhance the impression he makes on Michel and on the reader.

Ménalque awakens Michel's thought by anticipating it, as the Devil does in his famous dialogue with Ivan Karamazov. Listening to him, Michel would like to, but cannot, contradict; accordingly he becomes more annoyed with himself than with his interlocutor. He admits that Ménalque's remarks "did not teach me anything very new, but they suddenly laid bare my thought, a thought that I had been covering with so many veils that I had almost been able to hope it was stifled." Despite Ménalque's resemblances to the one whom Gide called "the great hedonist," is it not possible that he is also an *alter ego* of Michel (as we saw him to be a projection of the author in the *Nourritures*) and the conversations with him the exteriorization of an inner dialogue? In this sense Ménalque would represent a better, more mature, and more successful Michel.

Now, Ménalque, while inveighing against the constraint and imitation by which each man fashions himself a distorted, untrue personality, voices an idea toward which the protagonist is barely groping. He says: "The element of difference one feels in oneself is precisely the single rare possession one has, and it constitutes the value of each. . ." Much later Michel himself extends this thought, asking: "What further possibility lies in man? This is what it was important for me to know. What man has said up to now, is that all he could say? Has he overlooked nothing in himself? Is he condemned merely to repeating himself? . . . And every day there grew in me the vague feeling of untapped resources—covered, hidden, and stifled by cultures, proprieties, and moral codes." In such a reflection Michel transcends himself: he will fulfill his possibilities in an effort to know what man in general can achieve. From one point of view, then, his entire effort might be seen as a Promethean striving to realize progress for mankind.

Encouraged by Ménalque, Michel rapidly becomes a Nietzschean immoralist, defying traditions and moral codes, scorning the weak and exalting the strong, overriding every consideration of duty, decency, and love in order to assert himself and achieve his uniqueness. Like the Gidian Candaules, he admires himself for his daring; the novel's epigraph, from *Psalm* 139, would not be ironic to him, so closely does it reflect his attitude: "I will praise thee; for I am fearfully and wonderfully made." He starts, to be sure, with an act of will, and in this he differs from the Gidian Saul. But as he progresses, it becomes clear that he too, though less passive, is yielding to his inclination, taking the easy, selfish path while congratulating himself that he is blazing a difficult trail on which few will have the courage to follow. Most subtly Gide suggests the stages of his evolution from his interest in the Arab children as symbols of health to a preference for the unsubmissive and strong ones, and eventually for the bold and lawless Moktir, from his gradual self-identification with the emperor Athalaric, who chose to be a barbarian, to his affinity with the worst elements among the farm-workers and woodsmen in Normandy, from his neglect of Marceline during her miscarriage to his abandoning of her the night of her death. In case the reader has not foreseen the inevitable culmination of that development, the rapid last part of the novel contains many a clear indication. Pushed by Marceline, who clearly senses all that is implicit in his behavior, Michel is obliged to admit that "in each creature, the worst instinct seemed to me the most sincere." And soon thereafter, recognizing all he is destroying in both their lives, he concludes: "I have sought, I have found what constitutes my value: a sort of obstinate persistence in the worst."

Although Michel, who narrates his entire story to a group of friends, refers to "my crime, if you wish to call it thus," he dispassionately refrains from any judgment. He has called his friends to his aid; yet he is far from confessing total defeat and admitting, as Saul does, that he is dispossessed by his demons. Characteristically, he speaks rather of all *he* has suppressed, which he fears may some day take its revenge. He still cherishes, instead, a Nietzschean ideal of self-surpassing. At the very beginning of his narrative, he tells his faithful friends that he wants no other aid from them but to hear his story, which he feels he must tell. And he adds: "For I have reached such a point in my life that I can no longer go beyond." Strangely, no one has ever pointed out to what an extent that significant remark echoes Wilde's words to Gide before leaving Algiers to stand trial in London, as reported by Gide in December 1901 just after finishing *L'Immoraliste*: "But how can I be prudent? That would be retracing my steps backward. I must go as far as possible. . . I cannot go further. . . Something must happen, something else. . ." Likewise Gide's Oedipus will say after blinding himself: "I had reached that point which I could no longer go beyond except by using myself as a springboard."

Profiting from the teaching of Nietzsche and the example of Wilde, Michel seeks to define himself by trying to divest his instinctive self of the accretions of culture. In other words, he chooses "the old Adam" as the authentic man and opposes sincerity to morality. Deliberately (though half resisting in the beginning, and then acquiring momentum as he progresses), he lives a dangerous experiment already outlined in the *Nourritures terrestres*. To a friend in July 1902 Gide admitted that the two books were fundamentally the same, the story of *L'Immoraliste* being born between the lines of the *Nourritures*. In the same letter he described the novel as "full of bitter ashes, of dried tears, and of derision." Like the immediately preceding works, this first novel is a study in individuality; and, in so far as it can be summed up in Michel's disabused maxim that "Knowing how to free oneself is nothing; the difficult thing is knowing how to *be* free," it forms a critique of the doctrine expressed in the dithyrambic work of 1897. In Gide's original self-liberation he had intentionally cast off all restraint; but immediately he had recognized that discipline was inseparable from true freedom.

It is most important that in the course of writing his novel André Gide discovered the individualist anarchism of Max Stirner. Under that name the German Johann Kaspar Schmidt had advocated as early as 1845 the liberation of the individual from all social and moral bonds, total amoralism, and the complete supremacy of the individual. His major work, *Der Einzige und sein Eigenthum*, appeared in French in 1900 as *L'Unique et sa propriété* and in English seven years later as *The Ego and*

His Own. Gide's review of the French edition came out in the *Ermitage* in early 1900 as one of his "*Lettres à Angèle*"; at the end its composition is dated 10 December 1899—that is, ten months before the completion of *L'Immoraliste.* Hence Stirner may have contributed to the novel quite as much as Zarathustra did, for the review begins thus: "In connection with Stirner rather than with Nietzsche, I wish to speak to you briefly of 'the dangers of individualism.' I fear, Angèle, I fear the failures of individualism as much as all other failures. Let us leave failures and the second-rate to established religions; they will be better off; we too. Consequently let us not urge toward individualism what has nothing individual about it; the result would be woeful." And it ends with this exhortation: "For pity's sake, no individualism! For the sake of individuals. Never encourage great men; and as for the others: discourage! discourage! . . ." It is certainly possible to see Michel as an anarchist of the Stirner type, a failure of individualism because he had no individuality worth developing.

The moment *L'Immoraliste* appeared, readers criticized Gide either for holding Michel up as an example or for depicting so unattractive a character. Accordingly the author added to the second edition, which came out six months later, a very brief preface defending his right to present a spiritual crisis without judging or taking sides and claiming, as he had felt necessary with other books, that he had aimed solely to create a work of art. But privately he had already judged, and severely judged, his hero in a letter of 8 July 1902 to Arthur Fontaine, the sociologist and economist, stating: "The special plea would have begun if I had decorated my hero with very noble and sumptuous deeds. But no, I do not think him capable of them. Everything he does that is not childish is cruel or lamentably vile, and the exaltation of his thought (or of what gradually takes the place of it) contributes to no real beauty. He *is not* well; he has become so. He is not free; he is anarchical. [. . .] And what does he do, great gods of Greece? He shaves off his beard; he debauches while debauching himself; he covers himself with vermin; he kills his wife." Nothing could be more categorical or correspond better to the indignation aroused by Michel, for which no one, as Gide said in his preface, was grateful to the author.

Because the *Nourritures* had preached, readers sought preaching of the same kind in *L'Immoraliste*. Because the cynicism and immoralism of the original Ménalque had irritated them in that earlier work, they found the same attitudes expressed here. But they failed to notice that the new Ménalque had achieved equilibrium without sacrificing anyone else to his ends, that he was making a positive contribution to society, and finally that he possessed admirable virtues. But the Ménalque of the novel suffered also from the reprobation cast upon Michel. So did the author, for Michel had spoken throughout in the first person; when *Si le grain ne meurt . . .* became public in 1926, it was clear to everyone how largely Gide had drawn upon the facts of his own life in imagining Michel's. From that point on, few were the critics who could distinguish Gide's biography from that of his character.

Furthermore, the question of Gide's debt to Nietzsche—in all his works published between 1897 and 1903, but particularly in this novel—arose so often and formed the subject of so many studies animated by the desire to pin down precisely what would not admit of precision that Gide came to appear to some as a mere French disciple of the German thinker. To one student of the subject, Henri Drain, whose essay appeared in 1932, Gide wrote of the difference between his novel and *Thus Spake Zarathustra* as revealingly as he had written thirty years earlier to Arthur Fontaine: "It is easy enough for you to speak of the 'abyss separating them.' Obviously! *Zarathustra* displays a triumph; *L'Immoraliste* relates an error, a failure, the very parody of a Nietzschean triumph. One is a book of propaganda; the other is a book of warning. (Like *La Porte étroite,* moreover. The story of Michel, like the story of Alissa, is merely a plunge into the excessive, a case of the drunken Helot, and proof by the absurd.)'" Certainly this clearly defines Gide's intention in writing his novel. But it would be unjust to generalize from such a statement or to conclude, as Albert Thibaudet did in 1928, that, because Gide possesses a Norman sense of realism *à la* Flaubert and belongs to the noble tradition of French *moralistes,* "His novels offer much rather a gallery of infra-men (*sous-hommes*), like *L'Éducation sentimentale,* than an apotheosis of the superman (*surhomme*)." The realist in Gide begins to appear only with *L'Immoraliste,* for Philoctetes, Candaules, and Prometheus are far from deserving to be classed as infra-men, whatever may be said of Cocles, Damocles, Saul, and Michel. Even among the latter, as we have seen, there is a vast difference in the mere fact that Michel strives to surpass himself.

That not all readers accepted in the same spirit his failure to do so is evident from an enthusiastic prose-poem published by *L'Ermitage* in 1903 under the title "To the Immoralist." It had been written in July 1902 in Sweden by Jacques Copeau, then twenty-two years old, the same youth who a year before had thrilled to the voice that spoke to him from the pages of the *Nourritures terrestres,* and it ended: "O human type! do not let yourself be broken into fragments; do not let yourself be enslaved: we are lovingly awaiting your next crime, your supreme beauty. . ." The wait was a long one, for the next crime did not occur until twelve years later, when Lafcadio Wluiki thrust Amédée Fleurissoire from a moving railway carriage between Rome and Naples.

VII. OEDIPUS AND SELF–INTEGRATION

"For I wish you to realize, children, that as an adolescent each of us encounters, at the outset of his course, a monster that conjures up before him an enigma such as might keep him from advancing. And though to each one of us that peculiar sphinx addresses a different question, you may be sure that to each of his questions the reply is the same—yes, that there is but one and the same reply to such diverse questions; and that that single reply is: Man; and that that single man for each one of us is: Himself."

TO most readers in 1914 and for many years thereafter Lafcadio's unexpected and casual murder was the heart of André Gide's third *sotie*, *Les Caves du Vatican*, which has been variously entitled in English as "The Vatican Swindle" and "Lafcadio's Adventures" whereas it should be known as "The Roman Underground." That the crime serves as a catalyst here is obvious, but it has not been sufficiently pointed out that it precipitates the end rather than the beginning of the complex action. The novel (for, despite the author's reasons for avoiding that term, this is decidedly a novel) is divided into five books; the major plot, both in the sense of fictional scheme and in that of the conspiracy to extort money for the Pope's liberation, does not begin until the third book, and the murder of Amédée occurs only at the start of the last book. It behooves us to examine the first books to see whether or not they serve merely an introductory purpose as preparation for the climax of Lafcadio's strange act.

The first three books, or parts, of the novel are entitled respectively "Anthime Armand-Dubois," "Julius de Baraglioul," and "Amédée Fleurissoire." Together they present three very different brothers-in-law, all middle-aged and all rigidly determined as types. Anthime is the scientist and militant atheist; Julius is the conservative, right-thinking society novelist; and Amédée is the mousy provincial bigot. Incidentally they epitomize the three important social classes in French life of 1893, when the action takes place: the upper middle class, the nobility, and the lower middle class. But it is more significant that they represent respectively the self-made, closed world of the scientist who is equally isolated anywhere because of lack of contact with the outside; the exclusive society of Paris; and the narrow circle of Pau. Of all French provincial towns Gide chose this one probably not only because his sister-in-law, Valentine Gilbert, lived there, but also because it was near to Orthez, where Francis Jammes nourished his narrow and ostentacious Catholicism; besides, Jammes was instrumental in converting Valentine Gilbert, whose Christian name the author conferred upon the gullible Countess de Saint-Prix.

Anthime, Julius, and Amédée are all eminently "crustaceans" according to the distinction that Protos and Lafcadio established when still in school: ". . . a subtle man was one who, for any reason whatever, did not offer the same appearance to all people in all places. According to their classification, there were many categories of subtle men, more or less elegant and praiseworthy, to whom corresponded and was opposed the single, large family of *crustaceans,* whose representatives, from top to bottom of the social scale, strutted." Distinguished chiefly by their close-mindedness, the brittle brothers-in-law are the characters of *Paludes* grown up and matured. It is important that they appear to us as determined chiefly by their respective attitudes toward the Church. Suddenly, with no preparation or warning whatsoever, each one changes his thought and habits, uprooting himself from all his past and thereby acquiring a new fervor. The cause of such a brusque transformation is, in each case, external to the man. Anthime experiences a miracle that cures his sciatica and turns him into a devout Catholic. Julius, through spite at not being elected to the French Academy, adopts a new outlook diametrically opposed to his former conservatism. And Amédée, learning of the Pope's "abduction," acquires a mission to take himself outside of himself and, for the first time in life, a *raison d'être*. But once a crustacean, always a crustacean: it is noteworthy that each of the three men changes to a form quite as inflexible as he had formerly exhibited, embodying a classic type carried to the point of absurd exaggeration.

After his transformation, each one sounds like a parody of Ménalque's teaching or of Michel after his African awakening. Anthime says: "Nothing that concerned me yesterday any longer interests me today." Julius boasts: "My point of view has completely changed." And Amédée marvels: "This morning, before meeting you, I was able to doubt of my own reality, to doubt that I was myself here in Rome. . ." The many disguises of the Protean Protos, who is the very reverse of a "crustacean," and the ease with which he assumes them, caricature the revolutionary changes in the three brothers-in-law and serve to keep the idea of metamorphosis in the foreground. Perhaps even more important, however, is the initial falsehood on which Protos and his accomplices have constructed their vast swindle: the Holy Father himself is supposed to have been confiscated and supplanted by a false Pope. After Protos disguised as a priest has warned the naïve Amédée against the boy porter, and Carola the prostitute has warned him against the false priest, Amédée sees this intricate web of falsehood and suspicion as "at once the consequence and the proof of that initial vice, of that tottering of the Holy See: all the rest capsized at once.

In whom can one trust, if not in the Pope? And once that cornerstone yielded, on which the whole Church rested, nothing more deserved to be true." Although the substitution of the Pope is merely a clever fiction, the fact remains that Anthime, Julius, and Amédée actually substitute new selves for the ones that seemed immutably fixed by time and habit.

Chatting with Lafcadio in the *wagon-restaurant*, Professor Defouqueblize, of the Chair of "Comparative Criminology" at the University of Bordeaux, develops his thesis regarding the restraint that society imposes on each of us. "And even if there were no society to restrain us," he adds, "that group of parents and friends would suffice which we are unwilling to displease. To our uncivil sincerity they oppose an image of us for which we are but half responsible, which is very little like us, but to which it is indecorous, I tell you, not to conform." And because he has exceptionally drunk a glass of champagne and felt its effects, he claims that he is at the very moment escaping the conventional image people have formed of him, getting outside himself: "O vertiginous adventure! O perilous pleasure!" he exclaims. A little later, when he has revealed himself as a particularly alert and well-disguised Protos, he assumes that Lafcadio has rebelled against the rule of the "crustaceans" in the false belief that he could "get out of one society without falling into another."

However appropriate everything he says may be to Anthime, Julius, and Amédée, it does not apply to Lafcadio. Although the handsome youth has recently received a substantial inheritance from Count Juste-Agénor de Baraglioul, Julius's father, he knows that he must never claim to belong to that noble family. Lafcadio is the first of the many fortunate bastards in Gide's work who need take into account no past, who need fear no haunting atavism, for whom everything lies in the future. In addition to Lafcadio, the Bernard of the *Faux-Monnayeurs* and Gide's Oedipus are the shining examples of this form of *disponibilité* and rootlessness; Theseus would like to consider himself in their company by encouraging the legend that Poseidon fathered him. Consequently Lafcadio acknowledges no family and belongs to no society. A "creature of inconsistency," as he boasts, he has more curiosity about himself than about events. In him everything is possible and, as he has hardened no shell, he has nothing to change from. The unusual crime he commits in killing Amédée does not, therefore, change him. But it does serve as the agent that, once again, transforms Anthime and Julius.

Quite naturally, the sudden murder of his brother-in-law sobers Julius, though it provides him with just the unmotivated crime his next book and new aesthetic need. The arrival of his wife and daughter for the funeral with the news that he is now certain to win election to the Academy acts upon him like the renewal of the electric current after it has been turned off for a time. The cause of his former transformation now removed, he steps automatically back into the frame, becoming one with the image he has spent a lifetime in forming. As his wife points out to him that it is often sufficient in this world to wait for the good things, he adds: "And not to change. Faithful to you, to my thoughts, to my principles. Perseverance is the most indispensable virtue." He even begins to forget his deviation, his swerve from the normal line of his evolution, and, admiring the logic and constancy of his thought, he blames the entire confusion on the change of Popes. When he, in turn, attempts to console Anthime by telling him of the horrible substitution that has taken place in the Vatican, Anthime forgets his new rôle and chuckles at the thought that, if there are two Popes, maybe there are two Gods also. Suddenly and simultaneously he returns to his former atheism and his inveterate limp.

The only one of the three who does not change back to what he was originally is Amédée. "Poor Fleurissoire," says Julius, "is dead from having got behind the scenes. The simplest thing when one is simple is to cling to what one knows. That hideous secret killed him. Knowledge never strengthens any but the

strong." But that is Julius's rationalization. Amédée, it might
be said, does not transform himself a second time simply because it is too late; he is dead. From another point of view, he
had to be sacrificed in order to shock the other two back into
their former state. Furthermore, in losing his virginity with
Carola he had taken an irrevocable step that would have prevented his ever becoming the Amédée he was before.

For the distinguishing characteristic of the Amédée Fleurissoire who manufactured *papier-mâché* statues of saints at Pau
had been his purity. Although married for years, he had never
consummated his union with Arnica because of a solemn promise
made to his best friend and only rival. His extraordinary innocence, together with the nature of the perilous and sacred mission he undertakes, inevitably make one think of the most popular prototype of such saintly heroes: the Wagnerian Parsifal.
His wife herself sees him in such company when he wants to
share in the *Crusade for the Liberation of the Pope*: "The words
captivity, imprisonment raised before her eyes dark and semi-
romantic images; the word *crusade* exalted her infinitely, and
when, at last shaken, Amédée spoke of setting out, she suddenly
saw him in armor and helmet, on a horse." Like Parsifal, he is
a "guileless fool," and the moment he arrives in Rome he goes
straight to a "castle of perdition" filled with "flower-maidens"
who, naked under their flapping négligées, pass him on the
stairs. After succumbing to the charms of Carola Venitequa
(whose name pronounced in the Italian manner means "come
hither"), "he thought of his august mission, henceforth compromised; he moaned in a low voice: 'It's all over! I am no
longer worthy. . . Ah, it's all over! It's indeed all over!' The
strange accent of these sighs had meanwhile awakened Carola.
Now, kneeling at the foot of the bed, he was pounding his frail
chest, and Carola in amazement heard his teeth chatter as he
repeated among his sobs: 'Every man for himself! The Church
is collapsing!' " Even so, Parsifal, after resisting the enchantress
Kundry, falls on his knees and, seeing as in a dream the whole

seduction to which Amfortas succumbed, speaks of forgetting his mission in her embrace.

Immediately following his sin, the hitherto "spotless servitor" (as Amédée calls himself) displays a most noticeable and disquieting blemish, not unlike the incurable wound of Amfortas. While assuring him that his festering pimple is "not what he thinks," Carola asks how he got it and innocently arouses the following train of thought in Amédée: "Oh! what did the immediate cause matter, the razor's cut or the pharmacist's saliva? The profound cause, which had justly brought him this punishment, could he decently tell her? And would she understand it?" And though she does not bring him balm as Kundry did, nevertheless she gives him good advice.

Just as Kundry does the evil bidding of the sorcerer Klingsor, so Carola is the creature of the wicked Protos; yet, like her Wagnerian counterpart, she too reveals virtuous longings in her lucid moments. Both symbolize the genius of sensuality and perdition, the eternal seductress; and still, thanks to their contradictory character, both intermittently serve the knights of the Grail. Such duality on the part of the enigmatic Kundry sorely embarrassed the first commentators of *Parsifal*. Similarly, when Carola begs Protos not to harm Amédée, Gide frankly confesses: "I don't know just what to think of Carola Venitequa. The cry she just uttered allows me to suppose that her heart is not yet too deeply corrupted. Thus, occasionally, in the very depths of abjection are suddenly revealed strange sentimental refinements, as a bluish flower grows from a heap of manure. [. . .] But when a soul revolts against the ignominy of its fate, often its first struggles go unnoticed even by itself; it is only in the light of love that the secret resistance is revealed. Was Carola falling in love with Amédée? It would be risky to assert this. But, upon contact with his purity, her corruption had been stirred; and the cry I have reported had indubitably burst from her heart." It is probable that in thus insisting upon Carola's unexpected cry of pity Gide had in mind the piercing, sub-human cry uttered by Kundry as Parsifal makes the sign of the cross and routs Klingsor's magic.

The influence of the "naïve crusader" (as the author calls him) eventually redeems Carola, as the bouquet of asters indicates which she places on his grave just before her own violent death. But this is not all that the simple pilgrim accomplishes. By his death Amédée breaks the strange spell cast over his brothers-in-law Anthime and Julius. There is even a hint that his unwilling sacrifice may reform Lafcadio.

Now why should André Gide have indulged in so elaborate a parody of *Parsifal*, which was also so subtle as to have gone apparently unnoticed until now? The most obvious answer is simply that the plot of his novel suggested a parallel; after that, one detail merely led to another. During the writing of the *Caves du Vatican* there was much talk about Wagner, the centenary of whose birth fell in 1913, and particularly of *Parsifal*, which came into the public domain in 1912, just thirty years after its first production. The press of the world was full of discussion as to prolonging the exclusive rights to present *Parsifal* which had been enjoyed by Bayreuth. It happened that, almost alone among his literary contemporaries inoculated by Baudelaire and raised on the *Revue Wagnérienne*, Gide did not like Wagner. As early as 1908 he had replied to an inquiry conducted by the *Berliner Tageblatt*: "I hold the person and the work of Wagner in horror; my passionate aversion has grown steadily since childhood. This amazing genius does not exalt so much as he *crushes*. He permitted a large number of snobs, of literary people, and of fools to think that they loved music, and a few artists to think that genius can be acquired. Germany has perhaps never produced anything at once so great or so barbarous."

In ejecting Amédée Fleurissoire from the railway compartment, then, Lafcadio was rebelling not only against the deeply rooted, intricately ramified family and the whole régime of the hard-shelled crustaceans, but also by implication against Wag-

ner and Parsifal and all those snobs who had made a cult of
them. For the casual reader of the novel, Lafcadio's crime occupies the central point; it even seems as if the detailed depic-
tion of character (which went so far that the puppets Gide
started with actually began to take on flesh and blood), the
clever imagining of Protos's underground network, and the
numerous shameless coincidences were there simply to lead
up to the fortuitous encounter of Amédée and Lafcadio in a
railway compartment at night.

It is important to examine just why the youth kills the solitary traveler. The fact that Lafcadio is sorry for Amédée, who
looks so unhappy, is not sufficient reason. Much more revealing
is the fact that Lafcadio, bored, has been thinking over his
recent past, remembering how he helped an old peasant woman
across the mountains, and reflecting that he could just as easily
have strangled her. "One imagines *what would happen if,*" he
thinks, savoring his ambivalence, which he could not have
known was one day to be called Freudian, "but there always
remains a little gap through which the unforeseen creeps in.
Nothing ever happens exactly as one would have thought. . .
That is what leads me to act. [. . .] In love with what might
be. . . If I were the State, I should have myself locked up."
The strange, timid little man who slips into his compartment
just then suddenly offers an equally anonymous subject on which
to experiment. Lafcadio is a temperamental gambler, who likes
to play with sensations and emotions. At once he thinks: "An unmotivated crime, what an embarrassment for the police! [. . .]
It is not so much of events that I am curious as of myself. A man
thinks himself capable of anything and yet, before acting, draws
back. . . What a distance between the imagination and the
deed! . . . And no more right to cancel one's move than in
chess. Bah! if one foresaw all the risks, the game would lose
all interest!"

Inasmuch as he would rather be the agent of chance than
of a reasoned decision, he determines to push his innocent com-

panion from the train only if he sees a light in the passing countryside before counting to twelve. No deed could be less motivated by interest than his spontaneous crime. He might as well have cast the dice to decide whether or not to kill Fleuris-soire. Indeed, he does so a moment later to find out whether or not he should get out at Capua, but upon finding in the victim's pocket a ticket in the name of Julius de Baraglioul, he is seized by an unbridled curiosity to seek out his half-brother and to study "the impact of this event on that calm and logical mind."

Lafcadio did not even know that Julius was in Rome; consequently he could not have guessed the metamorphosis the Count had undergone. But the reader, who has seen Julius encounter Amédée just before the fatal trip to Naples and has heard him discourse about his work in progress, knows that he is building his plot around precisely such a crime as Lafcadio commits. For some time Julius had been worrying about the excessive logic of his characters and the way in which he dominated them; consequently he has imagined "a creature of inconsistency" (the very term Lafcadio uses about himself) who will not obey interested motives. Such a character will indulge in action as he would allow himself a luxury or play a game. Julius tries to explain this to the uncomprehending Amédée, who has other worries on his mind, with such arguments as the following: "I am of the opinion that since La Rochefoucauld we have been taken in; that self-advantage is not always the guiding principle of men; that there are disinterested actions. . . [. . .] By *disinterested* I mean gratuitous. And I believe that evil, what is called evil, can be as gratuitous as good."

Again André Gide inserts into his novel a novel in formation—which again happens to be the very one we are reading. By attributing to the novelist Julius some of his own reflections about his specific problems, as they would appear to Paul Bourget or Henry James, and by skilfully weaving those reflections into the very plot, he actually intensifies, not only the complexity of the action, but also the suspense for the reader, who remembers the irresponsible Lafcadio and suspects that he will come back into the novel. Hardly has Julius stated that "if one supposes the evil act, the crime, to be gratuitous, it becomes impossible to impute it to anyone and impossible to catch the one who committed it," than Lafcadio, as if to test the theory, acts suddenly and gratuitously.

What could be more piquant, after the real crime, than to bring together Julius and Lafcadio, the half-brothers who once represented opposite poles of intellectual and emotional response, now in agreement as one unwittingly illustrates the other's theories? Julius is imagining an unmotivated crime and trying to use the recent murder of Amédée as a starting-point, whereas Lafcadio, the unconfessed murderer, has only to consult his memory of the preceding night. Everything Julius says about his plot and his protagonist fits Lafcadio and his crime perfectly. As the two men talk, says Gide, they seem to be playing a game of leap-frog, each one pushing on farther from where the other left off. Lafcadio agrees heartily from his own experience when Julius says: "I don't want any motive for the crime; it is enough for me to motivate the criminal. Yes, I aim to lead him to commit the crime gratuitously, to desire to commit an utterly unmotivated crime. [. . .] Let's take him as an adolescent. I want the elegance of his nature to be recognized by the fact that he acts above all in a gambling spirit and that to his interest he regularly prefers his pleasure. [. . .] Let's inculcate in him a love of risk." Yet Lafcadio has to point out that whereas Julius reasons out the crime his hero simply commits it without reasoning.

Now Julius the theoretician (but not Lafcadio the doer) speaks of a disinterested action, an unmotivated crime, and a gratuitous act. Of all the strange things that have been written about André Gide in all languages, the most arrant twaddle has concerned the *acte gratuit*. From reading some commentators one would assume that all of Gide could be summed up in that single magic formula. And yet the concept becomes explicit in but three of his works of imagination, the three ironic *soties*. In the first of them, *Paludes*, the expression used is *acte libre*, about which Alexandre the philosopher discourses thus: "It seems to me, Sir, that what you call a free act would be, according to you, an act depending on nothing; follow me: detachable—notice my progression: suppressible—and my conclusion: valueless." The narrator comments simply: "According to my habit I said nothing; when a philosopher answers you, you no longer understand at all what you had asked him." It may not be irrelevant that no one has asked Alexandre anything; nor has anyone but him alluded to a "free act."

That was in 1895. Four years later, in *Le Prométhée mal enchaîné*, the term has become *acte gratuit*, about which the café waiter enthusiastically says: "A gratuitous action! Doesn't that mean anything to you? To me it seems extraordinary. For a long time I thought that was what distinguished man from the animals: a gratuitous action. I used to call man the animal capable of a gratuitous action. And then, later, I thought just the opposite: that man was the only creature incapable of acting gratuitously. Gratuitously! Just think: without a reason—yes, I see your objection—let's say without a motive; incapable!" Attempting to define what he means, he adds: "And please realize that this doesn't mean an action without profit, for if that were the case. . . No, simply gratuitous: an act motivated by nothing. You understand? Neither interest nor passion, nothing. The disinterested act, born of itself; also the act without a purpose; hence without a master; the free act; the autocthonous act." Here Gide has used all the qualifying adjectives that were to reappear in 1914 in the *Caves du Vatican*. But it is highly significant that the gratuitous act which moves the waiter to such an appreciation is committed by the Miglionaire Zeus, that is by the Deity. When, much later, the waiter asks the fabulous banker if it is not true that his actions are gratuitous, Zeus unequivocally replies: "Only he whose fortune is infinite can act with absolute disinterestedness; man cannot. Whence my love of gambling; not of winning, I beg you to believe, but of gambling. What could I win that I do not already possess?"

Thus the entire discussion in *Le Prométhée* has almost no bearing upon the later crime of Lafcadio. The very nature of the unmoved mover is to act distinterestedly, and if Gide insists upon the double act of Zeus, it is simply to point out that such providential interventions in the lives of men may be either good or evil—both in themselves and in their results. But irreverently he emphasizes the motive of gambling; and this is where Zeus and Lafcadio meet on common ground. For Lafcadio likewise gambles in a godlike way, oblivious of the consequences as he is unmindful of the welfare either of others or of himself.

Already in the *Nourritures* of 1897 Gide had glorified spontaneity, the instinctive performance of an action without judging whether it be good or evil. The suspension of moral considerations is essential to the gratuitous act, as Baudelaire had recognized in his remarkable prose-poem, "*Le Mauvais Vitrier*" ("The Poor Glazier"). In those four pages, which Gide knew, the poet speaks of "the spirit of mystification resulting from a fortuitous inspiration" and of the sudden prodigal courage (*courage de luxe*) which allows one to execute essentially absurd and dangerous acts. As an example he speaks of the man who "will light a cigar beside a barrel of powder, *just to see, to find out, to tempt fate*, to force himself to make a show of energy, to play the gambler, to taste the pleasures of anxiety, for nothing, as a whim, out of boredom." There is general agreement that Baudelaire must have been inspired in this instance by Poe's tale, "The Imp of the Perverse," with its definition of perverseness as "a *mobile* without motive, a motive not *motivirt*." Now, Lafcadio responds to just such a mysterious impulse and performs his destructive deed in the same spirit of curiosity.

Annoyed in 1927 when a journalist questioned a minor

writer about the gratuitous act and its false profundity, Gide disclaimed in his *Journals* that there was any profundity at all in the concept: "I merely meant that the *disinterested* act could well not always be charitable; but once this is said, you are free, with La Rochefoucauld, not to believe in disinterestedness at all. Perhaps I don't believe in it either, but I claim that the individual's potentialities and his inner meteorology remain a bit more complicated than you ordinarily make them, and that what you call the bad potentialities are not all egocentric. This is stated quite ridiculously; but I am writing in haste and plan to insist on this point soon—apropos of curiosity perhaps, the individual's perdition, but without it no progress would be possible." It was about this time that Gide began himself to show a disturbing curiosity for sudden unpremeditated crimes and to fill the pages of his *Nouvelle Revue Française* with newspaper clippings concerning the fifteen-year-old farm-hand who slaughtered seven people at Landeau and the twelve-year-old girl of Bari who impetuously drowned a three-year-old neighbor in a well. Obviously he was interested in the inexplicable aspect of such horrors, their disturbing and suggestive qualities: "what interests us is not the crime but the state of mind of the murderer," he wrote. One reader accused him of wishing to communicate to others the tormenting unrest of his own mind and aiming "to use this pan-Gidism to enlarge his field of investigation." By 1930 such investigations produced two collections of gory documents: *L'Affaire Redureau* and *La Séquestrée de Poitiers*, which appeared under the general heading of *Ne jugez pas* . . . (*Judge Not* . . .).

In the course of pursuing this morbid hobby, Gide *seemed* to be preaching the fullest expression of the least honorable instincts and glorifying the *acte gratuit*, which had become a rallying-cry for the Dadaists, essentially destructive anyway, and had generally won the enthusiastic and misguided support of his youngest admirers. Consequently, he felt it necessary to state definitively: "I myself do not at all believe in the gratuitous act, that is to say in an act not motivated by anything. It is essentially unthinkable. There are no effects without causes. The words 'gratuitous act' are a *provisional* label that seemed to me convenient to designate acts that elude the ordinary psychological explanations, the deeds not determined by mere personal interest (and it is in this sense, playing somewhat upon the words, that I could speak of *disinterested acts*). Yet, this too should be said: man acts either *with a view to,* and to obtain . . . something; or merely through inner motivation, just as a man walking can head toward something or simply go ahead without any other aim than to make progress, to 'go forward.' If the judge asks the former why he did something, he can give a motive (good or bad). The latter can merely reply: 'Because I wanted to do it.' "

Obviously the exploration of instinctive actions led back to further reflections on the nature of sincerity. Instinct appeared in contrast to reason, just as the sincere "old Adam" had stood opposed to the counterfeit man obtained through rigorous and artificial conformity with conventions. Yet Gide did not forget how *natural* it had once been for him to conform and how he, like his Michel after him, had had to make an effort to act in accordance with what he took to be his original self. Following instinct, he was well aware, does not inevitably imply letting oneself go in passive abandon, and for this reason he said of his Lafcadio: "Yet he never listened altogether to his desire and did not like yielding, even to himself."

An act of will, therefore, enters into even the gratuitous act, which is "gratuitous" solely because not dictated by self-interest and not obeying the ordinary laws of motivation. But for those very reasons it is free of secondary or extraneous implications. Apparently a deviation from the individual's normal development, an *irrelevance,* on the contrary it pierces through the stiff exterior and reveals the true personality beneath. Hence it often becomes the one essential act of his career, the only really relevant one. In giving up his invaluable bow and arrows,

Philoctetes performs a true gratuitous act that conforms to the usual sense of the word disinterested. Candaules is equally disinterested when he shares his wife with Gyges, though it might be impossible to decide whether his gratuitous act was essentially good or bad. Finally, from the moral point of view there can be no question about Lafcadio's crime. In all these cases, if the deed itself goes unmotivated, Gide has taken care, as Julius said he would do, to motivate the doer. Each of these acts, furthermore, represents the culminating dramatic moment in the protagonist's life, and we know each through his unusual acts. Likewise he comes to know himself thereby, asserting his individuality and integrating himself.

Like Proust's use of the involuntary gesture, the gratuitous act is no more than a device for revealing the profound personality, the real one hidden beneath the social personality. That superficial, external self which each man presents to the world is a false or counterfeit image. Gide did not wait until his long novel, *Les Faux-Monnayeurs* (*The Counterfeiters*) to express such an idea. In *L'Immoraliste* Ménalque says of the men around him: "Most of them expect to get nothing good from themselves save by duress; they like themselves only when counterfeited." Similarly Julius, during his momentary transformation, coins the maxim: "We live a counterfeit existence for fear of not resembling the portrait we have initially sketched of ourselves"; and Protos ironically tells Lafcadio: "People in society, like you or me, owe it to ourselves to live counterfeit lives." No one seems ever to have advanced the theory that Anthime, Julius, and Amédée—by momentarily slipping out of their respective shells—were not only supplanting the counterfeit man by the real man, but were even committing gratuitous acts. The same sudden, unpremeditated quality is present in their metamorphoses as in Lafcadio's crime, and even less motivation can be found in their characters. But Gide did not intend their dramatic transformations to be lasting; as an epigraph for Book II of the novel he uses the following words from

Cardinal de Retz: ". . . since one must never deprive anyone of the possibility of retracing his steps."

For all its complex and preposterous plot, which classes this novel among the most rollicking tales of adventure, for all its frank comedy and pointed irony, the *Caves du Vatican* is a further study in the nature of personality. Just what is the sincere, genuine man and how does he become himself? the author seems to be asking. However attractive, Lafcadio is obviously something of a freak because of his lack of upbringing and restraints; but Anthime, Julius, and Amédée are also excessive in their crustacean rigidity. Another epigraph used in the novel, even more revelatory than that from Retz, might justly serve for this whole preoccupation that dominates so much of Gide's writing. It comes from Conrad's *Lord Jim* and reproduces an odd dialogue: " 'There is only one remedy. One thing alone can cure us from being ourselves.'—'Yes, strictly speaking, the question is not how to get cured, but how to live.' "

The same problem of how to live dominates *Les Faux-Monnayeurs* (*The Counterfeiters* in America, *The Coiners* in England). That massive novel, which first appeared in 1926, had been in the author's mind since at least 1914, and consequently embodies his mature thought on the subject. Here the question, alluded to early in *L'Immoraliste* and implicit throughout *Les Caves du Vatican*, rises to the fore to be treated in sharper and more positive form. More than any other of Gide's works, this is a true *Bildungsroman*, a novel of growing up and finding oneself.

From among the many characters of this complex, Dostoevskian fiction, against the drab background of their conservative middle-class families, two adolescents emerge in the very first pages; and the novel tells the story of their self-integration. Bernard, bold and apparently assured, is close to Lafcadio. The discovery of his illegitimacy offers just the excuse he needs to revolt and break with his family. When he indulges in further daring by stealing Édouard's suitcase and seeking

ANDRÉ GIDE (1926)

out Laura, he wins our esteem by his show of energy. Olivier, despite Édouard's and the author's evident preference for him, loses some of our regard by missing his chance to hold his uncle and by falling, through spite, to the artificial Passavant, who serves as a sort of caricature of Édouard. But later, the night of the banquet, Olivier sacrifices his pride and achieves himself through self-renunciation. By the end of the novel, consequently, he is happy and integrated whereas his friend Bernard is still striving.

As the preceding paragraph shows, it is impossible to summarize the story of the two adolescents without constant reference to Édouard, for it is in relation to him that they both define and assert themselves. Yet Édouard, the novelist who is so much like Gide that even the most damning comments the author makes about him have been used against Gide, is not the hero of the novel. Despite the extent to which he holds the center of the stage, despite the large part of the book formed by his journal, he remains a marginal observer of others' actions. He is the commentator, and as such he is occasionally obliged to intervene in order to keep the action alive or to give it a sudden turn in another direction. Like the author himself, he serves as the point of intersection of the various plots. He is, above all, an original and effective literary device, the culmination of Gide's life-long experiment with *composition en abyme*, or the story within a story.

Commenting on Laura's almost tragic adultery, Édouard says: "It can happen to anyone to make a bad start. The important thing is not to persist. . ." The remark is more comprehensive than anyone but the author could recognize at the time it is made, for everyone in the novel makes a false step at the outset. Most of the characters remain permanently warped as a result, but a few, such as Laura, Olivier, and Bernard, make up for their bad start by correcting that false step later. They all do so by an act of will, without which there can be no genuine self-assertion.

As far back as one can go in André Gide's career, that element of will is present and consciously recognized. Under date of 1887, in one of his earliest journal-entries, which he incorporated into *Les Cahiers d'André Walter*, he wrote: "May will dominate in everything: make oneself as one wants oneself." Gide was not yet eighteen when he voiced such a resolve. Five years later, on 3 January 1892, he noted that instead of recounting his life as he has lived it, the artist must live his life as he will recount it; "In other words, the portrait of him formed by his life must identify itself with the ideal portrait he desires. And, in still simpler terms, he must be as he wishes to be." Again, in 1904, while prefacing an exhibit of Maurice Denis's paintings, he reduced the formula to "Will to be who one is."

This does not imply a mere fatalistic self-acceptance, but rather—as in the Pindaric motto "Become who you are," which Nietzsche used—a realization of one's best potentialities. In the capital conversation toward the end of *Les Faux-Monnayeurs* when Bernard asks Édouard's advice, the youth wonders whether or not it is necessary to fix one's eyes on an objective in life. "When Columbus discovered America," he asks, "did he know toward what he was setting sail? His objective was to go ahead, straight ahead. His objective was himself, and he who projected it in front of him. . ." Édouard tells Bernard to find his rule in himself, "to have as an objective the development of oneself." And when Bernard fears that in learning how to live he may meanwhile make mistakes, his mentor replies: "That itself will teach you. It is good to follow one's inclination, provided one go upward." How often that wise injunction was to be misunderstood by readers who, consciously or unconsciously, omitted or forgot its essential proviso! In the same spirit Gide speaks of Édouard's love for Olivier and the care with which he would have matured the boy: "With what loving respect would he not have guided, supported, carried him to his self-fulfillment?"

Such integration of one's possibilities and realization of the self is the theme of the novel. At one point Édouard voices the author's thought when he deplores the fact that literature, concerned with the hardships of fate, social relationships, and conflicts of passions and characters, has largely neglected another form of tragedy which is "the very essence of the individual." We know that he is here speaking for Gide because the latter stated the same idea more precisely in his lectures on Dostoevsky, delivered while he was writing his own novel. There he notices that in the Occident "the novel, except for very few exceptions, is concerned solely with relationships among men, relationships of passion or intellect, family or society relationships or those of social classes—but never, almost never, of the individual's relationships with himself or with God—which here take precedence over all others."

We have seen that Gide had done just this in his own writings—not all novels, to be sure, yet at least *L'Immoraliste* (1902) and *La Porte étroite* (1909) were novels. But in those works he had abstracted Candaules, Philoctetes, Michel, and Alissa, for instance, from society in general, showing how each one struggled with himself and progressed to his salvation or damnation in unreal isolation. At most, each one stands in contrast or in conflict with a single other person, at the expense of whose happiness, often, he finally achieves full expression. On the other hand, Dostoevsky showed Gide how the conquest of the individual can be attained even amidst numerous external relationships by a man deeply rooted in surrounding society. For this reason Gide had already praised Dostoevsky, in 1908 while writing about the Russian novelist's correspondence, for having reconciled individualism and collectivism: "And, opposite Nietzsche, he becomes an admirable example to show us how little conceit and complacency often accompany that belief in the value of the ego. He writes: 'The hardest thing in the world is remaining oneself'; and 'one must not waste one's life for any objective'; for, according to him, without individualism, as without patriotism, there is no way of serving humanity."

Les Caves du Vatican, with its numerous characters and

multiple plots all interlocking, had already marked a step in this direction. Yet Lafcadio committed his experimental act of self-assertion without reference to anyone else or to the rest of the novel. Only when it was beyond recall did he become aware that he had murdered his half-brother's brother-in-law, confirmed Julius's theory of the gratuitous act, and played into the hands of Protos. In his initial disregard for consequences, he had not stopped to think what a "crossroads" a mothy, provincial traveler can turn out to be. But Bernard of *Les Faux-Monnayeurs*, who begins with some of the same fine, careless abandon, progresses far beyond his predecessor. Gide tells us: "His struggle with the angel had matured him. Already he had ceased to resemble the carefree luggage-thief who thought that in this world it is enough to dare. He was beginning to realize that the happiness of others is often the price of one's daring." The Bernard who goes out into the world at the end of this novel is far more mature and integrated a personality than the Lafcadio whom we left waking up in Geneviève's arms at the end of the *Caves*.

Before his discovery of Dostoevsky, however, André Gide was aware of the interdependence of all—even in relation to the problem of self-assertion. In the *Nourritures terrestres* of 1897, just before the Envoi, he had inserted an allegorical, Dantesque "Hymn to serve as Conclusion" that seems completely out of harmony with the Dionysiac tone of the book to which it belongs. It was doubtless its abstract quality that permitted him to dedicate discreetly to his wife, under the initials "M.A.G." for Madeleine André Gide, this uncharacteristic fragment of a book of which she disapproved in general. The "Hymn" describes the stars in their ardent and fixed course through the heavens: "They are all linked to one another by bonds that are virtues and powers, so that each depends on another and the other depends on all. The course of each is marked out and each finds its own course. It could not change course without making all the others deviate, each being involved with every other one. And each chooses the course it *was to* follow; what it is to do it must do willingly, and that course, which to us seems decreed in advance, is the preferred course for each, for each has an independent will. A dazzled love guides them; their choice determines laws and we are dependent on them; we cannot escape." Obviously the stars, enjoying freedom of choice and yet obeying predetermined laws, parallel the human lot. In effect Gide is here expressing the same thought that Goethe voiced in his *Dichtung und Wahrheit*: "A man may turn whither he pleases, and undertake anything whatsoever, but he will always return to the path that nature has once prescribed for him."

The individual must *will* to become the man he is ordained to be, must, in Édouard's words, follow his inclination *upward*. The true self is not achieved without a struggle; hence Bernard's wrestling with the angel. Furthermore, such self-realization must take into account the human community and our inevitable interdependence. In the struggle many succumb, whereas others elude the problem by compromise or falsification of their true personalities. The latter are the counterfeiters who pass off upon the world an artificial, social self with nothing but the appearance of the genuine. Terms like "counterfeit" or "fabricated personality" occur throughout the novel, into which—as a further reflection of the theme—Gide has mischievously introduced the minor plot of the boys who circulate false coins. The anarchistic Strouvilhou talks of demonetizing sentiments, and Bernard, on the other hand, longs to "ring true" in every circumstance of life. Édouard, fascinated by what *might be* rather than by what has been, says: "I lean vertiginously over the possibilities of each individual and weep over all that the lid of conventions atrophies."

That lid presses most heavily on the older people in the novel, the representatives of conservatism and members of bourgeois families. Indeed, one of the most obvious themes in *Les Faux-Monnayeurs* is that of the decay of the middle-class family, living as it does on false and empty principles and unable to stand the inevitable conflict between the generations. Bernard's family and Olivier's, both belonging to what was once known as the *noblesse de robe* or magistrature, are disintegrating rapidly, until Pauline Molinier can finally confess: "I wish I had never had any children!" Behind its façade of hypocrisy, the numerous Vedel clan is even more decayed at the heart, its adulterous Laura, pathological Armand, and facile Sarah all rebelling against the grandfather's blind benignity and the father's sanctimonious agitation. Even the limited group formed by the old music-teacher, La Pérouse (the most Dostoevskian of Gide's characters), his wife, and his grandson crumbles before our eyes. Finally, Robert de Passavant belongs to a wealthy, noble family whose instability we sense during the vivid scene when little Gontran keeps vigil over his father's body. To be sure, the only reason for introducing the father and Gontran is simply to provide one more example for the demonstration.

The family is indeed the social cell, as Paul Bourget, the defender of tradition, claimed; but it is also, Édouard insists, a prison cell. Édouard has no family, save for his half-sister Pauline and her sons, to whom he hardly behaves in the usual avuncular manner. He belongs to the parents' generation by age and to that of the children by temperament; not involved in the struggle, he can observe and comment from the sidelines. He is not quite dispassionate, however, for he shares the attitude of the original Ménalque who cried: "Families, I hate you!" and of Gide, who longed to see children raised by anyone but their own parents. Édouard reflects that "The future belongs to the bastards. What significance in the expression: *a natural child*! Only the bastard has a right to the natural." Bernard owes his initial liberation, as Lafcadio owed his exceptional liberty, to his illegitimacy; but, as we now know, this is but a beginning of a solution to their problem. Inasmuch as the real difficulty lies in *being free*, there is no easy, a priori solution; everyone must pass through a struggle and attain the conquest of himself.

The self-affirmation of the individual through painful strug-

gle inspired, after the *Faux-Monnayeurs*, two other major works
of André Gide which clearly show that this problem preoccupied
the writer to the very end of his career. The legends of Oedipus
and Theseus had been much in Gide's mind as early as 1910 and
1911; but he did not write his play *Œdipe*, until 1930 or finish
his narrative, *Thésée*, until 1944. The play was published and
presented in 1931, and the tale was first brought out in 1946;
yet they belong together, and the American and English publishers did well to present them in a single volume entitled *Two
Legends*.

Oedipus, knowing that he had been found abandoned on a
mountain-top without status or identity, thinks he is illegitimate
and glories in the fact: "Indeed, I don't mind knowing I am a
bastard," he tells his conservative brother-in-law Creon. "So
long as I thought I was the son of Polybus, I strove to ape his
virtues. What had I that had not first been in my fathers? I used
to say to myself. Heeding the lesson of the past, I expected from
yesterday alone my prompting and approval. Then suddenly
the thread broke. Sprung from the unknown; no more past, no
more model, nothing on which to lean; everything to create—
nationality and ancestors—to invent, to discover. No one to resemble but myself." Theseus, on the other hand, while encouraging the legend that he might have been engendered by Poseidon, recognizes King Aegeus as his father. And, when Theseus
ventures into the labyrinth to kill the Minotaur, Daedalus gives
him as a "tangible image of duty" a mysterious thread, saying:
"This thread will be your bond with the past. Return to it. Return to yourself. For nothing springs from nothing, and it is
on your past, on what you now are, that everything you will be
depends." Such a recommendation from the pen of André Gide
may well surprise at first.

As an image of our link with the past, Ariadne's thread had
long haunted Gide, who expresses a certain ambivalence in his
attitude toward such a bond. In 1911 he speaks of it as *le fil à
la patte*—"the apron-string, to express it vulgarly"—which

forces Theseus to return after conquering his enemy. A few months later Gide sees it as "the secret thread of an inner fidelity" which assures the hero as he ventures into the unknown. In 1927 Gide groups Creusa, Eurydice, and Ariadne as symbols of the timorous woman who checks that advance, pulling Theseus back and making Orpheus turn round, afraid "to let go and to see the thread break which ties her to her past." But, thirty years before that, in the *Nourritures terrestres*, he had used the symbol much as he was to do in *Thésée*: "Memory of the past had just enough power over me to give unity to my life: it was like that mysterious thread which bound Theseus to his past love without preventing him from walking through the newest landscapes. Even were that thread to be broken. . ."

In the case of Oedipus the thread *had* suddenly broken, much to the tragic hero's delight. Or so he thought at least until, discovering his identity, he learned at the same time of the dreadful crimes he had committed. He then exclaims: "What! Beyond the Sphinx this is what was hidden! . . . And I who congratulated myself on not knowing my parents! . . . As a result I married my mother, alas! alas! and with her all my past. Ah, now I know why my virtue was sleeping. In vain the future called me. Jocasta was drawing me backward. . ." Gide's Theseus, however, takes his precautions against the backward pull by insisting upon holding the spool in his hands and thus remaining master of his progress. Without self-knowledge he could not have done that; as he tells his son, Hippolytus: "It is first essential to understand fully who one is; then it will be fitting to take one's inheritance to heart and in hand."

On the contrary, the distinguishing feature of Gide's Oedipus, at the beginning of the play, is his ignorance of self. The entire tragedy, in fact, traces his evolution from happiness in ignorance to unhappy knowledge. The first act depicts almost exclusively his intellectual smugness, his pride, and his scorn of the gods. Whatever he is he has won by the strength of his arm and the cunning of his ready wit. As the drama progresses, the high-priest Tiresias shakes his assurance by introducing into his mind the germ of unrest. After the King of Thebes has vaunted to his sons his conquest of the Sphinx and pointed out that the individual's answer to all riddles must be *himself,* Tiresias scornfully asks if that is the final word of his wisdom. No, he replies, it is rather the beginning of his wisdom, but his sons must carry on from there; he will leave it to them to find the other words. Then it is that, suppressing any supernumerary to identify Oedipus as the son of Laius, Gide skilfully has the high-priest waken him to a recognition of his double crime by a series of pointed questions in the Socratic manner. By the end of the second act the King's happiness is seriously compromised and his assurance shaken, though he can still look back to his fateful encounter at the crossroads and proclaim that he turned from the road to the Delphic oracle and took the one leading to the Sphinx because he was no longer worried about his identity: "What can one seek from a God? Replies. I felt myself to be a reply to I knew not what question. It was the Sphinx's question."

Oedipus claims never to have sought happiness, and even to have fled it by rushing forth from the court of Polybus at twenty "with taut sinews and clenched fists." But now he is forty, and for twenty years, since the meeting with the Sphinx, has lain back in a comfort compounded of error and ignorance, the very vices he abhors. Theseus has the inestimable advantage of having been taught as a youth the value of effort and discipline. By advising him to raise rocks in order to find the arms Poseidon had hidden for him, his wise father developed at once his muscles and his will. In later life Theseus is grateful to Aegeus, saying: "To be sure, he did right to raise up my own reason against me. To that I owe everything I subsequently became, to having given up a carefree life, however delightful such a state of licence might be. He taught me that one achieves nothing great or valuable or lasting without effort."

Not only the entire teaching of Aegeus, but that of Gide him-

self in this regard, can be summed up in the advice given to the
adolescent Theseus: "Show men what one among them can be
and plans to become. There are great things to be done. Achieve
yourself." Nathanael heard this in the *Nourritures* and Michel
from Ménalque and Bernard from Édouard. Oedipus thought
that by his bold reply to the Sphinx he *had* achieved himself.
But the moment he sees that he has been deceived by the gods
into committing crimes predicted before his birth, he revolts.
Instead of submitting, as Tiresias would have him do, and beg-
ging absolution, this proud humanist inflicts his own punishment upon himself, a punishment as horrible as his unwitting
crimes. In order "to escape the enveloping god, to escape myself," as he says, he would like to "invent some mad deed which
will amaze you all, which will amaze myself, and the gods!"
Thus, having reached that point which he cannot surpass without bracing himself against himself and springing into the unknown, he willingly sacrifices himself.

Now, it happens that André Gide had frequently maintained
that the triumph of individualism lay in renouncing individuality, in willingly sacrificing the individual. He considered as the
secret of classicism this doctrine he had discovered in the Gospels; and he developed it most fully in his little green notebook
of meditations on the Gospels entitled *Numquid et tu . . .?*
There, under date of 4 March 1916, we read this personal interpretation of John, xii, 25: "He who loves his life, his soul—
who protects his personality, who is particular about the figure
he cuts in this world—shall lose it; but he who renounces it shall
make it really living, shall assure it eternal life; not eternal life
in the future, but shall make it already, even now, live in eternity." Is this not what Oedipus does when chastizing himself
and giving up his throne to become simply "a nameless wan-
derer who renounces his possessions, his fame, and himself"?

No sooner had Gide given his *Œdipe* to the printer than he
began to imagine an epilogue containing a dialogue between
Oedipus and Theseus—"a decisive meeting of the two heroes,

each measuring himself against the other, and throwing light, each in opposition to the other, upon their two lives." And in the last chapter of his *Thésée* Gide has brought about such a supreme encounter; nothing, incidentally, so obviously justifies joint publication and parallel treatment of the two legends. There blind Oedipus, the victim of the gods, vaunts the inner world he has discovered by blacking out the world of the senses and opening up infinite new perspectives. That spiritual realm beyond the senses he now knows to be the only true one. "All the rest," he adds, "is but an illusion, which abuses and beclouds our contemplation of the Divine."

Theseus, the conqueror of the Minotaur and builder of Athens, is eminently a materialistic, positive man of action. He is now the anti-mystic that Oedipus himself was before his self-immolation; and naturally he is unable to understand such superhuman wisdom. As a resolute "child of this earth," feeling no urge to establish more intimate contact with the Divine, he clearly judges that he has come off better than Oedipus in his life. But the reader is warned by an unmistakable note of smugness in his final speech that Gide's view of him is not devoid of irony. Heroic though he be, he lacks one element of true greatness: the suffering of which Oedipus says: "You are amazed that I put out my eyes; and I am amazed myself. But in that rash, cruel deed there is perhaps something else: some secret need or other to carry my fortune to the breaking-point, to outdo my suffering and fulfill a heroic destiny. Perhaps I vaguely foresaw the august and redeeming quality of suffering which makes the hero loath to avoid it."

In contrast to the intuitive, mystic wisdom of Oedipus, the down-to-earth philosophic naturalism of Theseus seems rather one-dimensional. Against the man of action Gide has set the contemplative man; against the pagan hero, the Christian ideal. In 1946 most critics, yielding to the temptation to identify author and creature which had led them astray in judging so many earlier works by Gide, saw Theseus as Gide and the final speech

as the aged author's spiritual testament. But we know Gide to
have been a creature of dialogue for whom it would have been
only natural to oppose once more, as he had done in Candaules
and Gyges, Saul and David, Michel and Alissa, Bernard and
Olivier, two facets of his own complex personality. It was doubtless to establish this final equilibrium that he wrote *Thésée*.

The two heroes are equally noble. Both have lived their
lives and achieved themselves through a long process of self-
integration. Thanks to his peculiar blend of energy and discipline, each one has got the best out of his rich possibilities and
followed his inclination upward. Each one remains in a state
of continual becoming by straining toward the perfection of
his type. Although Oedipus starts with certain handicaps unknown to Theseus, he eventually rises higher through sacrifice
and renouncing self. And, above all, each remains within his
own limitations, brooking no outside interference and relying
on no external help, for everything is within man, the wonder
that Sophocles celebrates in a passage of the *Antigone* which
Gide uses as an epigraph for his play. Thus the sophisticated
sons of Oedipus have discovered that, in their advanced state
of civilization, gods and monsters have forsaken the skies and
surrounding countryside to take up their abode in men. In the
same spirit the subtle Daedalus speaks of the need of escaping
an inner labyrinth peculiar to each individual who succumbs
to the intoxicating vapors that cause him to fashion his own
imbroglio. And even the God that Oedipus eventually recognizes—altogether in accord with Gide's mature credo as we
shall see—is a God within himself.

VIII. ICARUS: ESCAPE UPWARD

" 'Poor dear child,' said Daedalus. 'Since he thought he could not escape from the labyrinth and did not realize that the labyrinth was within him, at his request I fashioned him wings that might allow him to fly away. He considered that the only possible escape was upward, all terrestrial paths being blocked. I knew him to have a mystical propensity and was not surprised by his desire.' "

WHEN the prodigal returns home in rags, defeated and dejected, in Gide's *Retour de l'Enfant prodigue (The Prodigal's Return)*, he attempts to explain himself in a moving dialogue with his sympathetic and bewildered mother. To her question as to what drew him away from home, he replies: "I don't want to think of it any more: Nothing. . . Myself"; and when she asks what he was looking for he answers in characteristic Gidian terms: "I was seeking . . . who I was." Sweetly she implies that such a question involves no mystery since he is but the son of his parents and a brother to his brothers; but the prodigal insists that he never resembled his brothers. Finally he confesses: "Nothing is more fatiguing than realizing one's dissimilarity. That pursuit eventually tired me."

Thus the most universally admired, doubtless because the most indisputably beautiful, of André Gide's writings turns upon a theme central to his thought since the *Nourritures ter-*

testres of 1897. We know that the brief prose-poem was written during a fortnight in early 1907, at a time when the novel *La Porte étroite*, on which Gide had been working for at least two years, was not progressing satisfactorily. From the *Journals* we also know that it forms a dialogue of his "spiritual reticences and impulses." Furthermore, we now know what inspired him to rewrite the parable, for in a letter of 2 July 1907 to Christian Beck, which was not published until 1949, he related the circumstances. The ardent Catholic poet, Paul Claudel, having found it easy to convert Francis Jammes and thus lead a lost sheep back to the fold, had decided to tackle Jammes's friend, Gide. Not unaware of the latter's Protestant heredity and upbringing, yet misled by Gide's deep admiration for Claudel's poetry, the proselytizer went rather far both in letters and in conversations. At this point the pastoral poet of Orthez intervened by promising Gide to write a dithyrambic article on him to celebrate his conversion. To avoid a misunderstanding, Gide explained himself to Jammes, who, feeling that Gide was escaping, abandoned plans for his article. "Nonetheless," Gide continues, "understanding in the very marrow of my bones both the INTEREST of the step that Claudel and he wanted to see me take and also why I did not take it—and how, if I had taken it, I could have done so only in the way MY Prodigal Son returned HOME to help his younger brother to leave home—I wrote this little 'topical' work into which I put my whole heart but also my whole reason."

Such was the motivation in Gide's mind when he interrupted work on his novel to make a rapid trip to Berlin in January 1907 with the painter Maurice Denis. The only notes he consigned to his *Journals* about that journey concern the masterpieces he admired in the Kaiser Friedrich Museum, among them a youthful, mannered John the Baptist by Michelangelo eating something bitter that puckers his mouth, a David by Pollaiuolo the folds of whose cloak, with corners caught in his belt, are "raised almost immodestly," and a Magdalen

anointing the feet of Christ by Dierik Bouts, in which a kneeling
donor balances the figure of the saint.

The day after his return to Paris, his memory glowing with
such impressions, he began to write. It is not strange that he
should see his work in pictorial terms and begin with this moving presentation: "As was done in triptychs of old, I have
painted here, for my intimate joy, the parable related by Our
Lord Jesus Christ. Leaving diffuse and commingled the double
inspiration motivating me, I am not seeking to prove the victory
over me of any God—nor yet my own. Still, if the reader insists
on some reverence in me, perhaps he will not vainly seek it in
my painting, where, like a donor in the corner of the picture, I
have knelt down, a counterpart to the prodigal son and like him
my face at once smiling and bathed in tears."

To the parable as recorded by Saint Luke, Gide has added
the mother and the younger brother of the prodigal. In other
words, he has embroidered on the theme provided by the Gospel
just as he was accustomed to reworking mythology. Curious
principally about the psychology of the returned vagabond and
the effect he makes upon the household, Gide tells the tale in
a prologue and four dialogues with the four members of the
family. In the first part, the author clearly identifies himself
with the prodigal: "I imagine the Father's embrace; in the
warmth of such a love my heart melts. I imagine a preceding
distress, even; oh, I imagine whatever you will! I see it all
clearly; I am the very one whose heart beats rapidly when,
through the dip in the hill, he recognizes the blue roofs of the
house he forsook. What is keeping me from rushing homeward,
from entering?—I am expected. Already I see the fatted calf
being prepared. . . Stop! Be not too quick to set the table!—
Prodigal Son, I think of you; tell me first what the Father said
to you, next day, after the celebration. Ah, though the elder
son prompt you, Father, may I hear your voice, occasionally,
through his words!"

We do hear that voice, for the Father questions and gently

remonstrates, admitting that he has spoken harshly only because the elder brother had insisted upon this. He even goes so
far as to say: "I know what urged you forth; I was awaiting
you at the end of your path. Had you called me . . . I was
there." The elder brother, on the other hand, frankly scolds:
"I know what the Father said to you. It is vague. He no longer
explains himself very clearly, so that one can interpret his
words as one wishes. But I know his mind thoroughly. I am his
only interpreter to the servants, and whoever would understand
the Father must listen to me." The priest does not speak differently, nor the Church herself. Years later, Gide will note in his
Journals: "But just as Christ told us: 'No man cometh unto the
Father but by me,' the Church would like us not to be able to
reach Christ save through her. . ."

At the age of twenty-seven, in his reflections on "Christian
Ethics" Gide had already expressed amazement that Protestantism had not rejected "the oppressive institutions of St. Paul,
the dogmatism of his epistles, in order to derive from the Gospels alone." That opposition is a constant throughout his
thoughts on religion, whether he regards Protestantism or Catholicism (in which later attitudes and exegesis seem to him to
have obscured the purity of the Gospels). For many years he
planned to write a work entitled "Christianity against Christ,"
which he abandoned only through fear of saddening his friends
and compromising his cherished freedom of thought. In 1929
he seemed to sum up much of his *Retour de l'enfant prodigue*
by writing: "When I seek Christ I find the priest and behind the
priest, St. Paul."

If the Home in his version of the parable represents any
Church whatever and its orthodoxy, then the elder brother is its
priest, governing the household, laying down the law, and inter-
preting the words of the benign, forgiving Father. Through the
person of his prodigal, Gide clearly indicates his simultaneous
attraction toward God and his dislike for the institutions and
ministers of God. This is his answer to Claudel and Jammes.

And by endowing the prodigal with a half-forgotten younger brother (lovingly modelled on the Renaissance representations he had seen in Berlin), Gide could end his prose-poem most beautifully on a recall of his theme of evasion. As in the *Nourritures*, a burst pomegranate symbolizes far places and strange thirsts. The swineherd had brought one to the younger brother after having been away three days. The prodigal recognizes it at once for a wild pomegranate; though it slakes no thirst, its tartness makes one love one's thirst. By eagerly asking the prodigal if he knows where to pick it, the boy evokes in his brother a nostalgia for the nomadic life: "It is a little forsaken orchard that one reaches toward evening," he replies. "No wall any longer separates it from the desert. There a stream flowed; some half-ripe fruit hung on the branches." "What fruit?" asks the boy. "The same as in our garden; but wild. It had been very hot all day." Though the prodigal himself has returned shameful and resigned, he starts his younger brother on his way to adventure and independence, placing high hopes in him and wishing that he may never return.

Unfortunately the prodigal does not pass on to the departing boy his newly acquired knowledge that there is no need to return home to find the Father. Perhaps this is one of the things that each man must discover for himself. Yet the *Nourritures* had already proclaimed: "Do not long, Nathanael, to find God elsewhere than everywhere" and "Wherever you go, you can but encounter God. 'God,' said Ménalque, 'is what lies ahead of us.'" The God of that dithyramb is clearly a pantheistic deity, but the need for him expressed therein reveals a regular impulse of Gide's nature. When, on Easter of 1892, at the age of twenty-two, he foresees that he will soon again hurl himself into a "frantic mysticism," he is doubtless recalling the exasperated state in which he wrote the *Cahiers d'André Walter*.

Prayers fuse with tears, poetry, and music in that first book by the young writer. It is fed by a pervasive mysticism, quickened by sharing with the beloved Emmanuèle, by mingling their prayers, illustrating their adoration with readings of the poets, communing with nature. Almost as insistently stressed as the opposition between body and soul, another dichotomy—that of mind and soul—runs throughout the work. Repeatedly the hero repudiates reason, which leads only to bigotry and artificial mysticism, and philosophy, which fails to stifle his heart's longing for the true God. As he begins to fear madness, he spends all night on his knees praying. He knows the spiritual dryness familiar to the great mystics, but he also knows ecstasy in the effort to embrace God. From *Si le grain ne meurt . . .* we know that André Walter's experience of mysticism faithfully reflects that of Gide.

A few years later, midway between the *Cahiers* and the *Nourritures*, Gide is already accepting the Goethean ideal when he states: "The laws of nature are those of God: happy is he who can know them and follow them; what has he to do with commandments? The tables of the law are eternal, for they are within us. Moses breaks the tables and they nevertheless continue to exist." Such an argument, he admitted, seemed to him an excuse for not kneeling on a prayer-stool. But whether the young André Gide finds God in the Gospels, in himself, or diffuse in nature, he *must* find God somewhere and associate himself with the divine.

In the years following the *Nourritures*, *Saül*, and *L'Immoraliste*, Paul Claudel—recognizing both Gide's manifest qualities and his urgent spiritual exigency—undertook to convert him. Attacking directly after their decisive meeting of late 1905, Claudel readily upset Gide's fragile equilibrium. The dialogue between the ardent Catholic convert of 1886 who had made his faith the substance of his art and the liberated Calvinist who had fled orthodoxy in order to achieve a more personal union with Christ rises to such a pitch of intensity in their published correspondence that it stifles literary considerations. At times Gide agilely side-steps or withdraws into silence; at other times he makes advances, seeming to ask for peremptory

spiritual direction. In 1905 he wrote to Jammes that he longed
to see Claudel again and yet feared to importune him because
he had long ago lost the key to "a certain secret room" in which
alone he could receive the poet properly. That Claudel understood the prodigal son's reticences and sensed the presence of
that secret room is clear from his statement to Gide in 1911:
"One of these days we shall have to talk like those Dostoevsky
characters who say such confidential things to each other that
the next day they don't dare look at each other and are seized
with a mortal hatred for each other." They did eventually talk
in just such a manner and with precisely the results foreseen;
for, after being profoundly shocked by the *Caves du Vatican*
and the revelations following it, Claudel abandoned his rôle of
catechist.

At the most fervent height of his correspondence with
Claudel, however, André Gide wrote his second novel, *La Porte
étroite (Strait is the Gate)*. Its laborious composition, begun in
May 1905, kept him busy until October 1908, during which
time he was most appropriately reading and rereading Pascal,
for this was to be a novel of religious mysticism. Here, coming
between *L'Immoraliste* of 1902 and the *Caves du Vatican* of
1914, neither of which Claudel or Jammes liked, was a book
by Gide that they could admire. Soon after its periodical publication in the first three issues of *La Nouvelle Revue Française*
(February–April 1909), Jammes, specifically calling himself
a Roman Catholic, enthusiastically reviewed it at length in
L'Occident for July 1909 as "the masterpiece of one of our
greatest writers." Gide had already predicted to Claudel that
he would find it "furiously, deplorably Protestant," and, indeed, the orthodox poet, while admiring the very human drama
of Alissa, did object that its form was Protestant and even
quietistic in the extreme. On the other hand, as Gide pointed
out in his outline of a preface for the novel, no Protestant periodical reviewed it, doubtless because Protestant readers refused to recognize the Jansenist heroine, whose purely mystical

devotion is without social results. To such an objection Gide replied that he was portraying a character and not a type. Still it was possible for his close friend, Henri Ghéon, when reviewing the novel in early 1910 for *Vers et Prose* to say: "Other readers, hypnotized by the book's Jansenism [. . .], thought they saw in *La Porte étroite*, if not a decisive act of faith, at least an act of progress toward faith. Christianity could not fail to welcome soon an additional lost sheep."

Neither Ghéon nor Jammes was so alert to the imputations of heresy implied in the terms Jansenism and quietism as was Paul Claudel. To his objections Gide replied: "You recognize that a religious and pure emotion prompts my book; the second acknowledgment, which I consider equally important, is that the very drama of the book exists only by virtue of its unorthodoxy. [. . .] Protestantism is a school of heroism, the error of which I think my book depicts rather well; it lies precisely in that sort of superior infatuation, of heady scorn for all rewards that offends you, of gratuitous heroism *à la Corneille*. But it may be accompanied by real nobility, and I shall have accomplished enough if I induce someone like you to pity and to love—with a love involving some admiration—my Alissa." This the beautiful book did achieve. It must also have proved conclusively to those who knew the author that Gide himself had truly just lived through a period of spiritual anguish and felt a strong impulse toward mystical fusion with God.

It was too much to expect Alissa's mysticism to take an orthodox Roman Catholic form. Her entire background, like her creator's, was Calvinist; and, like him, to supplement her reading of the Gospels she turned first to the masterpieces of French literature. In the Jansenists Pascal and Racine—natural choices after all—she found a passive devotional contemplation congenial to her own spirit. The important thing for the novel is that her own words and thoughts should be enlivened by a pure religious emotion, which could only be a reflection of her author's. After rereading some Pascal and sketching out two of the novel's dialogues, in fact, Gide noted in his *Journals* one day in June 1908: "Sublime style—direct emanation from the heart; it is only through *piety* that it can be achieved."

The autobiographic element in the novel is large indeed. Probably no one has ever read the book, knowing also something of the author's life from his memoirs, without seeing the spiritual relationship of the two cousins Alissa and Jerome as reflecting that of Madeleine Rondeaux and André Gide. The death of Jerome's father when the boy is eleven, the sketch of his widowed mother, and the fuller portrait of Miss Ashburton faithfully reproduce the details of Gide's life. The adultery and eventual flight of Alissa's mother correspond to the facts about Madeleine's mother related in the memoirs. Juliette might be considered a composite of Madeleine's younger sisters, Jeanne and Valentine; and Abel Vautier shares traits of Gide's two best friends during adolescence, Marcel Drouin and Pierre Louÿs. The pages devoted to the estate of Fongueusemare rather faithfully describe that of Cuverville, where Madeleine grew up and her cousin André spent most of his vacations; the substitution of Havre for Rouen was an easy one to make. Like the author, Jerome had to be an intellectual, and it required no great effort to make of him a student at the École Normale Supérieure, which Drouin had attended. In fact, so much seems borrowed directly from Gide's own adolescence that the reader automatically identifies Jerome with Gide and Alissa with Madeleine, as Francis Jammes did in his review.

That, however, is a mistake. Twice in the little essay written after his wife's death and published in 1951 under the Latin title *Et nunc manet in te* Gide protests against identifying Alissa with her. After asserting that "She served me merely as a starting-point for my heroine and I do not think she recognized herself much in Alissa," he returns to the subject and exclaims: "But what a mistake anyone would make who thought that I had sketched her portrait in the Alissa of my *Porte étroite!*" What he does not add is that the reality of the Gide *ménage* at

Cuverville from 1918 until 1938 came more and more to copy the fiction of *La Porte étroite* (as it had already copied that of *L'Immoraliste*), until Madeleine Gide seemed actually aiming to prove the truth of Wilde's paradox that nature copies art. Or it might perhaps better be said simply that the novel anticipated reality in an almost eerie way. At the time it was written, however, *La Porte étroite* did not portray the relationship existing then between André and Madeleine Gide. The author had merely borrowed from his past certain external facts to serve as framework of the novel.

Obviously Alissa is not Madeleine, because she actually *is* André Gide. As Flaubert said of his famous Emma Bovary, Gide might have proclaimed: *"Alissa, c'est moi!"* And just as Flaubert took for starting-point a banal case of provincial adultery occurring in a Norman community named Ry or Buchy, so Gide started from his recollection of his own rarefied love for his cousin during the André Walter period of his life. Since all the interest in the novel concentrates on Alissa, leaving Jerome the shadowy rôle of narrator and flabby foil to her noble aspirations, Gide could pour into her all his own adolescent yearnings toward heroism through abnegation.

Immediately upon finishing the manuscript he wrote to Claudel saying that he had had trouble disentangling from himself this story he had carried within him so many years. "And perhaps," he added, "you will be able to guess the secret element of confession that will enlighten you as to that childhood which you may have thought oppressed but which was so only by religion and ethics—or, as you will prefer, by Protestantism."

In other words, André Gide confesses himself in Alissa exactly as he had earlier confessed himself in Michel. The hero of *L'Immoraliste* represented one of the author's buds or dormant eyes isolated and brought to a monstrous flowering; similarly the heroine of *La Porte étroite* personifies another of his latent possibilities. And in like manner Gide here carries that potentiality to the point of excess, thus purging himself of it.

This is what he could not say to Claudel or Jammes or, even later, to any of his Catholic friends or critics.

According to his original theory of subjective objectivity, he had first to become the person he wanted to portray—that is, simply to isolate the latent mystic in him until he *was* Alissa, obsessed with sainthood and defining virtue as resistance to love. "I am Proteus," he wrote to Christian Beck a year after having finished the novel. "To maintain one's own style through such misleading transformations is the problem. But I believe that it is essential to admire here not so much the style as the transformation (if however I merely *lend* myself without compromising myself) and that the best of me lies in a gift of profound sympathy. Either I remain on the outside or else, if I penetrate another, I do so subterraneously. Whence, moreover, my need of narrating my tales in the first person. This 'I' is for me the height of objectivity. In *La Porte étroite* I consider this to have been a veritable *tour de force*, the feat of a human serpent slipping into a lamp chimney; that was *my* strait gate from which I came forth somewhat aching, not altogether dislocated after all, marvelously supple and clinging to myself." That feat might seem to apply to his succeeding in putting himself in the place of the flaccid Jerome who narrates the story, but elsewhere he had confessed to Claudel, referring to the *N. R. F.* periodical publication in three instalments, that "the first two parts are there to explain Alissa's journal which is, I believe, the best thing I have written. . ." We must not forget that there are *two* first persons in the novel and that even in Jerome's account the most interesting bits are the words of Alissa which he quotes. Even to Gide the book seemed like a nougat containing good almonds (Alissa's journal and letters) surrounded by a pasty filling.

It has become traditional to admire *La Porte étroite* at the expense of *L'Immoraliste* or vice versa, as if the technique were not the same in both. But repeatedly André Gide insisted that the two works belonged together and that the two subjects grew

up together in his mind, "the excess of one finding a secret permission in the excess of the other and the two together estab-
lishing a balance." Really the two novels ought to be published
under a single cover in order to be read together as two aspects
of the same problem. Whereas the one exposes the dangers of
individualism the other reveals the pitfalls of renunciation.

The moment he had finished writing *La Porte étroite*, Gide
told Claudel that the very idea of the book implied its criticism
within it, and Claudel, after a first reading, commented that it
contained. "a Dantesque suavity, but, beneath this, something
dreadfully bitter, I dare not say desperate." This shows that the
Catholic poet sensed, though he probably did not want to define,
Gide's act of catharsis. On the other hand, Henri Ghéon, Gide's
almost constant companion at the time, does not hesitate to state
in his review: "At the origin of *La Porte étroite*, however amazing that may seem, is found a satirical intent: the satire of self-
sacrifice. Yet what a tone of sincerity and affirmation rings forth
in the novel. The novelist has been won over by his heroine; he
has contracted her madness. Whether Alissa, Michel, or Candaules is involved, whether at first he condemns or approves his
creatures, as soon as he has begun to paint he has lost the power
to judge." A year later to a correspondent who, rejoicing over
an evolution in his work, had contrasted the second novel with
the first, Gide, perhaps thinking of Ghéon's remarks, had replied that *L'Immoraliste* offered a critique of anarchy whereas
there had been seen in *La Porte étroite* "a critique of Protestantism or of Christian abnegation (and saying critique is not saying satire—I am using this word in the sense in which Kant
could entitle his books 'Critique of . . .')."

The criticism is there as patently as in *L'Immoraliste*. No
matter how sympathetically and eloquently Gide presents Alissa's intense mysticism, he also makes clear how empty and useless it is. Besides thwarting Jerome without his complete consent,
it even fails to bring her satisfaction, and she dies miserably
alone, abandoned even of God. That she should spontaneously

think of sacrificing herself to her younger sister or to her lonely father is comprehensible and beautiful. That she should flee the brutalities of life as a result of the psychic trauma she had received in childhood and through fear of resembling her Creole mother is excusable. But after her sister has married and her father has died, when time has softened the recollection of her mother's sin, she should be freed from her scruples and inhibitions. Yet it is when she is most free that she feels most bound, when her sacrifice has become purely symbolic and gratuitous that she clings to it most tenaciously.

She has convinced herself that God has reserved her and Jerome for something better and nobler; "Not happiness but holiness!" she exclaims. In her diary, however, she reveals another, less attractive, motivation for continuing her sublime sacrifice. Finding Juliette surprisingly happy in her marriage, Alissa suffers to see that her sister did not need her sacrifice to attain happiness. Then she wonders if that sacrifice was really consummated in her heart. "I am as if humiliated that God no longer requires it of me. Was I then not capable of it?" she asks herself. At this juncture it is natural and quite in character for Alissa to continue in the path of renunciation just to prove, to God and to herself doubtless, that she *is* capable of doing so. Thus she provides Gide with a striking example of apparent virtue prompted by an egotistical motive.

That little clue lies buried in Alissa's diary, which comes to Jerome after her death, and nothing indicates that it opens his understanding of her. Many a reader may have missed it, to be sure. But whether one attributes her withdrawal from life and quest of God to a desire to prove her sincerity or to an obsessive need to flee the example of her mother, the motive remains selfish. And in any case she has ruined two lives that might have been happy and fruitful in marriage.

In the person of Alissa, André Gide has given free rein to his own impulse toward mysticism and pictured its futility. Little does it matter that the mysticism is heterodox; the point is that it is the mysticism he himself felt and might have in-dulged if he had not purged himself of it in this "critical" novel. We now appreciate better what he meant when he said that into *Le Retour de l'enfant prodigue* he had put his whole heart *but also* his whole reason. As Édouard was to say in *Les Faux-Monnayeurs*: "The forest shapes the tree. So little space is left for each! How many abortive buds! Each tree puts forth its boughs where it can. Most often the mystical branch results from stifling. There is no escape but upward." Gide, however, had his own ways of avoiding stifling, and the best of these was recourse to his own keen critical spirit. When the pressure became too great, as in the midst of writing *La Porte étroite*, he took time out and wrote a brief and beautiful rejection of orthodoxy in *Le Retour de l'enfant prodigue*. And when he had finally finished his novel, he could turn to other, very different novels such as *Isabelle* and *Les Caves du Vatican*, having put the mystical temptation behind him.

Yet his impulse toward mysticism did not altogether die, for in January 1916 he noted in his *Journals*: "I can believe in God, believe God, love God, and my whole heart inclines me to do so. I can make my heart dominate my mind. But, I beg you, don't look for proofs and reasons. That is where man's imperfection begins; and I felt myself to be perfect in love." Indeed, it was during the anguished years of the First World War that André Gide attained the highest point of mystical fervor of his life and maintained himself at that pitch for three years. This we know from his meditation on the gospels, which he entitled *Numquid et tu . . .?* when it was published anonymously in an edition of but seventy copies in 1922 and again in a trade edition in 1926. He took the title from John, vii, 52: "Art thou also of Galilee?"

In that special little green notebook, a sincere prayer to God to help him rise above his doubts and spiritual dryness, to which he kept adding between 1916 and 1919, Gide called on God's lightning love to "consume or vitrify all the opacity of my flesh, everything mortal that I drag after me!" He declared: "I am bored with everything in which I do not feel your presence and recognize no life that is not inspired by your love." Once he had begun to express what he asserts that he had put off writing for so many years, this man who was soon to be looked upon by many as a diabolic perverter sounded like St. John of the Cross. His friend Charles Du Bos, himself a Catholic convert, did not fear to state that *Numquid et tu . . .?* occupies in Gide's work the same place that the *Mystery of Jesus* does in Pascal's.

The unpardonable sin from the point of view of Du Bos, as doubtless from that of most Catholics was withholding the public, signed edition of this little spiritual journal until 1926 when it could appear simultaneously with the shocking personal revelations of *Si le grain ne meurt. . .* And, to make clear that he was no longer in the state of mind that had produced *Numquid*, Gide prefaced his meditations and prayers with a brief Foreword stating: "I am neither a Protestant nor a Catholic. I am simply a Christian. And as a matter of fact, I do not want anyone to make a mistake as to the testimonial value of these pages. Most likely I should still sign them today quite willingly. But, written during the war, they contain a reflection of the anguish and confusion of that period; and if, probably, I should still sign them, I should perhaps not still write them." Yet there was a certain justice in that double publication of 1926 (the same year, by the way, that saw the first edition of *Les Faux-Monnayeurs*), inasmuch as both works were composed of confessions, the one of a physical and the other of a spiritual nature. Quite possibly in their author's mind they were intended to strike a balance, and everything would seem to indicate that the revelations it cost him most to make were those regarding the spiritual state; for at that very time he stated that "the soul's recesses are and must remain more secret than the secrets of the heart and of the body."

No one who had read *La Symphonie pastorale* (*The Pastoral*

Symphony) of 1919 could have had any doubts as to the permanent "testimonial value" of *Numquid*. For that novelette, written during the year of 1918, contains the criticism of the very mysticism Gide was simultaneously expressing in his little green notebook. Coming after the *Caves du Vatican*, this tale seems rather an anachronism in his work; we know, incidentally, that the idea had been in his mind before his thirtieth year. Anyone who wonders why a realization that had been so long postponed finally forced itself upon the writer in 1918 will find the answer in a juxtaposition of *La Symphonie pastorale* with *Numquid et tu . . . ?* When he had almost finished the work of fiction, Gide noted in his *Journals* under date of 16 October 1918: "Today I have the greatest difficulty getting interested again in the state of mind of my minister, and I fear that the end of my book may suffer from this. In an effort to give life to his thoughts again, I have gone back to the Gospel and Pascal. But at one and the same time I long to recapture a state of fervor and I do not want to be taken in by it; I pull on the reins and wield the whip at the same time; and this produces nothing worth while." In the last remark he was wrong, for only by the co-existence of such contrary impulses could he have infused life into his fictional Pastor and at the same time have implied a judgment of him.

As in the other narrative works, André Gide has put himself into the Pastor with his lamentably good intentions, his sanctimonious hiding behind the Scriptures, and his blind self-deception. Thanks to his strict Calvinist background, Gide was most familiar with the moral climate that he evokes here. And all his life he had had a passion for teaching—like the Pastor who admits in an unguarded moment that he had promised himself great pleasure from educating his blind charge. Futhermore, Gide had spent the winter of 1894 in the icy Jura Mountains at inhospitable La Brévine, the scene he chose for his narrative.

Frequently the author has revealed the intention behind *La Symphonie pastorale*. At the same time that he referred to *La*

Porte étroite as "the criticism of a certain mystical tendency," he called the later fiction the criticism of "a form of lying to oneself." Later, adapting his terms to the Catholic priest to whom he was writing, he spoke of it as criticizing the dangers of "the free interpretation of the Scriptures." But the most revealing comment is found in a note on the Pastor inserted into a letter to an American scholar: "Through him, rather than trying to express my own thought, I have depicted the pitfall to which my own doctrine might lead, when that ethic is not rigorously checked by a critical spirit constantly on the alert and little inclined to self-indulgence. The indispensable critical spirit is completely lacking in the Pastor."

The Pastor's reading of the Scriptures corresponds exactly with that of *Numquid*. Capital passages of the little tale he narrates seem direct transpositions of the then unpublished spiritual meditation. Refusing to teach blind Gertrude the Epistles of Saint Paul, he raises her on the Gospels, in which he fails to see commandments or prescriptions. He considers the state of joy as not only natural but even mandatory for the true Christian. When Gertrude, cured of her physical blindness, discovers "the law" through reading St. Paul, tragedy ensues and everyone falls a victim to the Pastor's unconscious hypocrisy. Into the revealing, catalytic argument between the Pastor and his son Jacques, Gide has brought over almost unchanged the *Numquid* reflections dated 21 February 1916 about chapter xiv of the Epistle to the Romans.

Thus, around the Pastor who personifies the faith Gide had just voiced in his *Numquid et tu . . .?* but who utterly lacks the critical spirit that saved Gide, he constructed a parable of blindness in which the spiritual blindness is so much more dangerous than the physical blindness. Subtly yet emphatically by repetition, he established a parallel between Gertrude's actual blindness, her state of innocence, and the Gospels on the one hand, and, on the other, lucidity, the state of sin, and the Epistles.

Again André Gide had written a "critical" work to balance

the fervor that had almost swept him off his feet. The relationship of *La Symphonie pastorale* to *Numquid et tu . . .?* is precisely the same as that of *Saül* to the *Nourritures terrestres*: that of corrective or antidote. Thus Gide refused to relinquish any of his contrary tendencies, preferring rather to orchestrate throughout his work their various voices. Yet, apparently unmindful of this connection, friends and critics alike expected Gide to become converted after *Numquid*. Charles Du Bos laid great stress on a journal-entry of 1916 which figured in the original edition: "The three calls have the same sound: 'It is time. It is high time. It is no longer time.' So that you do not distinguish one from the other and already the third is sounding while you still think you are at the first." It was in 1922, the year of that first, limited issue of *Numquid*, that Mauriac prefaced a reprint of *La Tentative amoureuse* with these words, strangely sympathetic from the pen of so Catholic a writer: "Doubtless Claudel and Jammes, those good shepherd-dogs, scold and worry this lost sheep who carries his taste for conversion to the point of being converted every day to a different truth. Let us try, however, to understand in Gide a case of terrible sincerity: no trace in him of what Stendhal calls hypocrisy when he finds it in the men of the seventeenth century. It is true that the choice of a doctrine obliges us, at those moments when forces in us disown it, to continue doing it lip-service, until the return of grace. Gide is the man who would never be resigned to influencing, even for a moment, the automaton."

Gide himself admitted, a few years later: "I would not swear that at a certain period of my life I was not very close to being converted. Thank God, a few converts among my friends took care of this, however. Jammes, or Claudel, or Ghéon, or Charlie Du Bos will never know how instructive his example was for me." Indeed, the number and, most often, the quality of André Gide's friends who were Roman Catholic converts cannot fail to impress anyone who studies the first half of the twentieth century in France. Paul Claudel figures among them chiefly as a converter rather than as a convert because he himself heard the call as an adolescent in the eighties, long before Gide and the others knew him. After 1900, his religious zeal and Gide's admiration for his poetry misled them both for a time into thinking that they shared the same fervor, whereas Gide was drawn less by Holy Communion than by the desire to commune with a fellow-poet of different formation.

The first of Gide's literary friends to rally to Rome was Francis Jammes, like Claudel a few months older than he. In 1893 the two young writers were drawn together by a mutual affinity that kept them corresponding for three years before they met. They finally met in North Africa in 1896 during the Gides' wedding trip, on one of the very few occasions in life when the rustic poet allowed himself to be drawn far from his native Pyrenees. Jammes's monumental vanity and neurotic susceptibility were not tempered by his conversion in 1905. His increasing smugness, on the other hand, led to renewed clashes, and when for reasons of economy and spiritual hygiene, Gide followed the example of Ménalque and sold a large part of his library on the eve of setting out for the Congo in 1925, disposing of thirty-one autographed books and many manuscripts given him by Jammes, it was clear that the two writers had nothing more in common. Yet a few letters followed between them and the poet's death in 1938, the most astounding being that of 1931 in which Jammes asked permission to entitle his crude satire of Gide as *Lantigyde* (*The Anti-Gide*) and then expected his victim, without having seen the text, to find it a publisher in Paris!

In 1903 a young naval officer, Pierre Dominique Dupouey, deeply shaken by the *Nourritures terrestres,* came to Gide, acknowledging him as his liberator. By avocation he was a poet, essayist, and painter; a passionate admirer of English poetry and of the ancient Greeks, he was also a pianist and lover of music. The intellectual affinity between the two men was deep and many-sided. Gide introduced him to, among other things, the work of Claudel. In 1911 Dupouey married the devout and intelligent Mireille de La Ménardière, and his conversion to Roman Catholicism dated from about the same time. His son was born in 1913 at about the time that he joined the royalist Action Française movement. After spending the first months of the war on naval patrol in the Adriatic, he succeeded in getting transferred to commanding marines on the front line in the north of France, where he was killed in early April 1915. André Gide edited and prefaced his beautifully spiritual letters to his young wife, first published in 1922, with the admission that Dupouey's mysticism had echoed in him.

If he who had originally offered himself as a disciple had such an influence upon the "master," he exerted an even more decisive one upon Gide's closest friend, Henri Ghéon. For Ghéon, who had met Dupouey at the front in January 1915 and seen him only a few times, was actually converted through the example of the naval lieutenant's life and death. Gide and Ghéon had met in the mid-nineties when the one was about twenty-six and the other twenty. By the time of the First World War, Ghéon had shared an apartment with Gide in Paris, traveled with him in North Africa, Turkey, Italy, and Greece, prowled with him on the boulevards until early morning, and shared literary and artistic enthusiasms. Shortly before Ghéon left for the front at the end of 1914, Gide had a dream of his friend's conversion. That premonition seemed all the more preposterous because the young doctor had always professed a cynical incredulity and because Gide, annoyed at his deliberate refusal to read the Gospel, had vainly tried to get him to recognize Christ's teaching. His conversion was sudden. After the war the Ghéon who had distinguished himself as a young critic and had been closely associated with the founding of the *Nouvelle Revue Française* and the Vieux-Colombier theatre became a prolific writer of edifying miracle plays and syrupy hagiology.

The loss of Henri Ghéon as a constant companion struck Gide with particular force. In the long list of books that flowed from the convert's pen, there was never again a single one that Gide could wholeheartedly admire. The two men never broke off relations; they merely drifted apart, and in May 1917 Gide noted in his *Journals*: "I stiffen myself against grief, but it seems to me at times that Ghéon is more lost to me than if he were dead. He is neither changed nor absent; he is confiscated."

Nothing indicates that Gide was as deeply touched by the conversion of Jacques Rivière or that their relationship was in any way changed by it. The twenty-three-year-old Rivière met Gide in 1909, when the latter was approaching forty. At once Gide, struck by the young man's exceptional intellectual qualities and his spiritual eagerness, encouraged him to write for the recently founded *N. R. F.* His participation in the review rapidly grew in importance until he soon became managing editor under the general editorship of Jacques Copeau. Within the first months of the war, Rivière was taken prisoner; during four years of prison camp in Germany he wrote several moving essays, a spiritual autobiography, and a penetrating analysis of the German character. On his return to Paris in 1919, he became editor-in-chief of the *N. R. F.*, to which he devoted himself unstintingly until his untimely death in 1925.

Rivière had begun corresponding with Claudel, a consul in far-away China, in 1907; their stimulating exchange has been published in English under Claudel's name as *Letters to a Doubter*. Finally on Christmas day of 1913 he entered the Catholic Church. In the fat volume of homage which the *N. R. F.* devoted to him soon after his death, Gide wrote: ". . . certain people have striven to see Rivière as my disciple. We have been blamed—I for exerting a pernicious influence over him and he for not being able to protect himself against it. This showed ignorance of us both. [. . .] Rivière was one of those whose ever anxious conscience expects criticism from a friend rather than praise. He liked to be in opposition and to feel that others were in opposition to him. [. . .] The story of our relationship is that of our discussions." The critic Albert Thibaudet likewise defended him several years later against the myth created by Henri Massis of Rivière as a strangely respectable disciple of a perverse and satanic Gide; Thibaudet did this simply by pointing out how the young writer resisted influence and that, in any case, Claudel touched him much more deeply.

Rivière's Catholicism, which sacrificed none of his human qualities, in turn led Jacques Copeau back to Rome. Seven years older than Rivière, he had become enthusiastic for the *Nourritures terrestres* in 1901 and had met Gide the following year. During his years of literary apprenticeship as a perspicacious drama critic and even during his editorship of the *N. R. F.* and his Stanislavski-like revolution in the French theatre, he had remained an agnostic. One has only to consult the index of the *Journals* to see what a close friend of André Gide he was in those years. After the war he was tending toward a renewal of faith when Rivière's death, added to the example of such friends as Claudel, Charles Péguy, and Ghéon, led to a spiritual revaluation and gradual "conversion" in the years 1925–6.

The similar case of Charles Du Bos is complicated by the fact that he wrote a *Dialogue avec André Gide*, the deepest probing of Gide's mind that had been attempted, and underwent conversion to Roman Catholicism during its writing. The painfully sensitive, subjective critic (who reminds the reader of an amalgam of Walter Pater and H.-F. Amiel) and the complex modern moralist shared such a multitude of interests and yet offered such sharp differences in temperament that their dialogue cannot but fascinate. It is recorded not only in the comprehensive study of Gide that appeared in 1929, but also in the pages of Gide's *Journals* and the many volumes of Du Bos's *Journal*, to which must be added the collection of the letters they exchanged between 1911 and 1935. From the time when Du Bos wrote to Gide in English: ". . . more and more you are the only friend with whom it is possible to communicate on anything that is really deep down" to the moment in August 1929 when he fell into Gide's arms sobbing over the pain his book had caused his friend, we can follow the course of an enthralling private conversation that could not endure becoming public.

In addition to such close friends of André Gide, many others in the literary ranks went over to Rome, a few before 1914 and many more after 1918. Among the first, Jacques Maritain, the philosopher, and the poets Charles Péguy and Max Jacob were at most but acquaintances of Gide; Valery Larbaud, the subtle author of *Enfantines* and creator of *A. O. Barnabooth*, was a friend and an early contributor to the *N. R. F.*, but he was never a daily companion like Ghéon or literary associate like Rivière and Copeau. After the war, when conversion became epidemic, there were many sensational and not always lasting recantations. Inasmuch as Gide had long known Jean Cocteau and as both Maurice Sachs and René Schwob conferred with him and wrote books on him, he certainly was aware of their cases. Doubtless some thought of those younger men as disciples of Ménalque and brothers of Lafcadio—especially when Sachs was rumored to have wriggled out of his seminarist's cassock on the beach at Juan-les-Pins to reveal pink bathing trunks.

Gide may well have been thinking of such examples and the element of scandal connected with some of them when he wrote in his *Journals* in 1933: "There is not one of these conversions in which I do not discover some shameful secret motivation: fatigue, fear, blighted hope, malady, sexual or sentimental impotence." Four years later he doubtless had in mind several of his most intimate friends as well when he noted in a spirit of greater charity: "No, it is not exactly a fashion, for fashion comes from the outside, though responding to unconscious inner demands. But I believe that the war left all minds in a semi-emotional disposition particularly vulnerable to that sort of contagion."

Yet, feeling as he did, André Gide apparently made no effort to discourage his friends; he even actively encouraged at least Dupouey and Rivière. He did so probably because he could so readily appreciate their motives and put himself in their place.

Twice, in fact, he blames his self-doubt and intellectual modesty for having made him go to great lengths to understand the Catholic point of view and thus be unduly tolerant. An example of such tolerance can be seen in his suppression from *Numquid* of everything that the most orthodox Catholic could not approve.

In turn some of his converted friends became converters and attempted to proselytize him, encouraged by feeling in him a deep and permanent nostalgia for faith, which made him say in 1929 that he could slip into mystical ideas as into old slippers and feel at ease in them. Indeed, he was as keenly aware of his nostalgia as was anyone else and he struggled against it. "There are certain days," he confessed in a deliberately shocking image, "when, if I merely let myself go, I should roll directly under the Lord's Table. They think it is pride that withholds me. Not at all! It is intellectual integrity." By the mid-twenties, whatever his thwarted need for faith, he had taken his stand against the mysticism of his youth and of the war years.

To enter the palace of faith, he felt, one had to check too much at the entrance—even one's reason and *raison d'être*. He could admire Oedipus without being capable of deliberately blinding himself to achieve the inner illumination that guided Tiresias. "Under whatever form it appears," he wrote in 1927, "there is no worse enemy than mysticism. I have reason to know." Then he gives his definition of mysticism: "Whatever presupposes and requires the abdication of the reason." Four years later he defines it as "any blind belief." He resents the Roman Catholic monopoly of religious aspiration and the confusion of spirituality with mysticism. In other words, he would like to be allowed to be spiritual without having that impulse lead inevitably to Rome.

For many years certain ill-advised Catholic critics had regularly denounced Gide's work, personality, and influence. It was such attacks that strengthened his position of opposition and eventually made religious conversion impossible. Without them, he might never have become the enemy of the Church that he was in his later years. "I am not indifferent, or luke-warm," he stated as early as 1929, "and all my former fervor today turns against them. The conviction I have, which they force me to have, that their doctrine is mendacious and their influence harmful does not permit my mind that accommodating tolerance which people are too much inclined to believe a natural accompaniment of freethought." These remarks were written soon after Charles Du Bos's study of Gide, begun in admiration, had turned into an indictment.

No defection, however, could have caused André Gide such acute suffering as that of his beloved wife. That Madeleine, who represented his link with the past, whose very presence constantly reminded him of his Calvinist upbringing, should be drawn to Catholicism just when he was assuring his stand against Rome must have seemed a betrayal. To Claudel in 1911 he had described the obstacle to his conversion as lying less in heredity than in the "admirable, holy figures" who had surrounded his childhood and kept vigil over him; those "relatives and elders" who had lived in such perfect communion with God seemed to insist upon his fidelity to his early faith. Was not Madeleine Rondeaux one of those figures?

Both her sisters married Catholics, and in 1911 at Pau the widowed Valentine Gilbert joined the Roman Church herself. But in marrying her cousin André Gide, the eldest sister had remained within her communion. Little by little, nevertheless, she was drawn toward Catholicism. The influence of her best friend Agnès Copeau whose daughter Edi entered the Benedictine Missionary Order, and perhaps even more an unconscious protest against her husband may have given direction to her spiritual evolution, for as Gide wrote in 1922: "In Christianity, and each time that I plunge into it again, it is always she that I am pursuing. She feels this perhaps; but what she feels above all is that I do so to tear her away from it." Four years later he consigned the following bitter words to his *Journals*: "The slow progress of Catholicism on her soul; it seems to me that I am watching the spreading of a gangrene. Every time I come back, after having left her some time, I find new regions affected, deeper, more secret regions, forever incurable. And, if I could, would I attempt to *cure* her? That health that I would offer her, mightn't it be mortal to her? [. . .] And everything that constitutes my *raison d'être*, my life, becomes foreign and hostile to her." If the situation existing at Cuverville in the twenties and thirties reminds us of the tension between Michel and Marceline in *L'Immoraliste*, we must remember that the novel appeared in 1902 and was thus an anticipation. Furthermore, Mme Gide, whatever her intimate convictions, never entered the Catholic Church.

Eventually Gide must have come to accept more willingly his wife's growing Catholic devotion, for in an essay on Montaigne first published in 1929 he reflects on the death-bed conversion of skeptics which so often seems to give the lie to the work of a lifetime. He can readily accept such a contradiction when it is motivated by a desire to ease the suffering of a loving wife, since then the unbeliever yields "through affection, and the more willingly the more wrongs he is aware of having committed against her." Again in September 1948, on the eve of his seventy-ninth birthday, he recalls Paul Valéry's anger at the importance given to last-minute recantations, adding that he himself has so much respect for the sentiments involved in such a case that he would not resist. "And what more would that prove than, most likely, a great conjugal love, which is certainly worth sacrificing something to; that something, after all, not having so much importance when it is given the lie by the entire work." But at the time when he wrote these conciliatory words the problem was no longer a vital one for him, his wife having preceded him in death.

Certainly there is significance in the fact that so many of André Gide's closest friends were converted to Catholicism. It would be impossible to name any other figure of modern literature, not himself a convert, surrounded by a group of immediate associates who were so nearly unanimously drawn to a fervent and active faith. When the polemicist Henri Béraud violently attacked Gide and the whole group of the *Nouvelle Revue Française* under the title of *La Croisade des longues figures* (*The Crusade of the Long-Faced Men*), he was singularly ill-advised. For his thesis that the austere classicism and cult of authenticity preached by the review was a kind of Calvinist plot simply will not bear examination. The only Protestant in the group beside Gide (if, indeed, he could still have been considered one) was Jean Schlumberger. Rather, what annoyed Béraud and other journalists of the Paris boulevards, though they could never have said so, was the combination of uncompromising intellectualism and profound respect for spiritual values apparent in each issue of the *N. R. F.* Yet Béraud was right in sensing that, whatever were the qualities and shortcomings of the review, they were communicated to it by its founder and "gray eminence," André Gide.

A single fact, doubtless, can explain at one and the same time why there were so many converts in Gide's circle and why the Catholics who were stalking him never quite gave up hope of capturing him. The explanation lies in Gide's own spirituality, which involved also an extraordinary susceptibility to spiritual qualities in others. His mobile antennae quivered delicately in all directions and he was irresistibly drawn to those in whom he sensed a possibility of the same anxiety that tormented him. Born an ardent Christian, liberated from the dogma but not from the Scriptures, acutely sensitive to the voice of his own conscience, he constantly renewed the debate, keeping it alive also in others. Furthermore, the man who confesses to a friend usually elicits confessions by awaking an automatic impulse to emulation; and Gide's voice, low and vibrant with emotion and directed to each individually, always seemed to emerge from the grill of the confessional. As François Mauriac wrote, he was "conscious of the current of grace kept eddying about him by the successive conversions of his friends." Though he suffered from some of those conversions and even deplored them, he must have recognized in some deep recess of his soul that they were encouraged by the attitude of interrogation and receptivity he maintained in himself and in those who approached him. As late as 1941 he could still note in his *Journals*: "It is much rather a question of transparency of the soul that allows us to feel Him. The majority of men do not know that *state of communion*; but it brings the soul, the entire being, such a delightful felicity that the soul is inconsolable after once having known it and then allowed it to slip away. This is partly what makes me, without believing in any definite God, really enjoy only the company of pious souls."

Gide's sensitivity to the call of faith was certainly quickened by an acute feeling of guilt instilled in him during his puritanical upbringing. In the depths of intellectual torpor and spiritual dissatisfaction in 1905 he noted: "How can I call absurd a rule of conduct that would have protected me against this? At one and the same time my reason condemns it and calls out for it in vain. If I had a father confessor, I should go to him and say: Impose upon me the most arbitrary discipline and today I shall say it is wisdom; if I cling to some belief that my reason mocks, this is because I hope to find in it some power against myself." Then he added in a new paragraph: "As soon as a healthy day comes along, I shall blush at having written this." In part at least, then, Gide's yearning for faith, like his marriage, expressed a need for a protection against himself or a veto of the worst in himself. That yearning rose to the surface periodically, as we have seen, because it depended on the state of his physical and mental health. Each time that his psychosomatic condition dropped below a certain point of vitality, Gide became subject to a strong mystical urge.

Those moments were frequent in his life, and in the intervals between them he did not entirely forget them. This is what permitted Lieutenant Dupouey to write him in 1908: ". . . of all my friends you are the only man so tyrannically haunted by a faith—or by nostalgia for a faith." Claudel felt the same need in Gide; after *Numquid*, he wrote from Tokyo, where he was Ambassador of France, that Gide's tenacious concern with faith showed he was subject to divine grace, which had already brought about such transformations in him. Finally, as late as 1926, Claudel could still write in the last letter he was to address to Gide: "Your course is not finished; you are one of those whose existence has the value of a parable, who fully realize an evolution of which others merely suggest the crude start, and this is indeed one of the reasons for the interest I take in you, in which anxiety plays as large a part as hope. You are the stake, the actor, and the stage of a great struggle of which it is impossible for me to foresee the conclusion, but I believe that the best in you will eventually open its wings."

But Gide had, by that time, little confidence in wings. In fact he distrusted them. In 1932, years before writing his *Thésée*, he noted as if in reply to Claudel: "I used to compare myself to Icarus, lost in the labyrinth from which so many mystics think they can free themselves only by a leap toward heaven." His mature religious credo, his final serenity, had no place for such soaring flights.

IX. PROMETHEUS, SAVIOR OF MEN

"The constant drama of humanity is the struggle between Prometheus and Zeus, between spirit and matter, between love and brute force, between Christ and heaven's indifference."

IT might flippantly be said that the figure of Prometheus has particularly interested the French because he suffered from a peculiarly French ailment—liver trouble. But this would not explain why the son of Iapetus and Clumene plays an even more significant rôle in English literature. Baudelaire saw a more pertinent relation when, discussing Louis Ménard's *Prométhée déchaîné* (*Prometheus Unbound*), he said the legend furnished the most Protestant of subjects. It was, indeed, his proud independence and fearless championing of man against the gods which drew Goethe and Shelley to Prometheus and made Byron write:

"Thy godlike crime was to be kind,
To render with thy precepts less
The sum of human wretchedness,
And strengthen man with his own mind."

André Gide, the erstwhile Calvinist who led too sober a life ever to be bothered by his liver, was by nature inclined to see the Titan less as a symbol of a physical complaint than as an embodiment of spiritual anguish. The suffering liver interested him less than the eagle that fed on it. Few, if any, myths more insistently returned to his mind throughout life or established more intimate relationship with its personal problems. From his first published work of 1891 to the *Deux Interviews imaginaires* of 1946 (which I should like to call "Dialogues on God"), the name of Prometheus sounds through his career. At twenty, having already read the tragedy of Aeschylus, he discovered Goethe's *Prometheus*, of which he later noted that "no stroke of the scalpel" to outline his inner likeness ever cut deeper. Again and again he insists that "wisdom begins where fear ends, that it begins with the revolt of Prometheus." At different moments the Titan whose name means "Forethought" symbolized for him the uniqueness of the individual, "the vast sickly unrest of ancient heroes," the defence of man against the gods, "the devouring belief in progress," and even Christ himself.

The most sustained use Gide made of the myth is in his *Prométhée mal enchaîné* (*Prometheus Misbound*) of 1899. The struggle between Zeus and Prometheus in that *sotie* represents the conflict between determinism and free-will. The Miglionaire named Zeus, when Prometheus intercedes with him, refuses to intervene in order to save Damocles, who is dying of spiritual torment; he must preserve his incognito, as he says, though he makes no objection when the waiter points out that people are saying he is God himself. To be sure, the very name of Zeus should set the reader off at once on the right track. In the guise of Providence or Fate, the rich Banker blindly distributes good and evil to humanity in the persons of Cocles and Damocles, who prove that good may be a source of evil, evil a source of good. Prometheus, who has likewise received an eagle from Zeus in the past, tries to help humanity by teaching men awareness of their individual destiny and finally showing how one can dominate it, making it an integral part of oneself.

Although Cocles and Damocles are fully determined by Zeus the gambler, Prometheus, refractory and unsubmissive, acts freely in dominating his eagle. When he questions that bird three times in vain, we cannot but associate Prometheus with

Christ on the Mount of Olives thrice calling out to a silent heaven. The questions he asks are fundamental: "Who sends you? Why did you choose me? Whence do you come? Where are you going? Tell me: what is your nature?" And again: "Am I then to leave this earth without knowing why I love you? Nor what you will do or be, after me, on this earth?" The Gospels do not record the details of such an interrogation, but these are precisely the points on which Christ in Vigny's philosophical poem, "*Le Mont des Oliviers*," begs his Father's permission to enlighten man:

> "All will be revealed as soon as man learns
> Whence he cometh and whither he goeth."

That it is by no means fanciful to identify Gide's Prometheus at this point with Christ becomes apparent in the light of one of Gide's reflections published toward the end of his long career: "There can be no question of two gods. But I take great care not to confuse, under the name of God, two very different things, different to the point of being in opposition. On the one hand, the whole of the Cosmos and the natural laws that govern it, matter and force, energies. That is the Zeus aspect; and one may well call it God, but only if one divests that word of all personal and moral significance. On the other hand, the aggregate of all human efforts toward the good and the beautiful, the gradual mastering of those brute forces and their utilization to achieve the good and the beautiful on earth. This is the Prometheus aspect; and it is the Christ aspect too; it is the full blossoming of man, and all virtues contribute to it. But this God nowise inhabits nature; he exists solely in man and through man; he is created by man, or, if you prefer, it is through man that he is created; and any effort to exteriorize him through prayer is vain. It is with him that Christ has taken sides, but it is to the other that he speaks when, dying, he utters his cry of despair: 'My God, my God, why hast thou forsaken me? . . .'"

André Gide took a long time to come to this definitive credo, first published in 1946, when he was over seventy-five. Yet as

early as 1899, in what appears on the surface as merely a bur-
lesque *Prometheus Misbound,* he depicts the age-old antagonism
between God and Titan, even daring to suggest, so lightly and
implicitly that without the much later explicit passage one
might ignore it, a parallel between Prometheus and Christ. Before he was thirty, Gide had discovered that ideas can be put
forth in jest which would never gain a hearing if stated seriously. Over the years, concurrently with the periodic attraction
of mysticism, he gradually elaborated his private faith. The
playfully stated hint of *Le Prométhée* had to be put in such a
casual way, in fact, because it actually went beyond his mature
conclusions of that time. He was not for many years to dare a
categorical and clear statement of his belief in the opposition
between an impersonal Zeus and a God, son of man.

The first step for Gide was a Promethean revolt against the
concept of an omnipotent God. The idea of God, he stated in
1927, served usefully in the beginning to uphold the vault under construction; but once the vault is finished, such support is
unnecessary. It is but natural that against an all-powerful, impersonal God should be opposed Man, the strong, resourceful
individual. Many of the most constant strains in Gide's thought,
and particularly his devotion to ancient mythology, led him to
philosophical humanism. His Oedipus boasts: "I felt strong
enough to resist even God"; and his Theseus admiringly says
of the blind outcast of Thebes: "He had stood up to the Sphinx,
showed how Man could brave the enigma, and dared to oppose
him to the Gods." In his own experience Theseus found that
terror played a large part in religion, as everything inexplicable was called divine, and consequently heroism, such as
prompted his exploits, often seemed impious. Truly Gide shows
a consistent tendency to "remove God from the altar and put
man in his place," as he says.

Any eventual classification of Gide among atheists (such as
Time magazine risked even before his death) will note that he
frequently proclaimed his lack of belief, doing so twice even

during his last year of life. It will particularly quote a passage from his "Autumn Leaves" about weaning oneself from the idea of God and getting along "without a belief in an attentive, tutelary, and retributive Providence . . ." and refer, doubtless, to a journal-entry regarding the famous *philosophes* of the eighteenth century who "when forced into a corner [. . .] would have revealed more vague skepticism than a very definite and very decisive negative affirmation." And beside that reflection it will probably place Gide's statement, again from "Autumn Leaves" of 1947: "To Faith I do not oppose doubt, but affirmation: what could not be is not." Yet, categorical as such assertions seem, the author himself was aware that his pages were much less "subversive" than he had originally thought. In a postscript of May 1948 to the *"Feuillets d'automne"* he quoted a friend to the effect that the flexibility of the Catholic credo, constantly evolving, *could* make room for his reservations, for while voicing them he clearly showed that he was tormented by the idea of God and the need for God.

To this Gide protested that there must be some misunderstanding and that he wanted to be rejected once and for all. Regretting his destruction of the pages he had written on eternal life, which would have made it impossible for any orthodoxy to accept him into the fold, he closed with this peremptory statement: "That the life of the 'soul' is prolonged beyond the dissolution of the flesh seems to me inadmissible, unthinkable, and my reason protests against it, just as it does against the incessant multiplication of souls." Frequently he had already stated and would again express his inability to believe in immortality. And we now know from his final writing, appropriately entitled *Ainsi soit-il ou Les Jeux sont faits* (*So Be It or The Chips are Down*), that at the actual moment of his death on 19 February 1951 he had not changed his views.

Gide's philosophical humanism is, then, accompanied by an affirmative denial of the immortality of the soul and of the existence of a personal God. Yet, just as he had pointed out in

1897 that both Catholicism and Protestantism had long ago ceased being expansive to become restrictive formulas, so he could in 1929 state the same of atheism with the conclusion that "There is not a single exalting and emancipatory influence that does not in turn become inhibitory." In every domain, it is characteristic of Gide not to submit to classification. Not living in an age when men habitually gave their life for their ideas, he had other reasons than the humanists, the libertines, and the *philosophes* for hiding, avoiding, or simply postponing a definitive statement of his credo. The conflicting impulses of his own mind, indeed, sufficed to check any irrevocable self-commitment.

Furthermore, it was impossible for Gide to forsake Christ, to whose figure and teaching he remained, as we have seen, profoundly devoted. In the *Nouvelles Nourritures* (so dominated by his new Communism that the rather precious Nathanael has yielded to an equally precious "Comrade") he calls out: "I return to you, Lord Christ, as to God whose living form you are. I am weary of deceiving my heart. Everywhere I find you, when I thought I was fleeing you, divine friend of my childhood." The obvious way of maintaining his bond with Christ, in his evolving credo, was to annex him ever more to man, divorcing him from the God of natural forces. This Gide had already begun to do in 1929 by speaking ". . . of the antagonism between Christ and God—of Christ's *error* (wonderful to explain why that error was intentional and necessary) of claiming that he was closely associated with God—leading to the cry, at last revelatory: 'My God, why hast thou forsaken me?' "

When he returns to this theme in 1942, Gide can see in that "error" nothing but a tragic misunderstanding, for "the God of natural forces has no ears and remains indifferent to human sufferings, whether he attaches Prometheus to the Caucasus or nails Christ on the cross." And to the objection that the evil in men rather than natural forces crucified Christ, Gide replies:

"The God that Christ represents and incarnates, the God of Virtue, must struggle at one and the same time against the Zeus of natural forces and against the evil in men." This passage from the *Deux Interviews imaginaires* or "Dialogues on God" is a continuation of the one quoted earlier which distinguishes two aspects of divinity that Gide calls Zeus and Prometheus. By 1942 the identification of Christ with Prometheus, ever so allusively suggested in 1899, is complete.

It is perhaps significant that in the meantime Gide had seen the "great superiority" of Christianity over paganism to lie in the fact that, whereas Zeus crucifies Prometheus, God offers his Son to be crucified by men; but within a few months of the original publication of this remark in April 1929 he had changed the words "superiority over" to "difference between." Such a reflection and its emendation represent a step toward the identification of 1942.

In André Gide's life and work the revolt of Prometheus assumes a central position as symbol of the championing of the individual, of the downtrodden, and of mankind in general. In fact, the myths of Philoctetes, Oedipus, and Theseus, as Gide utilizes them, all lead to the exemplary figure of Prometheus who, in a sense, could be said to subsume them in the writer's "inner Olympus." During his last years, Gide was wont to glorify the *unsubmissive* as the salt of the earth who will eventually save the world. By identifying Christ with the unsubmissive Titan in the war against an inflexible Zeus, he integrated his personal devotion to the Gospels into his consistent faith in humanity and made of himself what might paradoxically be called a Christian atheist. In 1923 he noted in his *Journals*: ". . . there are two teachings whose virtue man will never exhaust: that of Christ and that of the 'Greek legend.' " At last he reconciled those two lessons in his mature religious faith.

Perhaps Gide was right in feeling that the one thing Catholics could not forgive him was his insistent attachment to Christ. Why else did Massis and others attack him particularly rather than Proust, who was indifferent, or Valéry, who was hostile? In one of his "Detached Pages" for 1925 which he did not maintain in the definitive edition of his *Journals,* Gide points out that Catholics such as Claudel dislike Jansenism even more than Protestantism because of its claim not to break with the Church, and Protestantism more than atheism because of its claim not to break with Christ. But Gide had made himself particularly vulnerable to anathema by his claim to have broken with *everything but Christ.*

Yet André Gide's novel and somewhat daring equation of Christ with Prometheus must not blind us to the essence of his credo: the relation between God and man. In the passages already quoted from *Deux Interviews imaginaires* he has clearly stated that the God of Virtue whom Christ represents and incarnates, who reveals the Prometheus-aspect of divinity as opposed to the Zeus-aspect, exists solely in and through man. Outside of those passages, his most satisfying expression of this belief is found in the same year (1942) in the *Journals*: "As soon as I had realized that God was not yet but was becoming and that his becoming depended on each one of us, a moral sense was restored in me. No impiety or presumption in this thought, for I was convinced at one and the same time that God was achieved only by man and through man, but that if man led to God, creation, in order to lead to man, started from God; so that the divine had its place at both ends, at the start and at the point of arrival, and that the start had been solely in order to arrive at God." This concept, however, of a circular evolution with God as both the end-result and point of departure, did not come to the writer as a novelty during the Second World War.

He had, in fact, been elaborating this theory for a long time. As early as 1916 he had decided that God was terminal rather than initial: "He is the supreme and final point toward which all nature tends in time," Gide continued. "And since time does not exist for Him, it is a matter of indifference to

Him whether that evolution of which He is the summit follows or precedes, and whether He determines it by propulsion or attraction." At that time he wondered whether or not he would ever be able to set forth his theory clearly. A few years later he expressed surprise that men could accept the principle of evolution by which centuries were required for the formation of man and not admit that even more time was needed to achieve the Supreme Being.

In his *Thésée*, completed during the Second World War, Gide communicated to the bewildered Icarus some of his own early groping confusion about this problem. For there, sharing the amazement of Theseus, we see a shadowy and handsome incarnation of the dead son of Daedalus, who escaped the labyrinth only by soaring upward on mystical wings, the misuse of which brought him to his end. His father explains that inasmuch as heroes, ever repeating the unfinished gesture originally performed in life, assume a symbolic value after death, Icarus remains the image of man's disquiet and of the impulse to discovery. That, indeed, is *his* inner labyrinth, which surrounds him even in Hades. Hence, still tormented by metaphysical anguish, he continues to wander in his father's house, oblivious to his surroundings, wondering how to reach God if he starts from man and, if he starts from God, how to reach himself. "Yet, just as much as God formed me," he says, "is not God created by man? At the exact intersection of the ways, at the very heart of that cross, my mind wants to abide." There Gide takes his stand too, but he has gone beyond Icarus and decided that God exists solely by virtue of man's virtue and that this is the meaning of the Tempter's words: *Et eritis sicut dei*—ye shall be as Gods. Thesus listening powerless to the anguished interrogations of Icarus somehow reminds one of the earlier scene of Prometheus in the sick-room of Damocles.

The concept that God is potential and that man is responsible for him was anticipated to some extent by Ernest Renan in his subtle and somewhat ambiguous definitions of God as the *summum* and the *ultimum,* the limit of humanity's aspiration toward truth and beauty, the form under which we conceive the ideal. André Gide could have subscribed to Renan's denial of the supernatural while preserving the divine, as to his statement at the end of *L'Avenir de la science* (*The Future of Science*) that he would die content in "the communion of humanity and the religion of the future." And, in return, all of Renan's reflections on faith might be summed up in Gide's comprehensive remark: "I am an unbeliever. I shall never be an ungodly man."

As a young man André Gide characterized as "madness and chasing after a shadow" the belief that humanity has any other end than the one it projects for itself. Fifty years later, he wrote to a young correspondent that we must achieve God, adding: "Could there be a nobler, more admirable rôle, and more worthy of our efforts?" And finally, a few months before his death, he noted in a matter of fact spirit: "I should give my life for God to exist. Yes, that makes sense. But giving my life to prove that God exists makes no sense at all. It simply has no meaning."

Consequently, although there is evolution in his religious thought, there is also a remarkable consistency. Gide's final, serene credo reconciles all the doubts and aspirations of his life, harmonizes his Christian and pagan impulses, and establishes, as in so many other domains, a dynamic equilibrium of opposing tendencies.

X. CORYDON, THE UNORTHODOX LOVER

"We always have great difficulty understanding the loves of others, their way of making love. . . And doubtless this is why we are
so lacking in understanding on this point and
so ferociously uncompromising."

"Probably there will always be delicate
readers, easily shocked, who prefer to see only
the bust of great men, who rise up against the
publication of intimate papers and private
correspondences. They seem to consider in
such writings solely the flattering pleasure
that mediocre minds may derive from seeing
heroes subject to the same infirmities as they.
In such cases they speak of indiscretion and,
if they have a romantic pen, of 'violating
tombs,' at the very least of unhealthy curiosity; they say: 'Let us forget the man; the
work alone matters!' Obviously; but the wonderful thing, and to me it is inexhaustibly instructive, is that *he* wrote it *despite that*."

A SHEPHERD figuring in Theocritus and in Virgil's *Bucolics* whose name has become conventional in pastoral
poetry—such is Corydon. The English tradition forgot or suppressed the strange love with which he burned for the fair
Alexis, but in French he has remained, as he was in Greece and

Rome, a symbol of the homosexual. André Gide had since early youth been drawn to Greek and Latin bucolic poetry, doubtless because of its "so frequently homosexual inspiration," and the fact that his own discovery of his unorthodox sexual tastes had taken place in North Africa, in a truly pastoral civilization where the young Parisian accompanied dark-skinned goatherds named Athman or Lossif as they led their flocks in the shade of the tall palms. In 1899 and 1906 he had used the names of two of Virgil's shepherds—*Mopsus* and *Amyntas*—as titles for his writings. Earlier, the happy Tityrus of the first *Eclogue* had become the smug protagonist of the book-within-a-book both of *Paludes* and of *Le Prométhée mal enchaîné* and appeared momentarily in the *Nourritures terrestres* in the company of such Virgilian friends as Amyntas, Menalcas, Meliboeus, and Mopsus. In great part, indeed, the "Fruits of the Earth" is itself a bucolic poem belonging to the purest pastoral tradition.

When Gide came to write a defence of homosexuality, it was but natural for him to name the principal of the two speakers and the book itself *Corydon*. To French readers such a title should immediately indicate the subject; furthermore, the subtitle of "Four Socratic Dialogues," added in the second printing, provided a respectable connotation while further suggesting the nature of the discourse. For the work could be called Socratic (in recollection of Plato's *Symposium*) even more because of the matter dealt with than because of the interrogatory technique of arriving at the truth. The dialogue form was a favorite with Gide; outside of his three plays already published, he had used it most effectively in *Le Retour de l'enfant prodigue*. In order to maintain an informal tone in the exposition of serious ideas, he needed a correspondent or interlocutor to interrupt, raise objections, and ask questions. For his literary criticism between 1898 and 1900 in *L'Ermitage* he had borrowed the naïve Angèle of *Paludes* and written "*Lettres à Angèle*," a form he was to resurrect in 1921 in the *Nouvelle*

Revue Française. In 1905 he had invented an even more anonymous, less clearly defined "interviewer" and for several months couched his critical remarks in *L'Ermitage* in a series of "*Visites de l'Interviewer.*" This device, a particularly happy one for Gide, was to reappear in 1943 in the *Interviews imaginaires.*

As to form, *Corydon* belongs among the Gidian imaginary interviews. But this time, instead of representing himself as being interviewed by a rather well-informed but not always quick-witted or tactful journalist, he has cast himself in the role of the interviewer, unsympathetic to homosexuality but eager to hear the arguments in its favor, who seeks out the well-informed Corydon, At least this is the reader's immediate impression, for the unnamed interviewer uses the first person singular. But the austere Corydon with his twofold interest in natural history and in art and his quiet devotion to truth is far closer to the author than is the interlocutor. It is characteristic that Corydon is writing a book on the subject and that what we have here is an informal preview of that book; hence Gide has again presented a book within a book. Much like the Ménalque of *L'Immoraliste*, Corydon, but for "the deplorable reputation his tastes were beginning to give him," is an admirable member of society. Known for a host of noble qualities, he had distinguished himself by his brilliant medical studies and gone on to research that had won the esteem of his colleagues; above all, he is not ashamed of his sexual orientation. Like André Gide, he is the masculine type of pederast and has no interest in defending effeminacy. In fact, he prefers not to speak at all of what he calls "inverts," who belong beside the neurotic misfits and the pathological types produced by heterosexuality; he suggests that perhaps society, by suppressing pederasty and making it a school of hypocrisy, is responsible for the frequency of such flaws in character. He expresses the longing for a martyr—"someone who would go forth to meet the attack, who, without swashbuckling or bravado, would endure reprobation and insult, or rather who would be of such recognized worth, integrity, and honesty that reprobation would hesitate at first. . ."

Corydon possesses those qualities, and probably Gide felt that he himself did also. At least there can be no doubt that, by his innate devotion to the principle of sincerity and his deep hatred for hypocrisy, he felt a vocation for martyrdom. His entire work reveals an awareness of the conflict between his involuntary impulse, for which he could feel in no way responsible, and the reprobation in which society holds that impulse. Most homosexuals outwardly accept the judgment of society and live a lie; but this Gide could not do. Although his friends did everything to dissuade him from publishing his dialogues, he felt strong in his scorn for the "applause, decorations, honors, admission to fashionable salons" which this book might prevent. This, of course, is precisely what *Corydon* did for its author; together with his memoirs, it effectively kept his name off the honors-lists which are so much a part of French literary life, while throughout his career he was to see younger writers, often those formed by his influence, crowned by prize-juries, decorated by the State, and admitted to the supreme honor of membership in the French Academy. By the time he received the international consecration of the Nobel Prize at the age of seventy-eight, he must have been aware himself of the rare distinction constituted by his unadorned lapel and the lack of honors in his biographical listing.

Despite his inclination, however, he did not rush into martyrdom without due deliberation. In 1911 he had *Corydon* privately printed in twelve copies under the enigmatic title of *C.R.D.N.* and without name of author, or publisher, or place of publication. At that time the work consisted of but the first two dialogues and a fragment of the third. Gide tells us that he put the entire small printing away in a drawer, and from his *Journals* we know that he continued to work on it for the next nine years until in 1920 a second private printing of twenty-one copies, under the same anonymous conditions and with the same abbreviated title, included all four dialogues with a page of Foreword. In 1924 finally a public edition, containing the Foreword of 1920 and a new and more eloquent Preface, comprised over five thousand copies for sale. At last Gide had taken the step he had so long been contemplating.

Was it mere timidity that had caused his long delay? In 1920 he ascribed his hesitation to a concern for public welfare which made him see his work as subversive. Yet in 1923 when the Thomistic philosopher and prominent Catholic layman, Jacques Maritain, urged him not to publish the work, André Gide argued that the book *had* to be written, that he was uniquely qualified to write it, and that not to do so would amount to shirking his duty and countenancing falsehood. In the final Preface, however, he analyzed his motives more keenly in a discreet allusion to his wife when he confessed that he had held back for fear of saddening a few—"one soul, in particular, which has from the beginning been dear to me above all. Who can say for how many delays, reticences, and evasions affection and love are responsible?"

Even though he then thought that his love for his wife had withheld him from expressing himself, at a later date he wondered whether, without the mute conflict that existed between the couple, he would ever have felt sufficient need to write *Corydon* or the second part of his memoirs. In other words, his wife's inability to understand and accept his sexual orientation prompted him to defend homosexuality and eventually to publish his confessions, while his profound spiritual love for, and consequent fear of hurting, her urged him to silence. This inner conflict lies at the basis of all of Gide's work. In the pages of his *Journals* which he reserved for posthumous publication, he recorded in early 1925: "Until *Les Faux-Monnayeurs* (the first book I wrote while trying not to take her into account), I wrote everything to convince her, to win her esteem. It is all but a long plea for the defence; no work has been more intimately motivated than mine—and no one sees deeply into it who fails to distinguish this." The mere thought that he might win her esteem with *L'Immoraliste, Corydon,* and *Si le grain ne meurt . . .* can only seem fantastic to whoever has studied the portrait he composed of her after her death. But his loathing for hypocrisy and devotion to truth at any cost were such that, against all the evidence to the contrary, he probably ascribed the same attitude to her.

A cognate reason for writing *Corydon,* he once confessed, was to disavow the false holiness with which his "disdain for ordinary temptations" clothed him in the eyes of relatives and friends. Again, from the fact that he wrote the preamble at one sitting as a reaction to his preface to the letters of Dupouey, we may assume that, like *La Symphonie pastorale* though in another direction, *Corydon* represented a revulsion from one of his flights into mysticism. All these reasons together might well justify the private printing of 1920—at least in the author's eyes. But after that symbolic gesture he need have gone no further. His most recent indulgence in mysticism was then far in the past; he could hardly have still retained much hypocritical saintliness in the eyes of those close to him; and Madeleine Gide had made it clear that she was not to be convinced. Yet he did take the irrevocable step of publishing his dialogues for all the world to read in 1924. The determining factor, which added to all the others fixed his decision, was undoubtedly provided by Marcel Proust—but not as some have assumed by setting an example of the free discussion of homosexuality.

Despite the paucity of documents, Gide's relations with Proust can be rather fully traced. The story properly begins with the *Nouvelle Revue Française* refusal, now almost incomprehensible, of the manuscript of *Du côté de chez Swann* (*Swann's Way*). As the unofficial director of both the review and its publishing house, Gide deserved the blame for failing to recognize one of the great books of the epoch, and one that decidedly belonged among those published by the *N. R. F.* His refusal—for he was the principal reader who made the decision

—was motivated by his recollection of Proust as a social butterfly of the nineties who spent his time among the snobs and
wrote detailed descriptions of ostentatious receptions for the
Figaro. The fact that Proust, whom Gide had not seen in twenty
years, offered to subsidize the edition of his novel simply confirmed the belief that he was not a serious writer. No one who
had lost track of him before 1896 (as it was so easy for all but
the society editors to do) could have expected anything but
frivolities from him in 1912. These, however, are but extenuat-
ing circumstances that by no means excuse Gide for having
failed to read Proust's manuscript carefully and discern in it
the qualities of genius. Great works of art always come as a
surprise; Gide knew this and was guilty of approaching *Du
côté de chez Swann* with a closed mind.

To some extent he compensated for his mistake by two con-
trite and admiring letters of January 1914 (at a time when
very few critics had yet appreciated Proust at his true value),
by his prolonged and successful efforts to acquire the rights
from Proust's original publisher and bring out the complete
A la recherche du temps perdu (*Remembrance of Things Past*)
under the *N. R. F.* imprint, and by his article of early 1921, in
which he declared that he had for Proust "one of the keenest
admirations I have ever felt for a contemporary writer." A
proof of that admiration can be seen in the journal-entry for
14 January 1918 where Gide admits disappointment with his
own unfinished memoirs and is overwhelmed when comparing
them to "Proust's marvelous book." Such a reference in 1918,
could only have meant *Du côté de chez Swann*, and Gide was
obviously contrasting two depictions of childhood. Later his
point of view was to change.

On the evening of 13 May 1921 André Gide spent an hour
with Marcel Proust, apparently for the first time in several
years. For the preceding four days Proust had sent a car and
chauffeur to fetch Gide every evening. Finally on the night
when the latter could come, the invalid, who had not been up

in some time, had dressed to go out. The meeting took place in the little salon at 44 rue Hamelin, with its hideous Barbedienne bronze on the mantel and the Jacques Blanche portrait of the foppish young Marcel on the next wall. To one the atmosphere seemed stifling, but the other, having just left a still warmer room, was shivering. The first part of Proust's *Sodome et Gomorrhe* (*The Cities of the Plain*) had recently appeared, with its stirring initial appeal for understanding of the plight of homosexuals: "Accursed race forced to live in falsehood and perjury because it knows its desire to be considered punishable and shameful, unable to show itself. . ." Gide had accordingly brought Proust a precious copy of his privately and anonymously printed *Corydon*, and the conversation quite naturally turned on this subject. "Far from denying or hiding his homosexuality," Gide recorded in his *Journals* the next day, "he exhibits it, and I could almost say boasts of it. He claims never to have loved women save spiritually and never to have known love except with men."

A few nights later, when Proust returned *Corydon* by his chauffeur, whom Gide accompanied back to the rue Hamelin, the invalid was in bed, wrapped in multiple sweaters. The next day Gide noted: "We scarcely talked, this evening again, of anything but homosexuality. He says he blames himself for that 'indecision' which made him, in order to fill out the heterosexual part of his book, transpose '*à l'ombre des jeunes filles*' all the attractive, affectionate, and charming elements contained in his homosexual recollections, so that for *Sodome* he is left nothing but the grotesque and the abject. But he shows himself to be very much concerned when I tell him that he seems to have wanted to stigmatize homosexuality; he protests; and eventually I understand that what we consider vile, an object of laughter or disgust, does not seem so repulsive to him."

That conversation marked the beginning of Gide's disappointment. For a few months he must have thought that Proust, a homosexual himself and a great writer whom he admired, would depict "the outlawed race" sympathetically in his work. But as the long novel continued to appear, Gide soon became aware that it contained no example of what he would call the "normal" homosexual to offset the "inverts"—more or less tainted with sadism or masochism—whom it portrayed. In December 1921 he read extracts from *Sodome et Gomorrhe* in the *N. R. F.* with indignation. "Knowing what he thinks, what he is," Gide commented, "it is hard for me to see in them anything but a pretense, a desire to protect himself, a camouflage of the cleverest sort, for it can be to no one's advantage to denounce him. Even more: that offense to truth will probably please everybody: heterosexuals, whose prejudices it justifies and whose repugnance it flatters; and the others, who will take advantage of the alibi and their lack of resemblance to those he portrays. In short, considering the public's cowardice, I do not know any writing that is more capable than Proust's *Sodome et Gomorrhe* of confirming the error of public opinion." From that moment onward, Gide must have thought of Proust as actually doing a disservice to the cause of understanding. Eventually he was to classify Proust with Wilde, because of his artistic hypocrisy dictated by the need for self-protection, and to call him "that great master of dissimulation."

Marcel Proust died in November 1922, just a few months after the second part of *Sodome et Gomorrhe* had appeared in book-form; and it was in that very month that Gide wrote his definitive Preface to *Corydon*. In it he states that he does not regret the delay in publishing his book because the intervening years have only confirmed his ideas. He mentions Proust's work as having not only accustomed the public to such questions but also, by adopting Dr. Hirschfeld's theory of an intermediary sex, misled opinion, paying attention only to such cases of inversion, effeminacy, and sodomy as *Corydon* ignores.

That Proust's entire work is marked by an obsession with the theme of homosexuality no one can deny. Some critics have felt that his insistent treatment of the subject encouraged Gide to issue his *Corydon* and to finish his memoirs. On the contrary, it was rather as a protest against Proust's uniformly ugly picture of love between men that Gide issued his two books. Some years later, he deplored the fact that when people speak of influence they are always thinking of direct influence, whereas influence through protest is often more important, a strong nature yielding to reaction rather than to direct action. This is assuredly what Gide did in this case. His reaction, to be sure, goes far beyond his *Corydon*—which, after all, was completely written before anyone knew that Proust was broaching the subject—and is much more clearly apparent in *Si le grain ne meurt . . .* and *Les Faux-Monnayeurs.*

Yet in all fairness it should be pointed out that Proust also reacted against Gide on the same score by writing in *La Prisonnière* (*The Captive*), which did not appear until a year after his death: "M. de Charlus himself would not have understood this, for he confused his mania with friendship, which in no way resembles it, and Praxiteles's athletes with amenable boxers. He was unwilling to admit that nineteen hundred years ago ('A courtier who is devout under a devout prince would have been an atheist under an atheistic prince,' as La Bruyère said) disappeared all socially accepted homosexuality—that of Plato's young men as of Virgil's shepherds, and that the only form to survive and to multiply is the involuntary, the neurotic one that is hidden from others and disguised to oneself." Such a remark may well have been inspired by those two evenings in May 1921 and by the reading of the still unpublished *C.R.D.N.* It is particularly ironic that, while unwittingly strengthening Gide's resolve, Proust should have left behind an anticipatory answer to the arguments of *Corydon;* such are the subtleties of literary influence.

But clearly, by presenting homosexuality in its least unattractive aspect, *Corydon* stands in contrast to the work of Proust. The entire little book argues that pederasty is a natural taste, whose expression does no harm to the individual or to society.

Drawing its three principal arguments from natural history, from history and the arts, and from sociology and ethics, it deserves the designation of "tract" that François Porché applied to it. Spurning all appeal to the emotions, Gide intentionally addressed himself to the head rather than to the heart. "I intend that this book should be written coldly, deliberately, and that this should be evident," he said in 1911. "Passion must have preceded it or at most be implied in it; but above all it must not serve as an excuse for the book. I do not want to move to pity with this book; I want to embarrass." Yet it is difficult, he recognizes, to be frank without seeming cynical in a domain where dissimulation has so long been mandatory. The first-person interlocutor refers to Corydon as an "outlaw," but this condition results, we are led to believe, from the injustice of the laws. Corydon himself speaks, somewhat reluctantly, of his "anomaly," but never uses a term like "abnormality."

The question of terminology is most important in any such discussion. In the work itself the words *uranism, pederasty*, and *homosexuality* are used interchangeably; but in the *Journals* Gide defines his terms more precisely:

"I call a *pederast* the man who, as the word indicates, falls in love with young boys. I call a *sodomite* [. . .] the man whose desire is addressed to mature men.

"I call an *invert* the man who, in the comedy of love, assumes the role of a woman and desires to be possessed.

"These three types of *homosexuals* are not always clearly distinct; there are possible transferences from one to another; but most often the difference among them is such that they experience a profound disgust for one another, a disgust accompanied by a reprobation that in no way yields to that which you (heterosexuals) fiercely show toward all three.

"The pederasts, of whom I am one (why cannot I say this quite simply, without your immediately claiming to see a brag in my confession?), are much rarer, and the sodomites much more numerous, than I first thought. I speak of this on the basis of the confidences I have received, and am willing to believe that in another time and in another country it would not have been the same. As to the inverts, whom I have hardly frequented at all, it has always seemed to me that they alone deserved the reproach of moral or intellectual deformation and were subject to some of the accusations that are commonly addressed to all homosexuals." These may not be the usual, scientific definitions of these terms but they are important to an understanding of André Gide, for he remained consistent in his use of them throughout his life.

To the average reader, the arguments of *Corydon* may not seem convincing. Yet the dialectical character of the book was dictated, as Ramon Fernandez saw, by the nature of the problem. Gide had first to establish the fact that the homosexual's desires were not unnatural and then proceed to show how their expression is harmful neither to morals nor to society. With this treatise Gide took his stand as a humanist, resolutely committing himself as opposed to the current rules of morality and the laws of the land. The book may not rank high among his collected works; it may even be deplored by the majority of his literary admirers; nonetheless it represents an act of exceptional courage in defiance of what seemed to its author an unreasonable taboo.

Even before the public edition of Corydon he had reproached the book for its prudence and timidity, regretting that he had given such good arguments to the opponent of his thesis. Far from admitting that his dialogues revealed an obsession (as friends and critics alike then thought), he insisted that they marked rather a release, for long ago he had solved his personal problem by facing it squarely. Through reading him, others should find similar release, he felt.

As time went on, Gide came to think of *Corydon*—probably because of the courage involved in writing so unwelcome a work and certainly because of the great social utility he attributed to it—as his "most important book." Still he rather regretted its form, going so far as to speak of it as an artistic failure; but eventually he withdrew even that reservation. By 1946, after his return to Paris from the exile of the war, friends were suggesting his eligibility to the French Academy, then sorely in need of new blood. The thought of so unconventional and unpopular a work as *Corydon* must have come to every mind, however, as a possibly insuperable barrier to that honor. Gide was nevertheless tempted to the point that he envisaged accepting election to the Academy if he were dispensed from the formality of announcing his candidature and paying official visits of solicitation to the "Immortals" who would have to vote for or against him. But his first act as an Academician, he promised in his *Journals*, would be a new preface for *Corydon* declaring it his most important and most useful work.

Perhaps that august body feared some such defiance as this; in any case, no exception to the traditional rules was made for André Gide. He had, accordingly, to wait another year until the Swedish Academy conferred on him an even greater honor and one for which no solicitation is necessary. Even then, when a journalist asked him if he regretted any of his books, he replied that he would have "bade farewell to the Nobel Prize" if he had had to disown anything to obtain it. Far from having to disavow any of his "subversive" writings, he had the pleasure of hearing them officially praised by the Perpetual Secretary of the Swedish Academy, who saw that those pages, which "by their almost unequalled audacity in confession" constitute a challenge, really combat pharisaism. And Mr. Osterling added: "One should nevertheless remember that such a procedure is a form of the passionate love of truth that, since Montaigne and Rousseau, has become a necessity in French literature. Through all the phases of his evolution, Gide appears, in truth, as a defender of literary integrity founded on the personality's right, and the duty incumbent thereon, to present deliberately and integrally all its problems."

Impersonal and unemotional as *Corydon* was, the mere fact

of having written a defence of homosexuality branded Gide, for only a homosexual could have felt the need of writing it. For all its superficial objectivity, it was obviously a plea *pro domo suo*. Yet Gide's passion for truth and need to legitimize could not be satisfied until he had openly identified himself with the "outcast race." He wanted no such hypocritical immunity as others achieved through concessions to the prevailing prejudice. When he saw the chastened Oscar Wilde at Berneval in 1898, the author of *The Ballad of Reading Gaol* praised the recently published *Nourritures terrestres*, but added that he wanted Gide to promise never again to write "I." He may well have been thinking of the allusions to pederasty contained in that already unconventional book; but when Gide later reprinted his account of the meeting he gave a more general application to these words by adding a paragraph in which Wilde clarified his thought thus: "In art, you see, there is no *first* person." In any case, whether this advice was dictated by purely aesthetic reasons or by considerations of personal prudence, Gide did not observe it.

Twenty-three years later Proust had to repeat the recommendation, and this time there could be no doubt as to the motive behind it. Upon lending Proust his anonymous *C.R.D.N.* and asking him not to speak of it to anyone, Gide said a few words about his memoirs; whereupon Proust exclaimed: "You can tell anything, but on condition that you never say: *I*." Recording that remark in his *Journals*, Gide added: "But that won't suit me." Certainly Proust's way was not his. He *had* to tell the truth about himself. The obvious way to do this was to make a detailed personal confession; and the determination to do so by publishing his memoirs during his lifetime antedates 1900. After a private printing of thirteen copies in 1920–21, *Si le grain ne meurt . . . (If It Die . . .)* appeared in 1926 in an edition of over six thousand copies. In a letter to the English critic, Sir Edmund Gosse, who had followed his work with increasing enthusiasm for many years but must have been shocked by these apparently unnecessary revelations, Gide all but described this book as a reaction against Proust and others when he said: "Perhaps I owe this to my Protestant upbringing . . . my friend, I have a horror of falsehood. I cannot reconcile myself to that conventional camouflage which systematically gives a false coloring to the work of X . . ., of Y . . ., and of so many others. I wrote this book in order to 'create a precedent,' to give an example of frankness, to enlighten some, to reassure others, to force opinion into taking account of what it doesn't know or pretends not to know to the great prejudice of psychology, of morals, of art . . . and of society."

Gide's way was to brave opprobrium with the truth, to go forth and meet attack—indeed, to invite it. Long before he finished the memoirs, he admitted to his *Journals*: "I am not writing these memoirs to defend myself. I am not called upon to defend myself, for I am not accused. I am writing them before being accused. I am writing them in order to be accused." Most readers must have recognized the entire memoirs to be motivated by the confession of the last part, the true "subject" whose deferment to the end Gide frequently deplores in the *Journals*. All the rest merely prepares for that revelation.

Gide's public confession represents the practical application of his lifelong cult of sincerity. In his book on Dostoevsky (in which he professes to have noted in his predecessor only those characteristics which found an echo in him), he manifestly delights in the Russian tendency to confess one's sins openly, even before an enemy, to accuse and humiliate oneself. He even tells the undocumented story of Dostoevsky's accusing himself before an uncomprehending and shocked Turgenev of a particularly loathsome crime. But Gide's many confessions correspond to a need of his nature deeper than a pathological urge to self-abasement. Convinced that "it is better to be hated for what one is than loved for what one is not," he forced the truth about himself upon a shocked and often unwilling public.

Such exaggerated sincerity must be considered as a corollary to Gide's fundamental need to legitimize his behavior. To a critic who had analyzed his homosexuality as springing from the attraction of the forbidden, Gide wrote: "No, the feeling of prohibition never awakened desire in me. Loathing for the forbidden long preceded the need of legitimizing in my own eyes my conduct and the intimate tendency of my being. And this is most important, for it is just that loathing for the forbidden which *forced* me to revise the code; I could not reconcile myself any more easily to living insincerely than to remaining outside the law." He has here linked the two impulses so closely as almost to confuse them; yet they are distinct. On the one hand, his hatred of insincerity made it impossible for him to do homage to the conventions by living as if he were a heterosexual, and on the other, his inability to reconcile himself to being a "sport" or an outlaw obliged him to argue that homosexuality was natural and that we must accept *what is.* He consistently needed to legitimize his conduct by analyzing and explaining it, as Roger Martin du Gard points out, "not for the satisfaction of proving that he was right to act as he did; but because he claims the right to be as he is and because, being that way, he could not act differently."

Consequently he wrote both an impersonal defence of homosexuality and a personal confession. Furthermore, both books transcended his individual problem, for he felt that his case had a general application, that *Corydon* would "release" many and *Si le grain ne meurt . . .* would "reassure" others who suffered from the same conflicts. In a sense, then, he had been impelled by duty to write both works. The legitimizing of not only his but *all* homosexuality undoubtedly appeared to André Gide as a desirable moral reform. The entire argument of *Corydon*, indeed, tends to prove that not only the unhappy individual, but even society as a whole would be improved thereby. Now the reformer, as Gide points out when discussing Dostoevsky's epilepsy, is invariably motivated by some "little physiological mystery, a dissatisfaction of the flesh, an anxiety,

an anomaly." Mahomet, the prophets of Israel, Socrates, Saint
Paul, Luther, Pascal, Rousseau, and Nietzsche—all suffered
from their demon, their "thorn in the flesh." In his *Journals*
Gide had elaborated this idea as early as 1918: "It is *natural*
that any great moral reform, what Nietzsche would call any
transvaluation of values, should be due to a physiological *lack
of balance*."

Surely André Gide could not have insisted so upon this observation without recognizing its application to his own case.
His own anomaly, his wound of Philoctetes, gave him a sense
of acute discomfort; and early in life he set himself to rectify
his feeling of unbalance, to achieve equilibrium as his highest
goal. It was this that drove him to write, rather than any hereditary conflict of North and South or of Catholicism and
Protestantism. Of the abnormal genius, such as Rousseau or
Dostoevsky, Gide writes: "Don't come and say: 'What a pity he
is ill!' If he were not ill, he would not have striven to solve the
problem created by his anomaly, to find a harmony that does
not exclude his dissonance." In writing both *Corydon* and the
memoirs, in writing all of his work in fact, this is precisely
what Gide was doing: *seeking a harmony that did not exclude
his dissonance.*

Inasmuch as the reform of which Gide dreamed was to
make it possible for the homosexual to live openly according
to his nature, the Gidian confession formed part of the self-
justification. Throughout his intimate writings, André Gide is
saying, in effect: "This is the way I am and this is the way I
have lived." Only by describing his dissonance and treating it
as quite natural could he hope to integrate it into a larger harmony. *Si le grain ne meurt* . . ., as we have seen, ends with his
engagement (incomprehensible in the light of what precedes) to
his cousin in 1895. In other words, it covers but the first twenty-
five years of his life. Until quite recently, the continuation of
the story had to be pieced out from the *Journals*—from which
Gide had systematically and somewhat regretfully suppressed

almost everything relative to his wife, leaving, "in the ardent place of the heart, but a hole." Consequently, even to those who had studied his work most attentively, the entire chapter of his conjugal life remained a mystery. Years after Mme André Gide's death on 17 April 1938, the most enlightened commentators did not even know her real given name and had to call her by the symbolic name of "Emmanuèle" which Gide had consistently given her in his writings. Until the American edition of *Madeleine* in 1952 reproduced a photograph from a family album, even her sad smile and bright eyes, that told so much, remained unknown. No indiscreet friend, so long as André Gide lived, provided impressions of her in print with which to fill out the muted sketch emerging from Gide's reticent prose.

From the memoirs we know that André Gide married after having discovered his homosexual tendency and returned to North Africa to confirm the discovery. And from an entry in his *Journals* dated in 1949 we learn that he did not love his wife "carnally." Between these two facts there lay, until after his death, an abyss that any reader could fill more or less as he pleased. To be sure, much could be gleaned from the *Journals*, where Gide reveals an ever keen susceptibility to adolescent beauty—whether in Donatello's David or in a young tailor's apprentice at the baths. The frequent references to one or another "X," to "little Guido" at Roquebrune, to "the little fellow" named Émile D. in Paris, to "François" at Tunis in June 1942 show in Gide, even down to his seventy-fifth year, a constantly alert sensuality and an unashamed rejoicing in its satisfaction.

Most of the encounters, it may be inferred, were accidental and fleeting. Yet one initial recurs rather insistently throughout a ten-year period (from 1917 to 1927), and by following it throughout the *Journals* one can capture the bare outlines of what Gide apparently considered an ideal relationship. In August 1917 the forty-eight-year-old writer, in a state of exceptional excitement, went to Switzerland to bring home "M."

after a month in camp. That he was decidedly in love with his young charge should be apparent from the following dithyrambic description, in which, identifying himself with the dashing, romantic hero of Stendhal's *Chartreuse de Parme*, he calls himself "Fabrice": "On certain days that child took on a surprising beauty; he seemed clothed in grace and, as Signoret would have said, 'with the pollen of the gods.' From his face and from all his skin emanated a sort of blond effulgence. The skin of his neck, of his chest, of his face and hands, of his whole body, was equally warm and gilded. He was wearing that day, with his rough homespun shorts, only a silk shirt of a sharp, purplish red, swelling out over his leather belt and open at the neck, where hung amber beads. He was barefoot and barelegged. A scout's cap held back his hair, which otherwise would have fallen tangled on his forehead, and, as if in defiance of his childlike appearance, he held in his teeth the brier pipe with an amber bit that Fabrice had just given him, which he had never yet smoked. Nothing could describe the languor, grace, and sensuality of his eyes. For long moments as he contemplated him, Fabrice lost all sense of the hour, of the place, of good and evil, of the proprieties, and of himself. He doubted whether any work of art had ever represented anything so beautiful." At that time the boy would seem to have been about fourteen or fifteen.

Frequent mentions of the same youth occur throughout 1917 and 1918. For one evening Gide is momentarily tormented by jealousy. They see each other frequently in Paris, visit friends together in Carantec, and go to Limoges for two days. By 1922 "M." has a mistress named "Bronja," an odd name that Gide borrows for the daughter of Mme Sophroniska in *Les Faux-Monnayeurs*. In May 1923 Gide takes him to Annecy-Talloires for a four-day holiday on the beautiful lake of Annecy, and in September of the same year they go to Tunis together. By May 1924 Gide fears that he is losing "M.," and in October of that year he postpones his trip to the Congo because of the youth's examinations. Happily this delay also permits the writer to finish his novel, *Les Faux-Monnayeurs*, on 8 June 1925. Five weeks later he sets out on the long voyage in darkest Africa which is to last until June 1926 and to produce two books, *Le Voyage au Congo* and *Le Retour du Tchad* (combined in English as *Travels in the Congo*).

Now, it is well known that André Gide was accompanied on that very important, year-long journey of exploration by young Marc Allégert, the fourth son of the Calvinist minister and missionary, Élie Allégret, who had served as Gide's tutor and best man at his wedding. André Gide considered Marc Allégret as his adopted son, and certainly the documentary film and numerous still photographs that the young man brought back from the Congo helped to launch him on his career as a writer of scenarios and film-director. If the initial "M." does not stand, then, for Marc Allégret in every instance, it certainly does in many cases. This assumption gains strength from the journal-entry of 9 June 1928 recording the giving up of a projected voyage to New Guinea with "Marc": "I fear, if I take him to New Guinea, doing him a disservice and getting him definitely out of the habit of work. It is the pleasure, the happiness of being with him, that leads me there, even more than any curiosity for distant places. That felicity, to which I surrender, seriously falsifies my thought. It was for him, to win his attention, his esteem, that I wrote *Les Faux-Monnayeurs*, just as I wrote all my preceding books under the influence of Em. or in the vain hope of convincing her." Finally, the posthumous revelation that Mme André Gide burned all her husband's letters to her in late 1918 confirms the identification, for Gide noted at the time: "She did it, she told me, just after I left for England. Oh, I am well aware that she must have suffered dreadfully from my departure with Marc; but did she have to take revenge on the past?"

In a strange, recent book entitled *A la recherche d'André Gide* (*In Quest of André Gide*), written in a spirit of Gidian sincerity that publicizes many a significant, hidden aspect of the famous writer, Gide's close friend, Pierre Herbart, rightly makes much of that incident, the first serious revolt on the part of the sacrificed wife. M. Herbart says: "At no moment does he bring out the essential fact: for the first time (at least so far as he himself admits) he had, with reference to his own ethic, *betrayed* his wife by going away with a boy *he loved*. That episode which suddenly ruins the whole structure of his moral code (love dissociated from desire) is told us by Gide solely through Madeleine and because it is necessary to an understanding of her destructive deed." This diagnosis is certainly correct. 1918 marks a great turning point in the life of André Gide because until then he could convince himself that he had successfully maintained the divorce between the spirit and the flesh, between love and desire, by giving all his pure, disembodied love to Madeleine and satisfying the demands of his flesh elsewhere. But suddenly it became clear to her that the ethics of André Walter had broken down and that he had robbed her of the little she had. In a gesture of understandable revolt, she destroyed her most precious possession—the collection of his letters, which he himself calls a most beautiful correspondence, recording from the days of childhood his consistent, disincarnate love for her. The relationship with Marc had given those letters the lie. Vainly André Gide wept for a solid week at the thought that the best of him, on which he was counting to balance the worst that he was making so flagrantly public, was now lost to the world. Yet nothing of what he wrote about that capital incident reveals that he sensed why she chose that particular form of violent revolt. Throughout the rest of his life, indeed, he continued the fiction that he had never really loved anyone but her.

Anyone who strove, during the life of André Gide, to determine under just what conditions he married Madeleine Rondeaux must have been perplexed by a wise letter he wrote to an unknown correspondent on 17 April 1928 and published in his works. It reads:

"You may be sure that in psychology there are nothing but individual cases and that, in a case like yours, too hasty generalizations may lead to the most serious errors.

"With this reservation, allow me to consider as most unwise a matrimonial experiment which, if it fails, will surely compromise a woman's happiness and very probably yours as well if your heart is in the right place. But let me repeat that all cases are individual, and, in order to advise you pertinently, it would not suffice for me to know you better; I should also have to know her to whom you would be attaching yourself.

"The question of a confession is as ticklish as can be. I am tempted to tell you: if you do not make one immediately (I mean before the marriage) never make it. But in that case you must manage never to have to make one—and you will surely need to make one sooner or later if you are not capable of behaving as a husband.

"As a general rule, it is better to sacrifice oneself than to sacrifice another person to oneself. But all that is theory; in practice it happens that one becomes aware of the sacrifice only long after it is accomplished."

Does this imply that he told his fiancée all about himself? Or rather that he was one of those who had to confess upon discovering that he was not "capable of behaving as a husband"? All that we know of the character of André Gide would contribute to the former supposition. On the other hand, a maxim of his published in 1925 in the little collection of *Caractères* would suggest rather the latter hypothesis. Like the "Characters" of La Bruyère, it is stated in general terms: "The worst suffering in love is probably not being deceived by the beloved but rather deceiving her oneself. It is perceiving that one has deceived her, disappointed her, that one is not the person she loved, the person one thought oneself to be when giving oneself to her; it is awakening as another in her arms. . ."

More convincing evidence appeared two years before Gide's death in the fat and fascinating volume of his correspondence with Paul Claudel. Shocked by a certain page of *Les Caves du Vatican*, the Catholic poet had written from Hamburg demanding to know whether or not Gide was homosexual. Gide replied immediately and categorically: "Now it is to the friend that I am speaking as I should speak to the priest, whose strict duty would be to keep my secret, before God. I have never felt any desire for woman; and the great sorrow of my life is that the most constant, the most prolonged, the greatest love could not be accompanied by any of what ordinarily precedes it. It seemed on the contrary that love prevented desire in me." But before making this definitive statement, in which the already familiar divorce of love and desire appears, he had warned: "I beg you to consider only this: that I love my wife more than life itself, and that I could not forgive you any act, any word on your part that would endanger her happiness." Surely this implies that in 1914 Madeleine Gide did not *know*, or rather that her husband *thought* she did not know. And if he had not confessed to her by then, there is little reason why he should have done so subsequently otherwise than in his books.

As if further to complicate an intriguing mystery of human relationships, the rumor circulated, in the last years of Gide's life, that he had an illegitimate daughter who had grown up in the south of France. Reference to the *Journals* showed frequent mentions, from 1926 on, of "little Catherine." After the war she began to be seen in his company—an attractive young woman with a marked resemblance to her father. By the time of the Nobel Prize, their photograph had appeared in newspapers, she was reported to have married the young writer, Jean Lambert, and Gide was known to be a grandfather. In the ensuing years the date of Catherine Gide's birth has been given as 1923 and her mother has been several times identified in print as the daughter of the painter Théo Van Rysselberghe.

So much could be pieced together during André Gide's lifetime by a careful reading of his works. By implication one got the impression that Francis Jammes summarized when he re-

Mme ANDRÉ GIDE (1897)

ferred to his friend's wife as "Madame Sainte Gide." Nonthe-
less, the intimate drama of Gide's conjugal life remained a mystery, as did the personality of the wife who had never shared his
fame.

With what keen curiosity and excited anticipation, then, did
we note a passage in the last *Journals* in which Gide, blocked
in German-occupied Tunis in March 1943, wondered if he
would ever see again the private papers he had left in Paris—
among which, he says, "the manuscript relating to Em., in which
I had transcribed the unpublished parts of my *Journal* and everything concerning that supreme part of my life which might
explain and throw light upon it." On his return to Paris he
found the precious documents intact and was thus able to have
them printed in Neuchâtel by his friend Richard Heyd under
the strange title of *Et nunc manet in te* and in a private edition
of but thirteen copies, each bearing the name of the recipient.
That was in 1947 at the time of his receiving the Nobel Prize.
But even then, to all but a handful of most intimate friends, the
bibliographical entry of a new Latin title for the year 1947 remained a tantalizing mystery until a few months after Gide's
death when, according to the author's wishes, M. Heyd issued
the text publicly. As for the Virgilian or pseudo-Virgilian words
Gide chose as a title, he interpreted them as suggesting that his
wife lived on solely in his memory; because of the ambiguity
of the title, I called my English version *Madeleine*.

It is in the pages of the previously unpublished "Intimate
Journal" appended to the essay proper (which was written
within a few months of Mme Gide's death) that the incident
of the burned letters is told for the first time. The account was
originally consigned to Gide's *Journals* under date of 21 November 1918 and then held up for posthumous publication. Yet significant and revealing as that episode is, it could not have been
fully appreciated without the preceding essay, in which Gide
portrays the devoted, selfless Madeleine André Gide and analyzes their conjugal life. He explains, for instance, that his love

seemed the more worthy of her the more ethereal it was, for he was convinced by the example of the austere widows and spinsters who had brought him up that desires belonged exclusively to men. The only woman in his family to whom it was possible to attribute "the least carnal perturbation" happened to be Madeleine's mother, and the daughter's reprobation for her mother's misconduct only contributed to his blindness. Furthermore, he says, because Madeleine "seemed to me all soul and, as far as the body was concerned, all fragility, I did not consider that it amounted to depriving her greatly to keep from her a part of me, that I counted all the less important since I could not give it to her. . ."

Nevertheless, worried by the nature of his own desires, he told his story to a doctor before becoming engaged. That worthy theoretician, who can be forgiven if at all only because of the age in which he lived, urged the young man to get married without fear and promptly forget all the rest, for he would soon find himself returning spontaneously to "the natural instinct." Gide doubtless had that consultation in mind when he wrote his letter of advice to a similar young man in 1928.

Although the essay contains no revelations as to André Gide's sexual life, it does reveal with what stupefying thoughtlessness (in a more sophisticated person it would be called revolting cynicism) he began yielding to his instincts even during his honeymoon in Italy and North Africa. One can only agree with his mature judgment that his pure love for his wife served to divide him more radically than he already was split, for heart and senses pulled him in opposite directions. Yet it is clear from every measured word he has written of her that Madeleine was necessary to his development, that her mute reproach constituted at times a check and at others an invitation to elements of his character whose conflict produced his varied literary work. Without her as witness of his life, he might never have resolved his contradictions in the equilibrium of art. In the large yellow house at Cuverville in which everything shone with polish and breathed bourgeois virtues, as in the obscure recesses of his mind, she served to maintain the systole and diastole rhythm to which he had early become accustomed. That in the process she was sacrificed, as those close to genius so often are, is now obvious; but, as her headstone proclaims, "Blessed are those that bring peace. . ."

Gide's second posthumous work, on the other hand, makes a number of specific statements about his sexual life. Written during his last year and a half as a kind of rambling self-portrait in the manner of Montaigne, the manuscript of *Ainsi soit-il ou Les Jeux sont faits (So Be It or The Chips are Down)* lay on his work-table until his death. After his fatal illness began, he continued to think of it, and the last lines were added in a trembling hand, in the middle of the night of 13 February 1951 just before he entered the final coma. A curious insistence, most notable toward the end of the work, constantly brings up his sexual life in a matter-of-fact manner that partakes neither of self-justification nor of defiance. Doubtless in his final and most informal communing with himself he felt impelled to state himself definitively about that controversial aspect of his nature. He says flatly, for instance: "As for my sexual tastes, I never hid them except when they might bother others: without exactly flaunting them, I let them be apparent; this is partly because I never thought them such as to dishonor me. It is lack of restraint, indulgent surrender to those tastes that dishonors; but this concerns no one but me." A few pages further on, he answers a popular misunderstanding by insisting that a moral or intellectual or sentimental interest that he took in anyone automatically excluded any erotic stimulation, so that his "numerous friendships remained wholly free of any sensual intrusion." To this those friendships owed their solidity and duration.

Everything Gide says about his sexual life here and elsewhere suggests a certain promiscuity or "varietism" as some specialists say; but how could the pederast whose interest is awakened exclusively by a certain transitory period of adolescence fail to be promiscuous throughout a long life? Like his character Édouard at the end of *Les Faux-Monnayeurs*, turning his attention away from the maturing Olivier and Bernard to the younger group of boys represented by Georges and Caloub, Gide must have constantly been attracted to new faces, as those in whom he had been interested grew out of the attractive age. It is possible, also, that he so completely divorced sex from affection that he found it necessary to avoid repetitions with one individual out of a perhaps unconscious fear that dependency might develop. In his sexual contacts, as in his life generally, Gide maintained his ideal of *disponibilité* that would allow of no entangling alliances. One paragraph in his last writing sheds considerable light on the mechanism of his desire. "I am going to risk," he says, "a very strange admission, that I can sum up in a few words: I have never (so far as I remember) *panted* after anyone. This requires an explanation: during my long life I have seen many individuals in love with a certain person of one sex or the other whom one could not see for a moment without thinking: this can only lead to tragedy. Nothing to be expected, nothing to be hoped for; no reciprocity is possible. As for me, this is enough to stifle all desire in me: an instinct warns me at once; this is one of the secrets of my happiness." This statement incidentally provides an answer to the painful and unnecessary little book of François Derais and Henri Rambaud entitled *L'Envers du Journal de Gide, Tunis 1942–43* (*The Background of Gide's Tunisian Journal*).

But this is not all that is contained in that outspoken final work, *Ainsi soit-il*. After evoking the voluptuous memory of the handsome boy whom the sultan added to his escort as a luxury during his expedition in the Cameroon, the now eighty-one-year-old writer longs to see again on his deathbed the gay smile of "sweet little Mala." Then he adds: "I don't care if these words scandalize some, who will consider them impious. I have promised myself to pay no attention to that. But I should like to be surer than I am that, if I should happen to reread them, I shall not be embarrassed by them myself. Is it really around the least spiritual in me that my last thoughts will gather?—although there would still be time, perhaps, to offer them to that God who is awaiting me, you say, and in whom I refuse to believe."

Whether the thought of Mala or of any similar encounter returned to comfort André Gide during his last moments we shall never know. In any case the last page that he wrote, six days before his death, contains no such allusion. Although still quite recognizably his, the hand is shaky at first, becoming firmer as it continues. In the first two or three lines certain words, through the repetition of a syllable, seem to stammer; but visibly the mind clears as the hand gains in suppleness. There is something infinitely pathetic in the observation that the old man, at the end of a literary career extending over more than sixty years, is tormented, between two periods of coma, by the thought that he may not have said all he had to say, that he may want to add something, he knows not what. Sleepy, but with no desire to sleep, he doesn't know what hour of the night or morning it is. Apparently seeing a clock, he is not sure whether it reads 2:40 or 8:12, and even this he records carelessly as "8:12 or 2:12." Then it is that he adds the final two lines, in which the old Gide fully comes to life again in a stylistically perfect and almost intentionally ambiguous sentence: "My own position in the sky, in relation to the sun, must not make me consider the dawn any less beautiful." Like Goethe's famous legendary *"Mehr Licht!"* these last words can, and probably will in time, lend themselves to endless discussion. Even now, one cannot but wonder whether they echo the materialism he himself expected or, on the other hand, belie his oft-repeated disbelief in an afterlife.

Such considerations, however, lie far afield from the subject at hand. The fact remains that until within a very few months of his death André Gide was still concerned with the subject of his own homosexuality. This fact would seem to corroborate those of his friends, even, who saw him as obsessed with the subject and the critic who characterized him as "a case of generalized inversion." The justification for such a feeling—and many inarticulate readers must have shared it—lies in the intrusion of this subject, not only into *Corydon*, the memoirs, the *Journals*, and all the writings of a personal nature, but also into the works of imagination.

When shocked by the *Caves du Vatican*, long before he knew of any of the personal revelations, Claudel wrote Gide: "If you are not a homosexual, why such a predilection for that type of subject?" To this Gide replied: "By what cowardice, since God calls me to speak, should I neglect that question in my books? I did not choose to be as I am." Ignoring this reply, Claudel promised Gide the absolute silence he requested, adding: "but you are the one who speaks out and makes a spectacle of himself. Such a thing has never been seen since the days of paganism. No writer, not even Wilde, has done that."

The fact is that, by that year of 1914, already the *Nourritures terrestres*, *Saül*, *L'Immoraliste*, and the *Caves du Vatican* contained overt allusions to homosexuality. And anyone who was looking for such implications could have easily read them into several other works. Claudel was quite justified, then, in speaking of a predilection for that theme.

Possibly the explanation for such an insistence on the part of Gide might be found in what he says himself of Dostoevsky's characters: "He is particularly attracted to disconcerting cases, to those that rise up as challenges to accepted ethics and psychology. Obviously in the current ethics and in that psychology, he himself does not feel at ease. [. . .] Let us recognize in his abnormal physiological state a sort of invitation to revolt against the psychology and ethics of the herd." How much more true would this be when, as in Gide's case, the "abnormality" is not simply physiological, as Gide classes the Russian novelist's epilepsy. Again, speaking of Oscar Wilde (and in this case the similarity is closer), Gide says: "Here, as almost always, and often without the artist's knowing it, it is the secret of the depths of his flesh that prompts, inspires, decides." But such an explanation rests wholly on unconscious motivation; and Gide, except in his extreme youth, was always eminently lucid about himself. In relation to almost every aspect of his life and work, one must be suspicious of explaining anything with reference to the unintentional. Gide was conscious to the point of self-consciousness.

Now, the conscious motivation for his regular insistence upon homosexuality lies first in his desire not to sacrifice to the conventions, as so many writers do, with a resulting distortion of psychology. Secondly, and this is probably even more important a consideration, he hoped, by treating the homosexual experience on exactly the same plane as the more familiar heterosexual experience, to legitimize and "naturalize" homosexuality. And, despite all the criticisms he thereby drew upon himself, he came as near achieving that end as any man could expect to do in a lifetime. "I shall teach you, Nathanael," as he says in the *Nourritures*, "that all things are divinely *natural*."

Without applying psychoanalysis to André Walter's erotic dreams (such as the one in which he sees a monkey raise the beloved's skirts to reveal nothing but black emptiness) or to Urien's visions of saffron-skinned pearl divers visited in their sleep by vampires from the nearby forest, one can still find overt implications in Gide's earliest writings. For example, one of André Walter's friends recommends liberating the soul by giving the body what it asks. "But," is the reply, "the body would have to ask for possible things; if I were to give it what it asks, you would be the first to cry shame;—and could I satisfy it?" Later, when André's reason is already undermined, he dreams of tanned children bathing naked in a river; the next day, in his solitude, he thinks of their supple bodies and would like to bathe with them and let his hands touch the softness of their brown skins. It is certainly significant that the shy and still inexperienced youth that Gide then was should interpret such a thought as a symptom of madness.

Le Voyage d'Urien contains more than one rejection of sensual pleasure, but the most pointed one occurs when the sailors and cabin-boys, sleeping on the open deck in tropical waters, dream aloud of love. As for the pure knights, "We remained standing, for we dared not lie down, and all night long we heard their sighs mingle with the sea's passionate swelling."

By the time of the *Nourritures terrestres*, however, sexual experience is welcomed gladly as the author had welcomed it at Susa and Algiers. Cabin-boys figure here too, but their rôle is openly recognized, for Ménalque tells how he equipped a yacht and set forth with three friends, a crew, and four cabin-boys, becoming enamored himself of the least handsome among them. The author tells of the postillion's coming to join him in the hay when he would go and sleep "deep in the barn-loft." And later he sings of the African goat-herd he loves. Yet neither Ménalque nor the author is presented as exclusively homosexual. When enumerating the different types of beds in which he has slept, the latter says: "There were beds in which courtesans awaited me; others in which I awaited young boys." Indeed, this can only reflect a conscious attempt on the part of André Gide to present the two varieties of experience on a footing of equality, with no distinction, moral or aesthetic, between them. Such a matter-of-fact handling of the subject—and with no more insistence than Virgil and Whitman had shown in somewhat similar works—undoubtedly contributed to the general impression of a glorification of the senses in every aspect.

But immediately afterward when he wrote *Saül*, Gide's attitude had changed. His deeply rooted puritanism had made him reproach himself for the life upon which he had just joyfully embarked; and the collapse and condemnation of his friend Oscar Wilde doubtless presented a frightening lesson to him. In reaction he had married the heaven of Madeleine, hoping thus to escape the hell he bore within him. Yet even during the wedding-trip he succumbed to the charms of the youths he encountered and abandoned his young wife to seek them. As he

wrote of that period many years later: "I acted like an irresponsible person. A demon inhabited me." Then it was that he
created the sombre character of the mad king of Israel, falling
in love with the naïve and handsome shepherd David, killing
his queen when she stands in his way, and dying consumed by
his demons. Again, as in the *Cahiers d'André Walter*, Gide was
ready to equate the direction of his sexual instinct with madness. His comment on the critics' indifference on the first presentation of the tragedy in 1922 clearly reveals his self-identification with Saul: "They saw nothing but declamation in it, as
they saw nothing but words in my *Nourritures*. Are you then
unable to recognize a sob unless it has the same sound as yours?"

L'Immoraliste was written during the same period and shows
much the same attitude. Claudel, in fact, saw Gide as struggling actively with the devil and almost succumbing to him in the
writing of both books. Certainly of all Gide's works of imagination, *L'Immoraliste* is the one that most obviously appears as a
homosexual document.

There is no denying that the novel does depict, with a detailed psychological penetration unmatched even in Thomas
Mann's *Death in Venice*, the emotional evolution of a pederast.
The progress from the convalescent's innocent interest in children as healthy little animals to Michel's preference for the
urchins his wife neglects and his awareness that her presence
embarrasses him when he is with the Arab boys requires but
nine pages. His unreasoning fear of the good children favored
by Marceline immediately precedes the scene of Moktir's theft
and Michel's sudden liking for him. And it is not long before
the "new man" in Michel has shaved his beard in protest against
the past (and also in an effort to make himself younger and
more attractive)—an act which necessitates the practice of
dissimulation with his wife. Any reader who had read carefully
to that point should not be surprised by the protagonist's later
attitude toward Charles Bocage, his complicity with Bute and
the Heurtevent family, his kissing the young coachman at

Taormina, or his relationship with the Kabyle child at the end of the story. Despite the fact that all of Michel's overt sexual acts are performed with female partners (Marceline at Sorrento, Moktir's mistress at Touggourt, Ali's sister at Sidi), the first readers were not misled as to the nature of his desires. In June 1902, in fact, Jammes wrote the author: "The lover's lane is a hospital, the husband a lamentable lunatic without the positive conviction of vice, an ineffectual sadist and homosexual." Whatever such readers saw in the novel Gide had consciously put there; yet he did not want them to look upon Michel's homosexuality as the central theme.

Inasmuch as Henri Ghéon and André Gide were daily companions at the time, we can assume that Ghéon's review of the novel in August 1902 represents the author's point of view when it states: "I wonder at certain critics who so readily penetrated it and reduced it to so little. One such saw in it only exactly what he was looking for, what remains secondary despite a few details, like a discreet corollary to the real action: I mean the sexual anecdote." A very few months later, in fact, when the second edition of *L'Immoraliste* appeared, Gide had added a Preface in which he said: "If some distinguished minds have deigned to see in this drama but the exposition of an odd case and in its hero but a sick man, if they failed to realize that some very urgent ideas of very general interest nevertheless inhabited it, the fault lies not in those ideas and that drama but in the author and specifically in his awkwardness—although he put into the book all his passion, all his tears, and all his skill." The common point of view on a first reading has centered on what Ghéon calls "the sexual anecdote" precisely because it is so skillfully treated, but thoughtful readers have gone beyond that to the basic problem of the tragedy of the weak individualist.

Perhaps Gide was unwise to put his passion and his tears into the novel, but he wanted to depict the utter collapse of a man through yielding to instinct; and the most imperious instinct

he knew was that of the homosexual, against which he had struggled in vain. Over a quarter of a century after *L'Immoraliste*,
Jacques de Lacretelle proved in his novel, *Amour nuptial* (*Married Love*), that the same story could be retold without the
homosexuality. Recounting his tale likewise in the first person,
Lacretelle's unnamed protagonist reveals the same selfishness
as Michel and suffers from the same dissociation of love and
desire. He says: "I often wondered how such a duality could
exist in a person, how the same brain could engender by turns
adoration for holiness and the desire for sensual excesses. The
word hypocrisy would be utterly false here, for the sincerity of
my fervor toward my wife was obvious, and, at the times when
I was subject to such contrary feelings, I was acting according
to the same natural penchant. I was obeying the same will to
fulfillment." Like Michel, he associates virtue with the naïve
and silly, comes to believe in the superiority of evil, and enjoys
discovering the vicious instinct behind the virtuous behavior.
Irresistibly drawn to prostitutes, he learns the value of dissimulation in his relations with his wife. Her prolonged illness, together with her irritating virtue, brings out in him a sort of
unconscious Nietzscheism. Abandoning her more and more in
the pursuit of his pleasures, he finally finds her dead on the
floor of their room one night—much as Michel finds Marceline.

The perfect utilization of Gide's familiar technique of the
tale in *Amour nuptial*, together with the close similarity of subject-matter, suggests that the novel was inspired by *L'Immoraliste*. Furthermore, although Lacretelle certainly could not have
wanted anyone to think of the novel as autobigraphical, he
made his hero a novelist engaged in writing Lacretelle's first
successful work, *Silbermann*. Possibly this shows the influence
on him of *Les Faux-Monnayeurs* and the logbook of that novel
which Gide kept during its writing and dedicated to Lacretelle
in 1926, three years before *Amour nuptial*. In any case, by keeping his novel so close to *L'Immoraliste* in all the essentials and
yet giving its protagonist a different sexual orientation, Jacques

de Lacretelle successfully illustrated the belief of Ghéon that Michel's homosexuality is anecdotal and almost incidental. In another novel, *La Bonifas* (*Marie Bonifas*) of 1925 Lacretelle had already depicted an unconscious female homosexual, but the book seems to owe nothing to *L'Immoraliste.*

If *L'Immoraliste* of 1902 reflects Gide's intimate life to a large degree and portrays, with but little transposition, his bitter struggle with his personal demon, *Les Caves du Vatican* of 1914, in its objectivity and gaiety, contains none of that. By the time he wrote the third of his *soties,* he has clearly learned to live with himself. Even so, he has still been unable, or unwilling, to omit altogether his homosexual preoccupation. Obviously the character of Lafcadio was created *con amore;* characteristically we first see him, even before we meet the handsome youth himself, over Julius's shoulder in a photograph taken on the beach at Duino when he was about fifteen, in which the naked boy is sitting astride an overturned canoe. Late Lafcadio explains that his "uncle" Fabian, Lord Gravensdale, had confiscated his clothes one whole summer so that he might live naked in the warm sunlight. Of another uncle he tells: "Bielkowski paid much attention to me, as did all those who wanted to make a good impression on my mother; but what he did was done, I believe, spontaneously, for he always yielded to his inclination, which sloped steeply in more than one direction. He paid attention to me even more than my mother knew; and I was not beyond being flattered by the special attachment he showed toward me." It was this kind of gratuitous detail (which nonetheless threw light on Lafcadio's upbringing and motivated his later actions) that caused Proust to write Gide after reading the first instalments of the novel in *La Nouvelle Revue Française*: "I should really like to know if all of Cadio's 'uncles' are 'aunties.' How interesting it all is!"

Appropriately all of the few references to homosexuality in *Les Caves du Vatican* employ the same easy, bantering tone. The page to which Claudel objected strenuously, even going so far as vainly to ask that Gide remove it, forms a narcissistic meditation of Lafcadio in the train shortly before Amédée Fleurissoire enters: "The priest of Covigliajo, so easy-going, did not seem in a mood to deprave greatly the child with whom he was talking. Certainly he was in charge of the boy. I should gladly have taken him as a companion—not the priest, good Lord, but the child! With what beautiful eyes he looked up at me, seeking to attract my gaze as nervously as I sought his, but I turned away at once. . . He was not five years younger than I. Yes, fourteen to sixteen, not older. . . What was I like at that age? A stripling full of covetousness, whom I should like to meet today; I think I should have liked myself considerably. . . In the beginning Faby was embarrassed at being enamored of me; he did right to confess it to my mother, for afterward he had a freer conscience. But how his reserve annoyed me! . . ." Such passages seemed dictated by a wilful cynicism, as if Gide intended to shock squeamish readers.

No such intention could be ascribed to *Les Faux-Monnayeurs*. The complexity of the novel's multiple plots and the variety of its characters probably obscure for most readers the fact that the central action hangs upon Édouard's love for Olivier. But this theme is handled so naturally and so directly that all but the most prejudiced tend to take it for granted here. As Fernandez so aptly says, *Les Faux-Monnayeurs* is "the poem of which *Corydon* expresses the theory." After all, Lafcadio is not a homosexual, although he can understand and sympathize with the pederast's desires; and Michel, without knowing anything of the subject intellectually, is a lamentably ill and unhappy individual. Édouard, on the other hand, is healthy, vigorous, well-balanced, and a creative artist. His own attitude toward his pederasty—as remote from the cynicism of Lafcadio as from the anguish of Michel—reflects Gide's mature attitude toward himself and somehow communicates itself to the reader.

Édouard, the "normal" pederast who knows himself and does not struggle against his penchant, stands not only far removed from the torment of Michel and Saul, but also just as far removed from the vice of Proust's Charlus. In fact, he, rather than Corydon, represents Gide's full answer to Proust. Inasmuch as Proust's work was not a tract or a book of memoirs but a novel, it was appropriate for Gide to present *his* view of the attractive homosexual in a work of fiction designed to counterbalance *Sodome et Gomorrhe*. And, in perspective, it would seem that *Les Faux-Monnayeurs*, as probably the most widely read of his works, did more for the tolerance he intended to teach than did *Corydon* and *Si le grain ne meurt* . . . together.

Within the novel even, Gide has constructed an opposition between the good homosexual (Édouard) and the bad homosexual (Passavant). That the latter is shallow, insincere, selfish, and scheming (the very portrait of the counterfeit man and counterfeit world to which Édouard and Gide are opposed) is tantamount to saying: "I do not claim that all pederasts are naturally admirable. There are bad representatives among *them* just as among heterosexuals." Passavant is also interested in Olivier and the superficiality of his interest, together with the way in which he begins to warp the boy's character, serves as a contrast to the beneficent influence of Édouard on the youth. Various attempts have been made to identify Passavant with this or that member of the Paris literary colony, as if this were a *roman à clef*, and one scholarly commentator has futilely analyzed the popular novelist's name into *pas savant* (not learned), *passe avant* (go before), and a reference to the *passavant* or gangway on a galley. It might have been more pertinent to point out that in one of his volumes that appeared while Gide was writing this novel Proust gives the war-cry of the Guermantes family as "Passavant." This should by no means lead us to assume that Robert de Passavant is a caricature of Marcel Proust, but rather simply that Gide, looking for a family name that would not lead to disputes, was struck by this noble *cri* with its aristocratic implications. At most, it may be that Gide half-consciously enjoyed borrowing from "that master of dis-simulation" the name of his master-counterfeiter.

At the time when André Gide made his own momentous self-discovery, homosexuality had no place in letters. Yet less than fifty years later, it had an official standing as one of the recognized themes of modern literature. To claim that so drastic a change was brought about solely by his need to legitimize his anomaly would be exaggerated. But his part in the annexation by literature of this new domain was probably greater than anyone else's. In a public debate that took place in 1935 he said: "Enthusiastically and almost systematically I become the advocate of whatever voice society seeks to stifle (oppressed peoples or races, human instincts), of whatever has hitherto been prevented from or incapable of speech, of anything to which the world has been, either intentionally or unintentionally, deaf. This is probably what leads me to attribute to certain instincts of man an importance that I should be quite ready to recognize as excessive, if I were not too often the only one to listen to their voice." At the height, then, of his Communist fervor, Gide saw his championing of the homosexual as parallel to his advocacy of other social causes. The idea that he was obsessed with the theme, however, is hardly justified in view of the fact that he used it significantly in but one of his eight plays and in but two of his ten novels.

Still, it is manifestly impossible to forget the capital fact of Gide's homosexuality in reading almost any of his works, for it colored his personality and frequently dictated his attitudes. With a different sexual orientation he would perhaps not have been the man divided, "the creature of dialogue," that he was —nor the great questioner of values and disturber of human complacency.

XI. FROM PAGAN DAEMON TO CHRISTIAN DEVIL

". . . I had no sooner *assumed* the demon than my whole biography was at once made clear to me: [. . .] I suddenly understood what had been most obscure to me, to such a point that this assumption took on the exact shape of my interrogation and my preceding wonder."

"There is no work of art without collaboration of the demon."

FOR some time André Gide's belief in an active force of evil served as a stumbling-block for many readers, who noticed with what disconcerting frequency the words Demon, Devil, and Evil One occur in parts of his work. "Satanism" implies worship of the Devil or at least trafficking with him; it suggests witchcraft, black masses, and such infamous figures as Gilles de Rais and the Marquis de Sade. Indulgent readers of Gide set it down as just one more of his contradictions that, by resurrecting the figure of Satan, he should seem to ally himself with such as these while spending much of his life combatting superstition. But since the novels of such Catholics as François Mauriac, Georges Bernanos, and Julien Green in France, since *The Screwtape Letters* of C. S. Lewis and the novels of Charles Williams and Graham Greene in England, there is a tendency to take more seriously this aspect of Gide's work.

Both Denis de Rougemont, an eminent Swiss Protestant, and Claude-Edmonde Magny, writing in a French Carmelite review, have described Gide as one of those rare spirits who show great familiarity with the Devil and talk intelligently of him.

Without ever worshiping Satan or, for that matter, dealing with him any more than the average man does, Gide certainly gave him his due. In fact, to write about the Devil in literature today without discussing Gide would be tantamount to omitting Milton or Blake or Dostoevsky. It is in the company of such writers that he belongs, in this regard, rather than in that of the fifteenth-century. Bluebeard and the man who gave a name to sadism, with whom one otherwise intelligent critic associated him on the grounds of a necessary link between Satanism and homosexuality. Nonetheless, Gide's sexual orientation does enter the discussion because it was the constant current of pederasty in his life, his ambivalent attitude toward his wife, and his consequent guilt-feelings that made him attribute a decisive rôle in his biography to the Devil. In the Spring of 1919, when he began to write the second and capital part of his memoirs, he had to make an effort to exclude from the drama an important actor —the Devil—whom he did not identify until long after the events. He complained to his friend, Roger Martin du Gard, that his task would be so much easier if he could bring the demon out into the open as an active influence. Still it was not quite possible for him to avoid altogether using Satan as an explanation, for the memoirs contain such remarks as this: ". . . in addition, as I have said, my love was almost mystical; and if the devil was deceiving me by making me consider as an insult the idea of any carnal admixture to it, this is something I could not yet realize . . ." or: "Since my adventure at Susa, to be sure, the Evil One had no further great victory to win over me."

Already during the dark years of the First World War, before composing those decisive revelations of *Si le grain ne meurt . . .*, Gide had come clearly to recognize the Devil's share in his tormented destiny. The whole of his "Detached Pages" for 1916 is devoted to this subject; and it is surely significant that they were written simultaneously with the first part of the mystical outburst of *Numquid et tu . . .?*, which they immediately follow in the editions of the *Journals*. For, although he protests that it is not necessary to believe in God in order to believe in the Devil, such a remarkable coincidence of beliefs suggests that he might never have accepted Satan if he had not been spiritually prepared to do so. "I had heard talk of the Evil One," he writes there, "but I had not made his acquaintance. He already inhabited me when I did not yet distinguish him. [. . .] I had invited him to take up his residence in me, as a challenge and because I did not believe in him, like the man in the legend who sells his soul to him in return for some exquisite advantage—and who continues not believing in him despite having received the advantage from him!" As he looks back on his life, Gide recognizes that many of the exhortations he had addressed to himself had contained a diabolic element, that in many a "specious dialogue" with himself he had had an interlocutor. On the other hand, his conviction of a positive external force is not inflexible, for he adds: "If someone should come along later and show me that he lives not in hell but in my blood, my loins, or my insomnia, does he believe that he can suppress him thus? When I say: the Evil One, I know what that expression designates just as clearly as I know what is designated by the word *God*. I draw his outline by the deficiency of each virtue." And a brief dialogue with Satan concludes the meditation with Satan's flattering remark:

"How well we know each other! You know, if you wanted to—"

"What?"

"What good friends we should be! . . ."

That was in 1916, at the height of Gide's mystical crisis. Actually his conviction of the demon's existence did not become firmly established until then. Despite the early representation of Saul's temptations in the guise of a horde of little black demons and the occasional, rather perfunctory mention of the demon pushing Michel madly southward with the ailing Marceline in *L'Immoraliste*, it may fairly be said that the Devil plays no significant part in Gide's work until after the age of forty-five. In fact, he was just that age when in a decisive conversation at Cuverville, Jacques Raverat, a young French artist who had recently married the granddaughter of Charles Darwin and settled in England, confessed to believing in the Devil before believing in God. "I told him," says Gide, "that what kept me from believing in the Devil was that I wasn't quite sure of hating him. Certainly there will be someone in my novel who believes in the devil." That conversation made a deep impression on Gide, for he was to refer to it often in the future and to remember it ten years later when writing *Les Faux-Monnayeurs*, where more than one character is tormented by such a belief.

Although Jacques Raverat's significant intervention in André Gide's life seems to be limited to that one crucial talk growing out of a reading of Milton, he left a profound mark by starting the writer on his absorbing identification of the demon. From then on, Gide's thought on the problem of evil was to burgeon and ramify rapidly, finding confirmation as it grew in his favorite writers. Less than two years later he describes himself as listening to the voice of the Devil despite himself. In the anguished spiritual autobiography of William Hale White, which Arnold Bennett wisely recommended to him in 1915, he found the sincere "Mark Rutherford" deploring, in words that he himself might have written, the popular dismissal of the notion of a personal devil: "No doubt there is no such thing existent; but the horror at evil which could find no other expression than in the creation of a devil is no subject for laughter, and if it do not in some shape or other survive, the race itself will not survive. No religion, so far as I know, has dwelt like Christianity with such profound earnestness on the bisection of man—on the distinction within him, vital to the very last degree, between the higher and the lower, heaven and hell. What utter folly is it because of an antique vesture to condemn as effete what the vesture clothes! Its doctrine and its sacred story are fixtures in concrete form of precious thoughts purchased by blood and tears." Mark Rutherford's thought here does not differ from Gide's apology for using such terms as "the soul" and "the Evil One"—implying, as he says, a certain mythology that "is the most eloquent to explain an inner drama."

It was, however, in 1921–2 that Gide's reflections about the Devil received the most encouraging confirmation—and from two very different literary sources. The first in time was Dostoevsky, whom he had been voraciously rereading and on whom he delivered a series of penetrating lectures at just that moment. In them he confessed to having used the Russian novelist as a pretext to develop his own thoughts, always seeking, like the bees of which Montaigne speaks, what would suit his own honey. Gide consistently did this with his favorite writers—whether Virgil or Whitman, Goethe or Dante or Nietzsche, Browning or Blake or Shakespeare—lovingly finding himself already in them rather than espousing a foreign thought. Charles Du Bos speaks of Gide's unerring faculty for discovering in his predecessors "that particle of virtual Gidism" which they contain. When polishing his Dostoevsky lectures for publication, annoyed that they should still take so much of his time after their delivery and keep him from the massive, Dostoevskian novel he had already begun, he noted: "But everything I find a means of saying through Dostoevsky and apropos of him is dear to me and I attach a great importance to it. It will be, just as much as a book of criticism, a book of confessions, to anyone who knows how to read; or rather: a profession of faith." He had already recognized himself in Dostoevsky before the war, when he wrote a long article on the Russian writer as he emerged from his correspondence. In that study of 1908, Gide had revealed an intimate knowledge of the novels as well as of the numerous collections of letters; and he obviously found a close spiritual relationship between Dostoevsky and himself, for he enjoyed stressing his familiar themes as handled by the Russian precursor.

Yet in *Dostoïevsky d'après sa correspondance* there is not a single mention of the demon—who looms so large in the later study. This simply proves that in 1908 André Gide was not yet ready to recognize the Devil; but in 1921–2 his own thought was so absorbed with that figure that he was pleased to discover what a place it occupied in Dostoevsky's work. He even granted that "some will probably see a Manichean in him."

The second confirmation of Gide's thinking that came to him at this time lay in William Blake. In January 1922, doubtless inspired by the first of the lectures on Dostoevsky and by private conversations with Gide, the critic Charles Du Bos sent him a copy of Blake's *Marriage of Heaven and Hell*. With his customary perceptiveness, the half-American Du Bos, as conversant with English literature as with French, had justly sensed a deep affinity. From a journal-entry of 1914 we know that Gide had already read some Blake "with amazement" in a borrowed volume of *Selections*. Now, after reading the little book he had just received, he noted: "Like an astronomer calculating the existence of a star whose rays he does not yet perceive directly, I foresaw Blake, but did not yet suspect that he formed a constellation with Nietzsche, Browning, and Dostoevsky. The most brilliant star, perhaps, of the group; certainly the strangest and most distant." Almost at once he must have begun translating *The Marriage of Heaven and Hell*—through a natural and already familiar desire to share his discovery with others—for his French version was finished by the beginning of June.

But an even more immediate reaction to Blake's prophetic work than its translation was Gide's introduction of it into his lectures on Dostoevsky. It is almost as if, in his spontaneous assimilation of their thought to his own, he had confused the English poet and the Russian novelist. In the fifth lecture, in fact, he quotes this paragraph as the opening of *The Marriage of Heaven and Hell* (it is not quite the opening) with the remark that Dostoevsky seems to have unwittingly appropriated it: "Without Contraries is no progression. Attraction and Repulsion, Reason and Energy, Love and Hate, are necessary to human existence." One can readily see how this statement, while justifying Gide's conflicts and the ambivalence he felt within himself, must have delighted him by making his beloved progress dependent on such contraries. This might be said to be the theme of Blake's little book, as Gide showed by quoting in that same lecture at least six of its "Proverbs of Hell":

"The road of excess leads to the palace of wisdom."

"If the fool would persist in his folly he would become wise."

"You never know what is enough unless you know what is more than enough."

"The roaring of lions, the howling of wolves, the raging of the stormy sea, and the destructive sword, are portions of eternity too great for the eye of man."

"The cistern contains: the fountain overflows."

"The tigers of wrath are wiser than the horses of instruction."

And, not content with quoting some of the best of Blake's subversive proverbs, Gide adds two of his own devising: "It is with fine sentiments that bad literature is made"; and "There is no work of art without collaboration of the demon." In order to substantiate the latter, indeed, he quotes further from *The Marriage of Heaven and Hell*: "The reason Milton wrote in fetters when he wrote of Angels & God, and at liberty when of Devils & Hell, is because he was a true Poet and of the Devil's party without knowing it." From 1922 onward, in memory of Blake, Gide occasionally entitles as "Proverbs of Hell" some of the pithiest remarks in his *Journals*, such as "Descend to the bottom of the well if you wish to see the stars." The form was a congenial one; to be sure, many other examples can be found in his work, without the label, even long before his encounter with William Blake. *Paludes* and *Le Prométhée mal enchaîné*, for instance, abound in them. Each reader could, in fact, make his own collection of infernal maxims from Gide's writings.

During the composition of his *Dostoïevsky*, Gide was also writing what he considered his only true novel, *Les Faux-Monnayeurs*; and from 1919 until 1925 he kept a special notebook in which he recorded "inch by inch" (as he said in English) the progress of the novel. It is not strange that in that workbook, originally published in 1926 as *Journal des "Faux-Monnayeurs"* (*Journal of "The Counterfeiters"* in America, and *Logbook of The Coiners* in England) and appreciated chiefly for its fascinating insights into the problems of literary creation, Satan should play a most important rôle. In early January 1921 Gide noted there that the more we deny him the more reality we give to the Devil, thus affirming him by our negation, and foresaw that this might become the central subject of his novel—"in other words the invisible point about which everything gravitates." A few days later he expressed the desire to let the Devil "circulate incognito throughout the entire book, his reality growing stronger the less the other characters believe in him. This is the distinguishing feature of the Devil, whose introductory motif is: 'Why should you be afraid of me? You know very well I don't exist.'" It was then that he wrote a dialogue entitled "Identification of the Demon" to explain that capital remark, which appeared to him as "one of the catchwords of the book."

From the fact that that dialogue did not find its way into the novel and the observation that the Devil hardly appears openly therein it has been assumed that Gide changed his mind on this point, as on so many others. But this conclusion overlooks the key-words "invisible point" and "incognito." It never entered Gide's intentions to list the Devil in the cast of characters. To be sure, the Demon fairly frequently shows the tips of his horns throughout the novel in more than a merely metaphorical sense. On the first page he influences Bernard to violate his mother's secrets and on the last page he persuades old La

Pérouse that the mysterious tapping on the wall is *his* infernal voice. Elsewhere he makes Bernard find a coin with which to withdraw Édouard's luggage, pushes Vincent to gamble the family savings and then smilingly watches him slip the little key into Lady Griffith's door, inhabits Olivier the night he receives Bernard's letter, and supplies Édouard with sophistries justifying his treatment of Boris.

It is Vincent Molinier, however, who best embodies the character Gide promised himself in 1914 to put into his novel: the person who actively believes in the Devil. Although we are told that his scientific education kept him from believing in the supernatural and thus gave the Demon a great advantage over him, we later see him reappear in Africa as a madman, probably a murderer, who identifies himself with Satan. Yet Vincent is himself a shadowy character at best whom we most often meet indirectly through Édouard's journal or the conversation of others; it is thus most appropriate that this last mention of him should occur in a letter written by a man who knows neither him nor his name and that the letter should be read by Vincent's brother, to whom it never occurs to identify him.

The key to Vincent lies in the *Journal des "Faux-Monnayeurs,"* where his creator said of him more than four years before the novel was published: "Vincent gradually lets himself be permeated by the diabolic spirit. He imagines he is becoming the Devil; it is when things go best for him that he feels the most damned. [. . .] In the end he believes in the existence of Satan *as in his own;* in other words, he eventually believes he is Satan." This, then, is the evolution of Vincent Molinier. But what Gide does not say is that he also stands as the *cause* of the novel's action. By leading Laura into adultery before the novel begins, he provokes Édouard's return from England to save her, Bernard's meeting with Édouard and Laura, and all that ensues. By handing over his brother Olivier to the vicious Passavant, he further complicates the plot sufficiently so that he can then leave the stage altogether. There are other diabolic characters in *Les Faux-Monnayeurs*—notably the mysterious Strouvilhou, Passavant himself, and to a smaller degree Ghéridanisol and even Armand Vedel; but Vincent's satanic rôle is even more central than theirs. In all his behavior one can hear echoes of that famous dialogue between Ivan Karamazov and the Devil which Gide so much admired. Is it not possible that it was in his person that Gide intended to make the Devil "circulate incognito" throughout the novel?

The moment he had finished writing *Les Faux-Monnayeurs*, Gide himself set out for the Congo on a year-long voyage. Instead of there identifying himself with the Devil as the unbalanced Vincent had done in the same setting (and as some of his readers were beginning to identify him), he flatly stated once and for all his disbelief in the Demon. On 21 September 1925 he wrote in his travel diary apropos of Bossuet's *Traité de la Concupiscence*, which he had been reading: "I know only too well for having often indulged in the practice myself: there is nothing in the life of a nation or in our individual life that is not susceptible of a mystical or teleological interpretation, in which cannot be seen, if one really wants to, the active opposition of God and the Demon. And that interpretation may even seem the most satisfactory simply because it is the most picturesque. My whole mind at present revolts against that complacent practice, which does not seem to me quite fair." In the case of Vincent Molinier, then, as in that of André Walter in his first book, André Gide had made his creature carry out to its logical extreme a tendency of his own nature, saving himself from the same fate, however, by that grain of common sense which he denied to his fictional character.

Over twenty years later Gide was to express no less categorically his mature attitude toward Satan by stating: "As for me, I look upon the Devil as an invention, júst like God himself. I do not believe in him; but I pretend to believe in him and gladly lend myself to this game. . ." Yet he wrote these words in his preface to *The Private Memoirs and Confessions of a Jus-*

tified Sinner by James Hogg, a book he wished to save from
oblivion just because it contains so vivid a characterization of
the Demon as "the exteriorization of our own desires, of our
pride, of our most secret thoughts." In other words, to the
very end of his life André Gide continued to play with the
concept of a personal Devil, employing traditional terminology, half convincing himself that he believed, and going out
of his way to adopt any literary work that personified the evil
spirit.

In brief, Gide's contradictory attitudes on the subject can
be summarized by stating simply that, whereas his conscious
mind rejected the idea of the Devil together with the idea of
God, he was constantly and obscurely drawn to posit both concepts as the extrapolation of an inner conflict. At the end of his
"Identification of the Demon" he formulated this theory: "Just
like the kingdom of God, hell is within us;" and a few years
later he found the same thought admirably expressed by Milton
in the line in which Satan says "Which way I fly is Hell; myself
am Hell."

It is dangerous to insist on the fact that evil is basic, for
he who does so is generally thought to be very wicked himself.
As Gide soon learned, the world has a tendency to think that
by merely admitting the existence of evil we somehow create
it. Perhaps none of Gide's provocative remarks has been more
often discussed or used against him than the first two of his own
"Proverbs of Hell" boldly inserted into his *Dostoïevsky*. Certain critics, perhaps wilfully ignoring the fact that he was cas-
tigating merely so-called "edifying literature," interpreted his
second proverb to mean that good literature is made only with
bad sentiments. Others reminded him that what he now called
the demon's collaboration he had named otherwise in 1895
when he wrote in the Foreword to *Paludes* of "that share of the
unconscious that I should like to call God's share," adding: "A
book is always a collaboration, and the more the book is worth
the smaller the scribe's share is. . ." But to this Gide might

have replied that he had only lately learned to identify his collaborator properly, and that, furthermore, as he says in the last of his "Proverbs of Hell" in 1941:

"The promise of the caterpillar
Binds not the butterfly."

In any case, the very phrase "collaboration of the demon" in this connection suggests some confusion in Gide's mind—it matters little whether it be intentional or unintentional—between the Christian concept of the Devil and the Greek view of the Daemon—that manifestation of divine energy, which may be good or evil, that element in man's fate which, according to Heraclitus, constitutes his character. It was this latter kind of demon (and a boundless confidence in his prompting) which Gide early found in Goethe and later felt had, in the comfort of Goethe's success, become rather stodgily middle-class. The principle is faithfully described by Stefan Zweig in words that Gide might have signed: "The daemon is the incorporation of that tormenting leaven which impels our being (otherwise quiet and almost inert) towards danger, immoderation, ecstasy, renunciation, and even self-destruction. [. . .] Whatever strives to transcend the narrower boundaries of self, overleaping immediate personal interest to seek adventures in the dangerous realm of enquiry, is the outcome of the daemonic constituent of our being. But the daemon is not a friendly and helpful power unless we can hold him in leash, can use him to promote a wholesome tension and to assist us on our upward path. [. . .] Restlessness of the blood, the nerves, the mind is always the herald of the daemonic tempest." So many of Zweig's expressions here correspond to favorite ideas of Gide—from the transcending of self to the upward path and from the value of renunciation to that of inquiry and unrest—that the passage almost seems to have been written by the French author. It was in just this sense that Gide quoted Goethe as saying: "That a man's strength and his force of predestination were recognizable by the demoniacal element he had in him."

In Gide's case the slipping from a neutral Daemon with as much potentiality for good as for evil to a stimulating and yet frankly evil spirit can be most clearly seen in his letter of 22 November 1929 (his sixtieth birthday) to Montgomery Belgion: "I believe it to be ill-advised, unprofitable, uninstructive to judge human actions, or more exactly to evaluate them, solely on the plane of *good* and *evil*. The comforting and reassuring idea of *good*, which the middle-classes cherish, invites humanity to stagnation, to sleep. I believe that often what society and you yourself call *evil* (at least the evil that is not the result of a mere deficiency, but rather a manifestation of energy) possesses a greater educative and initiative virtue than what you call *good*, and is thus capable of indirectly leading humanity toward progress." But if this is the clearest statement of Gide's eventual fusion of pagan Daemon with Christian Devil, the most revealing indication of this tendency on his part —because wholly unconscious—lies half-hidden in his *Dostoïevsky*.

There, after stating that the intelligence always has a demoniacal role in Dostoevsky and that the novelist invariably links the Devil with the intellect, Gide goes on to say: "The great temptations that the Evil One offers us are, according to Dostoevsky, intellectual temptations, questions. And I do not think I am getting far from my subject by considering first the questions that so long summed up the constant anguish of humanity: 'What is man? Whence does he come? Where is he going? What was he before his birth? What does he become after his death? To what truth can man lay claim?' and even more exactly: 'What is truth?' " It would seem, especially in view of the fact that Gide does not really consider these questions here beyond voicing them and does not develop the thought further, that he is indeed getting away from his subject. Yet if we remember that the questioning spirit is always a noble spirit to Gide, we shall recognize that first Dostoevsky, by insisting upon the interrogation, and then Gide, by attributing to him the questions that have forever haunted mankind, are ennobling Satan.

But even more significant is the fact that we have heard these very questions before in Gide's work. They are precisely the ones that Prometheus in vain asks his eagle. Gide seems to have been insufficiently aware, in fact, that Lucifer (the light-bearer) and Prometheus (the fire-giver) have much in common: both the archangel in revolt against God and the titan rebelling against Zeus are gravely punished for their pride in siding with man. Gide's interest in the Devil parallels his interest in Prometheus; more sophisticated and more subtle in its expression, it replaces that earlier interest. Perhaps because he had early traced a suggestive parallel between Prometheus and Christ, he hesitated to draw another one between Prometheus and Satan, those two arch-unsubmissive spirits who both symbolized progress in his mind. The Devil might be called a Christian counterpart of Prometheus, the greatest Daemon (both in the sense of demi-god and in that of energetic force) of them all. That at least once Gide nevertheless recognized the similarity between them is apparent from his words on Goethe written in 1928 in the outline of a lecture he was to give in Berlin: "No, all is not calm, smiling, and peaceful in Goethe and that is indeed what makes him so great. There is in him something demoniacal, untamed, something Promethean that relates him to the Satan of Milton and Blake, something restive that we still question, that will never reveal its secret or pronounce its final word because that final word is itself an interrogation, a question indefinitely deferred."

Clearly for Gide, as for Goethe, Nietzsche, Dostoevsky, and the other predecessors he admired, the daemonic spirit inhabited, in Zweig's phrase, the dangerous realm of inquiry. It made for progress precisely because it could not leave well enough alone. His own work is interrogative rather than affirmative in spirit, and this fact has contributed more than anything else to its deep and widespread influence. The Russian writer Georges

Adamovitch, whose comments Gide particularly liked, said of him in the course of a debate held in early 1930: "Gide's work is significant chiefly through the questions it raises: 'What is man? Whence does he come? Whither is he going?' Moreover, all great and lasting literary works are significant only in that way." Even Henri Massis, never favorably inclined toward Gide, admitted in another similar debate that "whenever criticism encounters Gide it inevitably touches something in the forefront of man's preoccupations today" simply because he had long been facing independently the principal problems raised by the crisis of modern civilization.

Surely no one could fail to notice that the fundamental questions singled out by Adamovitch as summarizing Gide's work are the very ones Gide had attributed first to Prometheus and later to the Devil. Now, in his *Dostoïevsky*, following on the Devil's questioning, Gide continues: "But since Nietzsche, with Nietzsche, a new question has arisen, one altogether different from the others . . . not so much grafted onto them as upsetting and replacing them, a question that likewise involves its anguish, such as led Nietzsche to madness. That question is: 'Of what is man capable? Of what is a man capable?' That question is accompanied by the dreadful apprehension that man could have been otherwise, could have been more, that he could still be more; that he is unworthily resting after the first stage without concern for his completion." Michel of *L'Immoraliste* had voiced precisely the same Nietzschean question, moved to anguish at the thought of man's untapped resources stifled by proprieties and moral codes. It was Gide's espousal of this daring idea— which he himself recognized to be an atheist's conception, the affirmation of man being motivated necessarily by the negation of God—that made the traditionalist Henri Massis state in his categorical execution of Gide that he had questioned "the very notion of *man* on which we live."

André Gide liked the phrase, feeling that it accurately summarized his intention, and even asked Massis's permission to use it as an epigraph in his next book. He did not do so; but in actual fact the statement might well stand at the head of all his work. As we have seen, the self-transcending of his Philoctetes and Oedipus and the self-realization of so many of his characters from Nathanael to Theseus mark what is probably the noblest and certainly the most consistent of his doctrines. In fact, Gide had already prefigured the debate between himself and Henri Massis as early as 1907 in *Le Retour de l'enfant prodigue*. For the Prodigal is urged forth toward other cultures, other lands, and the unblazed trails leading to them through a need to explore his own potentialities; and in his dialogue with his conformist elder brother he is told: "But what you will never know is the length of time it took man to elaborate man. Now that the model is achieved, let us keep to it." Except for the idea that it required ages for man to reach his present status and that he himself had anything to do with arriving there, this might be Massis speaking. In other words, the critic who represents the *Action Française* point of view is even more conservative and traditionalist than the elder brother of Gide's parable. Many years later, Gide's Oedipus was to complete the thought expressed in part in *Le Retour de l'enfant prodigue* when he tells his sons: "Convince yourself that humanity is doubtless much further from its objective, that we cannot yet even see dimly, than from its starting-point, that already we have ceased to discern."

For nearly forty years, from 1914 until the present, Henri Massis has regularly combatted what he considers the pernicious influence of André Gide. As the most articulate, reasoned and consistent of Gide's attackers, he deserves consideration in any study of Gide's mind and work. Partisan and moralizing in spirit, he early identified himself with such nationalists as Barrès, Maurras, and Léon Daudet, staunchly defending the Occident, or "Latinity" as he sometimes called the French tradition, against pan-Germanism, pan-Slavism, and the intellectual influence of Asia. He took such as Luther, Dostoevsky, Keyserling,

Spengler, and Gandhi as his personal enemies. Of his articles on Gide that he has carefully preserved in three separate collections, the first was inspired by Gide's *Morceaux choisis* of 1921, a fat little volume of selections from the writer's best critical and imaginative writings skillfully put together by Gide and interlarded with many previously unpublished pages, and the second, dating from 1923, was touched off by the *Dostoïevsky*. In both works Massis discerned a basic double desire to legitimize and to influence.

After the lectures on Dostoevsky, in fact, and after the translation of Blake, it was current in certain quarters to identify Gide, largely because of that influence, with Satan himself. Massis spoke of "the demoniacal character" of a work "whose whole art is applied to corrupting"; and the Jesuit Father Victor Poucel discerned "the fingerprints of a maleficent collaborator" in all his work. André Rouveyre, in an incoherent and turgid book purporting to reflect credit upon his misunderstood friend, saw in him "the cloven hoof [. . .] the devil's horns [. . .] and the derisive laughter of Mephistopheles." As the novelist François Mauriac wrote on the day of Gide's death, he had come to take on, at least for Catholic readers, the appearance of a Lucifer.

It would be tedious and otiose to cite all of Gide's numerous adversaries and detractors. Despite some isolated attacks and general warnings inspired by individual works of Gide before the First World War, the real offensive against him and his influence began in the early twenties with the articles of Massis, Eugène Montfort, and Henri Béraud. The time was appropriate because Gide's work—particularly the early *Nourritures terrestres*—did not become widely known until then. Reprints of earlier titles, originally published in limited editions, then appeared simultaneously with new works to help his influence to operate like a delayed-action bomb. Not having known any notoriety before 1914, under attack Gide now began to affirm himself, to become aware of his ruggedness, as he said. Although the Gidian legend kept growing until the caricature obscured his true image, there was some bitter consolation in the fact that the attacks had made him more famous in a few months than his books had done in thirty years.

The brunt of the offensive was directed at Gide's "baneful" influence. He was accused of being a destructive spirit (although he claimed to be destroying only what was already falling in ruins), of forming a vain and deliquescent generation, of relaxing the morals of an already disoriented epoch, and in general of being responsible for the bankrupcy of post-war youth. In brief, he became the scapegoat for everything in the restless age of the twenties—such as the romanticism of adolescence, the cult of unrest, and the aesthetic anarchy of surrealism—which moralists deplored. Hardly a crime was committed in France, or in Europe for that matter, by some pathological youth without Lafcadio's name being mentioned in the press, coupled with the magic formula *"acte gratuit."* One critic even linked Gide with the infamous Loeb-Leopold case in Chicago. To be sure, Gide contributed somewhat to the legend—not only by the publication of *Corydon* and his memoirs—but perhaps even more by his public interest in gruesome and vicious crimes as represented by his series of documents under the general heading of *Ne jugez pas . . . (Judge Not . . .)* and by his use of a school boy's enforced suicide in *Les Faux-Monnayeurs.*

Perhaps the most self-damaging of his writings, however, was a brief "Conversation with a German a Few Years before the War" which, noted in June 1904, the day after the single encounter, first appeared in the *N. R. F.* in 1919 before being included in *Incidences* of 1924. The German, who had come to Paris just to talk with Gide after getting out of prison, had said among other things: "Action is what I want. Yes, the most intense action . . . even to murder." After a long silence, Gide had replied: "No, action does not interest me so much by the sensation it gives me as by its results, its repercussion. This is why, even though it interests me passionately, I think it interests

me even more when committed by another. I am afraid, I beg
you to understand me aright, to compromise myself. I mean, to
limit by what I do what I might do. Thinking that because I have
done *this* I shall never be able to do *that* becomes unbearable.
I prefer *making others act* to acting myself." Years later, after
the last sentence had been frequently used against him, Gide attempted to explain that back in 1904 he had wanted to hold at
a distance an adventurer who, by adopting Gide's own ethic, had
forced him to the right of his real position. " 'If it may be that
my teaching leads to crime, I prefer that it should be you who
commit the crime.' This is what my sentence meant. Grève [the
name of the German, which Gide had not originally revealed,
permits us to identify him as the later translator of *Paludes*,
Saül, and *La Porte étroite*, then but twenty-five years old] was
playing the role of drunken helot in my presence. Through self-
esteem I tried to save face; but I felt his advantage and that he
got the better of me. I was beaten by my 'disciple' and was disavowing my ethic if that was where it was to lead." This is Gide's
belated explanation because others had conferred an unwelcome
notoriety upon his opposition between *faire agir* and *agir*. In
actual fact, the only people he ever caused to act in his stead
were his fictional characters—Saul, Michel, Alissa, Lafcadio,
among others—and it is not negligible that each of them suffers
the consequences of his action. Yet as early as 1896 he had
stated the same thought without incurring the slightest reprobation, doubtless because he then avoided the first person singular.
In his "Literature and Ethics" he had quoted Goethe thus:
"There are no crimes, however great, that on certain days I have
not felt capable of committing"; and then had gone on to comment: "The greatest minds are also the most capable of great
crimes, which they generally do not commit, through wisdom,
through love, or because they would limit themselves by so doing." The thought is true and suggestive; its expression became
dangerous only when Gide *seemed* to be cynically showing himself in the rôle of a criminal's inspirer.

But Gide may not have been either guiltless or shortsighted in this case, for it is difficult not to believe that when he published the conversation with Grève in 1919 and again five years later he was not motivated by a characteristic spirit of bravado compounded of scorn for his detractors and the pleasure of misleading opinion. Depicting himself in the company of a time-server who talked casually of murder doubtless flattered in him a puerile tendency to shock the conventional virtues. There was in Gide, in fact, a permanent complicity, probably by reaction to his own upbringing, with the outlaw and the sinner. In this he was like his own Michel—preferring the boy who stole the scissors, prowling at night in order to rub elbows with those who prowl, living vicariously a dangerous life of daring. The suspicious, the abnormal, the vicious in a man, an instinct, a behavior invariably elicited his interest—less for the individual himself or for the act itself than for what they could teach him about the human heart.

He had voiced the principle in his two articles of 1909 on "Nationalism and Literature" (which he long considered, according to Louis Martin-Chauffier, as his most important critical writing). There he expounded Carey's economic theory (in opposition to Ricardo's) that man first cultivates the easy, accessible, relatively poor lands: those on the heights. Not until much later does he think of turning to the richest lands, which must be disputed with the rising waters and with the most exuberant natural vegetation—"Luxurious and dark forests," said Gide, "where the tangle of undergrowth exhausts the advancing pioneer; lands peopled with cunning, fierce beasts; swampy, shifting lands full of noxious effluvia. . . Those unexpectedly fecund lands are the last to be exploited." Likewise for a long time literature limited itself to the readily cultivated plateaux, poor in top-soil: lofty thoughts and noble passions. "Racine," Gide wrote, "would not deserve so many honors if he had not realized, just like Baudelaire, the extraordinary resource offered the artist by the lower regions—wild, feverish, and unexplored—of an

Orestes or a Hermione, of a Phaedra or a Bajazet, and that the lofty regions are the poor ones. If he himself achieved the high plateaux of virtue, is this not a secret reason for his silence at the height of his career: the lack of depth he found in the subjects that suited his piety?" Dostoevsky, too, had exploited the rich virgin valleys, and this was clearly one of Gide's reasons for liking him. Long before he knew Freud's work, Gide was as interested as Dostoevsky or Baudelaire in the chartless underground of human psychology.

And this explains his curiosity for the criminal, the vagabond, the outcast, for whom he had a fellow-feeling as if studying in them what in other circumstances he might have become himself. His *Journals* show that everywhere he went he seemed to attract such individuals, some of whom even found their way into his books in the guise of Protos and Strouvilhou. The mere fact that he recorded such encounters gave credence to a libelous pamphlet of 1931 entitled *Un Malfaiteur: André Gide* (*An Evildoer*) and prefaced by the "Archbishop of Beaumont, happily deceased" (apparently the same who had "refuted" Rousseau's *Émile* in the eighteenth century). Among other things, it related how a young man of great promise had been "perverted, dissipated, and finally led to suicide by the influence of André Gide." Although Gide himself characterized the story as "a pure (or impure) invention, what the English call 'a forgery,'" Camille Mauclair repeated it on the first page of *La Petite Gironde* the same year and René Gillouin did likewise in the leading article of the Sunday supplement of the *Journal de Genève* for 7–8 February 1942.

It is characteristic of one polemicist simply to copy another, repeating the same falsehoods. Disseminated by men who had read Gide most carelessly and with most prejudiced minds, the image of an elusive, Satanic corruptor of youth in flowing cape and broad-brimmed black hat reached chiefly those who did not know Gide's work at all. Hence the most outrageous untruths circulated without verification; for his enemies, far from wishing to win him new readers with such publicity, aimed rather to warn *their* readers against a dangerous influence. Surely this explains why Gide himself initially refused to recognize his influence, even rejecting such sincere praise from a young writer as Marcel Arland's characterization of him as ". . . the contested, but veritable, master of contemporary letters, the writer who has exerted the deepest influence during the past twelve years, one of those rare spirits of whom it can be said that after them literature and thought are not as they were before." The very same issue of the *N. R. F.* that contained Arland's article, in fact, began the publication of *Œdipe*, in which, by attributing one of Arland's earlier essays to Eteocles, the youth who is seeking literary justification for his worst instincts, Gide scornfully repudiated all disciples.

But however Gide might deny any desire to influence others, his entire work was nevertheless there to give the lie to his statements. Had not Ménalque "lectured"—in the Socratic manner, to be sure—to Michel, Philoctetes to Neoptolemus, and the Prodigal to his younger brother? The Envoi of the *Nourritures terrestres*, indeed, had told Nathanael to throw that book away, but, after all, the little volume had been addressed to him and had couched in a vigorous hortatory tone a sort of reverse evangelism. And in the same key as the *Nourritures* and the *Nouvelles Nourritures*, Gide had noted in his *Journals* in 1934: "Companion of your solitude, young man who will read me later on, it is to you that I address myself. I should like you to derive from my writings strength, courage, and awareness, and scorn for false virtues. Do not sacrifice to idols." The fact of writing not for the present or even "for the coming generation, but for the following one" by no means precluded, then, a didactic intent.

In 1910 Gide had come across the remark that Nietzsche entered eternity as a corruptor of youth and had reflected: "This is perhaps the most tempting path." Thirty years later, when he himself was being similarly accused after the collapse of his country, he noted: ". . . that old accusation of '*corrumpere*

juventutem' is more likely than praises to assure fame; this is
generally known anyway, and how ill founded it usually is."
Like Socrates, and for the same reasons, André Gide was particularly vulnerable to the accusation. And, because of the homosexual implications it commonly carried, he especially resented
it. Martin du Gard reports one of his outbursts, shortly after the
vituperative pamphlet of 1931, against those who equate the
perversion of youth with the forming of young homosexuals by
taking advantage of their innocence and passivity. It particularly irritated Gide that, simply because he was an avowed pederast, the world could not believe that many young men turned
to him for moral and intellectual guidance. But wisely he never
stooped to answer such charges publicly.

In regard to the impress his writings made upon readers,
however, he never had any doubt. Though he might even there
have resisted being called a *corruptor,* he would certainly not
have objected to the term of *disturber.* The André of *Paludes*
had taught that one must cherish one's unrest, and thirty years
later Gide wrote in his own name a laconic and categorical statement that has come to summarize his entire position: "To disturb is my function." By that time he wanted to be known as a
disseminator of unrest, for, as he expressed it in a preface:
". . . it is to warn that I write, to exalt or to teach, and I call
a book a failure when it leaves the reader intact."

This was the fundamental attitude—especially since it was
coupled with a growing philosophical humanism—that André
Gide's critics and detractors could not forgive. The legend was
simply fabricated, by them or their petty lieutenants, to provide substance for their indictments. Now, it happens that Gide's
most consistent adversaries during the twenties—for in the following decade the Communists took up the chase on a different
terrain—were Roman Catholics. From Henri Massis by way
of Victor Poucel, S.J., and Francis Jammes to the great Paul
Claudel, who characterized him as "a poisoner," they shared a
common faith. So did the recent converts, Charles Du Bos and

René Schwob, who, though perhaps not justifiably grouped among the adversaries, wrote two of the most severe studies of Gide. And if *Un Malfaiteur: André Gide* was not written by Catholics, why did it cover itself with the spurious authority of a non-existent Archbishop?

It is not strange that Gide's first enemies should be Roman Catholics in a predominantly Catholic country where the best organized and most articulate defense of morals and traditions invariably stems from the Church. Nor was it odd for Gide, ever sensitive to attacks and somewhat touchy on the subject of religion, to react at once. The first thing he did, after the initial onslaughts of Massis, was to hasten the publication of *Corydon* and *Si le grain ne meurt . . .*, the frankest and, in the eyes of many, the most "subversive" books he had written.

Already in 1927, in a letter to Father Poucel, Gide foresaw the possibility of his becoming an enemy of Catholicism. "All the relentlessness of a Massis or of others," he wrote, "will never succeed in turning me into an enemy of Christ (and this certainly does not mean that I claim to have always lived in his light and that I am trying to make myself out less of a sinner than I am). If I ever subsequently happen to rise up against Catholicism, this will truly be because the Catholics have pushed me to it, forced me to it. Yet it will in any case be extremely painful for me to do so, for I count among them friends who remain very dear to me." The following year, reflecting that his forbearance toward Catholicism might some day be interpreted as fear, he noted in his *Journals* that he *was* afraid— but only of his own intransigence. Obviously a change had come over him: his bitterest comments on the Church of Rome date from the late twenties and the thirties. In general he accused its faithful of narrowness and prejudice, of intellectual dishonesty and bad faith, and of casting out all that they could not piously annex.

When the review *Latinité*, whose very title suggests Henri Massis's lifelong crusade, in January 1931 conducted a symposium on Gide's influence in Europe, with replies from half a dozen countries, many contributors annoyed Gide by assuming that he was much preoccupied with his influence. In his *Journals* he protested that "until quite recently" his sole desire had been to create works of art, which, if they influenced the reader at all, "could only help him to see clearly, to question himself, and force him to think. . ." Then he proceeded to specify his new attitude: "But it is certain that, of late, my position is not the same. This is also because I see more clearly in myself and want much more definitely and vigorously what seems to me much more clearly preferable. In any case, and whatever it may be, the thing I am most bitterly reproached with is having worked for the emancipation of the mind. This seems unpardonable to the group that, on the contrary, aims only toward the most complete submission to authority, to rules, to tradition, etc." By 1931—and this passage shows it as clearly as did *Œdipe*—Gide's humanism had clashed openly and irrevocably with Catholicism. From then on, he could neither be attracted by the Church nor make peace with it. Catholics had goaded and baited him until he felt forced to take a strong stand.

That the Church in turn should retaliate seems natural enough. André Gide himself would not have been surprised by the decree of the Suprema Sacra Congregatio Sancti Officii, dated 24 May 1952, putting his entire work on the redoubtable *Index Librorum Prohibitorum*. Rather, the wonder is that the ancient Holy Office—better known throughout the world as the Inquisition—should have waited until more than a year after the writer's death to anathematize him. Until his death there was evidently hope that the Prodigal might return to the fold, but after his unrepentant demise the condemnation had to be irrevocable, without the conditional clause *donec corrigantur,* which still appears after the works of Descartes. The decree, to which Pius XII gave his solemn approval on 3 April 1952, reads in part: ". . . *damnarunt atque in INDICEM librorum prohibitorum inserenda mandarunt* Opera omnia *ANDREAE GIDE*." This means that the humble and devout poetry of *Numquid* is condemned together with the shocking sincerity of the memoirs, the beautiful *Symphonie pastorale*, exposing a peculiarly Protestant free interpretation of the Scriptures, together with the homosexuality, illegitimacy, and suicides of *Les Faux-Monnayeurs*. It is appropriate, however, that the totality of Gide's work should be forbidden Catholic readers, for the Church was aiming to cast out, not this or that pernicious writing, but rather an integral humanistic philosophy, an influence, an attitude of mind. The sweeping expression *opera omnia* put André Gide at once, not in the same class with Balzac and Stendhal whose love-stories (*omnes fabulae amatoriae*) are forbidden, but rather in the noble category that includes—besides a host of obscure theologians from the Renaissance to the present—Giordano Bruno, Descartes, Hobbes, and Hume.

Decrees of the Holy Office, always published in Latin, are not accustomed to explain their sentences. But an editorial that the Vatican newspaper, *L'Osservatore Romano*, ran in the column next to the first publication of the decree condemning Gide offers explanations of an official nature. There Gide is accused of negating Christ, of living within Christianity but as a deliberate anti-Christian, of carrying profanation to the point of blasphemy, of assuming and maintaining a position of scandal, of corrupting generations of youths into now making a "filthy boast" of what once would scarcely have been whispered among mature people, of "asserting what respectable people negate and negating what respectable people assert even at the expense of their life." One of the strangest articles cited against him is: "He invented his own way of negating Christ, making use of carefully chosen words from the Gospels, even quoted in Latin indeed (*magari citate in latino*) and by way of a musical motif; and of assaulting the Church while remaining in the sacristy or in the presbytery." Yet this is but another way of saying, as Ramon Fernandez had already said, that Gide develops a new ethic and a new logic while using forms belonging to the very logic and ethics he is destroying, and thus takes on a Satanic appearance for traditional Christians. Gide, I believe, would have particularly enjoyed the eloquent oratory of the last sentence, which because of its position might seem to be the heart of the indictment: "André Gide, with that strong, suave voice that occasionally recalls the loftiest voice of the greatest France dared to reduce to a problem everything that was most certain, least debatable, most respectable—not, indeed, in order to affirm it in return with greater force and novelty but in order to negate it shamelessly and wantonly to lose his soul, thus acquiring fame, an income, and a prize."

Had the condemned writer been able to read that issue of *L'Osservatore Romano*, he might have lighted another cigarette, stared into space for a moment with narrowed eyes, and added a scathing page to his voluminous *Journals*. Or else he might simply have recalled that already in 1929 he had written: "It is in the name of God that Catholic critics condemn; they cannot be mistaken, for God inspires them; any hesitation, any counterbalancing, any nuance even, becomes a sign of compromise and, consequently, of lukewarmness. In order not to be cast out by God, they cast us out. [. . .] and the condemned man hasn't the right to protest or to complain, for it is in the name of Truth that the judge speaks, the interpreter of God, who condemns not so much an author as the evil and error that that author manifests and propagates, as every bit of Satan that laughs in the work of his henchman." Knowing doubtless very little about the secret functioning of the Holy Office, Gide nevertheless had learned to gauge the classic Catholic attitude. Twenty-three years before the irrevocable anathema was pronounced upon him, he had foreseen its very terms—even to its placing him among the followers of the Devil (*tra i seguaci dell'Avversario*).

Fortunately, not everyone considered as reprehensible his preference for problems over traditional certainties. In his homage of 1931, which Gide took such care to spurn, Marcel Arland summarized the view of many contemporaries when he wrote: "The importance of his work is made clear to me by the importance of the problems it raises even among his worst detractors." Even earlier the future novelist André Malraux had called him "a spiritual director" and classed him among the most important men of the day because "To half of those who are called 'the young writers' he revealed intellectual awareness." At about the same time another novelist who was to become famous, François Mauriac, specified in a preface: "Gide's mission is to throw a torch into our depths, to collaborate in our spiritual self-scrutiny." Mauriac was then, and has remained, a leading Catholic writer; yet even after Gide's unsanctified death, although he elsewhere showed some severity, he dared to repeat the same thought.

Such favorable witnesses for the defence deserve to be heard quite as much as does Henri Massis. Having profited from Gide's influence as directly as anyone, they can speak of it from firsthand knowledge—as could almost every one of the leading French novelists and critics of the double generation that includes Montherlant, Saint Exupéry, and Julien Green, Jacques Rivière, Ramon Fernandez, and Jean Hytier. Among those of the following group to reach literary maturity the most eloquent defenders of Gide's influence, which they too felt in their turn, are Jean-Paul Sartre and Albert Camus.

Outside of France that influence has similarly touched many of the best minds in each country, some of whom have specifically praised Gide's questing spirit. Thomas Mann, for instance, wrote even before Rome had officially spoken: "With time his figure has continued growing to attain that lofty spiritual dignity which accompanies philosophical torment. In defiance of simplistic morality that felt obliged to condemn him, he remained faithful to a conception that I can define only by saying that it constituted the extreme point of intellectual curiosity. At such an altitude, curiosity becomes a skepticism that is transformed into creative force." In English probably no statement is more pertinent than the one made by that eminently literate diplomat, Harold Nicolson. "The accusation levelled against Gide," he wrote in the London *Spectator*, "is that, with tranquil but daemonic subtlety, he destroyed the valuable certitudes of the young. Such a charge was brought by Meletus, Anytus and Lyco against the veteran Socrates two thousand three hundred and fifty years ago. I am angered by such an imputation. When I first came to read and to admire André Gide, I was every bit as young and malleable as were Lysis and Charmides. Am I conscious that the *Nourritures terrestres*, or even *L'Immoraliste*, seared the spring buds of principle or withered my young concepts of the beautiful and the good? Not in the very least. I do not remember even that I obtained any jubilant release from boyhood prejudices and inhibitions. The effect upon me was not negative but positive. His writings enhanced my curiosity and my zest; from them I derived a distrust of pragmatic injunctions and a delight in the variety of human life. I am certain that they did me not harm but good. [. . .] I became one of the band of his Nathanaels; my gratitude and my esteem for the modern Socrates are neither sporadic nor faint." This is a considerable personal testimony; it could be multiplied many times over, and in many languages.

In fact, the official biography of Gide published by the Swedish Academy at the time of his Nobel Prize noted that he had often been accused of "depraving and disorienting youth" and added: "This is the old accusation addressed to all emancipators of the mind. There is no occasion to protest; it is enough to note the value of his real disciples from Jacques Rivière to Antoine de Saint Exupéry. [. . .] It is probably thereby, as much as and even more than by his literary work, that he certainly deserved the signal honor that Sweden has just conferred upon him." Could the Nobel Committee have been aware that such a statement, from such a source, meant perhaps more to Gide than the prize itself?

Ultimately almost all attitudes toward André Gide reduce themselves to the question of his moral influence. Early in his career, when he delivered a lecture in Brussels entitled *"De l'influence en littérature"* ("On Influence in Literature"), Gide took his stand as the champion of all influences. In that year of 1900 he most likely classed himself among the influenced rather than among those who influence. Having already recognized himself in so many of his predecessors and experienced multiple influences, he felt naturally drawn to pronounce such an apology. He began by stating that many good influences do not seem so to all, that influences are good or bad, not in an absolute way, but merely in relation to whoever comes under them. Then, following an apology of the one who is influenced, he dismissed any apology of the one who influences—which would be simply an apology of the great man.

Nonetheless he added: "People have often spoken of the responsibility of great men.—Christ has not been so much blamed for all the martyrs Christianity has made (for the idea of salvation was involved) as this or that writer is still blamed for the sometimes tragic repercussion of his ideas. After Werther it is said that there was an epidemic of suicides. Likewise in Russia after a poem of Lermontov. 'After this book,' Madame de Sévigné said of La Rochefoucauld's *Maximes,* 'there is nothing to do but to kill oneself or to become a Christian.' [. . .] As for those that literature has killed, I think that they already had a germ of death in them; those who became Christians were wonderfully ready to become so; influence, I said, creates nothing: it awakens." It would nevertheless be wrong, Gide claims, to try to diminish the responsibility of great men. That responsibility must be considered as the heaviest and most frightening responsibility one can imagine. Yet it never makes any of them draw back.

And if such men use up a huge amount of human life, particularly the lives of those who come into contact with them, this is due to the fact that they are not sufficient unto themselves. Their energy extends beyond their personal limits. They need to live through others as well as in themselves; they need others to act out, to test out, their ideas for them. Each great man, says Gide, is tormented by the importance of the idea he bears within him. "He is *responsible* for it; he feels this. That responsibility seems to him the most important; the other comes second." How can one fail to hear an echo here of the capital note to *Narcisse* regarding the artist's necessity to *manifest* his idea and hence to prefer it to himself and everything else?

In *Le Prométhée mal enchaîné*, which one of the keenest critics calls the richest of Gide's works in "satanic" suggestions, Prometheus delivers a most stirring speech on the necessity of feeding one's eagle and cultivating one's awareness. The most tangible, if not the only result, of his lecture is that the susceptible Damocles, alone among the uncomprehending audience, falls mortally ill. Learning of this, Prometheus says to the ubiquitous café waiter: "I thought no one was listening. . . I insisted . . . If I had known he was listening. . ." "What would you have said?" asks the waiter, and Prometheus stammers: "The same thing."

XII. COMPASSIONATE PERSEPHONE

"Henceforth how could I
Heedlessly laugh and sing with you,
Now that I have seen, now that I know
How a thwarted multitude suffers
And waits endlessly.
O piteous host of shades, you beckon me.
Toward you I go. . ."

"The social question! . . . If I had encountered that great pitfall at the beginning of
my career, I should never have written anything worth while."

IN the early years of this century André Gide sketched out a
"dramatic symphony in four tableaux" entitled *Proserpine*,
which Paul Fort's review *Vers et Prose* published, in its frag-
mentary form, in 1912. It is easy to see why the writer was
attracted to that ancient myth of regeneration: it conformed to
his poetic interest in the seasons while also transferring into
allegory verses 24–25 of John xii, which had long dominated
his conduct and were to suggest the title for his memoirs. Furthermore, it embodies two powerful symbols that Gide had already most effectively appropriated: the narcissus and the
pomegranate. Perhaps he was secretly pleased to be able to use
the narcissus, with the authority of mythology, as a mirror of
desire revealing not the self but another, remote world; this
could serve as an answer to whoever might accuse him of nar-

cissism. The pomegranate, as is usual in his work, stands for the realm of sensual pleasure and sunlight. Into his rough schema for a musical composition—oratorio or symphonic suite depending on whether the actors sing or simply mime their parts—which lacked only a composer, Gide introduced the related myth of Orpheus and Eurydice to suggest the power of art to assuage and reclaim.

Nearly thirty years later, at the instigation of Ida Rubinstein and with Igor Stravinsky as collaborator, Gide went back to his early outline and produced a beautiful little opera that was first presented on 30 April 1934 under the title of *Perséphone*. A comparison between the two handlings of the familiar myth throws considerable light on the author's evolution. Whereas he was originally interested in the transformation of the anxious, sentimental Kore into the solemn, implacable Proserpina, Queen of Hades, he later used the theme as vehicle for a wholly social preoccupation that never entered his mind in the years before the First World War. Fusing the Greek legend with the Christian concept of redemption through renunciation, he now showed Persephone as moved by pity for human suffering to give up her advantages. For, seeing a destitute humanity in her narcissus-mirror, she willingly descends to the underworld for humanitarian reasons. Orpheus disappears from the final version, for Persephone herself, on her mission of benefaction, can take poetry to the wretched company of shades. Like another Prodigal—this time endowed with a keen sense of pity, however, Gide's Persephone abandons the world of security and peace to explore the mysteries of the shadowy otherworld and then returns to her mother, Demeter. But never will she forget what she has seen, which will periodically draw her back to the realm of Pluto. Henceforth her function is to carry to the suffering shades a little daylight, "a respite for their innumerable woes, a little love to offset their wretchedness."

That André Gide should have seen Persephone as dominated by a social consciousness is not strange, for he wrote his little opera at the height of his fervor for Communism, not many months after he had proclaimed that he would willingly give his life "to ensure the success of the U.S.S.R." Such statements evoked much the same excitement and scandal in French literary circles as had the earlier plea for homosexuality and the memoirs, causing a large part of the public to revile Gide while a minority was praising him exorbitantly for his sincerity. On the one hand, his approval of Soviet Russia raised another barrier between him and the conservative authorities who dispense official honors; but, on the other hand, the *Soviet Encyclopedia* hailed Gide's abandonment of "the world outlook of the middle-class *rentier*" in favor of a realization "together with the best representatives of Western intelligentsia" of the collapse of the capitalist system. In fact, Gide was one of the earlier of those almost countless intellectuals of unusual sensitivity who became converted to Communism. "They had a heightened perception of the spirit of the age," writes Richard Crossman, Member of Parliament and Assistant Editor of the *New Statesman and Nation*, "and felt more acutely than others both its frustrations and its hopes. Their conversion therefore expressed, in an acute and sometimes in a hysterical form, feelings which were dimly shared by the inarticulate millions who felt that Russia was on the side of the workers."

Two of Gide's closest friends, Jean Schlumberger and Roger Martin du Gard, have stated that he "discovered" social iniquity and took his stand against it during his trip through the Congo in 1925–6. Hurt by the implication that until then he had been exclusively concerned with himself and that it required direct experience of the oppressed black race to tear him away from his narcissism, Gide consistently objected to such statements. He pointed out specifically that, had he kept a journal during his first trip to Algeria as he did daily in the Congo, "most likely I should have spoken of the business of the Gafsa phosphates, which I was then able to follow closely, of the withdrawal of the White Fathers after the death of Cardinal Lavigerie, and especially of the arrival of barrels of absinthe to break down the natives, and of the expropriation of the Arabs by the device of the Cazenave bank according to a monstrous method that I would probably have exposed. . ." And he goes on to say that, had he *not* kept a diary in French Equatorial Africa, he would probably have brought back "only a few 'landscapes' for a new *Amyntas*." None of his friends seems to have remembered that, back in 1906 when *Amyntas* first appeared, one part of that book, dated 1903–4 and entitled *Le Renoncement au voyage* (*Renouncing Travel*), had stated in its Foreword: "When, for the sixth time, I took ship for Algeria, the book I hoped to bring back with me was altogether different from the one I am offering today. The most serious economic, ethnological, geographical questions were to be raised. It is certain that they interested me passionately. I took along notebooks that I wanted to fill with precise documents, with statistics. . . Are they really *these* notebooks?" Gide himself doubtless forgot that he had made that statement, remembering only that he had witnessed social abuses at that time and made nothing of them in his writing. The important thing, however, is not so much to blame him for having been so long blind to social considerations as to be grateful that, despite all his handicaps, he did eventually open his eyes.

Even though Gide grew up in a family that, without keeping a carriage in Paris, still felt it "owed it to itself" to live in a house with a carriage-entrance, he might nonetheless have been alert to the lot of the less favored. To be sure, he was; but three things kept such concerns out of his literary work: the influence of the symbolist school, the feeling of his own incompetence in those matters, and his conviction that moral questions came first. In direct reaction against the naturalist school, the young men who surrounded Mallarmé strove toward the "absolute" and aimed to write works of art free of the "contingencies" of ordinary life. "There was not so much ignorance and blindness among us, in regard to social questions, as scorn—a scorn born of misunderstanding," Gide wrote in 1935. Further-more, it was easy and natural to leave social problems to spe-cialists; and Gide never ceased, even after embracing Commun-ism, to proclaim his lack of competence in political, economic, and financial matters.

These first two considerations, however, are wholly nega-tive. The third and perhaps determining reason for Gide's ab-stention from social comment is a positive one: the overwhelm-ing priority he gave to moral problems. Some time before 1897 he wrote in his "Literature and Ethics": "Social question? Yes, indeed. But the ethical question is antecedent." And he went on to elaborate: "Man is more interesting than men. God made *him* and not them in his image. Each one is more precious than all." As late as 1923, in fact, he still clung to this attitude in an article on "The Future of Europe," in which he claimed that most social questions can be reduced to moral questions and that it is essential to reform man before reforming institutions. But by 1935 he was "convinced that man himself cannot change unless social conditions first urge him and help him to do so— so that attention must first be paid to them." And he saw this as the greatest and most significant change in his opinions.

What brought about the change? What, in other words, transformed André Gide from an utterly apolitical man ap-parently occupying a windowless tower high above the turmoil to one who wanted in 1931 to "cry aloud" his affection for Soviet Russia? It would be too easy to answer this question by simple reference to his well-documented experiences of social injustice, first as a juror in the Assize-Court of Rouen in 1912 and then as a tourist, thirteen years later, in the Congo and the Chad. Rather, one must seek an explanation in certain perma-nent and basic traits of Gide's character. Had it not been for them, he would never have seen in the law-court or in Equatorial Africa the abuses and exploitations that moved him so deeply.

The first and most fundamental of those traits was his power of sympathy and great susceptibility to pity. He never made a truer statement about himself than that his heart beat only through sympathy. It was this characteristic, indeed, that he attributed to his Persephone. As far back as one goes in Gide's life, one finds him putting himself in the place of others, sharing their suffering while weeping over it. In earliest childhood, for instance, when he learned that a playmate was going blind, he withdrew to his room to cry for poor little Mouton, and several days thereafter spent long periods with his eyes closed in an effort to feel what Mouton felt.

During the First World War, declared inapt for military service because of age and health, he devoted himself heart and soul to alleviating suffering as assistant head of the Foyer Franco-Belge. There, spending long days helping the refugees from the north, he lived "devoured by sympathy" for eleven months.

When he set out for the Congo in the summer of 1925, he could not foresee that the social questions raised by the treatment of the natives at the hands of the French colonizers would come to absorb him almost completely and become the chief interest of his journey. Yet he had been there only a few months and witnessed but one glaring injustice before he could write: "Henceforth a huge lamentation fills me; I know things to which I cannot resign myself. What demon urged me to come to Africa? What did I come looking for in this country? I was untroubled. Now I know; I must speak out." This is almost the language of Persephone after she has seen in her narcissus-mirror the tortured humanity of the lower world. The motivating emotion in both cases is that of overwhelming pity. Martin du Gard tells how Gide, back from Africa, was choked with sobs when he tried to read aloud an official report of 1902 describing the destruction of a native tribe through white exploitation, even though the events had taken place twenty-four years before!

As if seeking its most worthy object and true function, Gide's pity was awakened in turn by the petty criminals he helped to

AERIAL VIEW OF CUVERVILLE, GIDE'S NORMAN ESTATE

judge in Rouen in 1912, so often as utterly misunderstood by the court as by themselves, then by the inarticulate exploited Negroes of the Congo, often brutally punished for what was not a crime to them, and finally, in the thirties, by the political prisoners of the fourth Reich and of fascist Spain. In January 1934 he and André Malraux went to Berlin to intercede with Goebbels for Georges Dimitrov, acquitted of complicity in the Reichstag fire but still imprisoned. That same year he addressed the Spanish government on behalf of the political prisoners then being judged by military tribunals after the Asturian uprising. In June 1935 at the height of the Writers' International Congress for the Defence of Culture, over which he was presiding, he intervened, despite the protests of the pro-Soviet writers, in behalf of Victor Serge, then deported to Orenburg; and a few days later he wrote the Russian ambassador requesting Serge's release, which was effected. Meanwhile he shared with Malraux the presidency of an international committee for the liberation of Ernst Thaelmann, head of the German Communist Party, who had been arrested in March 1933 without any formal charges being brought against him. The struggle against fascism had given focus to Gide's natural compassion.

By the time that Gide presided over mass-meetings and sat on committees, he had an immediate audience, thanks largely to Communism. Richard Crossman speaks of the mortal loneliness of those who tried to fight fascism before it was normal and respectable to do so, a loneliness that made them hearken to the appeal of Communism. In this regard Gide's experiences on returning from the Congo marked his turning-point. Before then, he had left disturbing social questions to specialists, but in the heart of Africa there were no specialists—administrators sent out by the Colonial Ministry, businessmen, missionaries —who were not effectively silenced by duty or self-interest. Gide had stumbled onto certain flagrant abuses and, whether or not he was competent in such matters, he alone was able to denounce them. Realizing this new position, he noted in his travel diary: "But how to make oneself heard? Up to now, I have always spoken without concern as to whether or not I was heard, always written for those to come, with no desire but to last. I envy those journalists whose voice carries at once, even though it were to die out immediately afterward." At that very moment, however, he was himself beginning a new career as a journalist; and he was soon to discover how strong his voice was. A letter he wrote to the Governor brought about the indictment of a vicious administrator; a conversation with the Minister of Colonies launched a mission to investigate the high mortality-rate of natives working on a railway project; and his book, *Le Voyage au Congo* (*Travels in the Congo*), served as documentation in a session of the Chamber of Deputies resulting in a promise from the Minister that the big rubber concessions would not be renewed. Thus it was that his awakening to a social consciousness began when he saw the Negroes cheated, beaten, and ruthlessly killed by a handful of whites intent on quick profits. Like Persephone, Gide could never again be aloof.

It is not too much to say, then, that his championing of the oppressed and his eventual siding with Communism had their source in a particularly acute sentiment of pity that had been characteristic of him since childhood. A corollary of that humanitarian sympathy for the underdog was Gide's refusal to take advantage of his favored position in the world. Several times in his work he utilized a story told him by a survivor of the *Bourgogne* shipwreck, which had greatly impressed him. Seated in a lifeboat loaded to capacity, that man had seen some of his fellow-survivors beating swimmers over the head with oars or chopping off their hands to prevent them from climbing in and capsizing the boat. "Now, the feeling of being in the boat," Gide wrote to a friend, "of being safe while others are drowning close by—I want you to realize that that feeling can become unbearable. Then you come along with a whole series of arguments. I am not able to answer them, obviously. I merely cling to this: that I cannot admit a boat in which only a few are safe." Elsewhere he confessed that what brought him to Communism was not theories, but simply his hatred for the state of things that allowed one man to possess over and above another. He felt specifically that he himself had taken advantage of poverty inasmuch as his superabundance was compensated by what others lacked.

Christ taught such an equality among men as Gide dreamed of. To be sure, it should already be clear that Gide's Communism was simply the application of Christian ideals to a purely physical world. He was aware of this himself, as he showed by his journal-entry of June 1933: "But, I must admit it, what leads me to Communism is not Marx, it is the Gospel. It is the Gospel that formed me." To Gide, Communism seemed to be taking Christianity literally. In order to realize the fundamental equality of men, society had to be transformed; and this could be achieved only by an economic revolution. Some of Gide's friends saw that he was mistaken in looking for a lay form of Christianity in the U.S.S.R.; and he himself, when the interlude that he later called his "honeymoon" with Communism was over, recognized that when he thought himself a Communist he was merely a Christian without the faith.

Another consideration that drew André Gide toward Communism was his natural tendency to scrutinize most carefully, and generally to reject, such inherited notions as he owed to his class or to his favored situation in society. Constitutionally nonconformist, he early revolted against the society that had produced him, and now in Communism he found a mass revolt against that society, a systematic destruction of many of the false gods against which he had long been warring independently. He hardly had to force the note at all in order to state in a capital speech of 1935: ". . . of a bourgeois family, of bourgeois formation, I was obliged to realize, at the beginning of my literary career, that everything in me that seemed to me most authentic, most valid and valorous, stood in immediate and direct protest against the conventions, habits, and falsehoods of my environment."

Two of those conventions which Gide had regularly exposed to the greatest consternation of many readers were organized religion and the institution of the family. His attitude toward churches should already be abundantly clear. As for the family, besides crying in the *Nourritures*: "Families, I hate you! . . .," he had claimed it impossible to find any words of Christ authorizing the family and had deplored the fact that parents invariably influence their children in the direction to which the children are only too inclined by heredity. The family also appeared to him as opposed both to the individual and to the state and as inclined to foster a vicious form of interest. One can imagine his delight, then, on finding in Communism "a state without religion, a society without the family," for, as he added: "Religion and the family are the two worst enemies of progress."

Humanitarian pity, rejection of his favored social position, fervent acceptance of Christ's teaching, and innate nonconformism—these are the principal aspects of André Gide's temperament which led him to embrace Communism. To them might be added an ineradicable and optimistic interest in the future and an inveterate impatience. Martin du Gard suggests, for instance, that had he been younger and with more time ahead of him he might have been more circumspect, whereas his age made him commit himself somewhat blindly.

However startling his self-commitment in the early thirties, yet *Gide never became a member of the Communist Party*. At very most, like so many liberal and naïve idealists in all countries since then—intellectuals, artists, churchmen—he was a "fellow traveler." Infatuated as he was with the revolutionary principle (it would be too much to say with Marxism, as he never really mastered the Marxian dialectic), he still had enough critical spirit to write to the Association of Revolutionary Writers and Artists in 1932: "No, dear comrades. The only result of such an engagement would be immediately to keep me from ever writing anything again. I have declared as loud and clear as I could my sympathy (and the word is weak) for the U.S.S.R. and for all it represents in our eyes, in our hearts, despite all the imperfections that are still held up to us. I believe that my co-operation (and in my case very precisely) can be of more real advantage to your (to our) cause if I give it freely and am known *not* to be enrolled. Writing henceforth according to the 'principles' of a 'charter' (I am using the expressions of your circular) would make whatever I might write henceforth lose all real value; or, more exactly, it would spell sterility for me." From the beginning and at all times, Gide recognized that conversion to Communism, like conversion to Catholicism, implied accepting a dogma and an orthodoxy, giving up free inquiry. But all orthodoxies were suspect to him.

Perhaps it amused him to note that the present-day "mystics" were all among those who professed irreligion, but the fact that Communism represented a religion for many of the young frightened him. "This is too much," he wrote in August 1933. "I very well understand the need of calling on authority and of rallying the masses to it. But here I give up; or at least, if I remain with them, it is because my very heart and reason advise me to do so and not because '*it is written. . .*' Whether the text invoked be by Marx or Lenin, I cannot abide by it unless my heart and my reason approve it. I did not escape from the authority of Aristotle or St. Paul to fall under theirs."

It was such an unorthodox attitude as this that allowed André Gide, with complete disregard for the official "line" established by the statutes of the Association of Soviet Writers, to declare to the first Congress of Soviet Writers that the artist is always an individualist and that the U.S.S.R. must take into account everyone's individual peculiarities and found a "Communist individualism" if it were to have a valuable art. Then in his long speech before the meeting held in Paris on 23 October 1934 to celebrate that Congress, he did not hesitate to state:

"That literature, that art can serve the Revolution is obvious; but they have no need to be concerned with serving it. They never serve it so well as when they are concerned solely with the truth. Literature need not put itself at the service of the Revolution. A literature enslaved is a literature debased, however noble and legitimate the cause it is serving." Had he been a Russian and pronounced these words, he would at very least have been accused of "formalism" if not deported to a labor camp. Had he not been André Gide, he could not even have uttered them in Paris and been invited two years later to Russia by that very Association of Soviet Writers.

André Gide refused to enroll himself in order to preserve his freedom of thought and speech, fearing that the necessity of writing under orders would spell sterility for him. Yet the event proved that, even without signing away his liberty, his almost exclusive social preoccupation stifled his creative powers. In fact, between *Œdipe*, which he finished in 1930, and the amazing perfection of *Thésée*, completed in 1944, he wrote no major creative work. *Perséphone* (1934) is slight; the best of the *Nouvelles Nourritures* (1935) had been written much earlier, some of it even appearing in the *Morceaux choisis* of 1921; and the tale entitled *Geneviève* (1936)—from which he tried in vain to banish his new ideas—proved even stiffer and less dramatic than *L'École des femmes* (*The School for Wives*) and *Robert* of 1929, with which it forms a trilogy. His five-act play, *Robert ou l'Intérêt général* (*Robert or The Common Weal*), was conceived and written at the time of his Communist enthusiasm and, in Elsa Triolet's translation, would probably have been a success in Moscow, where plans for its production were dropped when Gide broke with the movement. For the next six years he struggled unsuccessfully to remake his social satire into a comedy of characters; but the best that can be said for the near thesis-play, first published in its final version in Algiers in 1944–5, is that it stands comparison with Mirbeau's *Les Mauvais Bergers* (*The Evil Shepherds*) and Curel's *Repas du lion*

(*The Lion's Share*), both typical of the social theater popular in the nineties.

Several years, in fact, were devoted to presiding over politico-literary congresses and anti-fascist meetings, helping to organize a Communist youth club, interceding for German, Spanish, Greek, Yugoslav, and Russian political prisoners, taking part in debates, prefacing pacifist and anti-fascist books, writing declarations and open letters in favor of conscientious objectors or Soviet films and against the Italian aggression in Ethiopia or France's non-intervention in the Spanish war, carrying on polemics with his attackers, and visiting the U.S.S.R.

By 1934 Gide could write, in words very close to Persephone's song used as an epigraph for this chapter: "For a long time there can no longer be any question of works of art. In order to listen to new, indistinct chords one must not be deafened by moans. There is almost nothing left in me that does not sympathize. Wherever I turn my eyes, I see nothing but distress around me. Whoever remains contemplative today gives evidence of an inhuman philosophy, or a monstrous blindness." Yet the same day, and immediately following this remark, he noted how unbecoming it is to attribute to virtue "the weariness of old age." Here Gide's critical spirit has again stepped forward and attempted to re-establish the balance, as it had two years earlier when he confessed: "If social questions occupy my thought today, this is partly because the creative demon is withdrawing from it. Such questions do not take over the field until the other has already surrendered it. Why try to overrate oneself? and refuse to recognize in me (what appears clear to me in Tolstoy): an undeniable diminution? . . ."

In other words, whatever his absorption in politics or in humanitarian endeavors, he did not sacrifice his art either willingly or gracefully. The mere fact that he struggled to write works of imagination at all during those years and "tiresomely persisted on the wrong track" indicates his reluctance to give up. Looking back in his eightieth year on the preceding two decades, he admitted: "I spent as much time spoiling *L'Intérêt général* and then *Geneviève* (of which I destroyed almost everything) as in successfully completing *Les Faux-Monnayeurs*. Everything that I wrote then, *invita Minerva*, remained unspeakably mediocre."

It was in such a spirit that he permitted his speeches, letters, declarations, and other circumstantial writings of the period 1930–7 to be gathered together by Mme Yvonne Davet and issued in 1950 under the ironic title of *Littérature engagée* (*Literature of Commitment*). By 1950, Jean-Paul Sartre and the Existentialists, with their insistence that a man's every act is a commitment, had conferred a special significance upon the word *engagement*. The Bruno of *Les Mains sales* (*Red Gloves*), like the Orestes of *Les Mouches* (*The Flies*) and the Mathieu Delarue (the man in the street) of Sartre's many-volumed novel, is tormented by the need to commit himself while still preserving his precious liberty. Such heroes, together with the protagonist of Camus' *La Peste* (*The Plague*), stand at the opposite pole from Gide's Lafcadio of an earlier, more carefree epoch.

Yet, while Sartre was still a student in the École Normale preparing for his career as a philosophy professor and Camus was a mere urchin playing on North African beaches, Gide was already committing himself irrevocably in *Corydon* and his memoirs and taking his first strong social stand in the Congo. After the Second World War, when the new work of men like Sartre and Camus was becoming widely popular, Gide reflected that perhaps the most obvious common denominator of his generation—and he mentions specifically Valéry, Proust, Suarès, Claudel, and himself—was their great scorn for things of the moment. The leaders of the new generation, on the contrary, seemed to him to gauge a work according to its immediate efficacy and consequently to aim for immediate success. "Nevertheless," he continues, "when there was a need to *bear witness*, I did not at all fear to commit myself, and Sartre admitted this with complete good faith. But the *Souvenirs de la*

Cour d'Assises (*Recollections of the Assize-Court*) have almost no relation to literature, any more than the campaign against the Great Concessionary Companies of the Congo or the *Retour de l'U.R.S.S.* (*Return from the U.S.S.R.*)." This is the sense in which the title *Littérature engagée* is ironic, then: from the author's point of view everything in that volume, including the social satire of *Robert ou l'Intérêt général,* is extra-literary.

Although André Gide definitively proclaimed himself, as early as July 1931, in favor of Communism and the U.S.S.R., he could not remain committed to that or any other cause against the evidence. Always loath to judge at a distance, he did not have the pertinent evidence at his disposition until the summer of 1936, when he spent two months in the Soviet Union as the guest of the Association of Soviet Writers. To let others take advantage of the extraordinary facilities of the trip and also in order to verify his personal observations, he took along five younger companions: the novelists Eugène Dabit and Louis Guilloux, both of humble birth; the Russian-born publisher Jacques Schiffrin; the journalist Pierre Herbart; and the Dutch writer Jef Last. Two of them spoke Russian and two were party-members; it was Last's fourth trip to the U.S.S.R., and Herbart had just spent six months in Moscow as a magazine-editor. At the outset all five shared Gide's conviction that the Soviet Union was an example and a guide for other countries, "a land in which Utopia was in the act of becoming reality." The group traveled widely by special railway car and by automobile, always accompanied by a female interpreter and guide; receptions were numerous and often pompous, and Gide delivered at least three important speeches. But, thanks to the unusual qualifications of his companions, he was frequently able to diverge from the official tour, as he had done in the Congo, and mingle with the people.

On the homeward journey, after seeing much that had surprised him, Gide wondered whether he should hide his reservations, declare anew his love for the Soviet Union, and lie by approving everything he had seen. But characteristically he decided: "No, I am too well aware that if I acted that way I should do a disservice both to the U.S.S.R. and to the cause it represents in our eyes. But it would be a very serious mistake to link one to the other too closely so that the cause might be held responsible for what we deplore in the U.S.S.R." Accordingly he brought out in November 1936, just three months after his return, a grave indictment of the Soviet State entitled *Retour de l'U.R.S.S.* Beginning mildly and with high praise for the evidences of beauty and progress he had found in Russia, he continued in discursive fashion to show how, from compromise to compromise, Stalin had betrayed the initial revolutionary ideal and established a one-man dictatorship. The vices Gide pointed out in the U.S.S.R. of 1936 were a universal conformism with corresponding stifling of the critical or revolutionary spirit, an appalling depersonalization of the individual and of home life, a cultivated ignorance of the outside world and resultant superiority complex, the revival of class distinctions with the re-creation of a *bourgeoisie*, and the regimentation of art. One of his strongest statements was: "I doubt if in any other country today (even in Hitler's Germany) the mind is less free, more bowed, more terrorized, more vassalized." In general he found the happiness of the Russian people made up of hope, confidence, and ignorance.

Like so many of Gide's writings, the book, which has been called "his classic statement of the Western case against Russian Communism," was an act of moral courage. It immediately brought down upon its author the vociferous condemnation of the Communist press of the world and outlawed him, of course, in Russia, where his books had previously sold more than 400,-000 copies in a few months. Eminent French Marxists, such as Romain Rolland, Jean Guéhenno, and Louis Aragon, condemned him publicly as a dilettante, a Trotskyite, even an agent of fascism. But Gide firmly stated: "As soon as falsehood enters in, I am ill at ease; my function is to expose it. I am attached to truth; if the Party abandons it, I immediately abandon the Party." He had written his pamphlet in exactly the same spirit as he had earlier reported the abuses in the Congo, he claimed, and those who were angered by his criticisms of the U.S.S.R. were the very ones who had most applauded "when the same criticisms were directed against the by-products of 'capitalism.' " In the one case he had been perspicacious, according to them, and in the other quite blind.

Like those who had aimed to discredit his testimony regarding colonial injustice, the Communists remembered Gide's avowed homosexuality and noticed his mention, in a footnote, of the new law against abortion and the older law condemning homosexuals to five years of exile. One of Gide's companions, Pierre Herbart, had given considerably more attention to the subject in his travel-diary, but because of Gide's reputation his implied protest against the harsh legislation seemed more significant. Consequently, from 1936 until the present, the official line has been that Gide's disappointment with the Soviet Union could be traced altogether to its outlawing of his kind. Like everyone else, to be sure, he had expected to find complete sexual liberty in the revolutionary state that had liberated man from the shackles of the past and abolished taboos; but, as he recorded in his posthumous *Ainsi soit-il,* he himself (perhaps benefitting from an extraordinary immunity granted him as a foreigner and useful fellow-traveler) never enjoyed elsewhere "such indulgence and connivance in that regard."

Gide probably felt more keenly than any of the official Communist attacks—which have continued using the same weapons to this day, insulting him on his death-bed and in his grave—the loss of the worldwide youthful following his adherence to Communism had brought him in his mid-sixties. He was surely infinitely more willing to abandon to the Association of Soviet Writers the immense royalties that had once accrued to him in Russia than he was to relinquish the host of belated Nathanaels with whom he felt that his Communism identified him. Some of them did follow him out of the Party, and many more would have done so had it not been for the Spanish war, which started while he was in Russia.

Just as he was an early anti-fascist, so Gide became an early anti-Stalinist. Before his book, few had spoken out with similar boldness; the most famous and effective of those few were probably Trotsky himself, Sir Walter Citrine, Bertrand Russell, Max Eastman, Boris Souvarine in his *Stalin*, Victor Serge, and the escapee, Vladimir Tchernavin. These were the men, also, whom Gide hastened to read on his return from Moscow and some of whom he cited, along with Marx and Engels, *Pravda* and *Izvestia*, in his *Retouches à mon Retour de l'U.R.S.S.* (*Afterthoughts on the U.S.S.R.*) which appeared in June 1937 to strengthen and document his accusations.

Gide's defection from the cause of the Third International was as sensational to the world at large as, five years earlier, his proclamation of affection for the Soviet Union. For Gide himself, it involved a severe wrench and that considerable suffering which always accompanies the collapse of an ideal. In his social conversion he had gone farther than he ever had in religious conversion, but in both cases the same spirit of free inquiry and skepticism had kept him from taking the final plunge. His whole Communist experience, to be sure, rather parallels that with the Roman Catholic Church. The moment he left the tabernacle, to those within he became an enemy and they cast anathema upon him. André Gide thus enjoys the perhaps unique distinction of figuring high on the *Index Librorum Prohibitorum* of two great rival organizations, both universal in scope.

Seen in perspective, Gide's Communist interlude may first appear as a deplorable deviation from his line of normal development. One must nonetheless recognize that it reflected a basic trait of his complex nature. For a time he simply gave precedence, an almost exclusive precedence, to one facet of his mind and heart. Even when he broke with the Soviet Union he was following the same impulse that made his Persephone forsake the ease of the upper world, for in his *Retouches* he wrote of the Siberian deportees: "I see and hear those victims; I feel them around me. Their muffled cries wakened me last night; their silence prompts these lines. I was thinking of those martyrs when I wrote the words against which you protest, because their tacit gratitude, if my book can reach them, is more important to me than the praises or imprecations of *Pravda*."

As most artists and intellectuals were to continue doing for some time, Gide descended into the arena, momentarily becoming a journalist in the sense that he once defined journalism as "everything that will be less interesting tomorrow than today." The most valuable lesson to be learned from his "treason" as an artist (to borrow the strong term that Julien Benda applied to the intellectuals who failed to remain above the fray during the years 1914–18) was the impermanence and futility of his commitment. After 1936 his example may have served to spare others such a wasteful and exhausting experience as his own. In any case, during the Second World War, the bitter memory of that political interlude in his life at least helped to preserve Gide himself from making political pronouncements and taking an active part in "psychological warfare."

During his last years André Gide considered it almost a mission to warn others against inconsiderately taking sides. Less than six weeks before his death, in fact, a letter of January 1951 told a Japanese correspondent: "Yet it is to individualism that I cling, in individualism that I see a hope of salvation. For though I am greatly embarrassed to say definitely toward what I am heading and what I want, at least I can declare with certainty what I cannot submit to accepting and what I protest against: and that is falsehood. I believe that we run the risk of dying stifled by falsehood, whether it come from the right or from the left, whether it be political in nature or religious, and I add: whether one use it toward others or toward oneself, and in the latter case often almost unconsciously."

After his detour into Communism, the idea of *engagement* (which younger writers were meanwhile exalting with an inquisitorial insistence) understandably came for him to be synonymous with abdication of the critical spirit, fossilization, refusal to learn and to progress. To a young unknown who had sought his advice he wrote in his seventy-seventh year warning all young men against the comfort of submitting to a rule, enrolling, and thus contributing to "the establishment of some form or other of 'totalitarianism' which will be hardly any better than the Nazism they were fighting." A year later, in his "Autumn Leaves," he generalized: "But the temptation that it is hardest to resist, for youth, is that of 'committing oneself,' as they say. Everything urges them to do so, and the cleverest sophistries, the apparently noblest, the most urgent, motives. One would have accomplished much if one persuaded youth that it is through *carelessness* and laziness that it commits itself; . . . if one persuaded youth that it is essential—not to be this or that, but—to be."

By 1947, then, all political passion spent, Gide had returned to the attitude expressed in *Les Faux-Monnayeurs* of 1926, in which Bernard resists both the lure of the Church and the temptation of enrolling himself in an idealistic youth movement, struggles alone with his angel, and receives from Édouard the advice to be himself—or rather, to *dare become who he is*. Over the years, that counsel simply echoes Ménalque's words to Nathanael.

Thus it may be said that in the serenity of his final period Gide reaffirmed his belief in the receptivity and readiness—the *disponibilité* in his own word—that he had preached so joyously in 1897. Without ever losing his interest in social problems and without abandoning the defence of mankind, lucidity, and justice, he was again free to return once more, enriched by witnessing the death of an illusion in another domain, to aesthetic and moral problems and the unimpeded practice of the art he had cultivated since early youth.

XIII. DAEDALUS, THE ARTIFEX

"The thing that means the most to me is my art."

ALMOST at the start of his literary career, André Gide had categorically placed the ethical question before the social question; and, indeed, with but one period of uncertainty during his sixties, he continued to grant it the same priority throughout his life. Yet he consistently held that moral problems themselves were secondary in his personal scale of values. In one of his provocative chronicles published by the review *L'Ermitage* in early 1905 he included this dialogue between an imaginary interviewer and himself:

"Do ethical questions interest you?"

"Of course! The very stuff of which our books are made!"

"But what, in your opinion, is ethics?"

"An annex to aesthetics."

Now, this hierarchy in which aesthetic considerations dominate all others is essential to an understanding not only of the young Gide who revered Mallarmé and frequented Pierre Louÿs and Paul Valéry, but of the mature Gide as well. Whatever his transformations and vacillations, all life long he was above all an artist. Few words recur as frequently or imply as much reverence in Gide's writing as "art" and "work of art." Imbued with the spirit of the French classics and marked by the more immediate influence of such predecessors as Baudelaire and Théodore de Banville, he naturally began life—as Proust and Claudel were doing at the same time—with a predisposition to make a cult of art. Willingly he espoused Oscar Wilde's paradox that life and external nature imitate art more than art imitates either of them. In words which an alert student of English literature would attribute, on an examination, to the closing pages of Wilde's *Decay of Lying* he said: "Every time that art languishes, it is referred back to nature, as an invalid is taken to a spa. Nature, alas, is at the end of its tether: there is a misunderstanding. I admit that it is sometimes good for art to take a fresh-air cure and, if it grows pale from exhaustion, to seek renewed vigor in green fields, in life. But our masters the Greeks were well aware that Aphrodite is not born by natural fecundation. Beauty will never be a natural product; it is achieved solely by an artificial constraint. Art and nature stand in rivalry on earth."

In the same spirit he applauded the aged Degas's crusty outburst against the landscapists who work directly from nature, and insisted that reality must serve rather than dominate art. Indeed, never quite able to believe in *reality* and its independent existence, he consistently objected to Gautier's famous remark that the artist is a man for whom the outer world exists; to him the artist had to be "somewhat of a mystic" who saw through the screen of phenomena. Rimbaud meant nothing different when he exalted the conception of the poet as a seer or *voyant*. In other words, as Gide was to state some years later, direct emotion and direct contact with life are essential; "but," he added, "I think it is an artistic error to paint from nature and that there is no art without transposition." The relationship between art and life, then, is a necessary one, and art is born from the pressure of superabundance; "it begins," Gide wrote in 1899, "where *living* does not suffice to express life. The work of art is a work of distillation; the artist is a distiller. For a drop of that refined alcohol, it takes a vast amount of life, which is concentrated in it." Realism must submit to "a proconceived idea of beauty," for art can be achieved only by constraint.

The concept of *la contrainte*, in fact, stands at the heart of the Gidian aesthetic. His lecture of 1904 on "The Evolution of the Theater" points out that, as with Kant's dove, the very condition of art's soaring upward is the resistance of the surrounding air. Consequently art longs for freedom and facility only in sickly periods, whereas the need for ever stricter forms torments genius in periods of overflowing life, such as the exuberant Renaissance. This explains Shakespeare's and Petrarch's use of the sonnet, Dante's choice of *terzarima*, Bach's affection for the fugue, Michelangelo's drawing the gesture of one of his figures from a defect in the marble, and Aeschylus's inventing the dramatic silence of Prometheus because of a traditional limitation of the number of voices on the stage. From this Gide concludes: "Art is born of constraint, thrives on struggle, dies of freedom." Thus it was that he early fought his natural penchants, in art as in life. What else, to be sure, was his marriage than a manifestation of the same will-power that made him decide to prefer Stendhal, who could teach him more, to Chateaubriand, to whom he felt naturally drawn? Early in life he recognized constraint to be his watchword, adding: "I want all my branches to be arched, like those the clever gardener torments to urge them to fruit." If the application of this principle to his art proved more successful than it did in the domain of life, this may simply indicate that his effort was more sincere and wholehearted where his art was concerned. Or it may simply be that, having already begun to apply his major effort of will to his art, he had not enough will left to sustain the effort elsewhere.

In *Les Faux-Monnayeurs* Gide put into the mouth of his novelist-character Édouard the remark that one can become an artist only on condition of dominating the lyrical state, although, in order to dominate it, one must first have experienced it. This is another way of saying, as Gide early did about Francis Jammes, that there is a sharp distinction between the poet and the artist: the first follows his inspiration and believes in his genius, whereas the second *questions* both. Or, in still other terms, Gide finally elaborated a lapidary formula to express much the same thought when he wrote at the age of seventy-one:

"The sole art that suits me is that which, rising from unrest, tends toward serenity."

It was such a distrust of inspiration and of the lyrical state that made the young Gide—in *Le Voyage d'Urien* and *La Tentative amoureuse*, for instance—deliberately flee the direct expression of emotion and describe landscapes designed to evoke the emotion he had felt. And for the same motives, doubtless, he professed to give an overwhelming priority to questions of form. As he wrote in his *Caractères* of 1925: "I tried to tell him (but he is still too young to grasp what I too failed to understand at his age): pay attention only to the form; emotion will come naturally and fill it. A perfect dwelling always finds a tenant. The artist's concern is to build the dwelling; as for the tenant, it is up to the reader to provide him." And that reflection, in the manner of La Bruyère, is followed immediately in that little collection by this corollary: "Like Chopin by sounds, one must let oneself be guided by words. The artist who complains that language is obdurate is not a true artist. The true artist realizes that the obdurate element is emotion, which gets in the way and must be dominated. It is never appropriate to let oneself be led by emotion rather than by the design, for emotion warps the design whereas design never distorts emotion. Any artist who prefers his personal emotion and sacrifices form to that predilection yields to self-indulgence and contributes to the decadence of art." Surely it was in this sense that he could write in a fragment of his memoirs, suppressed before publication but not before Charles Du Bos had quoted it in the *Dialogue avec André Gide*, that, more than anyone else, Chopin had taught him his technique as an artist.

There is no contradiction between this mature attitude and the aesthetic theory that the twenty-year-old Gide voiced in the famous footnote added to the second edition of *Le Traité du Narcisse*, which stated the necessity of manifesting and warned against preferring oneself to the idea or truth one is expressing. On the first appearance of that footnote in 1892, the artistic credo contained a paragraph that disappeared from later editions. It read: "That is what I should like to say. I shall return to this throughout life; I see in it all ethics, and I believe that everything can be reduced to this." Now, Gide's reluctance on second thought to bind himself for life to a youthful theory understandably explains his later suppression of these lines. But many years later one critic (who had probably not read the paragraph just quoted) claimed that he could schematically deduce all of Gide's works, together with their extreme consequences, from the single footnote of the *Narcisse*.

Such an early insistence upon the importance of the idea might seem to contradict the primary position given to form. But according to Gide form, or composition, is but the outward justification and symbol of the idea. "A well-composed work is necessarily symbolical," he wrote before 1897. "Around what could the parts group themselves? What could guide their arrangement except the idea of the work, which creates that symbolic arrangement?" Thus, it might be said that the work of art is the perfect expression of an idea carried to its fullest statement in sensual form.

Hence Gide can also state that art represents the only realization of perfect health, of an equilibrium outside of time. It is both voluntary and the product of reason. "For it must find in itself its adequacy, its end and its perfect reason," he said in his lecture of 1901 on "The Limits of Art"; "forming a unity, it must be able to isolate itself and endure, as if outside space and time, in a satisfied and satisfying harmony." The harmony or equilibrium results naturally from the fact that all art must of necessity be on a human scale. Consequently Gide suggested that art thrives in periods when the divinity or divinities are not remote from men, and flatly stated that "Skepticism is perhaps sometimes the beginning of wisdom, but it is often the end of art"; consequently he could make the Daedalus of this *Thésée* boast of having, in his sculpture, revolted against the traditional hieratic immobility of the gods and set free their limbs while at the same time aspiring "to mould mankind in the likeness of the gods."

If it is the human source and reference of art that gives it equilibrium, it is that equilibrium, in turn, which confers upon it permanence. The true artist aims always to survive, to "interest the men of tomorrow more than the men of today, and the men of the day after tomorrow even more." And it is the profoundly human qualities that assure such survival. But, as Gide pointed out in an essay on Baudelaire, those qualities often go unnoticed at first or, because they are presented in a new and unusual form, give the work a mysterious and even "unhealthy" appearance. Baudelaire and Chopin, whose perfection has such a subtle relationship to Baudelaire's, long suffered the stigma of that epithet, Gide enjoys pointing out. He might have added that no one becomes a classic in one generation.

Such is the body of aesthetic theory that can be laboriously extracted from André Gide's writing. Of course he never set down a credo in any systematic order, for, like all artists, he distrusted theories. "No theory," he wrote in 1909, "however interesting and important it be, ever served either to create a work of art or to negate or destroy it. . ." Years later he saw the necessity of going beyond any theory, or over-riding it, as the sole way of getting the good out of it.

Small wonder it is, however, in view of his predilection for problems of creation and form, that he twice warned readers and critics that the only point of view from which to judge his work soundly was the aesthetic point of view. But there was another reason for this insistence that his books be looked upon solely as a series of works of art. His adverse critics, by attacking his notorious "immoralism," his lack of an orthodox faith, and his "unhealthy" spiritual unrest, had begun to teach him how the conventional moral approach to his work could distort his intentions, falsify his message, and rob his writing of all beauty. If only, he doubtless thought, some unprejudiced critic would view his books simply as literature without striving to iso-

late the ethical implications of Ménalque, to see Candaules and
Michel as models of behavior, to exalt or mock Lafcadio as an
ideal. A resolutely and exclusively aesthetic attitude would, he
hoped, obviate such misunderstandings. He knew, after all, that
—apart from their moral, philosophical, or social overtones—
he had written his books primarily as works of art; and it was
not altogether unfair for him to want them to be judged as such.

To the world at large André Gide is probably most widely
known for his fiction rather than for his drama, journals, essays,
or literary criticism. Yet he claimed to have written but one
novel, although most readers would credit him with no fewer
than nine other novels, each of them shorter than the famous
Faux-Monnayeurs for which he reserved that designation. It
should be appropriate, then, to scrutinize the form of Gide's
fiction as a sample of his artistic achievement without proceed-
ing to apply the same method to the other *genres* he cultivated.

With *L'Immoraliste, La Porte étroite, Isabelle, Les Caves du
Vatican*, and *La Symphonie pastorale* behind him, Gide was already an accomplished novelist when he sat down in June 1919
to write what he called his first and only novel. Judging his work
from the inside, he is pleased to emphasize the differences between his *Faux-Monnayeurs* and all the rest of his fiction. In an
ironic and unused preface for that novel he claimed that he had
not classified his earlier works as novels for fear they might be
accused of lacking some of the essentials of the *genre*, such as
confusion, for instance. In the novel itself he makes his novelist
Édouard reflect that his earlier tales resemble those basins in
French parks, precise in contour, but in which the captive water
is lifeless. "Now," says Édouard, "I want to let it flow according to the slope, at one moment rapid and at another slow, in
meanders that I refuse to foresee." Between *La Symphonie pastorale* and the *Faux-Monnayeurs*, Gide's preparation for his lectures on Dostoevsky taught him, we have seen, many things.

But the break at this point in his career is less abrupt than
Gide implies in his personal writings. In actual fact the *Faux-*

Monnayeurs covers less ground both spatially and temporally than most of the tales. *L'Immoraliste* includes scenes in Paris, North Africa, Italy, and Normandy; *La Porte étroite* is laid in Rouen, Fongueusemare, Paris, Havre, and Aigues-Vives (near Nîmes); only *La Symphonie pastorale* with its limitation to La Brévine and nearby Neuchâtel rivals the economy of the *Faux-Monnayeurs*, which takes us out of Paris only for a brief stay at Saas-Fée in Switzerland. It is equally surprising to note, in view of the novel's complexity, that its action is concentrated within a few months, whereas *L'Immoraliste* records three years, *La Porte étroite* twenty years, and *La Symphonie pastorale* two years and nine months of life. Furthermore, for all their precise contours, not one of the tales is as balanced in composition as the *Faux-Monnayeurs*, with its eighteen chapters and 220 pages of the first part exactly paralleling the eighteen chapters and 225 pages of the third part.

The complexity and "confusion" of the novel must be attributable, then to the number of characters or rather to the number of plots, for the twenty-eight characters are necessitated by the multiple plots. Still, there is another reason for that apparent confusion. If growing up and becoming oneself is the principal theme of the novel, it is but appropriate that the novel itself should be in a state of becoming. Hence its impression of formlessness, created by the constant change of subject to avoid taking advantage of momentum, by the large sections devoted to Édouard's journal, by Édouard's numerous "asininities" (as he himself calls them) concerning *his* projected novel, and by the author's pseudo-naïve comments in the manner of Fielding or Sterne. Yet, despite the multiplicity of plots and the contrapuntal composition of *Les Faux-Monnayeurs* (which, together with the novel within a novel, were to inspire Aldous Huxley's *Point Counterpoint*), it proves on examination to be the work of a very conscious writer who has calculated every one of his effects—beginning with the suggestion of chaos and confusion which seemed to him in harmony with his theme.

Now, André Gide noted most loyally in his *Journals* for 1928 that Martin du Gard advised him to gather together the various plots, which, "had it not been for him, would have formed so many separate 'tales.' " Thus, without the example of Dostoevsky and the advice of a friend consummately skilled in the art of narration, Gide might never have renewed his fictional technique. On the other hand, despite his own conviction as to that renewal, readers can now discern the persistence of certain elements within that technique.

In the fascinating and invaluable *Journal of "The Counterfeiters"* (entitled in England *Logbook of the Coiners*), the novelty of Gide's approach throughout and his little youthful thrill of triumph at each new problem overcome prevent the reader from noticing how many of the apparent technical innovations had already found their place in the earlier tales. For instance, the first entry in that notebook reads: "For two days I have been wondering whether or not to have my novel related by Lafcadio. Thus it would be a narrative of gradually revealed events in which he would act as an observer, an idler, a perverter." Is this not again the first-person narration of the tales? To be sure, a month later Gide abandoned this plan after writing some pages of Lafcadio's journals (preserved in the Appendix); yet in doing so he added: "But I should like to have successive interpreters: for example, Lafcadio's notes would occupy the first book; the second book might consist of Édouard's notebook; the third of an attorney's files, etc." Surely this is the same technique as in *La Porte étroite* where, at a certain point, Jerome's account is broken to admit the diary of the dead Alissa.

In fact, it was not until much later that it occurred to Gide —possibly as a result of rereading *Tom Jones*—to resort to impersonal narration with frequent interventions of the author. At about the same time he decided to have events "exposed (and several times from different vantages) by those actors who will be influenced by those events," so that the reader will have to *reconstruct*. But this is already true of the tales. That there are two points of view in *La Porte étroite*—thanks to Jerome's account and Alissa's diary—is obvious. In *L'Immoraliste*, although Michel is the sole narrator, who is trying to report himself objectively, he is nevertheless judged by his wife, Marceline, and by his friend, Ménalque, not to mention the Arab youth, Moktir; and Michel strives to record those judgments— with the inevitable result that the reader has to re-establish the truth. Likewise in *La Symphonie pastorale*, where the lamentable minister is judged by his wife, his son, and the blind girl he loves.

After *Les Faux-Monnayeurs*, when Gide wrote *L'École des femmes* and its two sequels, *Robert* and *Geneviève*, he somewhat mechanically presented three views of the same family conflict, one to a volume . . . much as he had toyed with doing in *Les Faux-Monnayeurs*.

Thus Gide consistently called for a sort of collaboration, letting the reader enjoy the pleasure of getting the advantage over him by feeling more intelligent, more perspicacious, and more moral than the author. One might call this, in opposition to the technique of the omniscient author, that of the *nilniscient* author. This is why he left out of his novel all the non-essentials —such as the many deeds and remarks of his characters which any attentive reader could readily supply for himself. "I scrupulously ruled out of my *Faux-Monnayeurs*," he boasted, "everything that another might just as well have written, being satisfied with indications allowing one to imagine whatever I did not set out. I recognize that those neutral passages are the very ones that rest, reassure, and win over the reader; I alienated many whose laziness I should have flattered."

Another Gidian device that demands an effort of the reader is the artful implication that the novel *could* be continued almost indefinitely. Many of us have long admired the ending of the *Faux-Monnayeurs* with Édouard's suspensive remark: "I am very curious to know Caloub." And indeed, in his workbook the author noted: "This novel will end sharply, not through exhaustion of the subject, which must give the impression of inexhaustibility, but on the contrary through its expansion and by a sort of blurring of its outline. It must not be neatly rounded off, but rather disperse, disintegrate. . ." This too is less new in his work than Gide would have us believe. Do not the earlier novels likewise blur off, leaving the reader to reflect at length on the situation and emotions of the chief protagonist and narrator? Particularly in *L'Immoraliste* and in *La Porte étroite*, when the end is reached, the reader feels better informed—thanks to the technique of indirection—than is the bewildered narrator.

Finally, it must not be forgotten that in 1914—directly between *La Porte étroite* and *Isabelle* on the one hand and *La Symphonie pastorale* on the other—Gide had brought out *Les Caves du Vatican*. That thrilling novel has more in common with *Les Faux-Monnayeurs* than it has with the unilinear tales that precede and follow it. Comprising almost the same multiplicity of plots and contrapuntal composition as the later novel, it is narrated in the third person by a most conscious writer who even indulges in apostrophes and asides reminiscent of Fielding and Sterne to disclaim omniscience and responsibility; and it unfolds swiftly with all the complexity and compulsion of a novel of adventure. Furthermore, it includes a microcosmic novel within the novel, which Julius is writing almost at the dictation of Lafcadio. Clearly it is a try-out of the techniques to be used ten years later in *Les Faux-Monnayeurs*. Nothing is more natural than that Gide should have begun *Les Faux-Monnayeurs*, in his first draft, with the journal of Lafcadio, the charming and elusive hero of the earlier novel. His later rejection of Lafcadio reflects his characteristic desire not to take conscious advantage of momentum acquired in an earlier work.

Yet it was manifestly impossible not to benefit from unconscious momentum in the form of fictional techniques patiently elaborated over the preceding twenty-five years. Some readers will always prefer the concentrated, gem-like tales of Gide's early maturity, whereas others will choose the exasperatingly living, Dostoevskian qualities of *Les Faux-Monnayeurs*. But, whatever their differences, the men and women who have the good fortune to read those works a century from now will doubtless not hesitate for a moment to recognize the same hand in all of them.

Probably somewhat the same motives that made Gide insist on the aesthetic judgment of his works urged him to state in 1909, after a number of uncomprehending criticisms of *La Porte étroite*: "It will not be easy to trace the trajectory of my mind; its curve will reveal itself only in my style and will escape most people." Besides suggesting a desire to escape an implied commitment to this or that specific subject-matter, this statement shows the importance Gide always gave to style, his confidence in his own style, and his awareness of his stylistic versatility. That he should have attributed such capital significance to style is not odd, for style is the most obvious manifestation of formal preoccupations. When Paul Valéry differentiated poetry from prose on the ground that it is impossible to change or displace a single word in verse, Gide protested that the same was equally true of beautiful prose, claiming that he aimed to "satisfy an exigence just as rigorous (though often more hidden)." On another occasion he professed that he wanted to make his sentence "so sensitive an instrument that the mere displacement of a comma should be enough to destroy its harmony."

Despite the evident originality of his own language, André Gide was aware that few writers manage to achieve individuality of style and yet maintain correct usage. He also knew that when such originality is attained it is immediately attributed to affectation. Like Proust, Gide saw that the demands of sincerity lead inevitably to a new style that at first seems artificial and precious, for the public does not welcome the upsetting of its habits of vision and thought. The vigorous writer, precisely because he has new things to say, finds himself literally obliged to forge a new style. There is, then, a necessary relationship between style and subject; stylistic originality is "demanded by the very movement of the emotion or the thought."

Thus, when someone accused him of coquetry in stylistic matters, he objected that he liked only the barest necessity. "When I began to write my *Nourritures*," he continued, "I realized that the very subject of my book *was* to banish all metaphor from it. There is not a movement of my style that does not correspond to a need of my mind; most often it is but a need of order. The writer's eloquence must be that of the soul itself, of the thought; artificial elegance is a burden to me; likewise all added poetry." Of the many ways of saying a thing he invariably preferred the simplest. Reading Tacitus and likening him to Montesquieu, Gide contrasted the Roman's "wild austerity" with the often sugared grace of so many writers. That kind of grace he found in Renan, Barrès, and Loti among others, and he exclaimed: "Compared with that Asiaticism, how Dorian I feel!"

Such an attitude of mind naturally encouraged in him an innate tendency toward concentration, making him impatient of any writer who gains a reputation for fertility because he is merely avaricious and unable to suppress a thing he writes. In contrast Gide claimed: "I always long to draw the narrowest line, the most sudden and least expected." This is why he fled all devices of style, wanting his style to be so hidden as to be invisible. If he could realize that ideal, he would be—unlike his friends Régnier, Jammes, and Péguy—truly inimitable. For, without necessarily being mannered, each of them had developed a manner, whereas Gide wanted none but that which his subject demanded. This is why he rejected metaphors, not only from the *Nourritures*, but also from his first work, and thus drew from Heredia, master of the Parnassian poets, the reproach that he had written in a "rather poverty-stricken style."

To analyze the style of André Gide in detail with all its subtleties and chronological growth would require in itself a most scrupulous study fully as long as this one. Some day such an examination will be undertaken by a courageous scholar— doubtless in French and with Gide's voluminous French texts as primary documents. Meanwhile one can but recommend the thoughtful work of Ernst Bendz, *André Gide et l'art d'écrire* (*André Gide and the Art of Writing*), the too brief appendix to Ramon Fernandez's *André Gide*, and especially the most sensitive portrait contained in M. Saint-Clair's *Galerie privée* (*Private Gallery*).

As for the evolution of Gide's style and the "trajectory" of his mind that might be followed therein, one should recall his statement that progress in the art of writing comes solely from a progressive surrender of every cause for self-satisfaction. Hence we should expect his style to develop in the direction of simplicity and banality. At the beginning of his career, indeed, he indulged his every whim. Consequently, years later, the "jaculatory" tone of his first book exasperated him, as did his early predilection for such terms as "uncertain," "infinite," "indescribable," whose frequence in German writing had made that language seem to him particularly suited for poetry. Similarly much of *La Porte étroite* later struck him as affected and *Isabelle*, too full of nuances, made him long to write *Les Caves du Vatican* differently, deliberately placing a flat tone beside another flat tone. Little by little he learned to follow the genius of the French language, to prize precision and clarity above vagueness and suggestion.

On his best days, particularly when, seated on a bench along the quay, on a road embankment, in a train or the métro, he jotted down his thoughts in a little notebook that always accompanied him, he would write rapidly as if taking dictation.

This seemed to him a sort of "artesian welling-up" after a long subconscious preparation. At such moments he could correctly say: "Less a painter than a musician, it is certainly movement in preference to color that I wished my sentence to have. I wanted it to follow patiently the palpitations of my heart." For —even more than the subtlety of the syntax, the deliberate archaism of the vocabulary, the new meanings conferred upon old, worn words, the unexpected juxtaposition of familiar expressions, the startlingly emphatic displacement of a word or phrase—the distinguishing mark of Gide's style is its personal rhythm.

Anyone who has sensitively translated a page of Gide's writing into any language recognizes the wisdom of his recommendation to the author of one English version that the essential thing to catch was not so much his thought as his *gait*. In that first product of his adolescence, *Les Cahiers d'André Walter*, he wanted "so lyrical and sensitive a form that poetry would overflow it despite the rigid lines." He longed for a balanced, musical strophe without metre or rhyme, and, instead of writing in French, he dreamed of "writing in music." In more precise terms, he spoke in the same work of "an alliterative rhythm, the rippling of the sentence—and the interrupted recall of assonances." By 1914 he had begun to react against the cadence that balanced his sentences; but what he was fleeing was "that fatal number distinct from rhythm," an "indulgence toward eurythmy" that gave too much polish to his style.

A good example of what Gide means is the sinister attraction exerted upon him by the alexandrine, the classic French line of twelve syllables broken by a caesura precisely in the middle. In his "Detached Pages" for 1925 he flatly stated that prose which is shot full of alexandrines forms "a hybrid style of ambiguous charm" inasmuch as the rhythm of verse breaks that of prose. Yet his own prose frequently sins in this regard: the *Nourritures* abounds in irreproachable alexandrines sometimes following one another in succession; his first novel, *L'Im-*

moraliste, suddenly adopts the classic verse in a sentence of ridiculous effect because of the contrast between the thought and the regularity of the cadence:

"Il m'aurait paru beau s'il n'avait été borgne."

And in the drama *Philoctète* an attentive ear can detect the same rhythm not only in the final speech, but also in the closing stage direction!

As his early verses abundantly prove, Gide was never a poet; and in the impressive total of his highly personal prose such aberrations, conscious or unconscious, can be dismissed with a smile. The fact is that almost everything he ever wrote, with the notable exception of most of his *Journals,* nervously strains toward verse; if it occasionally goes too far in that direction, this merely reveals the force of the tension. In 1923 Gide admitted: "The exactingness of my ear, until the last few years, was such that I should have warped the meaning of a sentence for its rhythm." But he was wrong if he thought he had escaped that exigence, for eight years later he left obliged to note: "My ear, or some even more subtle precision-balance or other, remains just as hard to please. One foot more or less to my sentence and it shocks me like a bad line of verse. I cannot endure being quoted wrongly (as so often), even if it were with the best intention in the world." Again and more fully, as late as 1935, he was to include in his *Journals* a paragraph that would have shocked his then fervent Communist friends: "It is of no use struggling against what may seem to me (and quite wrongly, no doubt) an unjustified servitude: rhythm dominates my sentence, almost dictates it, clings closely to my thought. This need of a precise rhythm responds to a secret exigence. The scansion of the sentence, the placing of the syllables, both strong and weak, all this matters to me as much as the thought itself, and the thought strikes me as halting or distorted if it lacks a foot or has one too many. Thus it is that thought is worth nothing to me unless it participates in life, unless it breathes, becomes animate, and one feels through the words

and in their swelling, a heart beating." The vibrant pulsation
of a living organism combined with an inner tension are the
keys to André Gide's style; and the equilibrium they produce
echoes the dynamic balance achieved by his thought.

Such an equilibrium in both thought and style is eminently
classical. Now, no modern literature is more accustomed than
the French to revere the qualities of classicism; since the great
classic or neo-classic age of Louis XIV the French have habitually seen themselves as the only worthy heirs of Greece and
Rome. And no one among modern French writers, I believe, has
reflected more pertinently on the nature of classicism than has
André Gide. He frequently returned to the subject, on which
one of his most memorable conclusions first appeared in an
article of 1921: "Classicism—and by this I mean French classicism," he said, "tends altogether toward litotes. It is the art of
expressing the most by saying the least. It is an art of modesty
and reserve. Each of our classics is more deeply moved than
he allows to be seen at first. The romantic writer always remains
short of what he says; to find the classic writer one always has
to go beyond what he says. A certain gift for passing too rapidly, too readily, from emotion to speech is characteristic of
all the French romantics—whence their slight effort to seize
hold of the emotion otherwise than through speech, their slight
effort to dominate it. The important thing for them is not being,
but seeming, moved." According to this original definition,
Gide himself belongs among the classicists. Did he not as a
young man, after a certain amount of torment, choose *being*
in preference to *appearing*? And did he not also in his work
bend his effort to dominating emotion?

Gide achieved his classicism through an inner constraint.
As Denis de Rougemont has pointed out, his entire aesthetic is
founded on a sacrifice of the incidental to the essential, a self-
subordination and a conciseness that lead at once to an intellectual discipline and an ethic of expression: "The Calvinism
that the Prodigal was fleeing takes a vigorous revenge in the

style of the narration! Amazing paradox of a disciplined aesthetic regulating a work whose great message is that one must free oneself from rules." Gide himself would have agreed with this statement on condition that he could expand it somewhat, for in his reasoned reply to the symposium conducted by the *Renaissance* in 1921 he had written: "It seems to me that the qualities we like to call classical are moral qualities, and I am inclined to consider classicism as a harmonious assemblage of virtues, the first of which is modesty. Romanticism is always associated with pride, with infatuation. Classical perfection implies, not indeed a suppression of the individual (I am on the point of saying: quite the contrary), but the submission of the individual, his subordination, and that of the word in the sentence, of the sentence in the page, of the page in the work. It is the demonstration of a hierarchy. It is noteworthy that the struggle between classicism and romanticism exists likewise within each mind. And it is of that very struggle that the work must be born; the classic work of art relates the triumph of order and measure over the inner romanticism. The more refractory what is to be dominated the more beautiful the work. If the matter is submissive in advance, the work is cold and without interest. True classicism involves nothing restrictive or suppressive; it is less conservative than creative; it rejects archaism and refuses to believe that everything has been said." Gide's insistence on the problem of classicism doubtless reveals, not only an awareness that therein lies the secret of the French genius, but also, but especially, an intimate conviction that he too—like so many others from Montaigne and Racine to Valéry, from Ronsard and Molière to Flaubert—represents that genius.

And quite possibly the secret of crafty Daedalus patiently elaborating his complex labyrinth as a safe hiding-place for his subversive thought—a "lattice-work labyrinth" (as Charles Du Bos calls it) only in so far as its clarity protects it from unworthy intruders—is both the last and the most significant of the

metamorphoses of old Proteus. For over sixty years André Gide
worked to emancipate the minds of men. Many of his ideas have
already gained acceptance, and in the future others among
them will lose their shocking quality and become part of the
common heritage. At such time, his priority as the first to ex-
pound them will seem less important, doubtless, than the fact
that he expressed those ideas better than anyone else.

REFERENCES

IN ORDER to avoid reference symbols in the text of this book, I have repeated here the last words of each statement that is annotated. All references are to the French texts with the exception of the *Journal*, as yet unavailable in French in a single complete edition. *JAG* therefore refers to my edition in four volumes of *The Journals of André Gide* (New York and London, 1947–51); and the indication of dates or subheadings in such references makes it possible to find the text in *Journal, 1889–1939* (La Pléiade, Gallimard, 1939), *Pages de Journal, 1939–1942* (Gallimard, 1946), or *Journal, 1942–1949* (Gallimard, 1950). Every writing that is included in the fifteen-volume edition of *Œuvres complètes d'André Gide* (Gallimard, 1932–39) is referred to in that edition here abbreviated to *OC*.

Individual titles by Gide, after their first appearance among the references, are given in shortened form:

Cahiers for *Les Cahiers d'André Walter*
Grain for *Si le grain ne meurt* . . .
Numquid for *Numquid et tu* . . . ?
Prodigue for *Retour de l'enfant prodigue*
Prométhée for *Le Prométhée mal enchaîné*
Retour for *Retour de l'U.R.S.S.*
Tentative for *La Tentative amoureuse*
Urien for *Le Voyage d'Urien*, etc.

For writings not by André Gide and for all of his not included in the *Œuvres complètes* full bibliographical information is provided when they are first cited.

N.R.F. regularly stands for *La Nouvelle Revue Française*.

I. INTRODUCTION

p. 3.   . . . will allow."—*Dostoïevsky, OC*, XI, 157–8.
p. 4.   . . . of portraits."—Ibid., p. 283.
    . . . exaggeration of an idea."—*JAG*, I, 76 ("Literature and Ethics").
p. 5.   . . . has yet appeared.—*André Gide* (Algiers: Charlot, 1938 and Paris: Charlot, 1946).

p. 6.   ... circled the vase."—"Considérations sur la mythologie grecque," *OC*, IX, 147–8.

p. 7.   ... any of the gods."—*JAG*, II, 342–3 ("Detached Pages," 1923).

... each of them in turn.—*JAG*, III, 107 (30 May 1930).

... wanted to portray."—*JAG*, II, 306 (22 July 1922).

p. 8.   ... psychological significance.—"Pages retrouvées," *N.R.F.*, XXXII, 493–4 (April 1929).

... an inner fatality.—"Considérations sur la mythologie grecque," *OC*, IX, 149–50.

... profound truths."—*The Classical Tradition: Greek and Roman Influences on Western Literature* (London: Oxford University Press, 1949), p. 522.

II. INTERROGATING PROTEUS

p. 10. Epigraph—*Les Faux-Monnayeurs*, *OC*, XII, 292.

... labyrinth."—"Le labyrinthe à clair-voie" is the title of one section of Du Bos's *Dialogue avec André Gide* (Au Sans Pareil, 1929).

p. 11. ... reveals his sincerity."—*JAG*, II, 313 (29 Oct. 1922).

p. 12. ... cohabitation of extremes."—*JAG*, II, 343 ("Detached Pages," 1923).

... *who* they are."—*Journal des Faux-Monnayeurs*, *OC*, XIII, 54.

p. 13. ... as my loves."—*JAG*, I, 168 (10 Jan. 1906).

... of hating."—*JAG*, III, 269 (14 April 1933).

... lack of imagination."—*JAG*, I, 222 (13 Dec. 1907).

... ready sympathy."—*JAG*, I, 296 ("Detached Pages," 1911).

... not sympathize."—*JAG*, III, 306 (25 July 1934).

... a common emotion."—*Nourritures terrestres*, *OC*, II, 64.

... an artificial health."—*JAG*, I, 77 ("Literature and Ethics").

... wonderful about it."—*JAG*, I, 317 (Feb. 1912).

... to my lips."—*Cahiers d'André Walter*, *OC*, I, 157.

... believe in sin!"—*Nourritures*, *OC*, II, 89.

... are envied."—*JAG*, II, 183 (*Numquid et tu . . . ?*).

... listened to."—*JAG*, II, 205 (30 April or 1 May 1917).

p. 14. ... speaks in the desert!"—*JAG*, III, 342–3 (16 May 1936).

... misquotation . . .—Cf. *JAG*, II, 274 (29 Nov. 1921); III, 106 (30 May 1930); 170–1 (30 June 1931); 207 (14 Dec. 1931); 221–2 (9 Feb. 1932); 261 (8 Feb. 1933); 302 (6 June 1934); 308 (2 Aug. 1934).

... expressed by his characters.—Cf. *JAG*, II, 274 (29 Nov. 1921); III, 107 (30 May 1930).

... by his creatures.—Cf. *Dostoïevsky, OC*, XI, 311.

... blossoms."—*JAG*, II, 404 (June 1927).

p. 15.   ... simultaneous.—*Préface aux "Fleurs du mal," OC*, VII, 504.

... in contradiction."—*Si le grain ne meurt . . . , OC*, X, 341. Cf. *JAG*, II, 257 (5 Oct. 1920).

... remain faithful."—*JAG*, II, 282 (26 Dec. 1921).

... after his youth."—*JAG*, II, 281 (26 Dec. 1921).

p. 16.   ... I suffer."—*JAG*, I, 148 (24 Aug. 1905).

... take root?"—*A propos des "Déracinés," OC*, II, 437.

... of two faiths?"—*JAG*, III, 84 (2 Dec. 1929).

p. 17.   ... a sublime degree."—*Grain, OC*, X, 67.

p. 18.   ... had ever been."—Ibid., p. 47.

...·good literature."—R.-G. Nobécourt: *Les Nourritures normandes d'André Gide* (Eds. Médicis, 1949), p. 29.

p. 19.   ... extreme kindness."—*Grain, OC*, X, 38.

p. 20.   ... guile."—Ibid., p. 32.

p. 21.   ... late in life."—Ibid., p. 210.

... of the piece."—Ibid., pp. 44–5.

... affectionate words."—Ibid., p. 54.

p. 22.   ... never idle."—Ibid., p. 57.

p. 24.   ... act otherwise."—Ibid., p. 128.

... separate us."—Ibid., p. 129.

p. 26.   ... as possible."—Ibid., p. 67.

p. 27.   ... my exploit."—Ibid., p. 86.

... depicted."—Ibid., p. 96.

p. 28.   ... when I fell . . ."—Ibid., p. 149.

p. 29.   ... not yet finished."—Ibid., pp. 158–9.

p. 30.   ... touched them."—Ibid., p. 161.

p. 31.   ... these memoirs."—Ibid., p. 164.

... like the others!"—Ibid., pp. 172–3.

p. 33.   ... just now."—*Figaro Littéraire*, 21 May 1949, p. 6. Cf. G. Jean-Aubry: *André Gide et la musique* (Eds. de la Revue Musicale, 1945), p. 34.

p. 34.   ... more to me."—*JAG*, III, 412 (7 Jan. 1939).

... patience."—*Grain, OC*, X, 290.

... watching snails."—*JAG*, II, 142 (3 May 1916).

... unexpected color."—*Grain, OC*, X, 80.

p. 36.   ... delicate words."—*André Gide* (Eds. du Capitole, 1928), pp. 270–1.

p. 37.   ... of happiness."—*Grain, OC*, X, 267.

p. 38.   ... eager heart."—Ibid., p. 262.

p. 39.   ... repeat again."—*Traité du Narcisse, OC*, I, 207–8.

III. THE NARCISSUS POSE

p. 40.   ... Epigraph—*Narcisse, OC*, I, 209.
         ... convulsive movements."—*Grain, OC*, X, 167.

p. 41.   ... in consequence."—Ibid., p. 288.

p. 43.   ... of quintessence."—Ibid., pp. 276–7.

p. 45.   ... and scruples."—Ibid., p. 270.

p. 46.   ... intransigent conviction.—"Stéphane Mallarmé," *OC*, II, 453.
         ... carried along."—Ibid., p. 448.

p. 47.   ... to arrive too late.—*Cahiers d'André Walter, OC*, I, 68.
         ... of them all.—Paul Iseler: *Les Débuts d'André Gide vus par
         Pierre Louÿs* (Eds., du Sagittaire, 1937), p. 18.

p. 49.   ... at moonlight."—*Cahiers, OC*, I, 44–5.
         ... abstract speculation.—Ibid., p. 102.
         ... vagabond puberty."—Ibid., p. 107.

p. 50.   ... not known!"—Ibid., p. 108.
         ... obsesses me."—*JAG*, III, 115–6 (30 June 1930).
         ... he had a soul."—*Cahiers, OC*, I, 163.

p. 51.   ... your immortality."—Ibid., p. 165.
         ... our influences."—Ibid., p. 43.

p. 52.   ... personal catharsis.—Cf. *André Gide et la pensée allemande*
         (L.U.F., Egloff, 1949), pp. 125–9.
         ... without irritation."—*JAG*, IV, 53 (23 Nov. 1940).
         ... even mortification."—Preface to the 1930 edition of *André
         Walter: Cahiers et Poésies* (Œuvres Représentatives, 1930),
         p. 7.
         ... *in your outline."*—Iseler: *Débuts d'André Gide*, p. 88.

p. 53.   ... *d'intorno."*—*Cahiers, OC*, I, 50.
         ... *Porte étroite."*—*Le Dialogue avec André Gide* (Au Sans
         Pareil, 1929), p. 47.

p. 54.   ... *of Adolescence in France.*—By Justin O'Brien (N.Y.: Co-
         lumbia University Press, 1937).

p. 55.   ... of renunciation . . ."—*Le Jeune Homme* (Hachette, 1926),
         pp. 10–11.
         ... readily understood."—*Cahiers, OC*, I, 65.

p. 57.   ... acts and thoughts."—*Figaro Littéraire*, 5 Aug. 1950, p. 1.

p. 58.   ... spiritual value."—*Mercure de France*, II, 368 (June 1891).

p. 59.   ... a secret experience."—*La Wallonie*, 6e année, 175 (March–April 1891).

... breviary of virgins."—Letter of 9 May 1891 reproduced in 1930 edition of *André Walter*, p. 248.

p. 60.   ... from each other."—*Paul Valéry* (Eds. Domat, 1947), pp. vii–viii.

p. 61.   ... youthful *Novembre.*—Iseler: *Débuts d'André Gide*, p. 90.

... must believe."—Henri Mondor: *Les Premiers Temps d'une amitié: André Gide et Paul Valéry* (Monaco: Eds. du Rocher, 1947), pp. 69–71.

... through a misunderstanding."—*Grain*, OC, X, 305.

p. 63.   ... restored to him."—Ibid., p. 333.

... Hamleth"—This manuscript is in my collection.

p. 64.   ... beyond him."—*OC*, I, 202.

... Spring to come."—*OC*, I, 179–80:

"Il n'y a pas eu de printemps cette année, ma chère;
Pas de chants sous les fleurs et pas de fleurs légères,
Ni d'Avril, ni de rires et ni de métamorphoses;
Nous n'aurons pas tressé de guirlandes de roses.

. . . .

Il pleuvait. Nous avons ranimé les lampes
Que ce soleil rouge avait fait pâlir
Et nous nous sommes replongés dans l'attente
Du clair printemps qui va venir."

p. 65.   ... cast much light."—*OC*, I, 180:

"Mais tout ça, ça manque un peu de lyrisme
Et nos lampes ne font pas beaucoup de clarté."

... of green mud.—*OC*, I, 195.

... caused by it."—*OC*, I, 39.

p. 66.   ... delicate analogies."—Mondor: *Premiers Temps*, p. 24.

... it's too bad.)"—*Mercure de France*, XII, 354 (Dec. 1894).

... back to sleep.' "—*OC*, I, 198:

"Peut-être que tout cela c'est un rêve
Et que nous nous réveillerons.
                              Tu m'as dit:
'Je crois que nous vivons dans le rêve d'un autre
Et que c'est pour cela que nous sommes si soumis.'
Ça ne peut pas durer toujours comme ça.
'Je crois que ce que nous aurions de mieux à faire
Ce serait de tâcher de nous rendormir.' "

p. 67.   . . . glazing gleams."—"Ame de serre" in *Serres   chaudes*
          (Bruxelles: P. Lacomblez, 1900), p. 81:
          "Je vois des songes dans mes yeux;
          Et mon âme enclose sous verre,
          Eclairant sa mobile serre,
          Affleure les vitrages bleus."
          . . . rumpled water."—*OC*, I, 191:
          "Dans l'hémostatique eau fripée"
          . . . drills."—*OC*, I, 190:
          "Pendant que de ses vocalises mécaniques
          Un rossignol faisait des trous dans la nuit."
          . . . not learned."—*OC*, I, 195:
          "Et notre tristesse s'éplore
          En des lignes qu'elle n'a pas apprises."

p. 68.   . . . well and oft."—*OC*, I, 268:
          "Tout l'automne est dans mon grenier,
          Tout le printemps est dans ma grange,
          Tous les vins sont dans mon cellier:
          J'étais de toutes les vendanges."
          . . . within the germ."—*OC*, I, 268:
          "Ce qu'aujourd'hui d'hier avait reçu
          Demain le redira; le printemps futur
          Attend et sommeille dans le blé mur;
          Le printemps attend qu'un grain le ramène
          Et l'été revit à travers la graine."

p. 69.   . . . as a blank."—*OC*, I, 276:
          "Quand ils mourront, non satisfaits de leurs études
          Ils prétendront aussi qu'ils ont vécu
          Et se croiront de spéciales aptitudes
          Pour un ciel qu'ils auront imaginé tout nu."
          . . . good night.' "—*OC*, I, 277:
          " 'Et nous aurons navigué sous
          Des lignes vides de sirènes
          Sans que parvinssent jusqu'à nous
          Les chants qui sur la mer se traînent,

          Ni les parfums qui font déjà presque plaisir.
          Nous ne sommes pas morts de maladie.   Amen!' "
          . . . for poetry."—*Grain, OC*, X, 316–7.

IV. NARCISSUS AND THE MULTIPLE MIRRORS

p. 71.   Epigraph.—*JAG*, I, 16 (8 Oct. 1891).
         . . . *Poems in Prose.*—"Oscar Wilde," *OC*, III, 476–7.
p. 72.   . . . manuscript.—Mondor: *Premiers Temps*, p. 123 ff.
         . . . if it was."—*Narcisse, OC*, I, 210.
p. 73.   . . . of the unexpected!"—Ibid., p. 211.
         . . . all essential truth."—Ibid., pp. 212–3.
p. 74.   . . . subordinate himself."—Ibid., p. 215.
         . . . to adore."—Ibid., pp. 218–9.
p. 75.   . . . *Blessed Obscurity.*—*Leda* is reprinted in *Le Crépuscule des nymphes* (Eds. Montaigne, 1925).
p. 77.   . . . too is revelatory."—*JAG*, I, 268 (Aug. 1910).
p. 83.   . . . to Iceland."—*Grain, OC*, X, 348.
         . . . Academy of Sciences.—*Comptes-rendus hebdomadaires des séances de l'Académie des Sciences*, 114 (Jan.–June 1892), pp. 86–7 and 191–2.
         . . . *Voyage d'Urien.*—"De Lorient à Terre-Neuve," *Revue Scientifique*, 3ᵉ série, tome XIV, pp. 492–7 (15 Oct. 1887).
         . . . sperm whale.—*Revue des Deux Mondes*, vol. 90, pp. 625–50 (1 Dec. 1888).
         . . . biologist's death.—Cf. Arnold Naville: *Bibliographie des écrits de André Gide* (H. Matarasso, 1949), p. 219.
p. 84.   . . . with beauties . . ."—"Préface pour une seconde édition du *Voyage d'Urien*," *Mercure de France*, XII (Dec. 1894), 355–6.
         . . . just this time.—*André Gide et la pensée allemande*, pp. 70–3.
p. 86.   . . . of its folds . . ."—*Cahiers, OC*, I, 50.
p. 89.   . . . with oneself."—*JAG*, I, 29 (Aug. or Sept. 1893).
p. 90.   . . . purging of passions."—*OC*, IV, 616–7.
         . . . inner urge."—Henri Bergson: *Le Rire* (Félix Alcan, 1912), p. 171.
         . . . own incoherences.—*Dostoïevsky, OC*, XI, 161.
         . . . other body."—*The Letters of John Keats*, edited by M. B. Forman (London: Oxford University Press, 1931), I, 245.
         . . . to portray.—Cf. *JAG*, II, 306 (22 July 1922).
p. 91.   . . . Othello."—*JAG*, II, 392 (8 Feb. 1927).
p. 92.   . . . certain serenity."—Letter of 5 Nov. 1924 to André Rouveyre, *OC*, XII, 561.
         . . . puddles of his work."—*Goethe et Diderot* quoted by Gide in a letter of 21 Oct. 1929 to Henri Massis, *Lettres* (Liége:

A la Lampe d'Aladdin, 1930), p. 113.

p. 93.   ... for the portrait.—Cf. Wallace Fowlie: "The Fountain and the thirst," *Accent*, vol. 6, no. 2 (Winter 1946), pp. 67–76.

... more monstrous."—*Grain*, *OC*, X, 346.

... curves them."—*OC*, I, 337.

p. 94.   ... mature age.—Cf. *JAG*, I, 268 (Aug. 1910).

... theirs alone."—*Unforgotten Years* (London: Constable, 1938), p. 205.

p. 95.   ... drove me."—*Grain*, *OC*, X, 347–8.

... potential powers."—*JAG*, I, 33 (10 Oct. 1893).

... myself at all."—*JAG*, I, 27–8 (Aug. 1893).

p. 96.   ... without a struggle."—*OC*, I, 219.

V. THE FRENZY OF DIONYSUS

p. 97.   Epigraphs.—*Nourritures*, *OC*, II, 205, and *Grain*, *OC*, X, 435.

p. 98.   ... over-emphasize,"—*Grain*, *OC*, X, p. 350.

p. 100.   ... relaxing."—Ibid., p. 368.

... renewed."—*Nourritures*, *OC*, II, 71.

p. 101.   ... constraint."—Review of *Les Mille Nuits et une nuit*, translated by J.–C. Mardrus, in *La Revue Blanche*, XXI (1900), 474; reproduced in *OC*, III, 434.

... under palms."—Cf. *De l'influence en littérature*, *OC*, III, 256.

p. 102.   ... press my lips."—*JAG*, I, 23 (March 1893).

p. 103.   ... that is hard."—*L'Immoraliste*, *OC*, IV, 15.

p. 104.   ... my Nourritures."—*Grain*, *OC*, X, 386.

p. 105.   ... strange women.—Cf. *Urien*, *OC*, I, 300.

... other desires?"—*OC*, II, 129:

"Où sont, Nathanaël, dans nos voyages

De nouveaux fruits pour nous donner d'autres désirs?"

... bronze."—*OC*, II, 130–1:

"Trésor gardé, cloisons de ruches,

Abondance de la saveur,

Architecture pentagonale.

L'écorce se fend; les grains tombent,

Grains de sang dans des coupes d'azur;

Et d'autres, gouttes d'or, dans des plats de bronze émaillé."

... important to me."—*Grain*, *OC*, X, 386.

p. 106.   ... them of this."—Ibid., 386–7.

p. 110.   ... younger flowers.—Cf. Hermann Müller, *The Fertilization of Flowers* (London: Macmillan, 1883), pp. 517–8.

p. 113. ...his own words.—G. Apollinaire, *Anecdotiques* (Stock, 1926), p. 34.

p. 115. ...show in *Paludes?*"—Francis Jammes–André Gide: *Correspondance, 1893–1938* (Gallimard, 1948), p. 189.

...and I."—Ibid., p. 58.

p. 116. ...to 1890."—Paul Claudel–André Gide: *Correspondance, 1899–1926* (Gallimard, 1949), p. 46.

...universal thought?"—*Revue Blanche*, XII (1897), 236.

p. 117. ...one another.—Cf. Giraudoux: *Siegfried* (Grasset, 1928), Act II, scene 3, p. 102.

...as his life.—Letter to Bouhélier in 1897 quoted by Yvonne Davet: *Autour des Nourritures terrestres* (Gallimard, 1948), p. 14.

p. 120. ...my new law."—*Grain, OC*, X, 434–5.

p. 121. ...sixty years."—*Une Famille de haute bourgeoisie rouennaise: Histoire de la Famille Rondeaux par P.L.V.* (Rouen: Imprimerie Cagniard–Léon Gy–Albert Lainé successeur, 1928), p. 261.

...for 31 May.—Cf. *JAG*, III, 22 (4 Oct. 1928); and Jammes-Gide, pp. 46–7.

...frightened me."—*Grain, OC*, X, 443–4.

p. 122. ...withholding anything."—Ibid., 444–45.

p. 124. ...of wives."—Letter to F. Jammes, 23 Oct. 1895, in Jammes-Gide, p. 55.

...confounded."—Letter of 19 Jan. 1896 in Ibid., p. 63.

p. 131. ...pure lyricism"—Letter to Marcel Drouin in winter of 1894–95 quoted in Yvonne Davet, p. 55.

p. 132. ...of Grass.—Cf. Justin O'Brien, "Gide's *Nourritures* and Vergil's *Bucolics*," *Romanic Review*, XLIII (April 1952), 117–25; and S. A. Rhodes, "The Influence of Walt Whitman on André Gide," *Romanic Review*, XXXI (April 1940), 156–71.

p. 133. ...Davet.—Cf. R. Lang, *André Gide et la pensée allemande* and Y. Davet, *Autour des Nourritures*.

...great figure."—*JAG*, I, 44 (1895).

...true nature.—Cf. "Goethe" in *Nouvelle Revue Française*, XXXVIII, 373 (March 1932), reprinted in *Rencontres* (Neuchâtel: Ides et Calendes, 1948), p. 87.

...great heights.—Cf. letter quoted in Davet, p. 57.

p. 134. ...and small."—Letter quoted in Davet, pp. 61–2.

... the reply."—"Oscar Wilde," *OC*, III, 484–5.

p. 135. ... my gospel."—Quoted in Davet, pp. 145–6, from which the preceding statistics are taken.

... I told him . . ."—"Remarques intimes en marge d'un portrait d'André Gide," in *André Gide* (Eds. du Capitole, 1928), p. 112.

p. 136. ... of André Gide.—Jacques Rivière et Alain-Fournier: *Correspondance, 1905–1914* (Gallimard, 1926), II, 189 and 194.

... dividing him.—*Les Thibault III: La Belle Saison* (Gallimard, 1923), I, 39–41.

p. 137. ... of the artist.—Cf. *JAG*, III, 314 (19 Sept. 1934).

p. 138. ... regenerated."—Quoted in Davet, p. 22.

p. 139. ... everything one has.—Cf. *JAG*, I, 79 ("Christian Ethics").

p. 140. ... into one.—Cf. Jammes-Gide, p. 75.

... who bores him."—*JAG*, I, 217 (22 June 1907).

p. 141. ... recognized by you."—Both letters are in Jammes-Gide, pp. 112–3.

... posterity!"—Quoted in Davet, p. 22.

... by pleasure."—Ibid., p. 77.

... love of duty.—Cf. *JAG*, I, 45 (1895).

... of an idea,—*JAG*, I, 76 ("Literature and Ethics").

... boring to write.—Cf. Jammes-Gide, pp. 80 and 81.

p. 143. ... as it warns."—*JAG*, III, 14 (18 April 1928).

VI. PHILOCTETES: THE ANOMALY AND THE ART

p. 144. Epigraphs.—*Le Prométhée mal enchaîné*, *OC* III, 138 and *JAG*, III, 116 (3 July 1930).

p. 145. ... for generalities."—*JAG*, I, 73. Also included in the "Réflexions" following *Prométhée* in the first edition, p. 186.

p. 146. ... acceptance."—*OC*, IV, 216.

p. 147. ... Protestant.—Cf. Jammes-Gide, p. 139. The letter to Rouart is in *OC*, II, 485–8.

... suggested.—Cf. Yvette Louria, "Le Contenu latent du *Philoctète* gidien," *French Review*, XXV, 348–54 (April 1952).

p. 148. ... of disease."—*OC*, I, 415.

p. 149. ... of Nietzsche."—*JAG*, I, 80 ("Detached Pages," 1896).

... bound up together."—*The Wound and the Bow* (Cambridge, Mass.: Harvard University Press, 1941), p. 289.

p. 150. ... minister.—Cf. *JAG*, I, 217 (22 June 1907).

... *Noire*."—Cf. *Hommage à André Gide*, *N.R.F.*, Nov. 1951, pp. 175–6.

... laws."—*Galerie privée* (Gallimard, 1947), p. 160.

... of humor."—*JAG*, I, 77 ("Literature and Ethics").

p. 155. ... in a review).—Cf. "Lettres à Angèle," *OC*, III, 221.

p. 157. ... *give* them!" E. J. Kahn, Jr.: "Big Operator," *The New Yorker*, 8 Dec. 1951, p. 61.

... to *reconstruct*"—*Journal des F.–M.*, *OC*, XIII, 18 (21 Nov. 1920).

p. 160. ... *Roi Candaule.*—Cf. Jammes-Gide, p. 199.

... His verse-drama . . .—For a full treatment of Gide's drama, cf. James C. McLaren: *The Theatre of André Gide* (Baltimore: The Johns Hopkins Press, 1953).

... such difficulties."—*L'Art romantique* (Conrad, 1925), p. 171.

p. 161. ... swallowed it.—Cf. Book III, chapters 41–2.

p. 162. ... Schweinerei"!—*JAG*, I, 227 (12 Feb. 1908) and 224 (15 Jan. 1908).

p. 163. ... that ethic."—*L'Ermitage*, XVIII, 412 (Second Semestre 1899).

... in his favor,"—*Thus Spake Zarathustra*, II, 31

p. 164. ... March 1898.—Cf. Jammes-Gide, pp. 117 and 136.

p. 165. ... miserable flop.—Cf. *Notes sur André Gide* (Gallimard, 1951), pp. 31–2.

... surprising"—*JAG*, III, 178 (15 July 1931).

... choose *Saül.*—Cf. *Notes sur André Gide*, p. 31.

... charm me."—*Hommage à André Gide*, *N.R.F.*, Nov. 1951, p. 381.

p. 166. ... against me."—*OC*, II, 138.

... his demons."—*Mercure de France*, CCCVI, 619 (1 Aug. 1949); cf. *JAG*, IV, 207 (27 April 1943).

... throughout his life.—Cf. *JAG*, II, 117 (19 Jan. 1916) and *JAG*, III, 215 (21 Jan. 1932).

p. 167. ... their first reply."—Letter of 1 July 1922 in "Lettres d'André Gide à François Mauriac," *La Table Ronde*, no. 61, p. 93 (Jan. 1953).

p. 168. ... to the third . . ."—Letter of 26 March 1898 to Marcel Drouin in *Hommage à André Gide*, *N.R.F.*, Nov. 1951, p. 389.

... my head too."—*JAG*, I, 10 (10 June 1891).

... work of art."—*JAG*, I, 19 (11 Jan. 1892).

... live fully.—Cf. *JAG*, I, 24 (end of April 1893).

p. 169. ... all our powers."—*JAG*, I, 39 (end of September 1894).

... immorality."—*JAG*, I, 41–2 (13 Oct. 1894).

... their authors."—Letter of May 1902 in Jammes-Gide, p. 189.

p. 170. ... meant by that."—*OC*, II, 89.

p. 171. ... in the *Nourritures*;—Cf. *JAG*, III, 317 (24 March 1935).

p. 174. ... something else . . ."—"Oscar Wilde," *OC*, III, 489.

... springboard."—*Œdipe* (Gallimard, 1931), p. 117.

... of derision."—Jammes-Gide, p. 197.

p. 175. ... discourage! . . ."—*L'Ermitage*, XIX (1900), 60–4, reproduced in *OC*, III, 225–8.

p. 176. ... kills his wife."—Quoted by Yvonne Davet in her Introduction to *L'Immoraliste* (Lausanne: La Guilde du Livre, 1951), p. 16.

p. 177. ... by the absurd.)"—Quoted in Ibid., p. 16.

... *surhomme*)."—*N.R.F.*, XXX, 690 (May 1928).

... supreme beauty . . ."—*L'Ermitage*, XXVII (1903, III), 216.

VII: OEDIPUS AND SELF–INTEGRATION

p. 178. Epigraph.—*Œdipe*, pp. 80–1.

p. 185. ... barbarous."—*JAG*, I, 225 (25 Jan. 1908).

p. 189. ... asked him."—*OC*, I, 408.

... autocthonous act."—*OC*, III, 105.

p. 190. ... possess?"—*OC*, III, 141.

... boredom."—The italics are in the original.

p. 191. ... be possible."—*JAG*, II, 398 (1 May 1927).

... he wrote.—"Faits-Divers," *N.R.F.*, XXX, 843 (June 1928).

... investigation."—Ibid., p. 839.

p. 192. ... to do it.' "—Ibid., pp. 841–2.

p. 193. ... when counterfeited."—*OC*, IV, 107.

p. 196. ... wants oneself."—*OC*, I, 43.

... wishes to be."—*JAG*, I, 18–9 (3 Jan. 1892).

... who one is."—*OC*, IV, 419.

p. 197. ... all others."—*Dostoïevsky*, OC, XI, 149.

... serving humanity."—*Dostoïevsky d'après sa correspondance*, *OC*, V, 63.

p. 198. ... in general.—Cf. *Et nunc manet in te*, p. 37.

p. 199. ... cannot escape."—*OC*, II, 221–2.

... for him."—*Truth and Poetry*, Book IV, in *The Auto-Biography of Goethe*, trans. by John Oxenford (London, 1848), I, 105.

p. 200. ... their own parents.—Cf. *JAG*, II, 287–8 ("Detached Pages," 1921).

p. 201. ... and 1911;—Cf. *JAG*, I, 268 (Aug. 1910); 297–8 ("Detached Pages," 1911); 302 ("Detached Pages," 1911).

p. 202. ... his enemy.—*JAG*, I, 302 ("Detached Pages," 1911).
... the unknown.—*JAG*, I, 326 (Feb. 1912).
... to her past."—*JAG*, II, 403 (12 May 1927).
... to be broken . . ."—*OC*, II, 115.

p. 204. ... the individual.—Cf. "Réflexions sur l'Allemagne" of 1919, *OC*, IX, 114–5, and "Billets à Angèle" of March 1921, *OC*, XI, 36–7.
... in eternity."—*JAG*, II, 175 (*Numquid*, 4 March 1916).

p. 205. ... two lives."—*JAG*, III, 140 (18 Jan. 1931).

p. 206. ... wrote *Thésée*.—Cf. Roger Martin du Gard: *Notes sur André Gide*, p. 136.

VIII. ICARUS: ESCAPE UPWARD

p. 207. Epigraph.—*Thésée*, p. 65.

p. 208. ... and impulses."—*JAG*, I, 205 (6 February 1907).
... my whole reason."—"Lettres à Christian Beck," *Mercure de France*, no. 1032, p. 621 (1 Aug. 1949).

p. 209. ... of the saint.—Noted by Jean Guiguet: "La Quête gidienne," *French Review*, XXIII, 361–2 (March 1950).

p. 210. ... save through her . . ."—*JAG*, III, 371 ("Detached Pages," 1937).
... Gospels alone."—*JAG*, I, 78 ("Christian Ethics").
... regards Protestantism . . . —Cf. *JAG*, I, 261 (30 May 1910).
... of the Gospels).—Cf. *JAG*, II, 250–1 ("Detached Pages," 1918).
... freedom of thought.—Cf. *Grain*, *OC*, X, 436.
... St. Paul."—"Pages retrouvées," *N.R.F.*, XXXII, 501 (April 1929).

p. 211. ... frantic mysticism,"—*JAG*, I, 20 (Easter Sunday, 1892).

p. 212. ... continue to exist."—*JAG*, I, 42 (13 Oct. 1894).

p. 213. ... poet properly.—Jammes-Gide: *Correspondance*, p. 228.
... for each other."—Claudel-Gide: *Correspondance*, p. 187.
... greatest writers."—Jammes-Gide: *Correspondance*, p. 310.
... deplorably Protestant,"—Claudel-Gide: *Correspondance*, p. 90.
... in the extreme.—Cf. Ibid., p. 102.

p. 214. . . . social results.—Cf. *OC*, VI, 359–60.

. . . lost sheep."—"*La Porte étroite* et sa fortune," *Vers et Prose*, XXI (April–May–June 1910), 59.

. . . my Alissa."—Letter of 18 June 1909 in Claudel-Gide: *Correspondance*, pp. 103–4.

p. 215. . . . can be achieved."—*JAG*, I, 233 (22 June 1908).

. . . my *Porte étroite!*"—*Et nunc manet in te*, pp. 9 and 85.

p. 216. . . . by Protestantism."—Letter of 17 Oct. 1908 in Claudel-Gide: *Correspondance*, pp. 89–90.

p. 217. . . . clinging to myself."—Letter of 16 Oct. 1909 in "Lettres à Christian Beck," *Mercure de France*, I Aug. 1949, p. 629.

. . . I have written . . ."—Letter of 24 Feb. 1909 in Claudel-Gide: *Correspondance*, p. 99.

. . . pasty filling.—Cf. *JAG*, I, 240 (7 Nov. 1909).

p. 218. . . . a balance."—*JAG*, I, 318 (7 Feb. 1912). Cf. *JAG*, I, 240 (Sept.–Oct. 1909), *OC*, VI, 361 and 469–70.

. . . within it,—Cf. Letter of 17 Oct. 1908 in Claudel-Gide: *Correspondance*, p. 90.

. . . say desperate."—Letter of 10 May 1909 in Ibid., p. 101.

. . . to judge."—"*La Porte étroite* et sa fortune," *Vers et Prose*, XXI (April–May–June 1910), 63.

. . . Critique of . . .')."—Letter of 19 May 1911 to M. Deherme, *OC*, VI, 470.

p. 220. . . . but upward."—*OC*, XII, 393.

. . . perfect in love."—*JAG*, II, 122 (29 Jan. 1916).

p. 221. . . . by your love."—*JAG*, II, 181 (*Numquid*, 22 June 1916).

. . . in Pascal's.—Cf. *Le Dialogue avec André Gide*, p. 109.

. . . still write them."—*JAG*, II, 186 (Foreword to the 1926 edition of *Numquid*).

. . . and of the body."—Ibid.

p. 222. . . . his thirtieth year.—Cf. *Grain, OC*, X, 352, and *Incidences*, p. 53.

. . . worth while."—*JAG*, II, 235 (16 Oct. 1918).

p. 223. . . . to oneself."—"Feuillets," *OC*, XIII, 439–40.

. . . of the Scriptures."—Letter of 27 Nov. 1927 to Victor Poucel, *OC*, XIV, 408.

. . . in the Pastor."—Letter of 16 Oct. 1945 to M. H. Fayer published in the latter's *Gide, Freedom and Dostoevsky* (Burlington, Vermont, 1946), p. 2.

. . . to the Romans.—Charles Parnell examines the parallel passages in *Yale French Studies*, no. 7 (1951), pp. 60–71.

p. 224. . . . at the first."—*JAG*, II, 146 (19 Sept. 1916).

. . . the automaton."—*La Tentative amoureuse* (collection "Les Contemporains," Librairie Stock, 1922), p. 7. The same preface was added two years later to *Lafcadio* in the same collection.

. . . was for me."—*JAG*, III, 45 (5 March 1929).

p. 225. . . . formation.—Cf. Letter of Gide to Jammes, 16 May 1906, in Jammes-Gide: *Correspondance*, p. 238.

p. 226. . . . echoed in him.—Cf. "Préface aux *Lettres de Dupouey*," *OC*, VIII, 356.

. . . Christ's teaching.—Cf. *OC*, VIII, 365.

p. 227. . . . admire.—Cf. "Henri Ghéon" in *Feuillets d'automne*.

. . . confiscated."—*JAG*, II, 207 (19 May 1917).

. . . our discussions."—"Hommage à Jacques Rivière," *N.R.F.*, April 1925, pp. 498–9.

p. 228. . . . more deeply.—Cf. *N.R.F.*, XXX, 690 (May 1928).

. . . really deep down."—Letter of 17 June 1922 in *Lettres de Charles Du Bos et Réponses de André Gide*, p. 44.

p. 229. . . . bathing trunks.—Cf. Maurice Sachs: *Le Sabbat, Souvenirs d'une jeunesse orageuse* (Corrêa, 1946), p. 207.

. . . impotence."—*JAG*, III, 290 (14 Dec. 1933).

. . . of contagion."—*JAG*, III, 372 ("Detached Pages," 1937).

p. 230. . . . unduly tolerant.—Cf. *JAG*, II, 198 (1 March 1917), and III, 18 (6 July 1928).

. . . ease in them.—Cf. *JAG*, III, 60 (14 Aug. 1929).

. . . integrity."—*JAG*, III, 179 (17 July 1931).

. . . *raison d'être.*—Cf. *JAG*, II, 400 (7 May 1927).

. . . of the reason."—*JAG*, II, 421 (9 Nov. 1927).

. . . blind belief."—*JAG*, III, 166 (14 June 1931).

. . . with mysticism.—Cf. *JAG*, III, 50 (11 or 12 April 1929), 256 (4 Jan. 1933), and 373 ("Detached Pages," 1937).

p. 231. . . . of freethought."—*JAG*, III, 50 (11 or 12 April 1929).

. . . to his early faith.—Cf. Letter of 10 Dec. 1911 in Claudel-Gide: *Correspondance*, p. 185.

. . . Church herself.—Cf. Ibid., p. 184.

. . . away from it."—*JAG*, II, 315 (21 Dec. 1922).

p. 232. . . . hostile to her."—*JAG*, II, 381 (1 July 1926).

. . . against her."—"Suivant Montaigne," *OC*, XV, 63.

. . . the entire work."—*JAG*, IV, 295 (3 Sept. 1948). Cf. *JAG*, IV, 12 (15 Feb. 1940).

p. 233. . . . of his friends."—"Les Catholiques autour d'André Gide," in *Hommage à André Gide, N.R.F.*, Nov. 1951, pp. 103–4.

p. 234. ... pious souls."—*JAG*, IV, 82–3 (23 Aug. 1941).

... written this."—*JAG*, I, 149 (1 Sept. 1905).

p. 235. ... nostalgia for a faith."—Quoted by Gide in his preface to *Lettres de Dupouey, OC*, VIII, 359.

... transformations in him.—Cf. Letter of 12 Jan. 1924 in Claudel-Gide: *Correspondance*, p. 241.

... open its wings."—Letter of 25 July 1926 in Ibid., p. 245.

... leap toward heaven."—*JAG*, III, 247 (17 Oct. 1932).

IX. PROMETHEUS, SAVIOUR OF MEN

p. 236. Epigraph.—*Deux Interviews imaginaires* (Charlot, 1946), p. 51.

... of subjects.—Cf. "Prométhée délivré" in Baudelaire: *Œuvres* (Pléiade, Gallimard, 1938), II, 380.

p. 237. ... ever cut deeper.—Cf. *JAG*, III, 37 (15 Jan. 1929).

... of Prometheus."—*JAG*, III, 290 (14 Dec. 1933).

... ancient heroes,"—*JAG*, I, 80 (1896?).

p. 238. ... forsaken me? . . .' "—*Deux Interviews imaginaires*, pp. 35–6.

p. 239. ... is unnecessary.—Cf. *JAG*, II, 395 (6 March 1927).

... resist even God."—*Œdipe*, p. 106.

... to the Gods."—*Thésée*, p. 106.

... as he says.—*JAG*, IV, 277 ("Autumn Leaves").

... before his death).—Cf. *Time*, 7 June 1948, p. 112.

p. 240. ... last year of life.—Cf. *Ainsi soit-il ou Les jeux sont faits.* (Gallimard, 1952), pp. 150 and 174. Cf. *JAG*, IV, 16 (9 May 1940).

... Providence . . ."—*JAG*, IV, 278 ("Autumn Leaves").

... affirmation."—*JAG*, IV, 65 (17 April 1941).

... not be is not."—*JAG*, IV, 276 ("Autumn Leaves").

... of souls."—Ibid., p. 281.

... in immortality.—Cf. *JAG*, IV, 86 (15 Sept. 1941), 199 (10 April 1943), 300 and 302 (15 May 1949).

p. 241. ... restrictive formulas,—Cf. *JAG*, I, 78 ("Literature and Ethics").

... inhibitory."—*JAG*, III, 36 (13 Jan. 1929).

... of my childhood."—*Les Nouvelles Nourritures* (Gallimard, 1935), p. 52.

... forsaken me?' "—*JAG*, III, 36 (13 Jan. 1929).

p. 242. ... evil in men."—*Deux Interviews imaginaires*, pp. 37–8.

...difference between."—Cf. "Pages retrouvées," *N.R.F.*, XXXII, 499 (April 1929) and *Un Esprit non prévenu* (Eds. Kra, 1929), pp. 88–9.

...save the world.—Cf. *JAG*, IV, 264 (24 Feb. 1946) and "Two Declarations," *Partisan Review*, XVIII, 395–400 (July–Aug. 1951).

...Greek legend.' "—*JAG*, II, 322 (23 Jan. 1923).

p. 243. ...break with Christ.—Cf. *OC*, XIII, 425–6.

...arrive at God."—*JAG*, IV, 113–4 (June 1942).

p. 244. ...or attraction."—*JAG*, II, 122 (30 Jan. 1916).

...Supreme Being.—Cf. *JAG*, II, 294 ("Detached Pages," 1921).

...wants to abide."—*Thésée*, p. 63.

...be as Gods.—Cf. *JAG*, IV, 277 ("Autumn Leaves").

p. 245. ...an ungodly man."—*JAG*, II, 421 (6 Nov. 1927).

...projects for itself.—Cf. *JAG*, I, 75 ("Literature and Ethics").

...of our efforts?"—*JAG*, IV, 264 (24 Feb. 1946).

...has no meaning."—*Ainsi soit-il*, p. 166.

X. CORYDON, THE UNORTHODOX LOVER

p. 246. Epigraphs.—*Si le grain ne meurt* . . . , *OC*, X, 417–8 and *Dostoïevsky d'après sa correspondance*, *OC*, V, 51–2.

p. 247. ...inspiration,"—*Corydon*, *OC*, IX, 283.

...pastoral tradition.—Cf. Justin O'Brien: "Gide's *Nourritures terrestres* and Virgil's *Bucolics*," *Romanic Review*, XLIII, 117–25 (April 1952).

p. 249. ...might prevent.—Preface to the 1924 edition, *OC*, IX, 178.

p. 250. ...as subversive.—Cf. *OC*, IX, 181.

...falsehood.—Cf. *JAG*, II, 338–41 (21 Dec. 1923).

...are responsible?"—*OC*, IX, 178.

...of his memoirs.—Cf. *JAG*, III, 114–5 (29 June 1930).

p. 251. ...distinguish this."—*Et nunc manet in te*, p. 111 (Jan. 1925).

...and friends.—Cf. *JAG*, II, 246 ("Detached Pages," 1918).

...letters of Dupouey,—Cf. *JAG*, II, 220 (15 Dec. 1917).

p. 252. ...contemporary writer."—"Billets à Angèle," *OC*, XI, 44. The letters are reproduced in *OC*, VIII, 377–9 and in Marcel Proust: *Lettres à André Gide* (Neuchâtel: Ides et Calendes, 1949), pp. 9–12.

...marvelous book."—*JAG*, II, 222 (14 Jan. 1918).

p. 253. ...to show itself."—*Sodome et Gomorrhe*, I, 267.

. . . except with men."—*JAG*, II, 265 (14 May 1921).

. . . repulsive to him."—*JAG*, II, 267 (Wednesday, May 1921). For a study of how Proust transposed his recollections, cf. Justin O'Brien: "Albertine the Ambiguous: Notes on Proust's Transposition of Sexes," *Publications of the Modern Language Association of America*, LXIV, 933–52 (December 1949).

p. 254. . . . public opinion."—*JAG*, II, 276–7 (2 Dec. 1921).

. . . of dissimulation."—*JAG*, II, 409–10 (1 Oct. 1927).

. . . *Corydon* ignores.—Cf. *OC*, IX, 178–9.

p. 255. . . . finish his memoirs.—Cf. François Porché: *L'Amour qui n'ose pas dire son nom* (Grasset, 1927).

. . . to direct action.—Cf. "Dictées," *N.R.F.*, XXXIII, 15–6 (July 1929).

. . . to oneself."—*La Prisonnière*, II, 7.

p. 256. . . . applied to it.—Cf. Letter of 2 Jan. 1929 in *OC*, IX, 334.

. . . to embarrass."—*JAG*, I, 296 ("Detached Pages," 1911).

. . . been mandatory.—Cf. *OC*, IX, 328.

p. 257. . . . to all homosexuals."—*JAG*, II, 246–7 ("Detached Pages," 1918).

. . . of the problem.—Cf. *André Gide*, p. 181.

. . . of his thesis.—Cf. *JAG*, II, 308–9 (13 Aug. 1922).

. . . he felt.—Cf. *JAG*, III, 252 (29 Dec. 1932) and I, 296 ("Detached Pages," 1911).

. . . important book."—*JAG*, IV, 130 (19 Oct. 1942).

p. 258. . . . that reservation.—Cf. Ibid., 272–3 (18 Dec. 1946).

. . . useful work.—Cf. Ibid., 256 (Jan. 1946).

. . . obtain it.—Cf. Ibid., 275 (Nov. 1947).

. . . all its problems."—*Les Prix Nobel en 1947*, p. 48.

p. 259. . . . *first* person."—"Oscar Wilde," *OC*, III, 499. This paragraph does not appear in the original publication in *L'Ermitage*, XXIII, 401–29 (June 1902).

. . . won't suit me."—*JAG*, II, 265 (14 May 1921).

. . . antedates 1900.—Cf. Letter of Jan. 1928 to François Porché, *OC*, IX, 323.

p. 260. . . . of society."—Letter of 16 Jan. 1927 in *OC*, XIV, 400.

. . . to be accused."—*JAG*, II, 194 (19 Jan. 1917).

. . . in the *Journals*.—Cf. *JAG*, II, 156 and 195.

. . . humiliate oneself.—Cf. *Dostoïevsky*, *OC*, XI, 194.

. . . one is not,"—"Projet de préface pour *Si le grain ne meurt* . . . ," *OC*, X, 453.

p. 261. ... outside the law."—Letter of 10 Nov. 1924 to André Rouveyre, *OC*, XII, 562–3.

... act differently."—*Notes sur André Gide*, pp. 19–20.

... both works.—Cf. *JAG*, III, 41 (30 Jan. 1929). Cf. *Lettres de Charles Du Bos et Réponses de André Gide*, pp. 137–8.

p. 262. ... an anomaly."—*Dostoïevsky, OC*, XI, 292.

... *lack of balance.*"—*JAG*, II, 241–2 ("Detached Pages," 1918).

... his dissonance."—*Dostoïevsky, OC*, XI, 294.

p. 263. ... but a hole."—*JAG*, III, 413 (26 Jan. 1939).

... carnally."—*JAG*, IV, 301 (15 May 1949).

... David—Cf. *JAG*, I, 49 (30 Dec. 1895).

... at the baths.—Cf. Ibid., p. 98 (18 Jan. 1902).

... seventy-fifth year,—Cf. *JAG*, IV, 239 (April 1944).

p. 264. ... so beautiful."—*JAG*, II, 209 (21 Aug. 1917).

p. 265. ... convincing her."—*JAG*, III, 15 (9 June 1928).

... on the past?"—*Et nunc manet in te*, pp. 78–9 (21 Nov. 1918).

p. 266. ... destructive deed."—*A la recherche d'André Gide*, pp. 28–9.

p. 267. ... is accomplished."—*OC*, XV, 534–5.

... in her arms . . ."—*Caractères, OC, XII*, 8.

p. 268. ... desire in me."—Letter dated Florence, 7 March 1914, in Claudel-Gide: *Correspondance*, p. 218.

p. 269. ... light upon it."—*JAG*, IV, 184 (5 March 1943).

p. 270. ... it to her . . ."—*Et nunc manet in te*, p. 25.

... natural instinct."—Ibid., pp. 29–30.

p. 271. ... no one but me."—*Ainsi soit-il*, p. 192.

... intrusion."—Ibid., p. 194.

p. 272. ... of my happiness."—Ibid., pp. 193–4.

p. 273. ... to believe."—Ibid., p. 150.

p. 274. ... with the subject.—Cf. *JAG*, 1, 296 ("Detached Pages," 1911).

... inversion."—Charles Du Bos: *Le Dialogue avec André Gide*, p. 317.

... as I am."—Claudel-Gide: *Correspondance*, pp. 217 and 218.

... has done that."—Ibid., pp. 221–2.

... of the herd."—*Dostoïevsky, OC*, XI, 24.

p. 275. ... decides."—*JAG*, II, 409 (1 Oct. 1927).

... of psychology.—Cf. Letter of January 1928 to François Porché, *OC*, IX, 327.

... *natural.*"—*OC*, II, 166.

... emptiness) —Cf. *Les Cahiers d'André Walter, OC,* I, 169–70.

... nearby forest,—Cf. *Le Voyage d'Urien, OC,* I, 304–6.

... satisfy it?"—*OC,* I, 45.

... brown skins.—Cf. *OC,* I, 156–7.

p. 276. ... swelling." *OC,* I, 299.

... among them.—Cf. *OC,* II, 122.

... barn-loft."—*OC,* II, 151.

... goat-herd he loves.—Cf. *OC,* II, 196–7.

... young boys."—*OC,* II, 175.

p. 277. ... inhabited me."—*Et nunc manet in te,* p. 40.

... as yours?"—*JAG,* II, 305–6 (15 July 1922).

... both books.—Cf. Letter of 29 Feb. 1912 in Claudel-Gide: *Correspondance,* p. 194.

p. 278. ... and homosexual."—Jammes-Gide: *Correspondance,* p. 195.

... sexual anecdote."—"Les Lectures du mois," *L'Ermitage,* 13ᵉ année, II, 155 (Aug. 1902).

... all his skill."—*OC,* IV, 6–7.

p. 279. ... to fulfillment."—*Amour nuptial* (Gallimard, 1929), p. 201.

p. 280. ... toward me."—*OC,* VII, 196.

... it all is!"—Letter of 4 or 5 April 1914 in Marcel Proust: *Lettres à André Gide,* p. 35.

p. 281. ... annoyed me! . . ."—*OC,* VII, 329.

... the theory."—*André Gide,* p. 211.

p. 282. ... on a galley.—Cf. George Painter: *André Gide, a Critical and Biographical Study* (N.Y.: Roy Publishers, 1951), p. 140 *n.* 1.

... Passavant."—Marcel Proust: *A l'ombre des Jeunes Filles en fleurs,* II, 212.

p. 283. ... to their voice."—*André Gide et notre temps* (Gallimard, 1935), pp. 34–5.

XI. FROM PAGAN DAEMON TO CHRISTIAN DEVIL

p. 284. Epigraphs.—*JAG,* II, 189 ("Detached Pages," 1916) ; and *Dostoïevsky, OC,* XI, 280.

p. 285. ... of him.—Cf. Rougemont: *La Part du diable* (N.Y.: La Maison Française, 1943), p. 91 and Magny: "Satanism in Contemporary Literature," in *Satan,* edited by Bruno de Jésus Marie (N.Y.: Sheed and Ward, 1952), p. 453.

... homosexuality.—Cf. Magny in ibid., p. 461.

... after the events.—Cf. *Si le grain ne meurt* . . . , *OC*, X, 345–6.

... active influence.—Cf. Roger Martin du Gard, *Notes sur André Gide*, pp. 18–9 (dated Feb. 1920).

... yet realize . . ."—*OC*, X, 349.

... over me."—Ibid., p. 411.

p. 286. ... from him!"—*JAG*, II, 188 ("Detached Pages," 1916).

... of each virtue."—Ibid., p. 189.

... we should be! . . ."—Ibid., p. 190.

p. 287. ... in the devil."—*JAG*, II, 84 (25 Sept. 1914).

p. 288. ... blood and tears."—*The Deliverance of Mark Rutherford* quoted in *JAG*, II, 120 (25 Jan. 1916).

... an inner drama."—*JAG*, II, 129 (16 Feb. 1916).

... his own honey.—Cf. *Dostoïevsky*, *OC*, XI, 282–3.

... they contain.—Cf. *Le Dialogue avec André Gide*, p. 305.

... profession of faith."—*JAG*, II, 301 (22 April 1922).

p. 289. ... Manichean in him."—*Dostoïevsky*, *OC*, XI, 266.

... most distant."—*JAG*, II, 297–8 (16 Jan. 1922). Cf. Ibid., p. 71 (25 Aug. 1914).

... of June.—Cf. *JAG*, II, 302 (5 June 1922).

p. 290. ... of the demon."—*Dostoïevsky*, *OC*, XI, 279–80.

... see the stars."—*JAG*, III, 277 (4 July 1933).

p. 291. ... gravitates."—*Journal des Faux-Monnayeurs*, *OC*, XIII, 19.

... I don't exist.' "—Ibid., p. 21.

p. 292 ... of Boris.—Cf. *OC*, XII, 21, 549, 125, 65, 87, 251 and 318.

... with Satan.—Cf. *OC*, XII, 209 and 527.

... he is Satan."—*OC*, XIII, 44.

p. 293. ... quite fair."—*Le Voyage au Congo*, *OC*, XIII, 130–1.

... to this game . . ."—Preface to Hogg: *The Memoirs of a Justified Sinner* in *Préfaces* (Neuchâtel: Ides et Calendes, 1948), p. 141.

p. 294. ... myself am Hell."—"Pages retrouvées," *N.R.F.*, XXXII, 501–2 (April 1929).

... bad sentiments.—Cf. *JAG*, IV, 44 (2 Sept. 1940).

... share is . . ."—*OC*, I, 369.

p. 295. ... the butterfly."—*JAG*, IV, 60 (23 Feb. 1941).

... middle-class.—Cf. "Préface au Théâtre de Goethe," *Préfaces*, pp. 93 and 113.

... tempest."—*Master Builders: A Typology of the Spirit* (N.Y.: Viking Press, 1939), pp. 243–5.

...he had in him."—*Journal des Faux-Monnayeurs*, *OC*, XIII, 82.

p. 296. ...toward progress."—*OC*, XV, 553. Cf. *André Gide et notre temps*, p. 30.

...What is truth?' "—*Dostoïevsky*, *OC*, XI, 267.

p. 297. ...deferred."—"Feuillets 1928," *OC*, XV, 515–6.

p. 298. ...in that way."—*André Gide, Cahiers de la Quinzaine*, série 20, cahier 6 (5 April 1930), p. 30.

...civilization.—Cf. *André Gide et notre temps*, p. 19.

...his completion."—*Dostoïevsky*, *OC*, XI, 267–8.

...which we live."—*Jugements*, II (Librairie Plon, 1924), 48. Cf. Henri Massis: *D'André Gide à Marcel Proust* (Lardanchet, 1948), p. 34.

p. 299. ...his next book.—Cf. *OC*, XII, 555.

...keep to it."—*OC*, V, 13.

p. 300. ...to corrupting;"—*Jugements*, II, pp. 21 and 29–30.

...all his work.—*L'Esprit d'André Gide* (L'Art Catholique, 1929), p. 53.

...Mephistopheles."—*Le Reclus et le retors* (G. Crès et Cie., 1927), p. 140.

...of a Lucifer.—Cf. "André Gide," *Le Figaro*, 20 Feb. 1930, p. 10.

...as he said.—Cf. *JAG*, II, 324 (2 May 1923).

p. 301. ...thirty years.—Cf. *JAG*, II, 361 (3 Dec. 1924).

...in ruins)—Cf. *JAG*, III, 196 (19 Oct. 1931).

...in Chicago.—Cf. Pierre Lièvre: *Esquisses critiques*, 3ᵉ série (Le Divan, 1929), p. 174.

p. 302. ...acting myself."—*OC*, IX, 141–2.

...to lead."—*JAG*, III, 214 (18 Jan. 1932).

...by so doing."—*JAG*, I, 71 ("Literature and Ethics").

p. 303. ...exploited."—*OC*, VI, 16.

p. 304. ...his piety."—*OC*, VI, 18.

...a forgery' "—*JAG*, IV, 102 (15 Feb. 1942).

p. 305. ...recognize his influence,—Cf. *JAG*, II, 300 (22 March 1922).

...were before."—"André Gide," *N.R.F.*, XXXVI, 255 ʹFeb. 1931).

...to idols."—*JAG*, III, 308 (1 Aug. 1934).

...following one."—*JAG*, II, 312 (25 Oct. 1922).

...tempting path."—*JAG*, I, 268 (Aug. 1910).

p. 306. ...usually is."—*JAG*, IV, 34 (16 July 1940).

. . . intellectual guidance.—Cf. Roger Martin du Gard: *Notes sur André Gide*, pp. 97–8 (30 July 1931).

. . . my function."—*Journal des Faux-Monnayeurs, OC*, XIII, 61 (29 March 1925).

. . . reader intact."—Preface to the 1930 edition of *André Walter, Cahiers et Poésies, OC*, I, 203.

. . . a poisoner,"—Interview of 28 March 1947 in Claudel-Gide: *Correspondance*, p. 249.

p. 307. . . . he had written.—Cf. Massis: *D'André Gide à Marcel Proust*, pp. 42–3; Du Bos: *Le Dialogue avec André Gide*, p. 287 *n*; and L. Martin-Chauffier: *André Gide, Cahiers de la Quinzaine*, série 20, cahier 6 (5 April 1930), p. 18.

. . . dear to me."—Letter of 27 Nov. 1927, *OC*, XIV, 408.

. . . intransigence,—Cf. *JAG*, III, 18 (6 July 1928).

. . . piously annex.—Cf. *JAG*, III, 59 (11 Aug. 1929); 96–7 (13 March 1930); 133 (2 Nov. 1930); and 373 ("Detached Pages," 1937).

p. 308. . . . tradition, etc."—*JAG*, III, 145 (30 Jan. 1931).

p. 309. . . . *ANDREAE GIDE*."—*L'Osservatore Romano*, Città del Vaticano, 1 June, 1952, p. 1.

. . . of their life."—Ibid.

p. 310. . . . traditional Christians.—Cf. *André Gide*, p. 236.

. . . and a prize."—*L'Osservatore Romano*, 1 June 1952, p. 2.

. . . his henchman."—*JAG*, III, 59 (11 Aug. 1929).

p. 311. . . . worst detractors."—"André Gide," *N.R.F.*, XXXVI, 266 (Feb. 1931).

. . . awareness."—"Aspects d'André Gide," *Action*, 3ᵉ année (March–April 1922), p. 20.

. . . self-scrutiny."—Preface to *La Tentative amoureuse* in the series of "Les Contemporains" published by Stock, 1922, p. 11.

. . . same thought.—Cf. "André Gide," *Le Figaro*, 20 Feb. 1951, p. 10.

p. 312. . . . creative force."—*Hommage à André Gide, N.R.F.*, Nov. 1951, p. 11.

. . . nor faint."—*The Spectator* (London), 2 March 1951, p. 276.

. . . upon him."—*Les Prix Nobel en 1947*, p. 90.

p. 313. . . . it awakens."—*OC*, III, 271.

p. 314. . . . comes second."—*OC*, III, 272.

. . . "satanic" suggestions,—Cf. Fernandez: *André Gide*, p. 93.

XII. COMPASSIONATE PERSEPHONE

p. 315. . . . Epigraphs.—*Perséphone* (Gallimard, 1934), p. 21; and *JAG*, IV, 20 (30 May 1940).

p. 317. . . . U.S.S.R."—*JAG*, III, 232 (23 April 1932).

. . . capitalist system.—*Soviet Encyclopedia*, XXV, 390.

. . . the workers."—Introduction to *The God that Failed* by Koestler, Wright, Fischer, Silone, Gide, and Spender (New York: Harper and Brothers, 1950), p. 3.

. . . in 1925–6.—Cf. Schlumberger: "Gide rue Visconti" in *André Gide et notre temps* (Gallimard, 1935), p. 85; and Martin du Gard: *Notes sur André Gide*, p. 113.

. . . such statements.—Cf. *JAG*, III, 257 (4 Jan. 1933) and letter of 1 March 1935 to Jean Schlumberger in *André Gide et notre temps*, p. 87.

p. 318. . . . have exposed."—*JAG*, III, 257–8 (4 Jan. 1933).

. . . *these* notebooks?"—*Amyntas* (Mercure de France, 1906), pp. 107–8.

p. 319. . . . in 1935.—Letter of 1 March 1935 to Schlumberger in *André Gide et notre temps*, pp. 86–7. Cf. *Journal des Faux-Monnayeurs*, *OC*, XIII, pp. 37–8 (Aug. 1921); *Feuillets d'automne* (Mercure de France, 1949), p. 188; and *JAG*, III, 330 (17 Sept. 1935).

. . . financial matters.—Cf. *JAG*, III, 227 (5 March 1932); 237 (13 June 1932); 258 (4 Jan. 1933); and 275 (June 1933).

. . . than all."—*JAG*, I, 76 ("Literature and Ethics").

. . . institutions.—Cf. "L'Avenir de l'Europe," *OC*, XI, 135.

. . . to them."—*JAG*, III, 334 (30 Oct. 1935).

. . . Soviet Russia?—Cf. *JAG*, III, 179–80 (27 July 1931).

p. 320. . . . sympathy.—Cf. *Journal des Faux-Monnayeurs*, *OC*, XIII, 49 (15 Nov. 1923).

. . . Mouton felt.—Cf. *Si le grain ne meurt* . . . , *OC*, X, 37–8.

. . . eleven months.—Cf. *JAG*, II, 102 (9 Oct. 1915).

. . . speak out."—*Voyage au Congo*, *OC*, XIII, 189.

. . . years before!—Cf. *Notes sur André Gide*, pp. 89–90.

p. 321. . . . appeal of Communism.—Cf. Introduction to *The God that Failed*, p. 5.

p. 322. . . . afterward."—*Voyage au Congo*, *OC*, XIII, 189–90.

. . . impressed him.—Cf. *Souvenirs de la Cour d'Assises*, *OC*, VII, 73; *Les Faux-Monnayeurs*, *OC*, XII, 98–101; and *André Gide et notre temps*, pp. 61–2.

p. 323. ... are safe."—*André Gide et notre temps*, p. 62.
... above another.—Cf. *JAG*, III, 268 (14 April 1933).
... others lacked.—Cf. *JAG*, III, 285 (27 Oct. 1933).
... formed me."—*JAG*, III, 276 (June 1933).
... without the faith.—Cf. *JAG*, IV, 11 (7 Feb. 1940) and 74 (14 July 1941).
... in society.—Cf. *JAG*, III, 368–9 ("Detached Pages," 1937).
p. 324. ... my environment."—*Littérature engagée* (Gallimard, 1950), p. 93.
... authorizing the family—Cf. *JAG*, I, 78 ("Christian Ethics," 1897).
... by heredity.—Cf. *JAG*, II, 288 ("Detached Pages," 1921).
... form of interest.—Cf. *JAG*, III, 331 (6 Oct. 1935).
... enemies of progress."—*JAG*, III, 180 (27 July 1931).
... in the future—Cf. *JAG*, III, 160 (13 May 1931).
... blindly.—Cf. *Notes sur André Gide*, p. 100.
p. 325. ... sterility for me."—*JAG*, III, 250 (13 Dec. 1932).
... suspect to him.—Cf. *JAG*, III, 276 (June 1933).
... under theirs."—*JAG*, III, 281 (29 Aug. 1933).
... valuable art.—*Littérature engagée*, p. 55.
p. 326. ... it is serving."—Ibid., p. 58.
... with the movement.—Cf. Preface in *Littérature engagée*, p. 221.
p. 327. ... the U.S.S.R.—Cf. the "Chronologie" in *Littérature engagée*, pp. 333–44.
... monstrous blindness."—*JAG*, III, 306 (25 July 1934).
... diminution? . . ."—*JAG*, III, 243 (19 July 1932).
p. 328. ... mediocre."—*JAG*, IV, 297 (30 Jan. 1949).
p. 329. ... *from the U.S.S.R.*)."—*JAG*, IV, 288 (19 Jan. 1948).
... becoming reality."—*Retour de l'U.R.S.S.* (Gallimard, 1936), p. 15.
p. 330. ... in the U.S.S.R."—Ibid., p. 92.
... vassalized."—Ibid., p. 67.
... Russian Communism."—Richard Crossman: Introduction to *The God that Failed*, p. 8.
p. 331. ... abandon the Party."—*Retouches à mon Retour de l'U.R.S.S.* (Gallimard, 1937), pp. 67–8.
... of 'capitalism.' "—*JAG*, IV, 251 (15 Jan. 1945).
... in a footnote,—Cf. *Retour*, p. 63 *n*.
... his travel-diary,—Cf. *En U.R.S.S., 1936* (Gallimard, 1937), pp. 16 and 22.

... taboos;—Cf. Arthur Koestler: *The Yogi and the Commissar* (London: Jonathan Cape, 1945), pp. 128 and 174.

... that regard."—*Ainsi soit-il*, p. 126.

p. 333. ... of *Pravda*."—*Retouches*, p. 66.

... than today."—*JAG*, II, 289 ("Detached Pages," 1921).

... years 1914–18)—*La Trahison des clercs* was entitled *The Treason of the Intellectuals* in the U.S. and *The Great Betrayal* in England.

... almost unconsciously."—"Two Declarations by André Gide," *Partisan Review*, XVIII, 398 (July–Aug. 1951).

p. 334. ... were fighting."—*JAG*, IV, 263 (24 Feb. 1946).

... but—to be."—*JAG*, IV, 279 ("Autumn Leaves," 1947).

... *who he is.*—Cf. *Nouvelles Nourritures*, p. 141.

XIII. DAEDALUS, THE ARTIFEX

p. 335. Epigraph.—Statement by Gide in *André Gide et notre temps* (1935), p. 15.

... social question;—Cf. *JAG*, I, 76 ("Literature and Ethics").

... *to aesthetics.*"—*OC*, IV, 387.

p. 336. ... cult of art.—Cf. *JAG*, I, 339 (26 June 1913).

... rivalry on earth."—"L'Evolution du théâtre," *OC*, IV, 205–6. Cf. *JAG*, I, 299 ("Detached Pages," 1911).

... from nature,—Cf. *JAG*, I, 238–9 (4 July 1909).

... dominate art.—Cf. *JAG*, I, 139 (June 1905).

... screen of phenomena.—Cf. *JAG*, III, 114 (23 June 1930).

... transposition."—Undated "Feuillets," *OC*, XIII, 441.

... concentrated in it."—"Lettres à Angèle," *OC*, III, 197.

... by constraint.—Cf. Ibid., p. 209.

p. 337. ... dies of freedom."—"L'Evolution du théâtre," *OC*, IV, 206–7.

... naturally drawn.—Cf. *JAG*, III, 303 (12 July 1934).

... them to fruit."—*JAG*, I, 164 (18 Dec. 1905).

... experienced it.—Cf. *OC*, XII, 446.

... *questions* both.—Cf. *JAG*, I, 250 (30 Dec. 1909).

p. 338. ... toward serenity."—*JAG*, IV, 53 (23 Nov. 1940).

... decadence of art."—*OC*, XII, 9.

... *avec André Gide,*—Page 69.

p. 339. ... of the *Narcisse.*—Cf. F.–P. Alibert: "Au hasard d'André Gide," in *André Gide* (Eds. du Capitole, 1928), p. 58.

... arrangement?"—*JAG*, I, 76 ("Literature and Ethics").

... outside of time.—Cf. Ibid., p. 77.

... satisfying harmony."—*OC*, III, 407.

... a human scale.—Cf. *JAG*, I, 270 (July or Aug. 1910).

... remote from men,—Cf. "De l'importance du public," *OC*, IV, 191.

... end of art"—*JAG*, I, 153 (3 Nov. 1905).

p. 340. ... even more."—"Feuillets," *OC*, XIII, 442.

... appearance.—Cf. *OC*, VI, 314.

... destroy it . . ."—"Contre Mallarmé," *OC*, V, 292.

... out of it.—Cf. *JAG*, II, 238 ("Detached Pages," 1918).

... point of view.—Cf. *JAG*, II, 229 (25 April 1918) and 235 (13 Oct. 1918).

p. 341. ... to foresee."—*OC*, XII, 471.

p. 342. ... *Counterpoint*)—Cf. Justin O'Brien, "On Rereading the Modern Classics," *The Nation* (N.Y.), 28 Nov. 1942, pp. 579–80.

p. 343. ... tales.' "—*JAG*, III, 14 (17 April 1928).

... *Tom Jones—Journal des Faux-Monnayeurs, OC*, XIII, 51 (6 Jan. 1924).

p. 344. ... *reconstruct.*—Cf. Ibid., p. 18 (21 Nov. 1920).

... than the author.—Cf. Ibid., p. 45.

... flattered."—*JAG*, III, 181 (1 Aug. 1931). Cf. 165–6 (12 June 1931).

p. 345. ... disintegrate . . ."—*Journal des Faux-Monnayeurs, OC*, XIII, 60 (8 March 1925).

p. 346. ... most people."—*JAG*, I, 240 (Sept. and Oct. 1909).

... more hidden)."—*JAG*, III, 260 (16 Jan. 1933).

... its harmony."—*JAG*, III, 201 (5 Nov. 1931).

... correct usage.—Cf. *JAG*, III, 222 (14 Feb. 1932).

p. 347. ... and thought.—Cf. "Journal sans dates," *OC*, VI, 36–7.

... or the thought."—*JAG*, III, 222 (14 Feb. 1932).

... added poetry."—*JAG*, II, 287 ("Detached Pages," 1921).

... many writers.—Cf. *JAG*, IV, 100 (1 Feb. 1942).

... Dorian I feel!"—*JAG*, III, 239 (27 June 1932).

... least expected."—*JAG*, III, 88 (1 Jan. 1930). Cf. p. 137 (2 Jan. 1931).

... demanded.—Cf. *JAG*, I, 329 (7 May 1912).

p. 348. ... stricken style."—*JAG*, I, 302 ("Detached Pages," 1911). Cf. II, 287 ("Detached Pages," 1921).

... self-satisfaction.—Cf. *JAG*, II, 258 (28 Oct. 1920).

... for poetry.—Cf. *Grain, OC*, X, 301.

... as affected—Cf. *JAG*, I, 338 (March 1913).

... flat tone.—Cf. *JAG*, I, 280 (20 Oct. 1910).

... French language,—Cf. "Projet de conférence pour Berlin," *OC*, XV, 510.

p. 349. ... preparation.—*JAG*, II, 348 (14 Feb. 1924).

... of my heart."—*JAG*, II, 215 (3 Nov. 1917).

... *gait.*—Cf. *JAG*, II, 222 (7 Jan. 1918).

... in music."—*OC*, I, 96.

... of assonances."—*OC*, I, 135.

... his sentences;—Cf. *JAG*, II, 33 (4 July 1914).

... from rhythm,"—*JAG*, II, 287 ("Detached Pages," 1921).

... to his style.—*JAG*, II, 302 (11 July 1922).

... that of prose.—Cf. *JAG*, II, 371 ("Detached Pages," 1925).

p. 350. ... *été borgne.*"—*OC*, IV, 41: "I'd have thought him handsome had he not lacked an eye."

... for its rhythm."—*JAG*, II, 323 (23 Feb. 1923).

... in the world."—*JAG*, III, 158 (31 March 1931).

p. 351. ... heart beating."—*JAG*, III, 318 (24 March 1935).

... seeming, moved."—"Billets à Angèle," *OC*, XI, 40.

p. 352. ... from rules."—*Les Personnes du drame* (N.Y.: Pantheon Books, 1945), p. 158.

... has been said."—"Enquête sur le classicisme," *OC*, X, 25–6.

THE WORKS OF ANDRÉ GIDE

POETRY IN VERSE AND IN PROSE

Les Cahiers d'André Walter (Librairie de l'Art Indépendant, 1891)	The Notebooks of André Walter
Les Poésies d'André Walter (ibid., 1892)	The Poems of André Walter
Le Traité du Narcisse (ibid., 1891)	The Treatise of the Narcissus
La Tentative amoureuse (ibid., 1893)	The Attempt at Love
Le Voyage d'Urien (ibid., 1893)	Urien's Travels
Les Nourritures terrestres (Mercure de France, 1897)	*Fruits of the Earth (New York: Alfred A. Knopf, 1949; London: Martin Secker & Warburg, 1949)
El Hadj (ibid., 1899)	El Hadj
Amyntas (ibid., 1906)	Amyntas
Le Retour de l'enfant prodigue (Vers et Prose, 1907)	The Prodigal's Return
Les Nouvelles Nourritures (Gallimard, 1935)	*New Fruits of the Earth (New York: Alfred A. Knopf, 1949; London: Martin Secker & Warburg, 1949)

TALES

*L'Immoraliste (Mercure de France, 1902)	*The Immoralist (New York: Alfred A. Knopf, 1930; London: Cassell & Co.)

* The titles preceded by an asterisk have been published in English translation. Unless otherwise indicated, all translations are by Dorothy Bussy.

*La Porte étroite
(ibid., 1909)

*Isabelle
(Gallimard, 1911)

*La Symphonie pastorale
(ibid., 1919)

*L'École des femmes
(ibid., 1929)

*Robert
(ibid., 1929)

*Geneviève
(ibid., 1936)

*Thésée
(ibid., 1946; New York: Pantheon Books, 1946)

*Strait Is the Gate
(New York: ibid., 1924; London: Martin Secker & Warburg)

*Isabelle
(New York: ibid., 1931; London: Cassell & Co.; in *Two Symphonies*)

*The Pastoral Symphony
(ibid.)

*The School for Wives
(New York: ibid., 1929, 1950; London: Cassell & Co.)

*Robert in *The School for Wives*

*Geneviève in *The School for Wives*

*Theseus in *Two Legends: Theseus and Œdipus*
(New York: Alfred A. Knopf, 1950; London: Martin Secker & Warburg; trans. by John Russell)

SATIRICAL FARCES

*Paludes
(Librairie de l'Art Indépendant, 1895)

*Le Prométhée mal enchaîné
(Mercure de France, 1899)

*Les Caves du Vatican
(Gallimard, 1914)

*Marshlands and Prometheus Misbound
(London: Secker & Warburg, 1953; trans. by George D. Painter)

*Ibid.

*The Vatican Swindle
(New York: Alfred A. Knopf, 1925) or *Lafcadio's Adventures* (ibid., 1927) or *The Vatican Cellars* (London: Cassell & Co.)

NOVEL

Les Faux-Monnayeurs
(Gallimard, 1926)

The Counterfeiters
(New York: Alfred A. Knopf, 1927) or *The Coiners* (London: Cassell & Co.)

CRITICISM

Prétextes
(Mercure de France, 1903)

Pretexts

Nouveaux Prétextes
(ibid., 1911)

Further Pretexts

Dostoïevsky
(Plon-Nourrit, 1923)

Dostoevsky
(London: J. M. Dent, 1925; Secker & Warburg, 1949; New York: Alfred A. Knopf, 1926; New Directions, 1949; trans. anon.)

Incidences
(Gallimard, 1924)

Angles of Incidence

Journal des Faux-Monnayeurs
(ibid., 1926)

Journal of "The Counterfeiters"
(New York: Alfred A. Knopf, 1951; in *The Counterfeiters*) or *Logbook of the Coiners* (London: Cassell & Co., 1952); trans. by Justin O'Brien

Essai sur Montaigne
(Éditions de la Pléiade, 1929)

Montaigne
(New York: Horace Liveright, 1929; London: Blackmore Press; trans. by S. H. Guest and T. E. Blewitt)

The Living Thoughts of Montaigne
(New York: Longmans, Green & Co., 1939; London: Cassell & Co.)

Divers (Gallimard, 1931)	Miscellany
*_Interviews imaginaires_ (New York: Pantheon Books, 1943)	*_Imaginary Interviews_ (New York: Alfred A. Knopf, 1944; trans. by Malcolm Cowley)
Attendu que . . . (Alger: Charlot, 1943)	Considering That . . .
*_L'Enseignement de Poussin_ (Le Divan, 1945)	*_Poussin_ (London: *The Arts*, No. 2, 1947)
Poétique (Neuchâtel: Ides et Calendes, 1947)	A Definition of Poetry
Préfaces (ibid., 1948)	Prefaces
Rencontres (ibid., 1948)	Encounters
Éloges (ibid., 1948)	Praises

DRAMA

*_Philoctète_ (Mercure de France, 1899)	*_Philoctetes_ in *My Theater* (New York: Alfred A. Knopf, 1951; trans. by Jackson Mathews)
*_Le Roi Candaule_ (La Revue Blanche, 1901)	*_King Candaules_ (in ibid.)
*_Saül_ (Mercure de France, 1903)	*_Saul_ (in ibid.)
*_Bethsabé_ (Bibliothèque de l'Occident, 1912)	*_Bathsheba_ (in ibid.)
*_Œdipe_ (Gallimard, 1931)	*_Œdipus_ in *Two Legends: Theseus and Œdipus* (New York: Alfred A. Knopf, 1950; London: Secker & Warburg; trans. by John Russell)

*Perséphone
(ibid., 1934)

*Persephone in *My Theater*
(New York: Alfred A. Knopf, 1951; trans. by Jackson Mathews)

Le Treizième Arbre
(*Mesures*, No. 2, 1935)

The Thirteenth Tree

Robert ou l'intérêt général
(Alger: *L'Arche*, 1944–5)

Robert or The Common Weal

Le Retour
(Neuchâtel: Ides et Calendes, 1946)

The Return

MISCELLANEOUS

* *Souvenirs de la Cour d'Assises*
(Gallimard, 1914)

Recollections of the Assize Court
(London: Hutchinson & Co., 1941; trans. anon.)

Morceaux choisis
(ibid., 1921)

Selections

*Corydon
(ibid., 1924)

*Corydon
(New York: Farrar Straus & Co., 1950; trans. by Hugh Gibb)

*Si le grain ne meurt . . .
(ibid., 1926)

*If It Die . . .
(New York: Random House, 1935; London: Secker & Warburg, 1950; edition limited to 1,500 copies)

*Numquid et tu . . . ?
(Éditions de la Pléiade, 1926)

*Numquid et tu . . . ? in *The Journals of André Gide*, Vol. II
(New York: Alfred A. Knopf, 1948; London: Secker & Warburg; trans. by Justin O'Brien)

Un Esprit non prévenu
(Éditions Kra, 1929)

An Unprejudiced Mind

L'Affaire Redureau
(Gallimard, 1930)

The Redureau Case

La Sequestrée de Poitiers (ibid., 1930)	The Poitiers Incarceration Case
Jeunesse (Neuchâtel: Ides et Calendes, 1945)	Youth
Feuillets d'automne (Mercure de France, 1949)	*Autumn Leaves* (New York: Philosophical Li- brary, 1950; trans. by Elsie Pell)
Littérature engagée (Gallimard, 1950)	Literature of Commitment
Et nunc manet in te (Neuchâtel: Ides et Calendes, 1951)	*Madeleine* (New York: Alfred A. Knopf, 1952) or *Et nunc manet in te* (London: Secker & War- burg, 1953); translated by Justin O'Brien
Ainsi soit-il ou Les Jeux sont faits (Gallimard, 1952)	So Be It or The Chips Are Down

TRAVELS

Voyage au Congo (Gallimard, 1927)	*Travels in the Congo* (New York: Alfred A. Knopf, 1929; London: ibid., 1930)
Dindiki (Liége: Éditions de la Lampe d'Aladdin, 1927)	Dindiki
Le Retour du Tchad (Gallimard, 1928)	*in Travels in the Congo* (New York: Alfred A. Knopf, 1929; London: ibid., 1930)
Retour de l'U.R.S.S. (ibid., 1936)	*Return from the U.S.S.R.* (New York: ibid., 1937; Lon- don: Secker & Warburg, 1937)
Retouches à mon Retour de l'U.R.S.S. (ibid., 1937)	*Afterthoughts on the U.S.S.R.* (New York: Dial Press, 1938; London: Secker & Warburg, 1938)

The Works of André Gide

389

JOURNALS

*Journal, 1889–1939
(Gallimard, 1939)

*The Journals of André Gide
(New York: Alfred A. Knopf,
1947–51; London: Secker &
Warburg, 1947–51; 4 vols.,
trans. by Justin O'Brien)

*Pages de Journal, 1939–1942
(New York: Pantheon Books,
1944; Paris: Gallimard, 1946)

*Extracts from the Journals,
1939–1942
(in ibid.)

*Journal, 1942–1949
(Gallimard, 1950)

*Journal, 1942–1949
(in ibid.)

Deux Interviews imaginaires
suivies de Feuillets
(Charlot, 1946)

Dialogues on God

CORRESPONDENCE

Lettres
(Liège: A la Lampe d'Aladdin,
1930)

Letters

*Correspondance Francis
Jammes et André Gide, 1893–
1938
(Paris: Gallimard, 1948)

The Correspondence between
Francis Jammes and André
Gide

*Correspondance Paul Claudel
et André Gide, 1899–1926
(ibid., 1949)

*The Correspondence between
Paul Claudel and André Gide
(New York: Pantheon Books,
1952; London: Secker &
Warburg, 1952; translated by
John Russell)

Lettres de Charles Du Bos et
Réponses de André Gide
(Corrêa, 1950)

The Correspondence between
Charles Du Bos and André
Gide

Correspondance Rainer Maria
Rilke et André Gide, 1909–26
(Corrêa, 1952)

The Correspondence between
Rainer Maria Rilke and
André Gide

COLLECTED EDITIONS

Œuvres complètes   Complete Works
(Gallimard, 15 vols., 1932–9)

Théâtre   Drama
(Gallimard, 1942)

Théâtre complet   Complete Drama
(Neuchâtel: Ides et Calendes, 8
    vols., 1947–9)

INDEX